George Howe

D1737841

George Howe in the early 1950s.

GEORGE HOWE

Toward a

Modern American Architecture

ROBERT A. M. STERN

New Haven and London, Yale University Press

1975

Library of Congress catalog card number: 73-86918
International standard book number: 0-300-01642-5

Designed by John O. C. McCrillis
and set in Times Roman type.
Printed in the United States of America by
Halliday Lithograph Corp., West Hanover, Mass.

Published in Great Britain, Europe, and Africa by
Yale University Press, Ltd., London.
Distributed in Latin America by Kaiman & Polon,
Inc., New York City; in Australasia and Southeast
Asia by John Wiley & Sons Australasia Pty. Ltd.,
Sydney; in India by UBS Publishers' Distributors Pvt.,
Ltd., Delhi; in Japan by John Weatherhill, Inc., Tokyo.

Contents

List of Illustrations

The George Howe Collection at Avery Architectural Library, Columbia University, New York, is cited in this list as "Howe Archives." Unless otherwise noted, all buildings are credited to George Howe.

Frontispiece. George Howe in the early 1950s. (*Forum,* June 1955, p. 113)

Following page 34

Acknowledgments

This book was begun in 1961 when I was a student of Vincent Scully's at Yale, and such strengths as it may have are in large measure the result of his rigorous criticism then and since. At varying times Carroll L. V. Meeks, William Jordy, Richard Pommer, and Henry-Russell Hitchcock rendered assistance.

Many architects have been kind enough to share their recollections of Howe with me: Philip Johnson, Louis Kahn, Robert Venturi, Maxwell Levinson, Louis McAllister, Earle W. Bolton, Jr., Robert Montgomery Brown, William Lescaze, Oscar Stonorov, and especially Theo B. White, who, at the outset of this project, acted as my cicerone through the labyrinth of clubs and houses and families which describe Howe's world in Philadelphia.

Many friends and former clients of Howe's have been most generous. Among those are R. Sturgis Ingersoll, Robert McLean, Mr. and Mrs. Orville Bullitt, Francis Biddle, William Stix Wasserman, and Clara Fargo Thomas.

Charles Sawyer, former Dean of the School of Fine Arts at Yale, has been most patient with my questions about Howe's tenure at Yale. Lydia Wentworth and Helen Chillman, Dean Herman Spiegel and his assistant Gert Wood, all of Yale, have given invaluable assistance at many stages in the preparation of the manuscript, as has Adolf Placzek and the wonderful staff of Avery Library at Columbia, where Howe's papers and the drawings remaining from his practice are now on deposit.

Mrs. Walter West, Howe's older daughter, Helen, has been a continual source of assistance and, I think, a model of patience; she has answered questions, pieced together seemingly unrelated events, and garnered from diverse sources the remaining documents of Howe's years of practice.

At varying times, Mr. and Mrs. West, The Graham Foundation for Advanced Studies in the Fine Arts, and my parents have provided financial assistance for this project. My brother Elliot and my wife Lynn have been extremely helpful in the preparation of the early drafts of the manuscript, and Robin Bledsoe has given excellent advice and direction in the final editing.

ROBERT A. M. STERN

East Hampton, January 1974

George Howe

1. An American Case

The American of the emerging twentieth century was the loneliest man
in the world: the world of his fathers had vanished, and no America
had been created to replace it.

Waldo Frank, *The Rediscovery of America*

George Howe was born on 17 June 1886, in Worcester, Massachusetts. His
father, James Henry Howe, was a gentleman of wealth and leisure. A club
man, as the idiom of the day would have it, he drank a bit too much and died
of a heart attack while lifting a billiard table when young George was just past
his first birthday. On his father's side, George was descended from John Howe,
who came to New England around 1630 and founded a long line of New
England farmers and townsmen. Successive generations of the family prospered, leaving James Henry Howe in easy circumstances. For some years a
widower, he decided to marry for the second time and chose as his bride Helen
Fisher Bradford of Philadelphia. They were married in Philadelphia, at the
Church of St. James the Less, on 12 September 1883.[1]

A woman of good family, much younger than her husband, Helen Bradford
possessed uncommon intelligence and determination. Through the years the
Bradfords had, like the Howes, prospered while their Quaker fervor diminished. Helen Bradford's parents lived in Paris, where she was born on 7 June
1855; she was brought up and educated in convent schools in France as well
as in Torresdale, Pennsylvania. Her granddaughter, Helen Howe West, writes
that she "must have always been a fairly independent person. While at one
convent, when she was about twelve, she refused to be converted to Catholicism. She also announced, by her own admission, that she planned to marry
fairly late in life, to marry an elderly, wealthy man, to have one son by him, to
be widowed soon thereafter, in order to bring up this son to her own liking."[2]

1. Helen Howe West, letter to author, 2 Aug. 1973. The discussion about the Howe and Bradford families, and especially about Helen Bradford Howe, draws extensively on notes about the
family and a privately printed memoir of George Howe by his elder daughter Helen, now Mrs.
Walter West, *George Howe, Architect* (Philadelphia: William Nunn, 1973). Mrs. Howe's
Bradford lineage can be traced back to the Philadelphia printer William Bradford; her religious
heritage was Quaker.
2. West, letter to author, 2 Aug. 1973.

Although she did not choose to become a communicant of the Church of Rome, its aesthetic and cultural tradition was to remain with her always. Thus, for young George, a somewhat puritanical American background was enlivened with Gallic cosmopolitanism: Quaker propriety and the directness of New England puritanism modified by the skepticism of the French and the pageantry of the Roman church.

Mrs. Howe and her son set out for Paris shortly after her husband's death. Neither one was ever to return to Worcester, where George had been born only by chance. It was not unusual for Mrs. Howe to make important decisions rapidly and without hesitation. She possessed all the qualities deemed proper for a woman of her class as well as a rare intelligence special to herself. Her tastes were broad, and the liberality of her culture was founded upon a sense of history. George Biddle, the American painter who was one of Howe's closest friends, remembered that, on a visit to Paris in 1909, he was taken by Mrs. Howe to the Matisse exhibit, at which time they seem to have met Leo Stein.[3] At this time only a discerning few could see merit in Matisse's work; Mrs. Howe seems to have been among these, and in this respect she reminds us of another Philadelphian, Mary Cassatt. Such women do not belong at all to the tradition-bound European world depicted by Henry James but to the world which that writer found most clearly in Philadelphia, upon his return to America in 1907. It frightened and impressed him and made Philadelphia for him "strikingly . . . an American case."[4] Mrs. Howe was a woman of considerable force and daring. She was also domineering, and her son suffered accordingly. Almost from the first, she sought to direct the development of her only child. He was to be a man of learning and position, a gentleman, and, above all, an architect.

As a child, Howe displayed an interest in painting. He was later fond of recalling his "independent, though not remarkable gifts for drawing." Mrs. Howe, recognizing the limit of his talents, directed his thoughts toward architecture, which appealed to "her Quaker instinct as a reputable trade."[5] She was an admirer of Ruskin, and it was under the influence of his writings that young George's first view of architecture was formed. He was later to write: "I

3. Interview with George Biddle, Truro, Mass., Aug. 1962.

4. Henry James, *The American Scene/Together with Three Essays from "Portraits of Places,"* ed. W. H. Auden (New York: Scribner's, 1946), p. 283. A copy of this edition belonged to Howe; the passage from the quotation is excerpted and was underlined by him.

5. "George Howe, An Architectural Biography," *T-Square* 2 (Jan. 1932), 20–23. Maxwell Levinson, editor of *T-Square,* informed the author in an interview in August 1961 that the article was autobiographical; see also Levinson, "George Howe's Contribution to Contemporary Architecture," *USA Tomorrow* 1 (Oct. 1954), 42 ff.

was conceived an architect by my mother. . . . Before I knew what the name meant she told me I was an architect."[6]

The ancient monuments of Europe served as his textbook. Naturally, he was too young to understand the sciences of statics and proportion, nor was his mother competent to teach them. Instead she put to use her command of history and her ability as a storyteller to spin out the adventures of the lovers, tyrants, and money lenders who had once dwelled in the monuments they visited—men who, Howe recalled somewhat cynically, seemed "invariably to be the generators of the force that builds."[7] Mrs. Howe was well versed in the lives of these men by virtue of her early training in a convent where history was the only reading countenanced other than the Bible. For her son, she was able to infuse each building with a wondrous luminescence, to bring life back to old abandoned walls, walls behind which, in her memory, a pair of illicit lovers nearly always lurked. Toward these poor creatures, Mrs. Howe—herself a virtuous and somewhat humorless Victorian—was gently sympathetic.[8]

A tutor was engaged, and young George was made fluent in French, Italian, and German. He was drilled in each until his accent was impeccable, while at the same time his measured English cadence remained flawless. His remarkable skill as a mimic and actor probably had much to do with such success. He was also tutored in the classic French manner, by which history is learned through studying the French monarchs. So it was that Howe's earliest years were spent in an atmosphere that he remembered as prosperous and self-satisfied, "conservative though not reactionary."[9]

When he was eight years old, Howe met by chance John Stewardson, a distinguished Philadelphia architect who, with his partner Walter Cope, established in that city during the 1890s a successful practice in what has come to be described as the Collegiate Gothic style. Their picturesque work at Princeton is well known, but perhaps their finest achievement was the dormitory complex at the University of Pennsylvania. A skating accident ended Stewardson's life when he was just twenty-nine, and although Cope lived on for a few

---

6. Howe, foreword to his unfinished book, "Of Houses and Human Bondage. Reflections on Modern Architecture." Whether or not Howe's recollections were influenced by Frank Lloyd Wright's is a moot point, but if they were not it is interesting that the two men, so different in social background and in career, yet in later life such good friends, should share this earliest, subliminal introduction to architecture.

7. "George Howe, An Architectural Biography."

8. Helen Howe West writes: "Grandma Howe was not all *that* humorless. She was virtuous, & perforce Victorian—but she had a delicious chuckle & made those around her happy & jovial in an easy, relaxed way." Letter to author, 24 July 1972.

9. Howe, untitled talk delivered before the students of the Graduate School of Design, Harvard University, 1954, at the invitation of the dean of the school, José Luis Sert.

years more, the best work of the firm had already been done.[10] Stewardson was interested in young Howe's ability and showed him how to use a simple box of watercolors. If Mrs. Howe had not already done so, this served to fix his career.

When he was ten Howe was sent to a boarding school in Switzerland, and two years later he returned to America with his mother. After attending the Cloyne School at Newport, Rhode Island, he entered Groton in the fall of 1899. Mrs. Howe settled in Boston rather than Philadelphia, to be near her son.[11]

At the turn of the century, success at Groton, as at Harvard, might be pursued in three directions: athletics, the social graces, and leadership. As for scholarship, it was expected that a Groton boy would do creditably in his area as a matter of course. Howe did exceedingly well at everything. After the initial shock of his arrival, when the boys took to calling him "Frenchy" because of his fairly elaborate accent and manners, he soon became head of his class scholastically and athletically: football in the fall, crew in the spring. His good friend Francis Biddle, George Biddle's younger brother, recalls: "I had no intimate friends at Groton, with the exception of George Howe, who was, like me, a new boy and in my form. . . . He exhibited a sophistication which puzzled the Rector and made him a bit suspicious, but George's record in class and on the football field was so good that the suspicion never ripened into action."[12] Howe did not find the atmosphere at Groton completely to his liking. Its rigid code of behavior, conservatism, and coolness to scholastic achievement as an end in itself came as a shock to this cosmopolitan child. So did the zealous Christianity of the Reverend Endicott Peabody himself, whom he liked but whose religious attitudes, which have been characterized as an "unshaken faith in his particular God," were perhaps too restrictive. Worst of all, Groton tended to "smother—for a time at least—the creative spirit of a growing boy," as George Biddle has written, and the standard of excellence which Peabody held out was to prove far more useful on Wall Street than in the arts. Groton was a "chilly and uncongenial" place, Biddle was also to recall, "emo-

10. For the best recent discussion of the work of Cope and Stewardson, see George B. Tatum, *Penn's Great Town* (Philadelphia, Pennsylvania, 1961), pp. 118–20, 122, 198–99. See also Ralph Adams Cram, "The Work of Messrs. Cope and Stewardson," *Architectural Record* (hereafter *Record*) 16 (Nov. 1904), 407–38.

11. Mrs. Howe must surely have been like the "imperious" Sara Delano Roosevelt, whose "adored only son, Franklin . . . was the center of his widowed mother's life." See Arthur Schlesinger, Jr., *The Age of Roosevelt,* 3 vols. (Boston: Houghton Mifflin, 1957), 1:324.

12. Francis Biddle, *A Casual Past* (Garden City: Doubleday, 1961), p. 177.

tionally thinner than a modern kindergarten, since it straight jacketed play and human feelings; and it was avowedly medieval."[13]

Howe adjusted to Groton, but he never lost his sense of humor about it. Francis Biddle recalls him: a "new comer at the school drawing dogs with exclamation points for their bottoms, and lean, dirty cats; drawing Mr. Peabody falling down off a bicycle; drawing dour old Mrs. MacMurray, the housekeeper, whose face seemed to turn in on some central point; drawing the only pretty 'water nymph' who had ever been seen at Groton, with beautiful legs— the 'water nymphs' poured milk and water at table, and Mrs. MacMurray selected nymphs who were not much fun to look at, and this particular nymph did not stay very long."[14] Howe's adjustment to Groton was not without compromise, yet in later life he liked most to recall these school years. He came to love Groton as his memories of its puritanical aspects grew dimmer. It had americanized his cosmopolitanism.[15]

But the Groton attitude was not conducive to what was by now Howe's passion for architecture. Indeed, the practice of that art was "looked on as a rather futile if polite diversion," and he was forced to put thoughts of it aside until college.[16] Vacations were wonderful, especially the summers spent at Northeast Harbor on Mount Desert Island, Maine.[17] Francis Biddle remembered Mrs. Howe's house, called Holiday House, as the "prettiest and most comfortable in Harbor Side, its two blinking dormer windows watching the life of the little bay." Throughout the summer Mrs. Howe would arrange picnics on which a dozen or so, young and old, explored the countryside while she and a few of her contemporaries "plodded along slowly and comfortably,

13. George Biddle, *An American Artist's Story* (Boston: Little, Brown, 1939), pp. 65–66, 78. Biddle's bitter memories of Groton are colored in part by the social unrest of the period in which he wrote. He kept a diary at Groton, from which he quotes extensively in his book. See pp. 64, 66, for entries that refer to Howe.

14. Biddle, *A Casual Past,* p. 176.

15. Francis Biddle writes "Looking back I think that the religious training received at boarding school, and quickly discarded at Harvard, was not barren of good. The moral values which Groton stood for, and which were closely linked with its Victorian background, acted as a counterpoise to the esthetic and cultural standard which I had brought with me from home. And at the base of the teaching was more the sense of service than the function of worship, and for me public service came to achieve a good that no other way of life could reach. But, being something of a skeptic, I cannot go further than that, and suggest that service is the ultimate in life. But then I do not believe in ultimates." Ibid., p. 191.

16. "George Howe, An Architectural Biography," p. 20.

17. For a discussion of the special affection with which Philadelphians regard Northeast Harbor, see Nathaniel Burt, *The Perennial Philadelphians* (Boston: Little, Brown, 1963), pp. 535, 538.

as was her custom in life, so that she was never out of breath." An afternoon's hiking might take them over the small hills to Jordan Pond, where they would drink tea and eat toast and popovers smothered in a wonderfully satisfying jam which Mrs. Howe had prepared. "Pausing half way up a 'mountain,' as the sun pulled the shadows down around us, Mrs. Howe would supply raspberry vinegar, and large, round very thin ginger snaps . . . and Swiss chocolate bars, bittersweet and rich with milk."[18] There was a contentment in the salty air and the warm sun of the Maine coast that was not to be found in the gray, grim New England countryside around Groton.

In 1904 Howe entered Harvard College, having met the language requirements in advanced Greek, Latin, and French. If the years at Groton had been a period of repressed growth rather than of incubation, those at Harvard marked the beginning of intellectual maturity. During them, Howe donned the mask of that personality which he was later to present to the world at large. A mask it was, surely, a buffer and a disguise. Howe was ambivalent, uncertain, indecisive, at times almost neurotic, and plagued by internal conflicts throughout his life. To protect himself and others from these fundamental weaknesses, he adopted the facade by which most people remember him today: that of Edwardian elegance associated with the "Harvard aesthete" type, of refinement perhaps too refined, of cynicism, skepticism, and sardonic melancholy. George Biddle once wrote, "One cannot get through life without a mask. It is just as important—more so perhaps—than a face."[19] Unfortunately, few people ever saw beyond Howe's mask, and he wanted it that way. He wished to appear, as Francis Biddle remarked, "like a faun: no heart, no sense of responsibility, but great charm."[20]

Howe's sense of inadequacy, tending to produce the inability to act, was probably the result of his mother's domination. She had made all the decisions and they had seemed right. Partially, however, it was induced by the kind of society Howe found in America, at Groton, and to a lesser extent at Harvard. Its puritanical outlook and extroverted energy intimidated him. Its religion and its materialism alike ran counter to the aestheticism which he, perhaps more than most, substituted for a philosophy of life. Europe had made him skeptical; his mother had made him weak. He resolved to disguise himself, to guard his inner sensibilities until he was more certain of how to use or present them.

Howe suffered from another kind of split in personality. He was romantic

18. Biddle, *A Casual Past,* p. 199.
19. Biddle, *An American Artist's Story,* pp. 57–58.
20. Interview with Francis Biddle, Wellfleet, Mass., Aug. 1962.

and emotional in feeling but coldly, even dryly, analytical in mind. Because he possessed this rather intense combination of imagination and intellect, he felt himself incapable of acting without analyzing his actions. Each side of his personality distrusted the other; thus he could seldom convince himself that the kind of action to which he was instinctively drawn was truly worthwhile. To the ultimate degree, Howe was the perfect image of the pathetically and tragically handicapped Harvard graduate, whom Henry Adams characterized as "neither American nor European, nor even wholly Yankee; his admirers were few, and his critics many; perhaps his worst weakness was his self-criticism and self-consciousness; but his ambitions, social or intellectual, were not necessarily cheap even though they might be negative. Afraid of serious risks, and still more afraid of personal ridicule, he seldom made a great failure of life, and nearly always led a life more or less worth living."[21]

Everything at Harvard that fed Howe's imagination in these early years also helped form his public self. They seem worthy of some examination, as does the college itself, which was enjoying a remarkable flowering during the years that Howe was an undergraduate. His class, 1908, contained an unusually large number of preeminent individuals. Among them were George Biddle, painter; Van Wyck Brooks, man of letters; Samuel Eliot Morison, naval historian; George Richards Minot, distinguished physician and Nobel Prize winner; Edward Brewster Sheldon, playwright; John Hall Wheelock, poet and editor; Alfred Vincent Kidder, archaeologist; Paul Dudley White, heart specialist; Charles Louis Seeger, musician and musicologist; and Warren Delano Robbins, diplomat.

But the remarkable Harvard faculty was probably the most important measure of the college's distinction. This was still the Harvard of Charles Eliot Norton. Although he had retired in 1898, his mind, which "looked backward in time and across the sea," continued to set the tone. Norton, Van Wyck Brooks recalled, "never set foot in England without feeling that he was at last at home, and when, for the 'England' one substituted 'Europe,' with the Middle Ages and the history of art, one had the Harvard temper that I knew so well."[22] Henry Adams's gospel of despair, his inability to find anything satisfactory in the American scene, and his passionless devotion to medievalism as a means

21. Henry Adams, *The Education of Henry Adams* (New York: Random House, 1931), pp. 65–66. In *An American Artist's Story* George Biddle uses this quotation to open the chapter devoted to Harvard. Van Wyck Brooks also refers to it in his memories of Harvard recorded in *Scenes and Portraits. Memories of Childhood and Youth* (New York: Dutton, 1954).

22. Brooks, *Scenes and Portraits,* p. 107. Norton's influence on an entire generation of Harvard students was enormous, although he might have been surprised at the matured tastes of his

of escape from the present were part of that Harvard temper as well. So were Barrett Wendell's complaint that the world had been steadily going to the dogs since the time of Dante, and Irving Babbitt's conservatism—"humanism," he called it—which, with its authoritarianism and formalism, reflected a distinct dissatisfaction with democratic ideals. There was George Santayana, who chose to think of himself as an "American writer" because he could find no appellation that seemed more accurate. Santayana, like so many intellectuals in America, seemed always to be gazing over the heads of students "as if looking for the sail that was to bear him home," back to Europe. Like many at Harvard, he greeted with "smiling contempt" the efforts of "men to better the world." New England's traditional faith in progress and improvement was being dismissed as meaningless, and strong sentiment for a more authoritarian society seemed present. Both "the altar and the throne" seemed beautiful and suitable to the aestheticism and the malaise of fin de siècle Harvard.[23]

Pre-Raphaelitism, tending toward dilettantish Catholicism, flourished. Harvard was trying to recreate in New England what Malcolm Cowley had described as "an after-image of Oxford in the late 1890s." Harvard aesthetes "had crucifixes in their bedrooms, and ticket stubs from last Saturday's burlesque show at the Old Howard."[24] Reaction against the puritanism of New England ancestry was widespread among the undergraduates, and it found expression in Anglo-Catholicism and a cult of royalism. There also existed a cult of Dante and a tremendous interest in Italian art encouraged by Mrs. Jack Gardner's example. Her famous collection, gathered together by a recent Harvard graduate, Bernard Berenson, was more a reflection of this general interest in Italy than a generating force. Nonetheless, as Brooks notes, "it filled the Harvard mind with images that cropped out in scores of novels and poems—in Eliot's phrases about the Umbrian painters, for instance, and the trumpets and eagles that evoked Mantegna."[25]

To the roster of distinguished faculty, one should add the names of the philosophers William James, Josiah Royce, and Hugo Münsterberg. James seems to us perhaps the most appealing of all, and was probably so to Howe,

---

students. Not only did Howe travel a long way from the romantic naturalism of Ruskin and Norton, but so did, for example, Walter Conrad Arensberg, who, having purchased Norton's famous house Shady Hill as a residence for himself, went on to form what would become by around 1920 the most advanced and most carefully chosen collection of modern painting and sculpture in this country. See Fiske Kimball, "Cubism and the Arensbergs," *Art News Annual* 24 (1955), 117–22, 174–78.

23. Brooks, *Scenes and Portraits,* p. 107.

24. Malcolm Cowley, *Exile's Return* (New York: Viking, 1956), p. 35.

25. Brooks, *Scenes and Portraits,* p. 114.

who frequently turned to his essays in later life. His pragmatic outlook and his passionate belief in the constant metamorphosis of truth was, as Henry Steele Commager has written, "not single and absolute but plural and contingent," and in confronting "all dogma with skepticism and . . . [making] skepticism itself a dogma" he eschewed "all absolutes, causes, finalities, fixed principles, abstractions and rigidities, and embraced instead pluralism, uncertainty, practicality, common sense, adventure, and flexibility."[26]

At Harvard, Howe later remembered rather snobbishly, he "experienced for the first time the delight of discussion on equal terms with contemporaries of a like background and similar tastes."[27] After the starvation of puritanical Groton, Cambridge permitted an orgy of inquiry and experimentation, and he elected as many courses in the fine arts and architecture as could be found. In so doing, he came under the influence of Charles Herbert Moore, "white-haired and atrabilious,"[28] then in his last years at Harvard and at the peak of his powers. Moore's "insistence on structural significance as the only dignity of architectural style" had a profound effect on Howe's later career, although it seemed at the time unreasonably restrictive for a young romantic.[29]

Charles Herbert Moore was the last of the American Pre-Raphaelites. He was born in New York City and received very little formal education. A friend of Norton, he had known the architects Peter B. Wight, Russell Sturgis, and the protean Ruskin himself, and he had been a distinguished landscape painter in the 1850s and 1860s. Called to Cambridge by Norton as an instructor in freehand drawing, he and Norton later pioneered the famous Harvard laboratory method for teaching the history and appreciation of art, which emphasized learning by doing. Upon Norton's retirement in 1898, Moore, in addition to his Fine Arts One class, began to teach that part of the Fine Arts Two class—"Principles of Design in Architecture, Sculpture, and Painting"— which concerned itself with postclassical art and architecture.[30]

26. Henry Steele Commager, *The American Mind* (New Haven: Yale, 1950), pp. 93–94.

27. "George Howe, An Architectural Biography," p. 21.

28. Biddle, *An American Artist's Story*, p. 79.

29. "George Howe, An Architectural Biography," p. 21.

30. I have relied on Frank Jewett Mather's biography of Moore, *Charles Herbert Moore, Landscape Painter* (Princeton: Princeton, 1957). It is concerned primarily with Moore as an artist and is very brief in its treatment of his career as teacher, critic, historian, and first curator of the Fogg Art Museum at Harvard University. See also Peter Ferriday, "Professor Moore 1840–1930," *Architectural Review* 127 (April 1960), 271–72. Ferriday's principal focus is the influence of Moore's researches into Gothic architecture on English critical and historical writing, especially that of William Lethaby. See also D. H. Dickason, "The American Pre-Raphaelites," *Art in America* 30 (July 1942), 157–65.

In 1890 Moore published his most important book, *Development and Character of Gothic Architecture,* which in its insistence on structural as well as visual criteria, proved that pointed arches are not synonymous with Gothic architecture. In it he defined Gothic as "a system of construction in which vaulting in an independent system of ribs is sustained by piers and buttresses whose equilibrium is maintained by the opposing action of thrust and counter-thrust."[31] As much as Moore's philosophy of structure and form owes to Viollet-le-Duc and the nineteenth-century rationalists, it goes beyond theirs in its emphasis on the visual effects of structure rather than on its frank revelation.

True Gothic architecture, Moore insisted, resulted from a total architectural vocabulary, from an integration of structure and space where weight and thrust are given unmistakable visual expression through the plastic manipulation of vaults, buttresses, columns, and ribs. The significance of forms arose from neither structural advances over the Romanesque nor the use of the pointed arch, but from the brilliant statement in masonry of the dynamism of the structure. These forms dramatically expressed their purpose, and the grandeur of the space was the logical outcome. Moore's philosophy integrated Viollet-le-Duc's insistence on structural integrity with an aestheticism that recalls Ruskin and, somewhat more distantly, Ruskin's contemporary, the French aesthetician Charles Blanc. Moore himself wrote late in his life: "While Viollet-le-Duc dealt scientifically with principles of structure, . . . the prime motive with Ruskin was to set forth the beauty of them. The one was concerned with physical facts. The other with ocular impressions."[32]

The Harvard College catalogue listed Fine Arts One as: "Principles of Delineation, Color, and Chiaroscuro, with some consideration of historic forms of Art and the conditions which have influenced them. Lectures (once a week), with collateral reading. Practice in drawing and in the use of water-colors. Perspective." Fine Arts Two was "Principles of Design in Architecture, Sculpture, and Painting as exemplified in the Arts of the Past ages. Lectures (twice a week), with collateral reading. Practice in drawing." See also Charles Herbert Moore, *Examples of Elementary Practice in Delineation* (Boston: Houghton Mifflin, 1884).

31. *Development and Character of Gothic Architecture,* p. 30. Of this book, an anonymous reviewer wrote that it was only "a definition of Gothic structure; of engineering so to speak, and not yet of Gothic architecture. It is conceivable that a building which answered this definition might not yet be a work of architecture at all. It is only when the constructor becomes also an artist and sets himself to expound and accentuate and decorate his construction that he becomes an architect and it a work of architecture." *Record* 1 (July-Sept. 1891), 113–14.

32. Charles Herbert Moore, "The Writings of Viollet-le-Duc," *Record* 59 (Feb. 1926), 128–32.

Moore wrote three books of history: *Development and Character of Gothic Architecture* (New York: Macmillan, 1890); *Character of Renaissance Architecture* (New York: Macmillan, 1905); *The Medieval Church Architecture of England* (New York: Macmillan, 1912). In addi-

In its concern for structural integrity, Moore's theory leads to a conception of the art of building as the result of "artistic attitudes and constructive facilities," a synthesis of imagination and intellect.[33] The form and the way one builds it must be completely integrated, thus establishing architecture primarily as an art of construction. The disciplined disposition of structure, yielding "purposed expression of beauty transcending that of mere utility," distinguishes architecture from building. For Moore, structure, best referred to by the broader term "construction," is concerned not with engineering but with the "requisite knowledge of the strength of materials and their proper forms and adjustments." In other words, the principle of clarity of construction does not depend exclusively on that revelation of structure. The latter principle is the product of morality and honesty. The former derives from a thoughtful arrangement of the parts of the building which, when carefully studied, will yield a clear conception of the way a building was built. All historical styles of architecture should be studied in terms of their construction, in the broad sense, since "a habit of critical discrimination in [this] respect . . . cannot be formed too early."[34]

Moore believed that the great consideration in masonry architecture, beyond even the necessity of structural soundness, was the satisfaction of the eye, and that the thoughtful designer took into consideration the "imaginative sense of the material" as well as the "manual means by which it is realized."[35] He

tion to the article cited, the following articles by Moore in *Architectural Record* are relevant: "The Definition of Gothic," 40 (Sept. 1916), 274–78; "The Character of Renaissance Architecture," 44 (Nov. 1918), 465–69; "Some Principles of Design and Construction in Domestic Building," 45 (March 1919), 210–16; "Training for the Practice of Architecture," 49 (Jan. 1921), 56–61; "University Instruction in Architecture," 50 (Nov. 1921), 407–12; "Conditions Conducive to Architecture," 58 (Sept. 1925), 211–15; "Existing Conditions Favorable to Architecture," 58 (Oct. 1925), 386–90; "Mistaken Notions about Gothic Architecture," 59 (June 1926), 565–70.

For Charles Blanc, see Reyner Banham, *Theory and Design in the First Machine Age* (New York: Praeger 1960), pp. 15, 18. Blanc was librarian of the Ecole des Beaux-Arts, and his writings colored the impressions of such Americans at that institution as Ernest Flagg. See Flagg, "The Ecole des Beaux-Arts," *Record* 3 (Jan.-March 1894), 302–13; 3 (April-June 1894), 419–28; 4 (July-Sept. 1894), 38–43.

33. Moore, "Training for the Practice of Architecture," p. 60. A logical extension of this and other ideas found in Moore and Paul Cret can be seen in the work of the Philadelphia architect Louis I. Kahn. In his architecture and writings, Kahn expresses ideals resembling those prevalent at the Ecole des Beaux-Arts in the first part of this century. Kahn has always been close to that tradition through his training under Cret and his association with Howe as the latter's architectural partner, and as a professor in the Department of Architecture at Yale. For a fuller discussion of Kahn's philosophy, see Vincent Scully, *Louis I. Kahn* (New York: Braziller, 1962).

34. Moore, "University Instruction in Architecture," pp. 408–09.

35. Moore, "Training for the Practice of Architecture," p. 60.

suggested that the great obstacle to quality in modern architecture was the isolation of the architect from his materials. The student must be "exercised in the building craft" because a new, modern restatement of the craftsman's understanding for his materials, always present in earlier phases of architecture, could best be achieved through an understanding of the "manual processes" of building. For Moore, who was less interested in design than in construction, architecture was more concerned with how a building got to be than with the aesthetics of the building itself. The great architecture of the past has always been well within the "common tradition of building." Only the "inventive genius" and the "best inspiration" of men personally involved in that tradition "made their work their own in the proper sense."[36] For in the knowledge of the how lies the understanding of the what.[37]

Lawrence Grant White, Stanford White's son, was a classmate and close personal friend of Howe's. Perhaps it was he who introduced Howe to the works of his father's architectural firm, McKim, Mead and White. Or perhaps it was the Italianate elegance of many of their best efforts that captured Howe's fancy. At any rate, he came to love the work of this firm above that of all their contemporaries, even though he questioned the apparent lack of logic in their development of plan or construction.[38]

The work of McKim, Mead and White was not Beaux-Arts either in its forms or in its underlying theoretical premises. While recommending that aspiring architects study at the Ecole des Beaux-Arts because of its discipline, this mighty triumvirate seemed careful to discriminate in its own work between Beaux-Arts forms, sometimes referred to in the early twentieth century as

36. Ibid.

37. This idea is carried to its logical conclusion in the work of Kahn. See his statement, "Form and Design," in Scully, *Louis I. Kahn*, pp. 114–21. Earlier in his development, Kahn wrote: "I believe that in architecture, as in all art, the artist instinctively keeps the marks which reveal how a thing was done. . . . If we were to train ourselves to draw as we build, from the bottom up, when we do, stopping our pencil to make a mark at the points of pouring or erecting, ornament would grow out of our love for the expression of method. . . . The desire to express how it is done would filter through the entire society of building, to architect, engineer, builder and craftsman." See "Proposed City Hall Building," *Perspecta, The Yale Architectural Journal* 2 (1953), 23.

Moore's influence on Howe's thought was life long. When Howe, at the end of his career, became an architectural educator, he, like Moore in 1921, stated his educational philosophy as "Training for the Practice of Architecture." This paper was read before the Department of Architecture, Yale University, in September 1951 and was printed in *Perspecta* 1 (1952), 2–5. Howe's continuing concern for architecture as craft, in the sense that Moore articulates it, can be seen in his pedagogical attitudes at Yale, and especially in his support of the programs of Eugene Nalle. See chap. 8.

38. "George Howe, An Architectural Biography."

"Modern French," and Beaux-Arts technical methods and training. In the years after the World's Columbian Exposition in 1893, the bulk of their work was derived from the forms of imperial Rome or the Italian Renaissance. Rarely resorting to the direct copying of entire buildings, the firm nonetheless possessed a real understanding of the Renaissance and pillaged the Italian past in seeking architectural effects. Their buildings in the Renaissance style, usually designed by White, show a fine sympathy with its spirit. In the case of McKim, whose preferences were Roman, modern programs often conflicted with the desire to make pure statements. Windows and doorways—necessary modern considerations—confounded the grandiose intentions of their designer. Nonetheless, the spatial composition of McKim's Roman buildings is splendid and rivals anything produced by the Beaux-Arts school.

With the exception of a few buildings such as Pennsylvania Station, New York, the work of McKim, Mead and White does not reward those who seek formal innovation in architecture. They were not the "aesthetic adventurers" of their generation. But the cycle of American architecture has now come to a point not unlike the one which Herbert Croly and Henry W. Desmond predicted in 1906. "Americans of the next few generations," they wrote of the work of McKim, Mead and White, "will regard the best of their buildings, not as the relics of a superseded architectural fashion, nor merely as the progenitors of the still better buildings we hope may follow, but as architectural monuments, which satisfy a permanent and normal sense of beautiful form."[39]

Barrett Wendell often spoke at Harvard during the early years of this century of the affinity of contemporary American letters for the prose of Elizabethan England. His feelings about this kinship may easily have led Howe, as it did such architectural journalists as Croly and Desmond, to believe that "the gulf between ourselves and the Renaissance" could be more easily and more properly bridged by Americans than by the French or the English. Howe, "like the men of the Renaissance . . . fundamentally a sentimental traveller, a passionate pilgrim, among relics of an old world,"[40] thinking he could not

---

39. Henry W. Desmond and Herbert Croly, "The Work of McKim, Mead and White," *Record* 20 (Sept. 1906), 153–246. For an interesting discussion of the influence of McKim on Howe's generation, written at the time when Howe was preparing his autobiographical statement for *T-Square,* see John Wheelwright, "Architecture Chronicle. Masterpieces of Architecture in the United States," *Hound & Horn* 4 (July–Sept. 1931), 585–96. For the difference between McKim's and White's approach to design, with particular application to the Columbia and New York University campuses, see Charles C. Baldwin, *Stanford White* (New York: Dodd, Mead, 1931), pp. 223–35.

40. Wendell's remarks are quoted in Desmond and Croly, "Work of McKim, Mead and White."

justify this longing for the past along lines set down by Moore, perhaps found sustenance in Wendell's argument.

The powerful impression made on Howe by the work of McKim, Mead and White forced upon him a confrontation, at the beginning of his serious study of architecture, with an intellectual dilemma which was to plague him all his life, arising from the romanticism of his emotions and the rationalism of his intellect. Moore's philosophy seemed to take both of these attitudes into consideration, but the young student was slow to see this. He at first saw only Moore's rationalism—to be more accurate, his structural determinism. But in the work of McKim, Mead and White, he saw the kind of monumental splendor his emotions craved.

Harvard tended on the whole to value all manner of achievement—intellectual, athletic, and social—far more than any other college or university in America. Howe's grades, while hovering around a gentleman's "C," were nonetheless acceptable in a time when intelligence and learning were not measurable solely by a numerical rating received in class. Howe had a keen and inquiring mind, and his interest in learning and in new ideas for their own sake continued unabated throughout his life. He devoted much of his time to the Harvard *Lampoon,* eventually being elected to the position of "Ibis" or vice president. With its elaborate quarters a block or so from the Yard, "Lampy" had in the early years of this century the atmosphere of a cabal. Almost as soon as Howe arrived at Harvard, he contributed a drawing to the *Lampoon*—probably derived from those of Groton water nymphs—and an accompanying rhyme:

> A mermaid once wistfully sighed,
>   "Though to be like a man I have tried,
>   Though I've smoked, drunk and chewed,
>   Mrs. Nature, the prude,
> Has forbid that I e'er ride astride."[41]

Howe, although he could have succeeded on social position alone, did so on all terms. His wealth and family background made it possible. A superabundance of gifts—wit, musical and acting abilities, intelligence and charm—earned it. Howe had a rare ability to get on with anyone. Athletes, aesthetes, intellectuals, and club men all sought his company. He seemed to bubble with

41. *Harvard Lampoon* 48 (29 Oct. 1904), 38. Aside from the *Lampoon,* Howe's literary and artistic activities at Harvard were confined to membership in the Stylus Club. Here he enjoyed the company of fellow members George Biddle, Brooks, Wheelock, Sheldon, and Kidder.

a magic effervescence that made him seem the most desirable person in the world to know. He was the embodiment of the college undergraduate's ideal man of imagination. All of life seemed to be the material out of which he would fashion wonderful things. "If personality is an unbroken series of successful gestures," F. Scott Fitzgerald had Nick Carraway say of Jay Gatsby, "then there was something gorgeous about him, some heightened sensitivity to the promises of life, as if he was related to one of those intricate machines which register earthquakes ten thousand miles away."[42] Howe was that sensitive romantic, and his career was to be a remarkable seismograph registering the changing architectural philosophies of half a century.

There was an elusive quality to his personality, a remarkable mixture of blasé aestheticism with "innate sweetness and charm," as George Biddle has said, which made him fascinating. One felt compelled to talk with him, to know him.[43] There was a kind of unwordly perfection about him that made him seem pathetically beautiful as he made his way in a vulgar world. Popularity came to him naturally, as naturally as membership in the select Fly Club, the pinnacle of social success for a Philadelphian, although others might regard the Porcellian more favorably. Franklin D. Roosevelt, whom he had known at Groton, also belonged to the Fly Club.[44] Howe resembled Roosevelt in the distinct Groton-Harvard accent, the precise gestures, and the broad smile under a nose surmounted by a pince-nez. Yet he never liked Roosevelt and always, perhaps because their backgrounds and personalities were so similar, avoided him.[45] Howe belonged in the Fly Club in every way and yet he often railed against it, against his clubmates, and against the system that made both of them possible. Emotionally, he was part of this world, but his penetrating intellect gave him no peace. He enjoyed it all, and his enjoyment angered him.

This was the era at Harvard when, Francis Biddle writes, "one could stay out and drink all night, at one's club or at the dances for Boston debutantes at the Somerset, if one appeared, not too obviously drunk, in the next morning's classes." As a club man, Howe "wenched and drank enthusiastically," and, shortly after he became engaged at his mother's insistence to Marie Jessup Patterson of Philadelphia, he was " 'rusticated' for falling down in Professor

42. F. Scott Fitzgerald, *The Great Gatsby* (New York: Scribner's, 1925), p. 2.

43. George Biddle, letter to the author, 1963.

44. Roosevelt did not make Porcellian, "where Roosevelts were ordinarily welcome, and had to accept a lesser club. The failure to make Porcellian was a dismaying experience." Schlesinger, *Age of Roosevelt*, 1: 323.

45. For a typical "Grotonian" reaction to Roosevelt's personality as well as his politics, see Jeffrey Porter's vignette, "The Thing About Frank," *The New Yorker*, 10 Aug. 1963, pp. 70–74.

Walz's nine o'clock class in German 4, when suddenly called upon to recite."[46] His suspension lasted for part of his final year.

Mrs. Patterson and Mrs. Howe, long great friends, had arranged the marriage, a custom still common in 1907. According to Helen Howe West, Howe and his fiancee had "known each other from early childhood, travelled together, etc." Howe may or may not have been pleased. "Rumor has it that George was mad for her; sadly, for her . . . he was probably not ready for marriage," although Mrs. Howe "probably wanted him to 'settle down'. He was certainly showing signs of 'wining and wenching' in a rather persistent fashion."[47] The engagement had an opposite effect to the one intended, causing Howe to behave in a fashion best described as neurotic, and once, in a drunken moment, he told George Biddle, his roommate and confidant all through college, that he would commit suicide.

If Howe avoided decisions, it was because he had been allowed to make so few in the past; his mother had taken care of everything. Subtly and deftly, she had planned his life and nearly denied him his manhood in the process. But, almost despite herself, she had produced a perfect gentleman—intelligent, dignified, polite—one of the most civilized men of his generation. Howe was brilliant but, lacking strength, he was too trusting of others for his own good. He was a man as yet with little purpose in life and without direction from within.

46. Biddle, *A Casual Past,* p. 176; see also p. 221.
47. West, letter to author, 24 July 1972.

2. An Architect's Education

Architects and dogs are as good as their masters.

George Howe, 1954

Howe was graduated from Harvard on 26 June 1907 with honorable mention in the Fine Arts.[1] On 18 July he married Marie Jessup Patterson at Northeast Harbor, Maine. Their honeymoon on an island off the coast of Maine was arranged by his mother. It was followed by a year in Italy, where the couple traveled extensively, making side trips to Spain and Greece. Italy was, Howe later recalled, "the symbol of grace, the land of Botticelli and Brunelleschi rather than of the Caesars, or even of Giotto and Michael Angelo." Only later did he "take pleasure in the primitive or the powerful."[2]

In the spring of 1908, the young couple went to Paris, where Howe prepared for the Ecole des Beaux-Arts. On 7 December 1908 he was admitted to the Atelier Laloux, which was a favorite with Americans, whose high spirits and easy manners helped relieve the strict French discipline.[3] The esprit de corps

1. *The Harvard University Catalogue. 1907–08*, p. **275**. Howe's degree was entered in the *Quinquennial Catalogue* as of 1908.

2. "George Howe, An Architectural Biography," *T-Square* 2 (Jan. 1932), 21. Graduation at the end of the third year was frequent at Harvard at this time.

3. The examination problem was the design of a "building to regulate the flow of mineral water." It was to be built of stone and the ornament was to be in slate or iron.

Laloux's teaching method was based on a profound belief in the plan as the generator of architectural ideas. In his discussion of this method, Charles Butler wrote, "He should, I believe, be given credit for having done more to advance American architecture than any other man." In "Hommage à Laloux des ses Elèves Américains," *Pencil Points* 18 (Oct. 1937), 621–30. See also H. Bartle Cox, "M. Victor Laloux: The Man and His Work," *Amer. Architect* 51 (28 April 1920), 639–40; idem. (9 June 1920), 731–32.

American students of Laloux who enjoyed successful professional careers include: Chester Aldrich, George Applegarth, William Lawrence Bottomley, Arthur Brown, Charles Butler, George S. Chappell, John W. Cross, William Adams Delano, Ethan A. Denison, William Emerson, Otto Faelton, Howard Greenley, Frederic C. Hirons, Lloyd Morgan, William E. Parsons, Henry Shepley, Clarence Stein, Lawrence Grant White, and William Van Alen. The following French students of Laloux were later to come to America and, through their practice and especially through their roles as teachers, were to have considerable influence here: Jacques Carlu, Albert Ferran, Jean Jacques Haffner, and Jean Labatut. See James Philip Noffsinger, *The Influence of the Ecole des Beaux-Arts on the Architects of the United States* (Washington, D.C.: Catholic University, 1955). See also "Homage à Laloux."

that characterized the drafting room was traceable to Victor Alexandre Laloux, its genial master, always tolerant of the students' ways—so much so that he was usually willing to intervene on their behalf when some drafting-room prank brought the police down upon them.

The Atelier Laloux was the biggest and most successful of all the ateliers at the Ecole; it consistently produced more winners of the coveted Prix de Rome than any other. Howe was well suited to its atmosphere and to the student life in Paris, in general, with its belief in Art as a way of life and *la vie bohème*— provided one didn't carry it too far. Yet for Howe there were fewer of the careless good times than might have been expected. Though he enjoyed the student life, he was at the same time quite the responsible family man. Frederic Rhinelander King, one of his Harvard friends studying at the Ecole, remembers that Howe "worked diligently with enthusiasm, . . . was much admired by his fellow students and led a very domestic life."[4] It was in Paris on 28 May 1908 that his first daughter, Helen, was born. Shortly before her birth, Howe's mother arrived in Paris and rented an apartment on the same floor as her son's at 41 boulevard Raspail, taking charge of the situation immediately.

Howe has left us few of his memories of the Ecole. Only once, oddly enough in 1932 at the height of his interest in International Style modernism, did he reminisce at length, recalling that at the Ecole

> he became interested in mathematics and construction and learned from Victor Laloux the relation between plan and elevation. He took delight in

Laloux's designs for the railroad stations at Tours and the Quai d'Orsay in Paris, of 1897– 1900, were of enormous influence in the revolutionary organization of plan and section of this building type made possible by the use of electric engines. See Carroll L. V. Meeks, The Railroad Station (New Haven: Yale, 1956), pp. 98, 112, 159; Jean Schopfer, "The Modern Railroad Station," *Record* 11 (Oct. 1901), 557–80. The "spirit" of Laloux's atelier was described by Francis S. Swales as "joyously Germanic . . . Laloux impressed his ideas firmly in the minds of his pupils and during several years they went forth after the manner of the followers of Mahomet to impress the teachings of the prophet upon the world." "Draftsmanship and Architecture as Exemplified by the Work of Paul P. Cret," *Pencil Points* 9 (Nox. 1928), 688–704.

For student life at the Ecole, see Ernest Flagg, "The Ecole des Beaux-Arts," *Record* 3 (Jan.-March 1894), 302–13; (April-June 1894), 419–28; 4 (July-Sept. 1894), 38–43. See also George S. Chappell, "Paris School Days," *Record*, "1. The Projet," 28 (July 1910), 37–41; "2. The Atelier," 28 (Nov. 1910), 350–55; "3. The Charrette," 29 (Feb. 1911), 139–43. Another useful discussion, from the English point of view, is Arthur Davis, "The Training of the French Architectural Student at the Ecole des Beaux-Arts," *The Builder* 16 (23 May–6 June 1919), 515, 538–39, 557–59.

4. Frederic Rhinelander King, letter to author, 3 Sept. 1963.

the strict French logic but he also came indirectly under the influence of the contemporary Germans, with the result that his last design in the school was stigmatized by one of the academic critics as "très Boche." Nevertheless, the Italian influence remained strong. It was only slightly colored by an admixture of French and German modified by an emphasis on structural significance.[5]

Despite Howe's near-silence about his years at the Ecole, its effect on him was long lasting and stands, I believe, along with the influence of Moore, his teacher at Harvard, and Paul Cret, the distinguished Frenchman whose American career as an architect in Philadelphia and as the dominant figure in the School of Architecture at the University of Pennsylvania during the 1920s and 1930s was to influence an entire generation of architects, including Howe and Louis Kahn.[6] Cret was to remain Howe's lifelong friend, and that friendship continuously, no doubt, served to reinforce his convictions in the traditional architectural values which underlay Beaux-Arts thought. So strong was the impact of both Moore and Cret on Howe that their admonitions colored most of his important decisions through his forty-year career in architecture.

While it is difficult to characterize the exact nature of Howe's learning experience at the Ecole, I believe A. D. F. Hamlin's contemporaneous discussion of its influence on the architectural education of Americans offers a fair insight into its method and its spirit. Among the qualities Hamlin stresses are the "discipline" instilled in the student, the casting aside until the designer's maturity of the search for "originality and innovation" in favor of his doing "well and thoroughly the accepted and established thing."[7]

5. "George Howe, An Architectural Biography," p. 21.

6. See Arthur I. Meigs, "Paul Philippe Cret," *T-Square Club Journal* 1 (May 1931), 6–12. For recent discussions of Cret see George B. Tatum, *Penn's Great Town* (Philadelphia: Pennsylvania, 1961); Theo B. White, *Paul Philippe Cret, Architect and Teacher* (Philadelphia: Art Alliance, 1973).

When Cret arrived in America, he became involved in a debate over the value of the Beaux-Arts tradition in architectural education. In response to a spate of rather chauvinistic articles in the *Record* in 1908 and 1909, suggesting that the Ecole's influence might not be in the best interests of a developing American architecture, Cret wrote: "The Ecole des Beaux-Arts: What Its Architectural Teaching Means," *Record* 23 (May 1908), 367–71; "Truth and Tradition," *Record* 25 (Feb. 1909), 107–09.

7. A remark of A. D. F. Hamlin's can serve to explain why the Beaux-Arts theoretician, Julien Guadet, had such a powerful influence on Louis Kahn (1901–74), whereas he seems to have had considerably less effect on Howe. Hamlin wrote in 1908 that Guadet, "author of the famous treatise on the Theory of Architecture, still lectures at the Beaux-Arts. Feeble as he is, in his advanced years, his discourses on the fundamental principles are stimulating and suggestive

Near the end of his career Cret himself produced one of the clearest statements of the strength and weakness, as well as influence, of the Ecole's stress on the plan as the generator of architectural form:

> After five or six years of constant competition, the average student acquires a skill in abstract design, and a resourcefulness in discovering a number of solutions for a given problem, and then selecting the best one. Here he risks falling prey to a misconception. . . . The Ecole believed that the plan, more than all the other features of a design, should show the fitness of a building to its uses. This opinion is undoubtedly correct if we adopt the modernist's view that a house, for instance, is a "machine à habiter." From this, in spite of the Professor's protests, it was only too easy for immature minds to conclude that elevations and sections were relatively unimportant. Thus the Ecole, hypnotized by the search for the "parti" (that is, what characterizes a building), soon began to lavish every effort in the plans. By the end of the nineteenth century, the students went ever further, and almost lost interest in all questions of architectural forms. . . . The plan became a decorative composition, usually over-complicated, and a "beau plan" was a pleasing picture in itself, instead of a necessary diagram for achieving a good organic arrangement of rooms, with opportunity for well-designed facades and good interior treatment.[8]

Only four of Howe's student projects remain. Three of these, awarded prizes, were published in the official records of the Ecole. The first, a sketch design for paper money, though reasonably well drawn, is of only passing concern. The second, a somewhat conventional design for an oceanographic institute, is interesting for the composition of the axes and building elements

---

but for American students what he has to say of the planning of theatres and libraries, hospitals and schools and churches, is either so far removed from American ideas and practice or so far behind them as to be a detriment rather than an advantage to the American." "The Influence of the Ecole des Beaux-Arts on our Architectural Education," *Record* 23 (April 1908), 241–47. Thus Howe would have seen Gaudet at his worst, old and feeble and seemingly irrelevant, while Cret, older than Howe, would have heard him in a more vital phase of his career and would be able to convey to his greatest student, Kahn, an inspiring version of Guadet's ideas and method. For a brief summary in English of the section of Guadet's book dealing with professional practice, see "The Architect's Profession," *Pencil Points* 7 (July 1926), 391–93. It is interesting to note that Hamlin's son Talbot, at the end of his career, sought to revive Guadet's method in terms of modern American practice in his *Forms and Functions of Twentieth Century Architecture* (New York: Columbia, 1954).

8. Paul P. Cret, "The Ecole des Beaux-Arts and Architectural Education," *Journal of the Society of Architectural Historians* (hereafter *JSAH*) 1 (April 1941), 12–15.

at the end of the garden near the entrance. Betraying none of the mannerisms of the Laloux style of "Beaux-Arts Baroque,"[9] the elevation is severe and carefully conceived in terms of the expressive use of masonry.

The third project, a scheme for a post office, testifies to Howe's ability to handle the "Beaux-Arts Baroque" with skill and enthusiasm (*fig. 1*). Its beautifully worked out plan, a good example of Beaux-Arts axial composition, is complemented by an exuberant exterior with a giant order of columns flanked by end pavilions surmounted by globes. A mansard roof sits on a low attic above the frieze. Not a remarkable design, to be sure, but more than competent; Howe's special touch can be seen in the charming figures that people the foreground of the drawing of the elevation. Howe's last project, his thesis, was "the complete plans, structural and mechanical details for the house" High Hollow, which he was to build for himself in Chestnut Hill, Philadelphia, shortly after his return to America in 1913.[10]

"If fortunate is the man as well as the nation who has no history," Howe wrote in 1923, "then the five years of peaceful married life, occupied in travel and the study of architecture in Europe, that marked the beginning of my postgraduate career, must have been the happiest in my life." It was with a "sense of elation," nonetheless, that he returned to America in June 1913 "to take up the daily task in earnest."[11] Friends recommended that he settle in New York and open his own office. Philadelphia, it was felt, offered few opportunities

9. This term was used by Vincent Scully in *Modern Architecture* (New York: Braziller, 1961), pp. 16, 29. The more usual term, "Neo-Baroque," although acceptable, emphasizes stylistic mannerisms at the expense of the underlying principles that help to distinguish the style from its seventeenth-century prototype. Alan Burnham, in *New York Landmarks* (Middletown: Wesleyan, 1963), uses the term "Beaux-Arts Eclectic." This he regards as a "rather free French interpretation of classic architecture" (p. 49). It is useful more as a description of the overall stylistic attitude throughout the century than as a description of the Garnier-Laloux variant, a freely conceived variation on the baroque, combining Art Nouveau influences with others, that was characterized by A. D. F. Hamlin in 1908 as the " 'cartouche architecture' [which] has become a byword in New York." "Influence of the Ecole des Beaux-Arts." Another writer of the period defines the Beaux-Arts style as "an amalgamation of Louis XVI detail, L'Art Nouveau inspiration and other influences emanating from an ingenious desire to express structural form." Stanely D. Adshead, "A Comparison of Modern American Architecture with that of European Cities," *Record* 29 (Feb. 1911), 113–25. See also Claude Bragdon, " 'Made in France' Architecture," *Record* 16 (Dec. 1904), 561–68. For a recent general description of the Beaux-Arts style and method, see also William H. Jordy, *American Buildings and Their Architects. Progressive and Academic Ideals. Turn of the Twentieth Century* (Garden City: Doubleday, 1972), pp. 278–80.

10. King, letter to author, 3 Sept. 1963.

11. "George Howe," in Harvard University, *Class of 1908, Secretary's Fourth Report* (Cambridge, Mass., 1923).

for large commissions and was, besides, hidebound by strict conventions in architectural taste as in everything else. But Howe's wife wanted to go to Philadelphia, her family home. Howe was rich, with limited ambitions, and William Penn's "Greene Countrie Towne," however restricted its apparent opportunities for artistic success, at least seemed to guarantee an orderly life in an established social context. So Philadelphia was right enough for both.

While Howe looked for a job, the young couple rented an old house in Chestnut Hill, a rather clumsy Victorian relic, which the fledgling architect remodeled slightly and decorated with furniture and objets d'art purchased in Europe. Harold D. Eberlein thought well enough of it to illustrate it in an article he wrote for the *Architectural Record* in November 1914.[12]

During the summer of 1913, Howe made inquiries about jobs in a rather desultory fashion, eventually taking a position with "an ancient and honorable firm of Philadelphia architects more noted for its probity than its artistic gifts, where I spent three years in comparative affluence."[13] That firm, Furness, Evans and Company, was in its dotage. Long before his death in 1912, its driving force, Frank Furness, had been beaten down by the wave of academic neoclassicism that swept America after the World's Columbian Exposition of 1893. Furness, in earlier days, had been the idol of young Louis Sullivan, who was amazed by the brusque Philadelphian's ability to "make buildings out of his head."[14] By the time Howe was asked by Allen Evans to become a full partner in November 1913, what had once been the most wildly original firm of architects in Philadelphia, and probably in the country, had degenerated into a routine "plan factory."

Considering Howe's relative lack of office or field experience and his extreme youth—he was twenty-seven—Evans's offer of partnership seems remarkable. But Howe's education at the Ecole had provided him with a fine background and it was probably hoped that this charming and well-educated young man would be able to infuse new life in the "outworn Victorian traditions" of the firm.[15] Howe's first undertaking as full partner was the supervision

12. Harold D. Eberlein, "Current Tendencies in the Arrangement of Interiors," *Record* 36 Nov. 1914), 394–420. Photographs of Howe's drawing room and dining room are on p. 418.

13. "George Howe," in Harvard University, *Class of 1908, Secretary's Fourth Report.*

14. Louis Sullivan, *Autobiography of an Idea* (New York: Dover, 1956), pp. 190–91. For Furness, see James F. O'Gorman et al., *The Architecture of Frank Furness* (Philadelphia: Museum of Art, 1973). Vincent Scully suggests that Furness's architecture can now be seen as the most directly French-derived of the Philadelphia architects. Furness's French influences were from the writings of Viollet-le-Duc and the neo-grec work of R. M. Hunt, his early master.

15. "George Howe," in Harvard University, *Class of 1908, Secretary's Fourth Report.*

of the detailing and the preparation of working drawings for the Commercial Trust Building—a gloomy combination of Renaissance forms and Victorian heavyhandedness built at Fifteenth and Market Streets in Philadelphia. He had little to do with the design of the building, and it is cited only as a curiosity typical of Furness, Evans and Company's late work.

Howe enjoyed considerable self-assurance as a result of his success at Furness, Evans and Company. His family was growing (his second daughter, Ann, was born on 3 January 1914), and early in 1914 he decided to move out of his "Victorian relic" of a house into one more suitable to his needs and tastes, one of his own design. He called the house, which he designed and built between 1914 and 1917, High Hollow.[16] Though adapted from his thesis at the Ecole, this complex suburban villa is not a dry working out of academic rules dutifully learned but a combination of Howe's thoroughly romantic formal predilections and Beaux-Arts principles of composition and expression.

At High Hollow the principles of particulate space and rationalized structure were given threedimensional form in a composition of such restraint, sensitivity, and strength that it established the standard for fashionable country house design around Philadelphia for the next twenty years (figs. 2-9). Often imitated, this beautiful house, certainly a minor masterpiece, was never surpassed by Howe or by the many architects who came to design in his manner.[17]

Located in the farthest extremities of Chestnut Hill and bordering Fairmount Park, High Hollow enjoys some of the most spectacular scenery in the Philadelphia area. The work of a man who knew Italy well, its long vista reminded Paul Cret of the Villa d'Este, and its secluded spaces evoked for him some "peaceful Italian cloister" while its relationship to its hill site seemed as integral as "the terraces and houses of Amalfi are [to] the cliff over the bay."

16. Louis E. McAllister, one of Howe's draftsmen, believes that the name was suggested by Cret. Letter to author, 7 March 1963. The house was sold by Howe in 1928 to Mr. and Mrs. Samuel Crozer, for whom he added a swimming pool. The Crozers in turn sold it to Mr. and Mrs. Samuel Paley, who willed it upon their death to the University of Pennsylvania for use as a conference center.

17. Another member of Furness, Evans and Company was Charles Willing, who in the twenties, as a member of the firm of Willing, Sims and Talbutt, was to become a most successful imitator of the Mellor, Meigs and Howe style. Talbutt's early work, like some of Mellor and Meigs, was in the Pennsylvania colonial style. See Harold D. Eberlein, "Two Good Moderate-Cost Houses," *Record* 36 (Sept. 1914), 198–211; for the work of Willing, Sims and Talbutt, see Eberlein, "Latin Feeling and English Tradition Combined in One House," *Arts and Decoration* 22 (Dec. 1924), 30–32, 68. Robert Rodes McGoodwin was another architect who worked to considerable advantage in the manner established by Mellor, Meigs and Howe. See his "A French Village, Chestnut Hill, Pennsylvania," *Amer. Architect* 135 (20 April 1929), 499–509; and R. R. McGoodwin, *Monograph on the Work of Robert R. McGoodwin* (Philadelphia: Fell, 1942), esp. pls. 29–49; 62–63, 65–84, 105–11.

But beyond the languid Italianate spell which High Hollow seems to cast, there are more fundamental qualities that Cret recognized when he wrote that it was "quite free from imitation of historic precedent in its details. Were not the phrase 'modern art' somewhat discredited for having been a cloak for a multitude of sins, I would see here a very typical example of what modern art ought to be: a logical combination of the best traditions. It is free from archaeological imitation as it is devoid of a pretentious striving for originality."

High Hollow, extremely refined, is nonetheless infused with considerable sculptural force. Though it undoubtedly reminds one of Italy, and especially of the Villa Madama, its sensitive use of materials—Philadelphia red brick and local stone—and its careful siting make it an interesting effort toward the development of a modern vernacular architecture. As Cret noted, it is "picturesque without affectation." It has a strong "affirmation of individuality . . . and a distinctive elegance achieved only by a highly developed culture."[18]

The plan consists of a main rectangular block containing the family quarters and a service wing situated diagonally to it. This is a *parti* frequently employed in what Vincent Scully has called the Shingle Style.[19] Its plan bears great similarity to that of 1891 for the E. S. Hand House at Southport, Long Island, designed by Wilson Eyre, another and highly influential architect of Philadelphia and in the teens and twenties a good friend of the Howes.[20] But Howe sweeps aside the informality of Eyre's scheme, with its wide palette of building materials, and imposes a disciplined geometry of masonry. This formality is not without surprises, as in the case of the small balcony that connects the two principal bedrooms on the second floor, and the brilliantly conceived main stairway, with its dazzling spatial and optical effects. Its cantilevered landing, at the halfway level above the main floor, forms a bridge as it crosses the hall; it allows one to perceive from the entrance hall the quite unique arrangement of the house upward as well as downward on the three different levels, and

18. The quotations are from Paul Cret, "A Hillside House . . . ," *Record* 48 (Aug. 1920), 83–106; reprinted in *A Monograph of the Work of Mellor, Meigs and Howe* (New York: Architectural Book Publishing Co., 1923), pp. 24–27. Hereafter cited as *Work of Mellor, Meigs and Howe*.

19. Vincent Scully, *The Shingle Style* (New Haven: Yale, 1955). In addition to the George D. Howe House discussed below, other plans illustrated in Scully's book similar to that of High Hollow are the G. N. Black House, Manchester-by-the-Sea, Mass., by Peabody and Stearns, ca. 1882; and the W. B. Howard House, Mount Desert Island, Me., by William Ralph Emerson, ca. 1883–84.

20. See "House at Southport, L.I., New York," *Amer. Architect* 36 (4 June 1892), 154, pl. 858; Julian Millard, "Work of Wilson Eyre," *Record* 14 (Oct. 1903), 280–325. For a recent discussion of Eyre, see James D. Kornwolf, *M. H. Baillie Scott and the Arts and Crafts Movement* (Baltimore: Johns Hopkins, 1972).

draws the eye to an almost limitless vista across the garden and valley beyond.

While the connection with Eyre's design might be dismissed as coincidence, High Hollow's relation to another Shingle Style house employing this organizational *parti* is far more direct. For Howe knew well the house of his aunt and uncle, Mr. and Mrs. George D. Howe, Cliffs, Smith's Point, Manchester-by-the-Sea, Massachusetts, designed by Arthur Little about 1886 (*figs. 10, 11*). It was a favorite vacation spot of Howe's mother's; he visited there often as a child, and it was there that he was to be reunited with his family upon his return from service in World War I.[21]

Whereas Eyre and Little attach their diagonal service wing directly onto the main block, Howe, composing according to Beaux-Arts principles, uses a cylindrical form (in this case a turretlike stair tower) as a pivoting element. This is as appropriate in terms of function as it is successful in terms of composition. Everywhere at High Hollow, then, there is an attempt not to make rooms out of areas or functions but to compose spaces that have their prime basis in use and their definition in structure. As volumes, moreover, these spaces are composed with far greater freedom and imagination in section than the symmetrical and rather formal plan would at first seem to indicate.

The relationship between the interior and exterior spaces also illustrates this principle. The disposition of the grounds themselves reflects Beaux-Arts compositional theories, with spaces as separate and specific as those indoors: devoted to sitting, walking, and working, and, as Paul Cret remarked, "each of these in the proper place and with the special character it deserves. . . . The general layout has, in the . . . division of spaces . . . the quality of the well-planned industrial plant where each process of fabrication is in fact in the right relation to the preceding and succeeding processes."[22] One need not emphasize this point, for we can be certain that Howe's intentions hardly lay in the direction of that awakening machine consciousness which was just beginning to affect European architectural thought. Yet Cret's remarks of 1920 are interesting in light of Howe's later career.

Because Howe conceived of both indoor and outdoor spaces as parts of a

21. In fact, as Walter Knight Sturges points out, Cliffs and High Hollow have something in common in addition to their plan: each set a style for its generation of architects and yet each architect turned away from it. "Arthur Little and the Colonial Revival," *JSAH* 32 (May 1973), 147–63. See also Helen Howe West, *George Howe, Architect* (Philadelphia: William Nunn, 1973), pp. 5–6; Helen Howe West, letter to author, 24 July 1973.

22. Cret, "A Hillside House." In this context, it is interesting to observe certain formal relationships between High Hollow and LeCorbusier's Villa Favre-Jacot of 1912. See Charles Jencks, *LeCorbusier's Tragic View of Architecture* (Cambridge: Harvard University Press, 1973), pp. 38–39.

total composition, the exterior wall assumed an extremely important role as a space divider. To this end, the windows on the first floor are actually glass doors deeply recessed into the plane of the wall in order to reveal its thickness. When opened, they slide into the wall with great elegance, admitting generous amounts of light and allowing ease of access. All the same, the integrity of the wall—as much a continuous surface as a cage of masonry—is maintained. Frank Lloyd Wright faced similar problems in his lifelong efforts toward "the destruction of the box."[23] In the work of his first mature period, like the Larkin Building of 1904, Wright separates buildings into as many component parts as possible: piers are articulated in the manner of a skeletal cage; walls are treated as weightless skins, distinct wherever possible from the structure. Howe, on the other hand, despite his articulation of bearing and nonbearing structure, seeks a fusion of parts emphasizing the continuity of the surface of the box.

Despite all the words that have been spent on the integration of indoors and outdoors, neither Howe nor Wright lost sight of the need to structure each environment according to its own characteristics, nor confused the natural with the man-made. Howe's was a static conception; Wright's a dynamic one. It was the young Europeans, basing their work on Wright's forms as seen in photographs and applying them to a highly regularized structure that did not grow out of those forms, such as Mies's Barcelona Pavilion, who destroyed this classic relationship between space and structure. Wright himself, in later years, became more concerned with the "space within" as the "reality of the building" than with the building fabric itself, and Howe, then directly under his influence, came to feel that architectural form and style occupied a position of importance secondary to the quality of enclosed spaces.[24]

High Hollow testifies to Howe's confidence in the possibilities of a masonry architecture; it is a logical outgrowth of his work at the Ecole and relates directly to his student project for an oceanographic institute. Although the specific formal references may at first glance seem foreign to the Philadelphia region, there is almost no recognizably eclectic detail, and the plan, probably because of its strong central-hall organization, seems almost a cross between

23. Wright used this phrase frequently toward the end of his life. See "Organic Architecture" in Frederick Gutheim, ed., *Frank Lloyd Wright on Architecture: Selected Writings, 1894–1940* (New York: Duell, Sloan and Pearce, 1941), pp. 177–91.

24. For Howe's attitudes toward interior space, see Edwin Bateman Morris, "Architecture of Today and Tomorrow," *A.I.A. Journal* 4 (Nov. 1945), 203–10. Scully develops this point at length in "Wright, International Style and Kahn," *Arts* 36 (March 1962), 67–71, 77. See also Scully, "Wright Versus the International Style," *Art News* 53 (March 1954), 32–35, 64–66, and the ensuing discussion in *Art News* 53 (Sept. 1954), 49–50.

Georgian and Shingle Style as sifted through a French sensibility.[25] Most noticeable is the simplicity and directness with which natural seam-faced stone of dark brown and red hues is combined with red brick and with wood trim painted a dull blue. The stone was selected with great care: a long-abandoned local quarry was opened up to secure the proper type of Philadelphia ledge stone, which was then laid up by experienced masons. It is not the quality of the brick nor the stone itself, finally, that is most important, but the effort spent in the consideration of the nature of the materials and of the forces in the wall. Great care was taken in the detailing of floor levels by means of brick string-courses and in the differentiation between bearing and infill walls, retaining walls, relieving arches, and so on, to make the clearest possible expression of the building as a constructed object. It is composed of separate elements—literally put together piece by piece—not only functionally and spatially but structurally as well.

High Hollow marks the beginning of Howe's search for a resolution between his rationalism and his romanticism. It is rational in the disposition of spaces and the handling of materials, romantic in the formal configurations extracted from those spaces and materials. Howe's search was halting and haphazard, and his instinctive ability to handle brick and stone and to compose shapes seemed to delay rather than to accelerate his progress. Design came easily to him, as George Biddle has suggested. One senses a progressive spirit at work—an open mind awkwardly reaching to the future but without direction.

High Hollow is Howe's first and certainly one of his best houses. The large sliding windows, the spatially complex stair, the almost complete absence of ornamental detail, and the profound respect for the realities of masonry construction all contribute to its success and testify to the freshness of its approach. It is architecture in the great tradition; a way of building that, as Cret wrote, owes "so little to precedent [and] is true to the best tradition of art, finding the soul of our art instead of the cast-off clothing of former time."[26]

25. See Bruno Zevi, "George Howe, An Aristocratic Architect," *A.I.A. Journal* 24 (Oct. 1955), 176–79. This article was translated from the Italian by Carroll Purves. The original appeared in *Chronace* 16 (July 1955).
26. Cret, "Hillside House."

3. Wall Street Pastorale

> It was little enough to look back on; but when he remembered to what
> the young men of his generation and his set looked forward to—the
> narrow groove of money-making, sport, and society to which their
> vision had been limited—even his small contribution seemed to count,
> as each brick counts in a well-built wall. He had done a little in public
> life—he would always by nature be contemplative and a dilletante—but
> he had had high things to contemplate, great things to delight in. . . .
>
> Edith Wharton, *The Age of Innocence*

Howe had been taken into Furness, Evans and Company "with the avowed
intent of infusing life into its outworn Victorian traditions . . . [but] finding
the arteries of these traditions so hardened by age as to be sensitive to no artificial stimulus, either external or internal," he decided "after a three years'
trial . . . to pulsate in freer channels." He left Furness, Evans and Company in
1916 and joined a "young firm, though of established repute," Mellor and
Meigs, which then assumed the name of Mellor, Meigs and Howe.[1]

Walter Mellor was born in Philadelphia on 25 April 1880.[2] He was graduated from Haverford College in 1901 and from the School of Architecture at
the University of Pennsylvania three years later. After working in the office of
T. P. Chandler in 1904-06, he joined Arthur Ingersoll Meigs to form the firm
of Mellor and Meigs.[3] Mellor was extremely quiet, as conservative in his tastes
as in his social and political opinions. His Quaker restraint was in great contrast to the garrulousness of Meigs. Born on 29 June 1882, Meigs, a graduate
of Princeton, seems never to have received formal training as an architect or
any practical experience prior to joining Mellor in 1906.[4] Meigs was more like

1. "George Howe," in Harvard University, *Class of 1908, Secretary's Fourth Report*
(Cambridge, Mass., 1923).

2. He died on 11 Jan. 1940. See C. M. P. [C. Matlack Price], "As He is Known, . . : Walter
Mellor," *The Brickbuilder* 24 (Aug. 1915), 208; "Walter Mellor," *Country Life* (U.S.) (Oct.
1921), 47.

3. T.-P. Chandler is best remembered as the founder, in 1890, of the Department of
Architecture at the University of Pennsylvania. For a brief account of his work, see George B.
Tatum, *Penn's Great Town* (Philadelphia: Pennsylvania, 1961), pp. 118, 182, pl. 86.

4. Meigs died on 11 June 1956.

Howe than Mellor was; he came from a prominent Philadelphia family and was an enormously rich, sensitive, and apparently very difficult man. Spoiled, positive of the rectitude of his thought, he could belabor the most insignificant point for hours in an effort to force another person to see it his way. Intelligent but bull-headed, his conservatism always assured him a place ten years behind the time.[5]

The work of the young firm of Mellor and Meigs enjoyed a fine reputation among Philadelphians and in the pages of the architectural press in the years just before World War I. It seemed to strike a progressive note and it was often linked with contemporary English efforts and with the late, medievalizing work of Wilson Eyre. Its eclecticism, though free of the "period" styling so characteristic of the time, did not, however, grow out of a specific concern for the Philadelphia vernacular such as that underlying High Hollow. The country house as designed by Mellor and Meigs, and many others, was almost completely derived from the work of Eyre, whose long career as a designer of residences spanned fifty years and who may be classed with M. H. Baillie Scott, C. F. A. Voysey, and Edwin Lutyens as a skillful manipulator of picturesque form and traditional materials.[6] In terms of larger-scale work, his position in the history of domestic architecture in America between Richardson and Wright is in many ways similar to Sullivan's.[7]

The architecture of Mellor and Meigs was one of mood; that is to say, its formal basis was arrived at through literary analogy rather than through struc-

5. Helen Howe West notes that Meigs's Ingersoll family connection "ties him to many clients—(and therefore also ties G. Howe as his partner). . . . Many clients were attracted to Mellor, Meigs, and Howe by some of these social things; and/or actually were related to one of the partners." Letter to author, 4 Aug. 1973. For a discussion of the Bullitt House in this regard, see chap. 4.

6. For a discussion of tendencies in Philadelphia domestic architecture, with emphasis on the influence of Eyre and an incisive characterization of the work of Mellor, Meigs and Howe, see C. Matlack Price, "The Country House in Good Taste," *Arts and Decoration* 23 (Oct. 1925), 42–44, 95. See also "Twenty-Second Annual Philadelphia Architectural Exhibition," *Amer. Architect* 109 (31 May 1916), 353–58; "Twenty-Third Annual Philadelphia Architectural Exhibition," *Amer. Architect* 111 (4 April 1917), 209–13.

7. The placement of Eyre between Richardson and Wright is suggested by remarks made by Vincent Scully in *The Shingle Style* (New Haven: Yale, 1955), pp. 121–25, especially: "That this sense of extended horizontal plane and intensified, 'positive' scale evident in Eyre's work became a later component in the work of Wright . . . represents, however—as Wright's work later represents in a much more complicated way—the pulling together of the free architecture of the 80's into a stronger and more coherent order. It simplifies, unifies and intensifies. It reveals, especially in plan and space, the development of an integrated, disciplined design." See also James D. Kornwolf, *M. H. Baillie Scott and the Arts and Crafts Movement* (Baltimore: Johns Hopkins, 1972).

ture or function. Thus the Charter Club at Princeton University (1913) was English Georgian;[8] the Phi Gamma Delta Fraternity House at the University of Pennsylvania, Collegiate Gothic.[9] At the same time, in the design of country residences and farm buildings, where specific images were not so pronounced and any number of historical "styles" were considered appropriate, the architects did allow themselves considerable freedom. Beginning with a rather obvious attempt to revive traditional Pennsylvania Dutch forms in their remodeling in 1909 of a stable in Germantown owned by Walter Mellor's brother Alfred, there is in their domestic work a gradual progression toward an architecture displaying great craftsmanship and using, in a single building, elements from many styles rather than concentrating on one specific set of formal references. Typical of these later designs is the Caspar W. Morris House built at Haverford, Pennsylvania, in 1916.[10] Loosely composed and many gabled, it is completely picturesque. Although each material is handled with great care and each element (gables, chimneys, doors, windows, and the like) is skillfully designed, the total conception lacks vigor and coherence. This is an architecture of impressions, a broad eclecticism in which suggestions of many previous forms are all rather casually combined as one might have composed them in one's mind after a fleeting trip across the English countryside in a train. It lacks discipline and order. These Howe could provide.

The offices at 205 South Juniper Street, built in 1912 by Mellor and Meigs for their own use, were probably their finest work.[11] With a limited budget and a restricted site in an urban residential neighborhood surrounded by architecture of the highest quality, the architects produced an admirably simple two-story brick structure. Next door, at the corner of Juniper and Locust Streets, is Wilson Eyre's house of 1890-91 for C. B. Moore,[12] which in turn neighbors the same architect's house for Joseph Leidy, now the Poor Richard Club. Though Mellor and Meigs's scheme is restrained, it is marred by such stylistic appendages as a cupola and an indecisiveness in the handling of the gable at the Juniper Street end of the so-called Big Room. Nonetheless, the planar structure in brick, with window openings cleanly cut into the wall, especially on the north side, has about it enough toughness and severity to ensure compatibility with the Victorian masterpieces that adjoin it.

8. See *Work of Mellor, Meigs and Howe*, pp. 148–54.

9. Ibid., pp. 155–64.

10. Ibid., pp. 1–13.

11. Ibid., pp. 184–89.

12. See "House at the Corner of Locust and Juniper Streets, Philadelphia, Pa.," *Amer. Architect* 37 (24 Sept. 1882), 201, pl. 874.

Howe's effect on the firm was immediate and all for the best. It can be seen in the second remodeling of an old stable for Alfred Mellor. The first remodeling was an addition built in 1909. To accommodate it, the masonry of the original exterior was repainted and a white mortar was substituted for the original gray to simulate the stonework used by the Pennsylvania Dutch. Similarly, the woodwork was painted white, and shutters and a double door were added. The result is thin and too bright, principally because painting makes the stonework lose its texture and appear synthetic. In 1916, after Howe had joined the firm, the stable was enlarged.[13] The contrast between the new wing and the portion remodeled earlier is remarkable. Presumably under Howe's influence, the stable became gracious, solid, and inviting. Local stone was used with a dark mortar to create a sheer wall plane with a slight texture. Great attention was given to the articulation of structure, especially where high springing arches carry the second floor over an arcade. As in High Hollow, Howe's reticence is manifest in a design at once powerful and refined.

The new partnership of Mellor, Meigs and Howe had hardly taken effect when America entered the European war in April 1917. Meigs, commissioned in the field artillery, joined the Fourth Division in the Argonne. Mellor, slightly deaf, was not able to serve. Howe sailed for France in May 1917, after enlisting as a private in the reserve corps of the Pennsylvania Hospital Medical Unit (Base Hospital no. 10).[14]

World War I came, Howe later wrote, and "the beautiful fabric of the leisurely bourgeois structure collapsed about my ears." His first "vivid recollection as an enlisted man," he later recalled, "was of endless sick and wounded rolls . . . , evacuation lists, death notices, and parti-colored 'chits,' in the British Base hospital we had taken over." Life in the army was dull, and Howe's "preferred professional relaxation was arguing with the French owner of the one sanitary pump in town against his claim that he was too busy to evacuate the cess-pools." When it was not dull, it was certainly grim enough, and Howe's memory of the first German mustard gas attack was of "burned and congested men, a new horror, in from the battlefield today, out to the transports and to England tomorrow."[15]

13. *Work of Mellor, Meigs and Howe*, pp. 140–44.
14. "George Howe," in Harvard University, *Class of 1908, Secretary's Third Report* (Cambridge, Mass., 1920). See also Helen Howe West, *George Howe, Architect* (Philadelphia: William Nunn, 1973), pp. 5–6.
15. "George Howe," in Harvard University, *Class of 1908, Secretary's Sixth Report* (Cambridge, Mass., 1933).

But Howe, with his command of the French language and his continental background, was wasted in the medical corps. He wrote: "Before long my existence and my remarkable talents were brought to the attention of the powers that be, and I was summoned to GHQ. Here I was commissioned First Lieutenant in the Corps of Interpreters and ultimately sent as Assistant A. M. to Berne to become by turns opéra-bouffe spy, clerk, accountant, property officer and potential defendant in a series of threatened courts-martial. A friend of mine was to say, I held the front line of desks with unexampled fortitude."[16]

After the Armistice of November 1918, Howe was demobilized in France. He was not allowed to return home, and in February 1919 he was sent by the Peace Commission on a diplomatic mission to Munich. Bavaria had been the first of the German republics to declare its independence. Its revolution had been successful and a Socialist government established, with Kurt Eisner as prime minister. The events of 1919 in Germany have faded from our memory in light of the horrors that succeeded them in the next three decades. Nonetheless, the roots of that later trouble can be traced to the violence of this first postwar year: the Communist-inspired Sparticist uprising, led by Rosa Luxemburg and Karl Liebknecht, and the reprisals of the reactionaries. Howe witnessed these in dangerous proximity.

Eisner was the strongest of the Socialists in Bavaria, but even he could not ward off the tide of national conservatism. The workers' and soldiers' councils were disappointed and disillusioned with the state of affairs after the war. Tensions were building up among the populace, and, when Howe arrived in Munich, the city was in the grip of fear. He dined with Eisner and Auer on the night of 20 March 1919. Eisner had reconvened the Diet; it was to meet on the following day, at which time he would announce his resignation. On his way to the session, he was shot dead by a young student, a counter-revolutionist, Count Arco-Valley. As Rudolf Coper has written, "the Diet began its session. Auer was shedding tears over the crime just committed when the door of the chamber opened. A man walked slowly across the floor, the worker Lindner. He shot two bullets at Auer who he thought was responsible for Eisner's death. Then he killed a police officer who tried to stop him. Auer was severely wounded but soon recovered."[17] That Howe was one of the last people to talk to Eisner and Auer before these events was of little importance to the course of history. But the impact of the events on Howe's still

16. Ibid.
17. Rudolf Coper, *Failure of a Revolution: Germany in 1918–1919* (Cambridge: New Press, 1955).

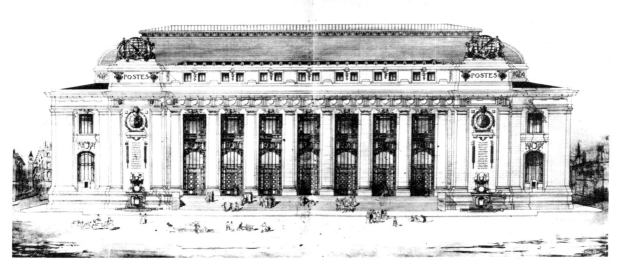

Fig. 1. Post office. Student project, Ecole Nationale des Beaux-Arts, Oct. 1912.

Fig. 2. Photo from Howe's files, labeled "Italy" by him.

Fig. 3. High Hollow, George Howe House, Chestnut Hill, Pa., 1914–16, plan.

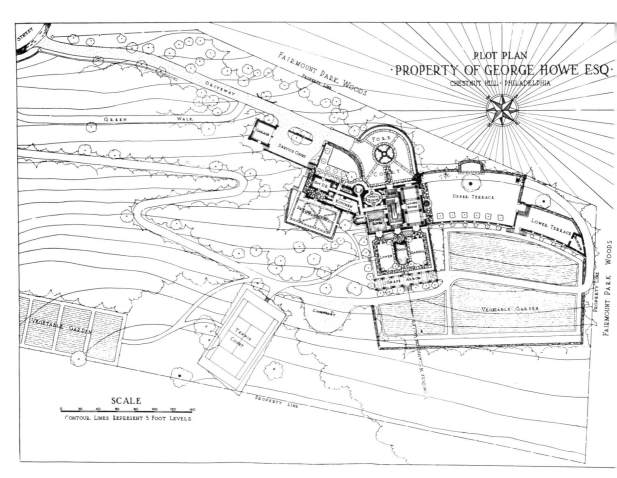

Fig. 4. High Hollow from the driveway.

Fig. 5. High Hollow, living room from the forecourt.

Fig. 6. High Hollow from the lower terrace.

Fig. 7. High Hollow from the lower garden.

Fig. 8. High Hollow, stair hall from entrance door.

Fig. 9. High Hollow.

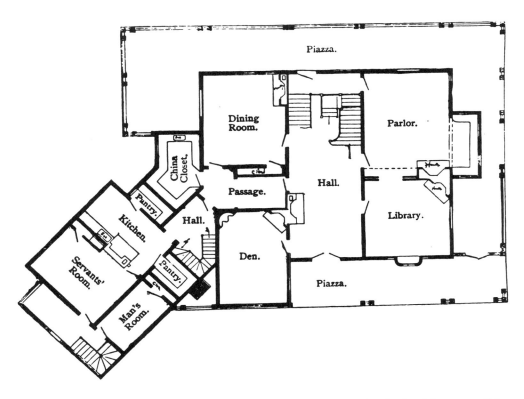

Fig. 10. Arthur D. Little. Cliffs, George D. Howe House, Manchester-by-the-Sea, Mass., ca. 1886, first-floor plan.

Fig. 11. Cliffs, general view.

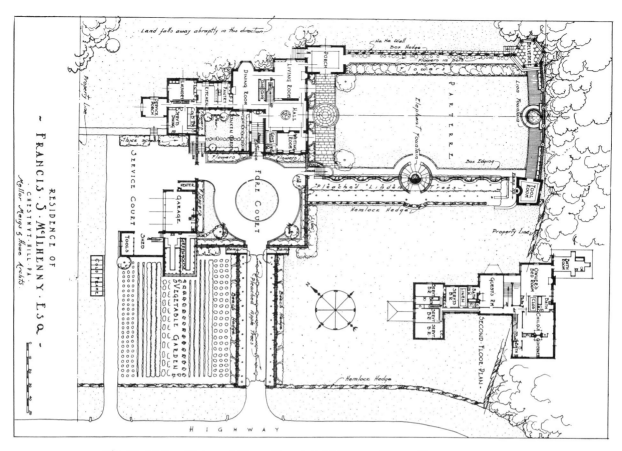

Fig. 12. Mellor, Meigs and Howe. Francis S. McIlhenny House, Chestnut Hill, Pa., 1916–18, 1921, plan.

Fig. 13. McIlhenny House.

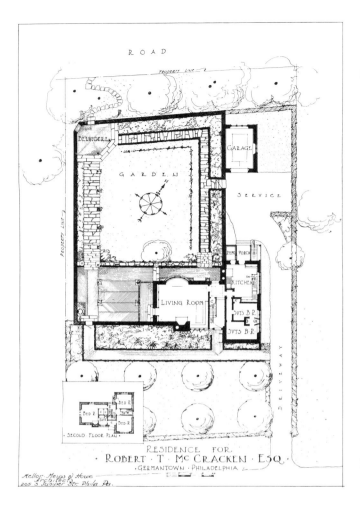

ROAD

PROPERTY LINE

BELVIDERE

GARDEN

GARAGE

SERVICE

PROPERTY LINE

SIDE PORCH

KITCHEN

LIVING ROOM

SVTS B R

SVTS B R

DRIVEWAY

BED R

BED R

BED R

SECOND FLOOR PLAN

RESIDENCE FOR
· ROBERT · T · MᶜCRACKEN · ESQ ·
· GERMANTOWN · PHILADELPHIA ·

Mellor Meigs & Howe
Architect
205 S Juniper St. Phila Pa.

Fig. 14. Mellor, Meigs and Howe. Garth, Robert T. McCracken House, Germantown, Pa., ca. 1920–21, plan.

Fig. 15. McCracken House, entrance side.

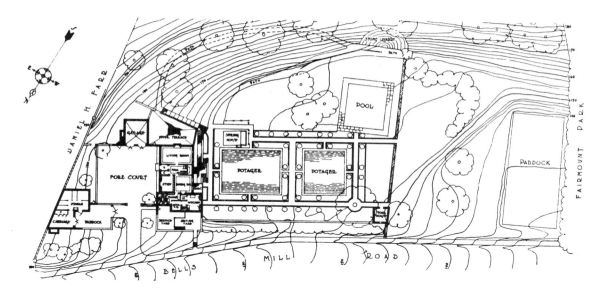

Fig. 16. Mellor, Meigs and Howe. Benjamin A. Illoway House, Chestnut Hill, Pa., ca. 1922, plan.

Fig. 17. Illoway House, view of entrance court.

Fig. 18. Illoway House, view from lower garden.

Fig. 19. Illoway House, staircase.

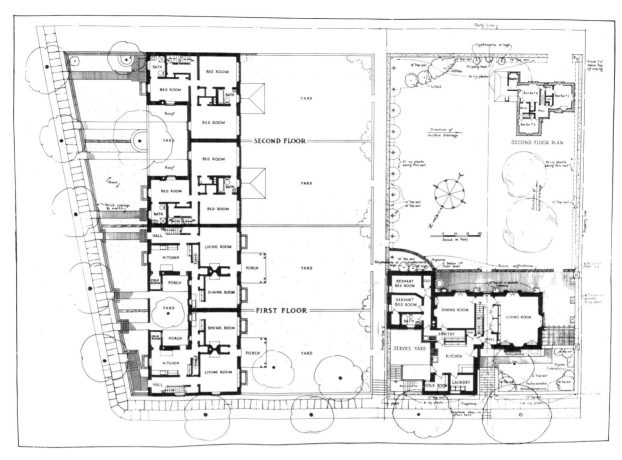

Fig. 20. Mellor, Meigs and Howe. Four-house development and Howe-Fraley Residence, Chestnut Hill, Pa., 1921, plans.

Fig. 21. Four-house development.

Fig. 22. Howe-Fraley Residence, garden facade.

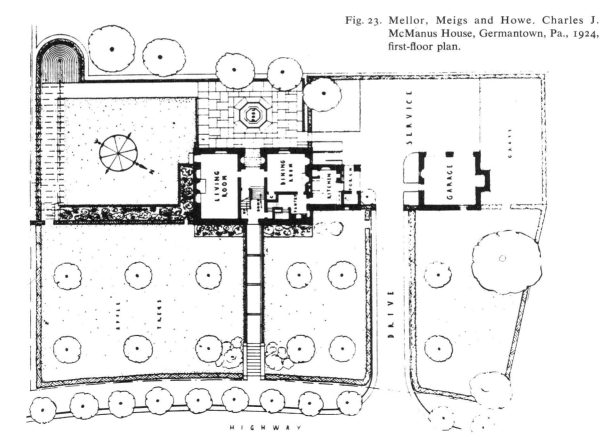

Fig. 23. Mellor, Meigs and Howe. Charles J. McManus House, Germantown, Pa., 1924, first-floor plan.

Fig. 24. McManus House, garden facade.

Fig. 25. Photo from Howe's files, labeled "Farm near [Etange?]" by him, ca. 1921.

Fig. 26. Mellor, Meigs and Howe. H. F. C. Stikeman House, Chestnut Hill, Pa., 1921–23,
view from road.

Fig. 27. Stikeman House, view from garden.

Fig. 28. Mellor, Meigs and Howe. Carl E. Siebecker
House, Bethlehem, Pa., 1925, plan.

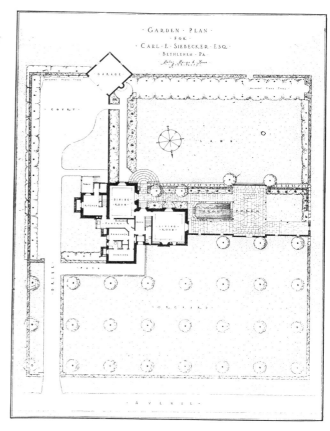

Fig. 29. Siebecker House, garden facade.

Fig. 30. Siebecker House, view of garage.

relatively unshaken complacency was considerable. The war, uglier and less romantic than he had thought it would be, had retained up to that moment enough swagger to satisfy his cravings for freedom in romance. The gnawing agony of what followed the war was a different matter. For Howe it was to become almost unendurable.

Later in 1919 Howe was appointed American representative on the Interallied Teschen Commission, whose aim was to resolve the political future of the Duchy of Teschen (Upper Silesia). We do not know Howe's exact role on this commission, but he later wrote of the effect the negotiations had on him: "In Teschen, I knew the people, the unhappy state of the individual without a government. From there I made journeys to visit and confer with Marsaryk and Benes in Prague, Paderewski in Warsaw. I lived for the first and only time behind the scenes of world politics where the actors, great and small, are human beings instead of puppets on a newspaper stage. It was an illuminating, exciting and distressing experience."[18]

His work on the Interallied Commission over, Howe was able to return to America in August 1919, after two and a quarter years abroad. Like so many others, he was faced with the inevitable disillusionment that follows periods of intense altruism; he personally chose to suppress, at least for the present, his memories and his ideals and to subside into the security, however illusory, of Chestnut Hill. It seemed desirable, indeed imperative, to forget the war. Howe set out with great intensity to reweave the torn threads of his weakening family life and to entrench himself deeply in acceptable social and professional patterns.

Chestnut Hill is an upper-class enclave within the geographical and political borders of the city of Philadelphia. Considered more civilized and dignified than the Main Line suburbs, it has the atmosphere of a small village, and its residents enjoy more than the usual amount of pride of place. Its houses are large and comfortable but not usually palatial. Built close together on easily maintained properties, these small estates have been the principal reason for the area's stability through the years.[19] Francis Biddle, who lived on Schoolhouse Lane in neighboring and similar Germantown during the twenties and thirties, accurately defined its spirit and that of Germantown when he wrote in the first volume of his memoirs that his life in Philadelphia "hardly touched

18. "George Howe," in Harvard University, *Class of 1908, Secretary's Sixth Report.* See also Maxwell Levinson, "George Howe's Contribution to Contemporary Architecture," *USA Tomorrow* I (Oct. 1954), 42ff.

19. See Willard S. Detweiler, Jr., Inc., *Chestnut Hill, An Architectural History* (Philadelphia: Chestnut Hill Historical Society, 1969).

the tightly held together and closely knit group that spread along the Main Line, played golf at the country clubs, knew what they wanted in life and got it. . . . [Main Line society] was a pleasure-loving society, more rooted to the land than that of most American cities, solid and prosperous, but lacking in imagination and curiosity."[20] Chestnut Hill, on the other hand, is a simpler place than the Main Line and, despite its fundamental conservatism, one not closed to the consideration of ideas.

Howe found it natural to settle into this familiar atmosphere of ease and gentility. Successful and relaxed and more than a little lazy, he seemed content to assume the role of suburban gentleman for which his Edwardian youth had prepared him so well. His life assumed a regular pattern. During the day, he would be driven by a well-tailored chauffeur in an exquisite Isotta-Fraschini car to his office on South Juniper Street in downtown Philadelphia or to the golf club to join in a game with one of his friends—who were also his clients. In the evening there were dinner parties at which, as Francis Biddle remarked, "the same faces appeared and reappeared each year, each season a little older, the cautious well-bred talk, and the amiable and routine minds, not so much disillusioned as devoid of curiosity and of any passion." But there was also a small group that gathered informally: a dozen or so spirited men and women, mostly in the arts, who, rather than going to more cosmopolitan New York, chose to remain in Philadelphia. Biddle captured the flavor of these gatherings and of the personalities:

> Arthur Carles, who was cynically drinking himself to death, and was bent on breaking down the courage of the others who tried to make a living by painting; . . . Leopold Seyffert, turning out dozens of well-paid portraits, very fashionable at the time, sometimes saved from mediocrity by help from Henry McCarter, who had taught him at the Academy of Fine Arts, and Adolphe Borie, . . . [who] was French to his fingertips, . . . with delicate, overrefined perceptions, more articulate than creative. His friendly sweetness and good manners made him universally popular, and concealed the dark melancholy that may have been connected with his turning from his fashionable success as a portrait painter to try other less effective experiments in paint.
>
> There was Franklin Watkins—in 1931 he won the first prize at the International Exhibit of the Carnegie Institute with his "Suicide in Costume"—painting his portraits with the inner eye for half-hidden traits. . . . Now and then Joseph Hergesheimer would turn up, pleasantly ribald and

20. Francis Biddle, *A Casual Past* (Garden City: Doubleday, 1961), pp. 385–86.

lively. He had written his best novels and had turned to describing dress
and furniture rather than men and women. Stokowski, whose particular
friends were Carles and McCarter, was too absorbed in what he was
doing to waste himself in our pleasantly aimless drinking and skylarking.[21]

Francis Biddle himself was a successful and high-minded lawyer who described his own personality in those years as one of "restless impatience,
resulting from an over-vitality of nerves always wound tight," finally impelling
him to leave Philadelphia and launch the distinguished career in public life
that culminated in his service as attorney general of the United States under
Franklin D. Roosevelt.[22] His wife, Katherine Garrison Biddle, a charming
woman with instinctive friendliness, enjoyed considerable success as a poet.
George Biddle, his older brother, just then becoming recognized as a painter
of merit, was also part of this group, although he spent most of his time
away from Philadelphia. Since Groton, he had been Howe's closest personal
friend, and his awkwardly American outlook, charm, and directness were extremely refreshing in this somewhat overrefined atmosphere.

And there was Howe, as charming and carefree in his manner as he was
careless of his talents. Always a delightful guest who never failed to acknowledge a handsome object, beautiful garment, or fine wine put before him, he
was something of an Edwardian dandy in his attitudes and conversation:
formal and somewhat precise, detached and willing to participate in individual
events while reserving judgment on the entire spectacle of life itself. In this
way Howe succeeded, as did many other nearly middle-aged men during this
time, in living in two worlds, the nineties and the twenties; the former had
shaped so many of his values and manners while the latter was a time when he
was mature enough to exercise them and old enough to find them challenged
by a restless younger generation.[23]

At these gatherings Howe would beguile the crowd with delightful conversation. He liked to act out charades, particularly with Katherine Biddle, who
"when the mood was on could turn herself inside out and be unexpectedly disorderly or scabrous." Frequently, they would be joined by Paul Cret, whose
specialty was a grave and "correctly infantile playing [of] an illegitimate Biddle

21. Ibid. Carles was a particular friend of Howe's, and Robert McLean writes of "his
efforts to pull Arty out of his depression and the fund he raised to send Carles to Paris for a
year where he attempted to regain his earlier skills, but with limited success." "A Few
Recollections of George Howe," in West, *George Howe*, p. 35.

22. Biddle, *A Casual Past*, p. 398. For an account of Biddle's later years, see the second
volume of his autobiography, *In Brief Authority* (New York: Doubleday, 1962).

23. This similarity between the nineties and the twenties is pointed out by Frank Freidel,
intro. to Thomas Beer, *Mauve Decade* (New York: Random House, 1961). p. xi.

baby in Rittenhouse Square." Cret's wife Marguerite "had the acuteness of the French educated *bourgeoisie,* and could analyze Philadelphia gossip with a deft yet discreet touch." R. Sturgis Ingersoll, then just beginning to amass his remarkable art collection, completed the group.[24]

These early years of the twenties were quiet ones for Howe. They were also "charmingly dull."[25] His marriage was not a success. Mrs. Howe thrived on the more mundane aspects of the suburban life of Chestnut Hill. Of absolutely no intellectual aspirations, Maritje, as she was called, was uncomfortable in the presence of the strange guests Howe often brought home. She was not snobbish; hers was the shyness of the incurious. The tragedy of the marriage lay deeper than incompatibility. Mrs. Howe had never been interested in her husband's work. She seemed almost afraid of ideas, and as Howe became more dissatisfied with the limited boundaries of his world, she retreated more and more into herself. With the passing years, as he began to involve himself in engrossing architectural theories and experiments, the fabric of their marriage gradually disintegrated. Mrs. Howe became increasingly eccentric, substituting a vast number of pets for the affection she seemed no longer to obtain from her husband. Immovable and irreconcilable, she gradually retired from active life.[26]

One of Howe's friends, Owen Wister, who came from an old Philadelphia family, was always a welcome guest. Author of *The Virginian,* he was the most distinguished Philadelphia man of letters. He was not a great writer, but his gentleness of wit and subtle satiric skills endeared him to a considerable and conservative audience. Howe provided the illustrations for two of Wister's less memorable books. The first, a collection of satirical rhymes titled *Indispensable Information for Infants; or Easy Entrance to Education,* contained a number of "careful charts" drawn by Howe. These were in the form of line drawings that illustrated the satirical clerihews, such as:

Edgar Allen Poe

> Edgar Allen Poe
> Never could bear Harriet Beecher Stowe.
> He said that she would talk about slaves
> When he wanted to talk about graves.[27]

24. Biddle, *A Casual Past,* p. 388.

25. Howe, untitled talk delivered before the students of the Graduate School of Design, Harvard University, 1954.

26. They were divorced in 1948.

27. Owen Wister, *Indispensable Information for Infants;* . . . (New York: Macmillan, 1921).

In 1923 Wister wrote a play, *Watch Your Thirst,* a spoof on Prohibition, which took as its motto the sentiment, "You may lead a man to water but can you stop his drink?"[28] It was set in mythical times, and Howe's drawings are witty and satiric characterizations of the Roman pantheon.

In 1923 a lavishly illustrated folio, *A Monograph of the Work of Mellor, Meigs and Howe,* was published. It enjoyed considerable success and became, as Howe wrote, "a sort of handbook for the Young Romantic."[29] It established the firm of Mellor, Meigs and Howe in the forefront of the profession as architects of freely conceived country houses. Wister contributed a preface which, though gentle, was not without spice. He suggested that "charm and beauty" need not be crowded to the wall by "Commerce [which] juts up from the face of the world like a host of warts, huge clumps, long welts, mills, mean rows of houses." Industrial buildings "with a true expression growing from their structural necessities need not be an offense to the eye; but least unimpeded and most ready to our hand is the dwelling house, and no one has shown better than Messrs. Mellor, Meigs and Howe how this may keep the expiring spark of beauty alive and clothe our domestic moments with a form of grace."[30]

Wister pointed out that "life determines the true character of any building," a notion that Howe developed in an essay written especially for the *Monograph.* Ostensibly a discussion of four buildings designed by the firm (Bird House for the Philadelphia Zoo; workshop for Samuel Yellin; garden building for Charles Biddle; offices of Mellor, Meigs and Howe—all with the possible exception of the Bird House designed before Howe became associated with Mellor and Meigs), it used them merely as touchstones in a vague though complex theoretical consideration of the true nature of function in architecture. Using a botanical metaphor, Howe characterized this function as the "outcome of an agreeable human necessity."

> Human necessity is the sea from which springs architectural design, and by necessity design is foreordained, not only in its general outline, but in its every detail, as the form and feature of a plant are determined before the first shoot has burst its sheath. Furthermore, as a plant will inevitably develop some special and satisfying quality—if not the fragrance of the rose or the strength of the oak, at least the humble succulence of the cabbage—if allowed to follow its natural development from the seed,

28. Owen Wister, *Watch Your Thirst;* . . . (New York: Macmillan, 1923).

29. "George Howe," in Harvard University, *Class of 1908, Secretary's Sixth Report.* The monograph was reviewed anonymously in *Architectural Forum* (hereafter *Forum*) 39 (Oct. 1923), 26, where it claimed: "Few offices where domestic architecture is chiefly followed have been more successful than that of Mellor, Meigs & Howe."

30. Wister, preface to *Work of Mellor, Meigs and Howe,* pp. 5–7.

unwarped and unblighted, so will every building develop some special and satisfying quality, however humble it may be, if allowed to follow its inevitable growth from the seed of human necessity. This special and satisfying quality constitutes the essential beauty of a building as of a plant, and on this essential beauty the by-product of mere external beauty is utterly dependent.[31]

Apologizing for this long exposition of architectural theory, Howe wrote that, although the "halls of our schools of design resound, and the pages of our technical publications are black with the word 'organic,' and with lengthy dissertations on its meaning, important dictates of organic growth to architecture are more honored in the breech than in the observance when it comes to practice." This essay marks the earliest formulation of Howe's philosophy of functionalism. Like that of Louis Sullivan to whom it probably owes a debt, it is beclouded with psuedo-scientific comparisons.[32] Howe would nurture this philosophical premise during the coming years, shedding the outworn biological metaphor as he studied the mathematical developments of the day and sought to relate architecture to the so-called space-time continuum, an unhappy juxtaposition but fashionable until recently. Through all this, however, he never lost sight of "human necessity" as the motivation for architectural design.

Life was sweet for Howe during the few years immediately after his return from the war, almost sickeningly so. The shame of it was its waste. Together with his partners, Howe built well, expending effort and considerable talents on buildings of no special importance for clients who desired little more in architecture than to be pleased. By 1925 the firm of Mellor, Meigs and Howe enjoyed a position second to none among American architects who designed residences.[33] Howe, although anxious to bring the best to his art, was content

31. Howe, "Four Buildings," in ibid., pp. 169–72. The interdependence of the Mellor, Meigs and Howe office and the workshop of Samuel Yellin was a particularly close one. The Arch Street Studio, which Mellor and Meigs designed for him in 1910, saw the production of the most beautiful ornamental metalwork that graced High Hollow, as well as virtually every work of the firm. See Myra Tolmach Davis, "Samuel Yellin's Sketches in Iron," *Historic Preservation* 23 (Oct.-Dec. 1971), 4–13.

32. In 1924 Sullivan's eloquent statement of biological metaphor was published, his *System of Architectural Ornament* (New York: A.I.A.); see also Donald Drew Egbert, "The Idea of Organic Expressionism in America," in Stowe Persons, ed., *Evolutionary Thought in America* (New Haven: Yale, 1950), pp. 336–96.

33. "Among those architects designing in the 'picturesque,' [with] very indirect European derivation," Mellor, Meigs and Howe were, according to C. Matlack Price, "the most brilliant [having] achieved a quality of technique. . . . definitely their own. . . . [They] have made an unusually intelligent and imaginative use of precedent. They have seen it as a point of de-

with his quiet success. His romanticism, growing out of a desire to escape the modern world, contrasted with the romanticism of the European modernists, which grew out of an intense desire to participate in that world. Edmund Wilson's criticism of F. Scott Fitzgerald, written in 1922, can well serve for Howe, older in years but, like the flappers' hero, the master of his craft though not yet of his art. Fitzgerald had been given, Wilson wrote, "imagination without intellectual control of it; he has been given a gift for expression without many ideas to express."[34] Howe's imagination and intellect lay ready and as yet virtually unused.

Although technically a partnership, the firm of Mellor, Meigs and Howe was actually organized as a collaborative association, with the three architects (and especially the two better-known and more gregarious of the trio, Howe and Meigs) practicing more or less independently. Each project was handled by the partner who brought it into the office. The staff was at the service of all the partners, and there was, of course, considerable discussion about each project as it was being designed. Mellor appears to have chosen to pursue a more passive role in the firm, concerning himself more with running the office than with securing clients or designing.

Arthur Meigs brought to the firm a sense of picturesque, asymmetrical composition derived from Wilson Eyre and the English Arts and Crafts. Howe, on the other hand, exhibited a sure skill in the expressive handling of material and functions according to principles of particulate composition learned at the Ecole. In the early twenties, as Nathaniel Burt has written, Meigs's influence dominated the firm and his version of the Norman farmhouse was a "not very chic perhaps but awfully well-bred and 'nice' kind of house of native stone with steep roofs, graceful, cosy, rambling, roomy, one that adapted itself to the hilly sites, terraces, walled gardens, cobbled forecourts and other nostalgic Europeanized detailed for which the cultivated and traveled patrons of the past Philadelphia generation yearned."[35]

---

parture rather than a thing to copy and because of their imagination they have been able to adapt subtly from the English country house and the French farm house and to avail themselves, for variety, of a slight Italian accent, yet always to design houses that seem undeniably at home in the countryside about Philadelphia. . . . [Their] work is a rich contribution to American country house architecture, for it is not only genuine and beautiful in itself, but it raises a certain standard by which other work is measured." "The Country House in Good Taste." Even as late as 1928 the work of Mellor, Meigs and Howe was held in high esteem; see C. H. Blackall, "American Architecture Since the War," *Amer. Architect* 133, (15 Jan. 1928), 1–11.

34. Edmund Wilson, "Fitzgerald Before the Great Gatsby," in Alfred Kazin, ed., *F. Scott Fitzgerald: The Man and His Work* (New York: Macmillan, 1962), pp. 78–84.

35. Nathaniel Burt, *The Perennial Philadelphians* (Boston: Little, Brown, 1963), p. 363.

The house in Chestnut Hill for Francis S. McIlhenny, called Ropsley, begun in 1916 and developed through the early years of the twenties, is typical of the firm's medium-sized house design (*figs. 12, 13*). The house had originally been designed in a free Italian manner, with low roofs, a more spread out version of Eyre's Cochrane House of 1891, but, as the project developed, this scheme was discarded in favor of the simpler one in which no period style is dominant. It reflects the French-Italian spirit of High Hollow as well as Howe's interest in the use of Chestnut Hill stone.[36] The McIlhenny House is, as Meigs wrote, both functional and appropriate. "Whether the results are good or bad is open to question, but certain it is that, from the standpoint of the designer, much more pleasure and benefit may be derived from the planning of a house, up from the ground, rather than down from a style."[37]

The house for Robert T. McCracken, built in 1919–20 in Germantown, also shows the strong influence of Meigs, who probably designed it while Howe was still in Europe (*figs. 14, 15*). A small house on a restricted lot, its plan is straightforward and compact with a combined living-dining room. Its relationship to the site and to the courts and gardens was carefully planned to extend vistas while maintaining privacy.[38]

The success of the McCracken House, as with most of the firm's small houses, depends to a considerable extent on the knowledgeable use of natural materials. The use of Chestnut Hill ledge stone in conjunction with brick, cast concrete, and shingles was regarded as a most important characteristic in

36. See Harold E. Dickson, *A Hundred Pennsylvania Buildings* (State College, Pa.: Bald Eagle Press, 1954), p. 87. Dickson's descriptions of the firm's work are most articulate and especially important in their contextual implications, establishing links not only with Wilson Eyre but also with Lutyens.

Two renderings of the original proposal may be found in Arthur I. Meigs, "The Design of a House at Chestnut Hill, Philadelphia," *Forum* 31 (Oct. 1919), 119–22; reprinted in *Work of Mellor, Meigs and Howe*, pp. 33–60. For Eyre's Cochrane House, see "Residence, Corner Thirty-sixth and Baring Streets, Philadelphia," *Inland Architect* 22 (Jan. 1894), pls.

37. Meigs, "Design of a House." Meig's account of the design of the McIlhenny House goes a long way toward justifying the claim that modern architecture, like any other style, is a question of form and not function or constructional technique. The composition of elements according to the demands of orientation as well as the considerable use of cast concrete—mostly for ornament—does not alter the fact that this house, like all the others of the firm, was fundamentally traditional in its appearance.

38. The McCracken House was enlarged in 1926; see Arthur I. Meigs, " 'Garth,' " *Record* 64 (Nov. 1928), 355–78. Jonathan Lane has shown that, despite the conservatism characteristic of American domestic design in the twenties, economics, if nothing else, made compact, open planning necessary, preparing the way for the stylistic revisions of the thirties. The McCracken House is an excellent example of this tendency. "The Period House in the Nineteen Twenties," *JSAH* 20 (Dec. 1961), 169–78.

the development of a local style in Philadelphia.[39] The critical response to the
directness of these houses was immediate, and there was general agreement
that, from both aesthetic and sociological points of view, their simplicity
of mass and their skillful siting marked an important step toward a domestic
architecture that would take into account the growing informality of American
life as well as the gradual diminution of size that characterizes suburban development during the last fifty or sixty years.[40]

Unquestionably, new values affecting American life and American domestic
architecture were coming into play after the war. By 1919 Charles Herbert
Moore, Howe's teacher at Harvard, was turning from the strictly historical
formulations that had been his concern during the previous fifteen years or
so. In that year he devoted the first of a series of theoretical essays, which were
to appear in *Architectural Record* during the following ten years, to a consideration of domestic architecture. American designers, he complained,
seemed to lack "good taste," a quality he defined as that "which forbids the
incorporation of borrowed fancies or features that are unnecessary or inappropriate in any given case." His complaint was accompanied by a plea
for a simple architecture in which "construction alone may give ornamental
character." As to structure, it "may be concealed—it is largely so of necessity
in every organism—but that it must not be falsified is an immutable law."[41]

Howe's first commission after his return from the war in August 1919 was
the house for Benjamin Illoway on Bells Mill Road, Chestnut Hill, which was
designed and built in 1919–20 (*figs. 16–19*). He probably had little time to
work on this design, for what he produced was essentially a reworking of the
parti employed at High Hollow, which it overlooks. The emphasis was shifted
from the composition and expression of interior volumes to the composition
of dense shapes built of ledge stone, intended to define exterior spaces. The
shapes themselves are symmetrical with relatively small openings cut cleanly
into the walls. This compositional device, the asymmetrical arrangement of

39. In *The American Spirit in Architecture* (New Haven: Yale, 1926), Talbot F. Hamlin
wrote that the "garden front of the McCracken House shows the charm of the stratified
masonry of this Pennsylvania stone, and shows how it can furnish the keystone for the whole
design" (p. 334); see also p. 265.

40. C. Matlack Price," "Attaining the Ideal in the Small House," *Arts and Decoration* 15
(Sept. 1921), 28–86; reprinted in abbreviated form in *Work of Mellor, Meigs and Howe*, pp.
61–64. Russell Lynes describes with only half-exaggeration the extraordinary triviality of much
work of the 1920s, a good deal of which was based on such prototypes as were inadvertently
supplied by Mellor, Meigs and Howe and other skilled practioners in romantic effects and traditional design. *The Tastemakers* (New York: Harper, 1954), pp. 237–41.

41. Charles Herbert Moore, "Some Principles of Design and Construction," *Record* 45 (May
1919), 210–16.

symmetrical shapes, frequently used by Mellor, Meigs and Howe, is most successful on the garden side of the Illoway House, where a complex interplay between walls and changing levels creates a base for the house as well as a series of delightful small terraces along the steep downward slope of an extremely difficult site. The differentiation between the parts of the building fabric is less precise here than at High Hollow, but the consistent use of one material throughout most of the construction gives an impression of clarity. Still, in relation to its prototype, the Illoway House remains a somewhat stiff variation.

A four-house development on Germantown Avenue, designed by Howe in 1921 as a variation on the Philadelphia row house, is rather calculated and archaeological in its use of American Georgian detail—a response, in all likelihood, to the "colonial" character of the buildings along Germantown Avenue (*figs. 20, 21*). Of considerably more interest is the house Howe designed in the same year, around the corner at 10 West Chestnut Avenue, for his mother and aunt (*fig. 22*). Its plan is straightforward. Situated between high walls and close to the street, to which it turns an almost blank facade, the house opens at the back to a small secluded yard. The forms are French in origin but so devoid of detail that almost all the visual interest is achieved through the extreme severity of the silhouette and the boldness of the projections. A strong pattern develops from the contrast between the exposed concrete frame and the stuccoed infilling. Thus the concrete, made to simulate cut stone, is used to define openings, casually express floor levels, and give visual strength to the corners. At the entrance, where these materials are used in combination with local stone and exposed half-timbering, this technique fails to convince—as where the concrete and stone intermingle at the entrance steps—but in the rear elevation, where only two materials are used, there is that quality of abstraction and toughness and complexity of composition that one associates with the best architecture in Philadelphia and especially with the work of Furness.

Closely related to the Howe-Fraley House but much gentler in its form is the small residence for Charles J. McManus in Germantown (*figs. 23–25*). It is a compact plan with a split in level which, though it anticipates one ranch-house design of the 1950s, gives the entrance facade of the house a monumentality belied by its actual size. The McManus house is perhaps the most explicitly dependent on historic precedent of all the firm's work, though the overall strength of the design does not lie in its historicism but in the simple geometry of the composition.

The house of H. F. C. Stikeman, built on Hampton Road in Chestnut

Hill in 1921–23, is beautifully adjusted to the difficult, steep site (*figs. 26, 27*).[42] The garage and bedrooms are at street level; the living and dining rooms and their attendant spaces are one level below; and below them, forming a base for the house, is a high basement containing laundry and mechanical spaces. Built of wood and local stone, the house reflects Howe's concern for the composition of distinct shapes that are closely related to functional, spatial, and structural demands. The "separateness" of the Stikeman House is in distinct contrast to Meigs's more picturesquely conceived house for Robert T. McCracken. A variation of the Stikeman house, probably designed by Meigs, is the residence for Ralph J. Baker, Harrisburg, Pennsylvania, which employs an L-shaped plan in order to obtain privacy on the street and give the illusion of spaciousness on a restricted site.

Yet another relatively small house of the period is that of Carl E. Siebecker at Bethlehem, Pennsylvania (*figs. 28–30*). Here a more complicated plan is reflected in a restless composition of juxtaposed boxes of brick capped by pronounced shingled roofs and punctuated with exaggerated dormers and bays built in cast concrete. A wooden porch pavilion and a garage complete the composition. The house sits on a platform; the site drops off in gentle increments toward the open country. Walls extend out across the landscape in a manner reminiscent of Mies's country house projects of the period, though probably imitative of Lutyens's work. Although no direct connection to European modernism is implied, it is interesting to note that Howe, writing of the "style" of his work almost thirty years later, referred to it as "Paleo-Plasticism, since it corresponded closely in duration with Neo-Plasticism."[43]

All these houses fade into insignificance beside the best known of the firm's designs, the estate of Arthur E. Newbold, Jr., at Laverock, Pennsylvania, a project that occupied the firm's attention from 1921 to 1928 (*figs. 31–38*). The Newbold Estate, now demolished and subdivided for tract housing, must be considered, even by pre-World War I standards, an extensive residential building project. A gentleman's farm on an enormous scale, it should not be considered as typical of the firm's work nor representative of its best efforts, but as the quintessential example of the architects' romanticism, combining generous amounts of architectural make-believe with sound building in a composition that Howe was fond of describing in his later years as a "Jumbo,

42. The site was a portion of Howe's original holdings at High Hollow, which he sold to Stikeman. See West, *George Howe*, p. 7.

43. Howe, "Some Experiences and Observations of an Elderly Architect," *Perspecta* 2 (1953), 2–5.

Anti-Economy, Romantic Country-House Package, complete with sheep folds, duck ponds, dovecotes and immemorial elms, transplanted at great expense."[44]

For the architects, as for the client, the Newbold Estate offered an elaborate escape route from the unpleasant realities of the Machine Age to the security, however false, that the pre-industrial and bucolic past seemed to have offered. The modern farm, Meigs wrote, exists for one purpose, "the desire to make money," whereas the traditional farm was directed toward the "desire or necessity of making a living." The specialization of the modern farm has with it "all the ugliness of money-making in general" while "the process of making a living out of a farm—that is out of the land—will, by its very essence, produce results resembling nature in their beauty, since the elements that are being dealt with are natural, and any organic arrangement of natural elements cannot fail to produce a beautiful whole." At the Newbold Estate the intention was simply "to surround a pleasant country dwelling with some of the appurtenances that properly belong to country life, some of the elements . . . that go with an old-fashioned farm, instead of living in a suburban villa that differs only from a house in town by being less advantageously situated."[45]

One can easily criticize this psychology, as well as the theatricality of the estate's sagging roof lines and the other details contrived to give an appearance of age, but it would seem more profitable to seek out the virtues in its defects. Reflecting on his work in the twenties in general and the Newbold Estate in particular, Howe once asked himself:

> What were we trying to do, we Romantics? . . . Were we merely trying to recreate a picturesque past without any higher purpose than to arrive at sense-soothing and soporific forms? I venture to say no.
>
> As I look back on the conviction with which we imposed ducks, sheep, doves and cows on rueful stockbrokers, I am convinced these animals represented to us a "Symbol," the symbol of the fruitful soil as opposed to the hundred-acre suburban lot with its dreary monotony of lawn and landscaping. . . . That we . . . gave these symbols a "configuration" out of the past shows merely our incapacity to invent a better one.[46]

The commission for the Newbold Estate probably originated with Meigs, who unquestionably took the initiative in the design, but Howe, with his sure sense for constructional detail, supervised its execution. Attribution of its

---

44. Ibid.

45. Arthur I. Meigs, *An American Country House* (New York: Architectural Book Publishing Co., 1925), pp. xxciii–xxix.

46. Howe, "Some Experiences."

authorship was a sore point with Howe, and many years later when Howe was terminating his relationship with his partner William Lescaze he wrote the following, with particular reference to the Newbold Estate:

> That is the way it worked out with Mellor and Meigs. I loyally tried to uphold the unity of the firm authorship, even including in it my own house which Meigs never saw until it was completed, and asserting far and wide that Meigs and Mellor and I always worked together on all our projects, so that we were all jointly responsible. However, I found that when the medal of the Architectural League was awarded [in 1925] necessarily not to our work in general but to the particular work exhibited that year [the Newbold House], Meigs was not slow to seize the opportunity to publish a monograph on this work in which it was set forth how he individually and personally conceived and executed this monument of domestic architecture.[47]

The book, a lavish folio called with some pretension *An American Country House,* was published in 1925 and was to enjoy wide circulation. In it, Meigs, who regarded himself as somewhat a man of letters, claims to have planned to write a book about the "unconscious" architecture of the French countryside. But he was interrupted when Arthur Newbold mentioned to him in the winter of 1921 that he planned to keep sheep. "The idea fitted in pretty well with all that I had been thinking and trying to write about," Meigs wrote later, "so I abandoned the book for the time, and made him an extremely rough perspective scrawl on a piece of brown wrapping paper of the manner in which I conceived he could keep sheep."[48] This led directly to the design of the pigeon tower, sheepfold, goose pond, and farm court, which were completed during the summer of 1921. In 1922 the avenues of trees were planted, and the cottage, *potager,* and tennis court were constructed; in the following spring the alterations to the house—which had been built ten years earlier by other architects—were begun. These continued until 1924. The only major addition after 1924 was the swimming pool designed by Meigs in 1928, a Gothic fantasy that Howe found particularly offensive and that served as the actual point of dispute in the breakup of the partnership (see chapter four).[49]

At the Newbold Estate the architects attempted to extract the maximum in

47. Howe, letter to Lescaze, 5 November 1934.
48. Meigs, *An American Country House,* p. xi.
49. Interview with Louis E. McAllister, Philadelphia, July 1961.

picturesque charm from the presence of animals as well as human occupants, from the emphasis on the buildings as useful components of a working farm, and from the structural and functional components of the buildings themselves. Careful study will reveal that it is function, not in the dismal utilitarian sense that the architects of the *Neue Sachlichkeit*[50] emphasized but in the realm of the imaginative interpretation of use, with which both the anonymous Norman buildings and the firm of Mellor, Meigs and Howe were concerned. The elaboration of joints and intersections as well as gates, railings, and door handles gave a richness to the strong geometric forms. The architects sought, according to Meigs, to "bring back forgotten functions and clothe them with a form of grace."[51] Returning the animals to the main entrance and the vegetables to a position in the immediate front of the whole design, they pursued not so much the forms as the methods of the Norman builders down to the smallest detail. For example, as Meigs described it: "The door locks have been pulled out of their holes and set again where they may be seen and enjoyed. The treatment and decoration of function has been the controlling force throughout the entire design, and since function is everywhere in domestic architecture, function becomes the motif of the place. . . . Function and the revelation of construction."[52] Thus the fabric of the wall was made to express as clearly as possible the nature of the building process as well as to indicate important arrangements in the interior. Permanent and simple materials were used everywhere, always with an eye toward clarity of articulation. For example, the treads of the stairs are expressed on the exterior of the tower, as are the landings. At the same time, the cylindrical tower asserts itself against the rectilinear forms of the hall and the upstairs bedrooms.[53]

Only once did the architects revert from their concern with constructional expression to a more easily comprehended though exaggerated kind of struc-

50. For a discussion of this term see chap. 4.

51. Meigs, *An American Country House*, p. xvi.

52. Ibid. In this regard Meigs indulges in an elaborate discussion of the "chessmen" that were used as doorpulls in the owner's bedroom suite. According to McAllister, these were designed by Howe as chessmen and adapted for use as hardware by the firm.

53. Meigs writes: "The Tower runs through the center of the design and everything must make way for it. We find indications of its presence throughout three floors, not only when we are in it, but in all the spaces which adjoin it. It intrudes itself upon the Hall, Mr. Newbold's Bed Room, the Tower Room, and all the adjacent smaller spaces and closets. Nowhere in its vicinity are we allowed to forget its existence. The construction of the Stairs forces itself equally upon our attention; it may be seen from above or below, and not only from within but from without, as each step runs through the thickness of the wall and marks the Tower as Stair Tower from without; the evidences thereof appearing and disappearing as the stairs wind upward." Ibid.

tural revelation. As Meigs wrote, "the beams, where they show in the ceilings are heavy, far heavier than necessary to achieve a roof that could stand, using the minimum amount of material, and extra strength has been thrown in by way of good measure. We like to look at a beam that is capable of carrying its load two or three times over, if necessary."[54]

Of the farm buildings, the sheepfold is perhaps the most interesting. Sited across the downward slope of the land, it was deliberately curved in plan so that it would sit more naturally. This curve was continued not only in the ridge but through the entire roof. Meigs wrote: "An extremely satisfactory impression of strength is imparted to the whole, very similar to the impression of strength produced by the curved lines of a ship, not only in its plan, but in the curved sections of its hull and of its decks as well—while in the case of this building it seems almost to cling to the land on which it stands."[55]

The roof of the pigeon tower is also noteworthy. It is constructed entirely of courses of brick laid in concentric rings, each separate ring of laid header, arching itself and thus becoming self-supporting. The quoins and lintels used about the openings of the sheepfold and pigeon tower are of concrete colored to resemble limestone. The lintels were cast in place whereas the quoins were cast on the ground. In the case of the latter, the forms of "rough lumber" were made by a carpenter and the surface of the concrete was left untouched after their removal—"a pleasant texture being thus easily obtained."[56] It was not until after World War II that so-called modern architects operating in an idiom that has come to be described as Brutalism—Le Corbusier being the foremost among them—came to realize the expressive possibilities of overstated structure and the articulated use of rough formwork used in concrete construction.[57]

The origins of the forms of the Newbold Estate lie in the peasant architecture of the Normandy region of France, which both Meigs and Howe felt derived its richness from the expression—indeed, the overexpression—of the elements that made up the building fabric (*figs. 39–41*).[58] During the war

54. Ibid., p. xvii.
55. Ibid., p. xxix.
56. Ibid., p. xxx.
57. See Reyner Banham, *The New Brutalism* (London: Architectural Press, 1966).
58. Sympathy for Norman France was stimulated by the publication in 1904 of Henry Adams's epochal book, *Mont-Saint Michel and Chartres* (Boston: Houghton Mifflin). Adams's constant references, snobbish and sentimental, to the Anglo-Saxon-Norman heritage, appealed to a whole generation of Americans desperately seeking roots in the pre-industrial European past. See esp. chap. 1, "Saint-Michiel de la Mer del Peril," and chap. 4, "Normandy and the Ile de France."

they had both seen a good deal of that region and had come to find in its masonry buildings an unaffected simplicity which Meigs was to call "unconscious."[59] Late in the summer of 1920, Meigs and Howe returned to Normandy for six weeks to study these buildings more thoroughly. With an archaeologist's zeal, they photographed and measured them and prepared elaborate drawings, especially of Le Manoir d'Archelles, which was to influence considerably the design of the Newbold Estate.[60] Of course, the source may have been even more direct: this first specifically francophile farm design of the firm's may have been influenced by Wilson Eyre's Farm Group at Glen Isle, Chester County, Pennsylvania, which was published by Elisha Harris Janes in 1919. It is interesting to note that Janes's article begins with a long discussion of the "effect" on American "country boys" of French and Italian farm complexes, with their "dove cotes, gate lodges, etc., each with its individual charm and beauty. . . . Let us hope, "Janes continues, that the experience or the war will influence American taste, "and that when the silo is to be built the coming farmer will think of Normandy, or if it is to be a barn, he will recall the one he was billeted at and take out his snapshots and say to his dad, 'Let's have something like that.' "[61]

The impact of the Newbold Estate on the architectural profession as well as on the general public was widespread; the ensemble apparently came to symbolize a kind of grandeur combined with a simplicity that clients and architects alike recognized as essential to elegant living. The estate was thus also assured an important role in the critical literature of architectural reform, which during the middle twenties was growing more insistent in its tone

59. Meigs, *An American Country House*, pp. ix-x.

60. Ibid., pp. x-xii. Meigs does not mention, in recounting his European trips, that Howe and sometimes Maritje Howe accompanied him (Meigs was at this time a bachelor). Helen Howe West recalls that her parents did not really care to travel with Meigs, who boorishly almost always acted the stereotyped role of the American tourist—insulting the local population, getting drunk, and at least once landing both Howe and himself in jail for disturbing the peace. Letter to author, 4 Aug. 1972.

61. Elisha Harris Janes, "Buildings for the Modern Farm," *Forum* 30 (March 1919), 63–74. There is also a second part: 30 (April 1919), 109–14. The specific sources for some of the firm's work are illustrated as part of Richard H. Pratt's "Where Small Houses Come From," *House and Garden* 49 (Jan. 1926), 55–59, 130, 132.

Unquestionably, the war rekindled interest in historic architectural form, especially in vernacular buildings of the relatively remote countryside, which, in a time before the automobile, was little visited. These pragmatic building forms, usually ignored in history books, had a strong and predictable impact on a great many American soldiers. John E. Burchard and Albert Bush-Brown have restated Janes's interpretation of the war's effect on the architectural taste of the doughboys, in *Architecture of America* (Boston: Little, Brown, 1961), p. 314.

as well as more influential. Especially so were the articles of Lewis Mumford, who wrote about the estate in 1925, shortly after it had been awarded the coveted Gold Medal for Excellence in Design by the Architectural League of New York—the most valued architectural honor then awarded in the United States. Mumford singled it out as an especially characteristic example of the architectural sickness of the time, which he called "architectural anesthesia," writing that the

> malady of the unreal is a deep one in western civilization . . . but in our own time this homesickness [for nature] is coupled with a number of other ailments: the desire to recapture the past; the desire to create more permanent homes than our metropolitan rent warrens; and, finally, the desire to cut loose from an environment in which the day is announced by the alarm clock, instead of the birds, and finished by the blare of the radio instead of the crickets and the katydids. . . . The critical weakness of the romantic architect is that he is employed in creating an environment into which people may escape from a sordid workaday world, whereas the real problem of architecture is to remake the workaday world so that people will not wish to escape from it. Mr. Meigs's inspiration, Mr. Meigs's values are fine and efficacious, but they must be applied to real problems, and not to such grand evasions as the American Country House.[62]

The Newbold Estate, with its concern for volumetric relationships rather than surface textures, with its walls considered simply as constructed space definers, relates to puristic tendencies in advanced French painting and architecture. At once volumetric and massive, these architectural shapes, if we imagine them stripped of their detail and textures and painted white, qualify as the cones, spheres, and cylinders so often praised during the twenties by Le Corbusier. What the American work lacks is a sense of the possibilities inherent in the machine. On the other hand, the work of Le Corbusier, at that date, lacked Mellor, Meigs and Howe's comprehension of the possibilities inherent in a close relationship between function, structure, and space. The Citrohan House scheme of 1923, for example, employed a confusion of structural systems—columnar as well as bearing-wall. The parallel between

62. Lewis Mumford, "The Architecture of Escape," *The New Republic* 43 (12 Aug. 1925), 321–22. Three years later Mumford wrote, with the Newbold Estate presumably in mind, "These new country houses are not bad of their kind; the point is that their kind is irrelevant." "American Architecture Today," *Architecture* (New York) 57 (June 1928), 30.

the unmodern architectural shapes at the Newbold Estate and those praised and used whenever possible by Le Corbusier, whose dedication to modernity was passionate but whose belief in American technology conflicted with his preferences for elemental geometry, is not surprising for, as Reyner Banham points out: "The theory and aesthetics of the International Style were evolved between Futurism and Academicism, but their perfection was only achieved by drawing away from Futurism and drawing nearer to the Academic tradition. . . . In cutting themselves off from philosophical aspects of Futurism, though hoping to retain its prestige as Machine Art, theorists and designers . . . cut themselves off not only from their own historical beginnings but also from their foothold in the world of technology."[63]

The Newbold Estate and the attitudes of its designers can be compared also to the buildings and theories of Hugo Häring, a German architect whose experimental farm of 1923 at Garkau successfully used local building techniques, employing brick and wood as well as concrete (*fig. 42*).[64] He combined them to make a highly expressive set of original shapes as romantic as those French-inspired forms used at the Newbold Estate. Not concerned with a Machine Style, Häring attempted to find a basis for form not in the past, nor in platonic geometric shapes, nor in the forms of machines, but in his response to the programmatic requirements and the inherent characteristics of the building materials chosen. His rejection of geometric purity in his architecture and thought is summed up best in an essay of 1925 called "Approaches to Architectural Form": "We want to examine things and allow them to discover their own images. It goes against the grain with us to bestow a form on them from the outside, or to impose some abstract modulor on them."[65] Häring's method, as outlined by Jürgen Joedicke, consisted of first making an intellectual analysis of the program and then deriving from this a plan that

63. Reyner Banham, *Theory and Design of the First Machine Age* (New York: Praeger, 1960), p. 327.

64. Banham, in his *Guide to Modern Architecture* (New York: Van Nostrand, 1962), pp. 31–32, writes: "From 1912 to 1922—from Hans Poelzig's water tower in Posen to Eric Mendelsohn's hat factory at Luckenwalde—there flourished in German-speaking countries a school of so-called expressionists who genuinely strove to find new forms for new functions. The last major work of this movement, Hugo Häring's school at Gut Garkau, was rapidly pushed into the limbo labelled *romantic* by the uniformed conformists of the teenage period, only to emerge again with force and authority as a prophecy of what would happen to modern architecture in the fifties: it could almost be a mature work of Alvar Aalto."

65. Hugo Häring, "Approaches to Architectural Form," quoted by Jürgen Joedicke, "Häring at Garkau," *Review* 127 (May 1960), 313–18. See also Joedicke's essay, "Häring," in Gerd Hatje, ed., *Encyclopedia of Modern Architecture* (New York: Praeger, 1964), pp. 146–47.

would function and a type of construction that would implement it; from these, then, the form would derive.

Häring himself brought the argument around in a kind of full circle. Commenting on the relationship between his approach to architecture, which he called "the new way of building," and that of Le Corbusier, he stated that Le Corbusier's interpretation of function was geometric, introducing "an external point of view. . . . Le Corbusier does not evolve his designs from within." Häring felt that Le Corbusier's use of concrete did not give sufficient expression to "the organic forces at work. . . . He only makes use of it in order to produce the pure forms of geometry. . . . Since Le Corbusier is interested in pure forms only, he is not concerned in establishing a primary relationship with his material, which remains merely a means to the end of geometric form."[66]

Mellor, Meigs and Howe entertained a desire similar to Häring's: to establish a "primary relationship" with materials as well as with function. The significance of their domestic work lies not in its individuality but in the development of a consistent approach to design, direct in the disposition of interior spaces and in the unaffected use of local materials. But by their unwillingness to experiment with vernacular forms, Mellor, Meigs and Howe failed to achieve a truly local character in their work. Their houses "were elastic in plan, frank in their use of local materials, but, for all their simplicity, traditional and eclectic in the elements of design."[67]

The firm's tendency to overromanticize the forms of French architecture was kept in check by their concern for fundamental principles of architectural construction and composition: they were imagists, but they were builders as well. Their command of domestic architecture as an expressive art was impressive: every variation in use or in material was carefully calculated for its potential as an expression of the nature of the structure. Their concern

66. Häring, quoted by Joedicke, "Häring at Garkau." See also Julius Posener, *From Schinkel to the Bauhaus* (New York: Wittenborn, 1972), esp. the chapter "Häring, Scharoun, Mies and Le Corbusier." Posener concludes with an anomaly related to current practice: "The younger architects who, at present, condemn functionalism have frequently acclaimed (and claimed) Häring as a leader in their own 'anti-rationalist' struggle. In actual fact, Häring has been the purest of functionalists. One may go so far as to say that only *his* theory can be termed functionalist, whereas the architecture of the Bauhaus which has been hailed and, in our own time, condemned under that name has been informed by machine-esthetics, Cubism, the 'Stijl' movement and possibly even Giedion's concept of the space-time continuum as an agent in architecture" (p. 34).

67. Henry-Russell Hitchcock, "Howe and Lescaze," in Alfred Barr et al., *Modern Architecture. International Exhibition* (New York: Museum of Modern Art, 1932), p. 143.

for architecture as a constructed work of art was itself craftsmanlike. Their determination to reveal the nature of the building process was scrupulous. It was as though they wished to give reality to a romantic object by stripping it bare and sending it forth, a revelation of its materials and processes.

Nonetheless, it is not wise to go too far in the separation of form from content in architecture as in any other art; if the form is not intimately related to the content—if it is not indeed inseparable from it, growing naturally out of the processes of its construction as well as out of the occasion of its commissioning—then its integrity is compromised. It is precisely this compromise with integrity that denies the country houses of Mellor, Meigs and Howe ultimate significance.

4. *Crise à Quarante Ans*

Only the art whose purpose is to change the purpose of the beings to whom it is addressed is a fine, freeing art. The artist must be a messenger of discontent.

Edgar Singer, *Esthetics and the Rational Ideal*
(frequently quoted by Howe)

In five years, the entire picture has changed. The energies that worked below the ground so long are now erupting in a hundred unsuspected places; and once more the American architect has begun to attack the problems of design with the audacity and exuberance of a Root, a Sullivan, a Wright. In a sense, we have at last caught up with 1890.

Lewis Mumford, "American Architecture Today," *Architecture*,
April 1928

Howe's complacency was challenged as early as 1925. Lewis Mumford's strenuous criticism of the Newbold Estate in *The New Republic* probably disturbed him, although we have no record of his reaction to it. The discrepancy between the intellectual facts of the time and his work was brought closer to home in this article than it had been since the war. Howe's personal unhappiness, especially his increasingly unsuccessful marriage, no doubt also contributed to his discontent. It is not surprising, then, that his house for Robert F. Holden, built at Haverford in 1926, reflects his wavering commitment to his old ideals: ideals shaken, though not yet to the point of collapse (*figs. 43–45*). Unwilling or unable to free himself from the shackles of historical form, he abandoned the firm's well-known formula for the more exotic forms of the Spanish Colonial style of the seventeenth and eighteenth centuries.[1] With simple massing and decoration of an obviously applied character

---

1. The late work of Bertram Goodhue, who had recently died, was receiving considerable attention, and the solidity of its stripped forms may well have encouraged Howe's choice. See Charles Harris Whitaker, ed., *Bertram Grosvenor Goodhue, Architect and Master of Many Arts* (New York: A.I.A., 1925), esp pls. 198–205; Howell Lewis Shay, "Modern Architecture and Tradition," *T-Square Club Journal* 1 (Jan. 1931), 12–14. Of the many evaluations, Lewis Mumford's essay, "B. G. Goodhue," *The New Republic* 44 (28 Oct. 1924), 259–60, is the most intelligent.

concentrated at isolated points, this style lent itself to the kind of proto-modern composition toward which Howe, in his dissatisfaction, was already moving. In the Holden House, despite the client's initial preference for an Italianate design,[2] Howe introduced the character of the Spanish Colonial style with mannered gestures. The local stone is covered with a pinkish stucco; the awkwardly placed entrance is heralded with an obviously false arched shallow niche housing a ship's bell; the unornamented walls are treated as broad, solid planes with huge windows kept flush with the outer surfaces of the walls to maintain the continuity of the wall plane from the outside; the roof of the principal mass is pitched so gently as to be almost invisible from eye level, while a simply curved, concrete cornice gives definition to the skyline and enhances the impression of solidity.

The almost deliberate hesitancy of conception is, under the circumstances of Howe's own dissatisfaction with his firm's work, not surprising. Not only do the faintly Spanish forms sit uneasily in the suburban landscape, but they are not even master of the composition itself. A delightful loggia at the rear is, for example, more in the spirit of Brunelleschi's Foundling Hospital than of the California missions. The interiors also reflect this directionless eclecticism. Not even the ingenuity of the plan with its double-height main hallway is strong enough to conquer the rectitude and banality of the pine-paneled neocolonial main rooms.

The Holden House is of marginal interest compared with the revealing series of branch banking offices designed for the Philadelphia Saving Fund Society between 1923 and 1927.[3] These branch banks retain a twofold interest for us today: they document Howe's thoughtful and halting search for suitable modern architectural expression and they are uncommonly important statements about the Beaux-Arts style, its limitations and its potential, its preferences for masonry, its stultifying classicism, and its tendency toward archaeology and the kind of eclecticism that almost always smothered its more fundamental principles.[4] These bank designs show the limitations of Beaux-

2. "The Robert F. Holden House, Haverford, Pennsylvania," *Record* 63 (Jan. 1928), 105–12. See also Clare Ledoux, "Spanish Influence in a Unique Modern Home," *Arts and Decoration* 31 (July 1929), 56–57, 82. It is interesting to note that Ledoux gives credit to Howe and Lescaze for the design despite the fact that their partnership was less than a month old (see chap. 5).

3. The chronology of these offices is rather confusing. The Renaissance banks were built in 1924; those in extended Beaux-Arts forms date from 1926. The temporary branch was not built until 1927; that is, after one design for a tall office building and designs for the two Beaux-Arts branch banks had already been submitted.

4. Howe asked Walter Creese to include in his dissertation the two branch banks among

Arts forms in practice, although later designs for PSFS, as we will see, demonstrated the wider applicability of its principles.

The first branch banks designed for PSFS—in fact, one design for two identical branch banking offices—were completed in 1924, at the peak of Howe's success as a designer of romantic country houses (*fig. 46*).[5] The decision of the oldest saving institution in America to construct branch offices was arrived at only after much sober deliberation, and it was the hope of James M. Willcox, the Society's president, that the new branch offices would invoke in the minds of the depositors a degree of awe mixed with reassurance similar to that produced by the venerable main office at Seventh and Walnut Streets. For Howe, such programmatic requirements constituted a considerable departure from his country house work. The new offices had to be more monumental than anything he had thus far undertaken to design and, more importantly, had to respond to explicit iconographic and symbolic requirements.

For a number of reasons, Howe chose to respond in the language of the Italian Renaissance, toward which he had long been attracted. It is not unlikely that he recalled his own student work at the Ecole, and the principles enunciated by Auguste Choisy, Julien Guadet, Victor Laloux, and others as well as their insistence on the continuity of the classic tradition.[6] Indeed, so much of what these distinguished teachers had to say was inextricably interwoven in Howe's mind with the masterpieces of the classical tradition which they cited as illustrations that only with great difficulty could he separate the fundamentally irrelevant forms from the still potent theoretical principles. Of greater immediacy, perhaps, was the tendency toward a literary conception of architecture that was so much a part of the psychology of American revivalist architects and their clients alike. In America during the twenties, a bank was Greek, Roman, or, even better, Italian Renaissance in style. Nonetheless,

---

the "buildings designed in a composite modernized traditionalism. . . . If you look at these buildings," he confirmed, "you won't find they go very far, but you would be astonished could you return to the day in which they were built and realize what a furor of opposition and criticism they aroused. At the time it seemed incredible and it still does." Letter to Creese, 12 Aug. 1946. Dean Creese has generously entrusted to my care two letters from Howe, which were eventually incorporated into his valuable and pioneering doctoral dissertation, "American Architecture from 1918 to 1933, with Special Emphasis on European Influence" (Harvard, 1949). These are now on deposit in the Howe Archives.

5. One twin, the so-called North Office, stands at Eleventh Street and Lehigh Avenue. The other, the so-called South Office, may be found at Broad and McKean Streets.

6. For a discussion of the relationship of French theory to the modern movement, see Reyner Banham, *Theory and Design in the First Machine Age* (New York: Praeger, 1960), pp. 14–67.

despite the deadness of their forms, buildings such as Howe's first branch banks testify to the tenacity of Beaux-Arts principles and the ability of Beaux-Arts designers to apply them with understanding. In these branch banks, Howe grafted onto a simple floor plan his intentions to give form to "the double function of the savings bank building, first as a magnified strong box, and second as a working space."[7] The heavy rustication and the nail-studded oak doors enhance the image of strength and enclosure while the large windows indicate an ample, well-lighted working area. Most important, the design conforms to "accepted tradition" for banking architecture.

In 1926 Howe was called upon to add electric signs to his "Renaissance" banks. He declined, pointing out to James Willcox the inappropriateness of such an anachronistic feature. "But why," the client asked, "if my business will benefit by it, shouldn't I have it?" On reflection, this seemed reasonable to Howe, and he promised to "incorporate the most blazing and beautiful specimen in existence" in his next building for the Society. Howe was later to remark that "though this concession to the machine age necessitated a superficial change in . . . method of design it did not involve a complete abandonment" of his accustomed approach.[8]

Howe's next design, again for twin buildings, is freer in conception and represents his growing awareness of an architecture reconciled to "modern commercial practice (*fig. 47*)." Abandoning the idea of a strongbox, with its literary associations of treasure house and private stronghold, Howe still worked to preserve "solidity of aspect." Thus he eliminated the fortified base of the first banks in an attempt to make each building "more inviting to the timid public." Once again he conceived a design with a double intent: a "large hospitable entrance door," closed at the bottom only by a richly ornamental grille; illuminated inscriptions that necessitated, or rather suggested, service balconies; and multiple wrought-iron reflectors that formed the chief features of the elevations.[9] The inclusion of the illuminated sign and the simplification leading to a less forbidding exterior reflect not so much Howe's concern for an increasingly demanding machine technology as the realities of

7. Howe, "The Philadelphia Saving Fund Society Branch Offices," *Forum* 42 (June 1928), 881–86.

8. Howe, "Why I Became a Functionalist," paper read before a Symposium at the Museum of Modern Art, New York, 19 Feb. 1932. A portion of these remarks are included in "Symposium: The International Architectural Exhibition," *Shelter* 2 (April 1932).

9. Howe, "PSFS Branch Offices." The first of this pair, the so-called West Office, is at Fifty-second and Ludlow Streets. The second, the so-called Logan Office, is at Broad and Ruscomb Streets.

business practice. The needs for advertising and for an unforbidding bank were satisfied without compromising design or composition.

The simplicity of this scheme, predicting Paul Cret's Folger Shakespeare Library in Washington, D.C. (not under design until 1928), is remarkable. In contrast to Cret's ambivalent combination of Tudor entrails and classic skin, Howe's design is a simple geometrical statement entirely consistent in its structure, space, mass, and detailing. A masonry building with slag roof which demands no cornice, its neoclassicism is well rooted in the tradition of John Soane. Clear and crisp, it is also, within its inherent limitations, logical and straightforward.

The spark that was to ignite Howe's discontent was provided in April 1926, when he was asked by the Philadelphia Saving Fund Society to prepare designs for a large bank, store, and office building combination (*fig. 48*).[10] His first solution tacitly acknowledged his need to reinvestigate thoroughly his architectural philosophy. Here was a problem that could not be solved within the masonry tradition and was not compatible with a conception of architecture as sculpture in mass. Again, in his confusion, Howe turned toward the theories of the Beaux-Arts, almost none of which dealt directly with the problem of the skyscraper, which was in the early years of our century a specifically American building type. Only a few successful precedents for skyscraper design were even vaguely compatible with Beaux-Arts theory. Graduates of the Ecole, when they tried to apply its principles to this difficult problem, tended to substitute for the Beaux-Arts ideal of structural-functional-spatial unity a concern, almost negative in its restrictive tone, for the applied skin (or revetment) of the facade. Carrère and Hastings's Blair Building in New York stands in the forefront of these elegantly detailed, though ultimately weak, experiments. For the critic Montgomery Schuyler, Ernest Flagg's Singer Building, despite its free eclecticism, was, along with Sullivan's tall buildings, a "hopeful experiment" in the design of skyscrapers—a building marked by expressive articulation "in the handling of its masses and the partial revelation of its structure."[11] Only Sullivan, a renegade but also a Beaux-Arts *ancien,* was able to cope with the problem intelligently and, in part, as some perceptive

10. This proposal was not published until 1962, when William Jordy and I jointly presented it as part of the discussion of PSFS in *JSAH* 21 (May 1962), 47–102. See chap. 5, n. 51.

11. Montgomery Schuyler, "The Evolution of the Skyscraper" and "The Woolworth Building," in William H. Jordy and Ralph T. Coe, eds., *American Architecture and Other Writings* (Cambridge, Mass.: Harvard, 1961), 2: 434, 608. For the Blair Building, and in fact for a most complete contemporary overview of the French influence on the design of tall buildings, see H. W. Desmond, "A Beaux-Arts Skyscraper," *Record* 14 (Dec. 1903), 436–63. Desmond's discussion deserves serious attention because it articulates more clearly than most the frustra-

contemporary observers noted, according to the logical precepts of French theory.[12]

American theorists took up the problem of the skyscraper only occasionally. Schuyler's writings were historical and critical rather than theoretical; Sullivan's were frequently misunderstood and often dismissed as the work of an eccentric radical. Charles Herbert Moore, Howe's former teacher at Harvard, did, ironically enough, take up the problem beginning in the early 1920s. Moore believed that the great architecture of the past had been built with masonry, and that without masonry there could be no great architecture. Because tall buildings were the products of excessive industrialism, and because of the "haste and cheapness" of their construction, they were not, according to Moore, worthy of real architectural thought. A steel-framed building could never be a pleasant object to behold: if such buildings must exist, let them at least have the honesty of articulated structure. Moore denied the claims of some architects, engineers, and potential clients when he stated, "There are no new conditions, and there is no call for new methods; though new forms may be evolved in the future as in the past. The only materials suitable for architecture have been long established, and are the same now as in former times. The present use of iron and steel—which indeed requires new methods—comes of no need of architecture. It is destructive of architecture if it is not kept apart from it." For Moore, the demands of the business and industrial community were economic and not architectural. Functionalism, the making of buildings for "utilitarian ends," led to a dangerous confusion of roles and intentions between architects and engineers. Out of this confusion was produced not an architecture of significant form and structure but one merely of expedient use. Thus Moore, in relegating the tall building to an inferior architectural position, and in emphasizing structural articulation and regularity, may well have reinforced the direction of Howe's thought, leading him to attempt, like so many other architects wrestling

---

tion felt by some over the failure not only in Sullivan to abandon matters of metaphorical expression in favor of the frank revelation of the frame, but also in Ernest Flagg, the architect of the Singer Building, for having almost given in to a literal structural expression. On the other hand, the notion of masonry skin or revetment as the expression rather than the revelation of the structural fact of the steel frame is explored in the Blair Building, which Desmond discusses in detail.

12. See Montgomery Schuyler, "Architecture in Chicago: Alder and Sullivan," in Jordy and Coe, *American Architecture*, 2:377–404. See also William H. Jordy, *American Buildings and Their Architects. Progressive and Academic Ideals. Turn of the Twentieth Century* (Garden City: Doubleday, 1972), pp. 83–179.

with the problem of high buildings, a synthesis between architectural mass and articulated structure.[13]

Howe's proposal of 1926 is an indication of his almost unbelievable caution in his first attempt at designing a tall building. Going out of his way to produce a scheme that would be, above all, clear in its expression of construction, he sheathed the building in a revetment of stone that expressed the steel structure it concealed but was visually appropriate to masonry. Thus the band of stonework above the banking room, in spirit similar to a cornice, conceals and expresses the trusswork. The big steel columns that carry the trusses are expressed by broad stone panels set between the high windows of the banking room. The two mezzanines of that space are also expressed at the south end of the Twelfth Street facade. The sheathing is bolted to the structure, and the bolts are left exposed to clarify the nature of the construction technique while indicating in an ornamental way, without fully revealing, the structure.

The building, conceived as a column rather more literally than Sullivan had done, except in his writings, was given an imposing space at the ground level. The elaborate twenty-sixth floor includes board rooms, a kitchen, and an employees' dining room. Although the building had been intended by the Society as a branch office, the provision of this executive space was the result of Howe's faith in the new location and in the building as a better symbol for the bank than the old main office at Seventh and Walnut Streets (designed by Sloan and Hutton in 1868–69 and enlarged by Furness, Evans and Company in 1900).

The forms employed by Howe in this scheme of 1926 relate closely to the work of Secessionist architects two decades before. In his well-known Postal Savings Bank of 1904–06 in Vienna, Otto Wagner used "thin masonry sheets hobnailed with aluminum bolts but to a masonry wall, and not, as his famous central housing chamber inside with its exposed frame would suggest, to a metal skeleton."[14] The fenestration of Howe's scheme, similar to Wagner's, is carefully controlled in an effort to articulate columns and bays. The proliferation of spheres at the top and at each setback echoes Wagner's use of stylized figures and panels to enliven the skyline of his building. The illuminated spheres resemble even more closely the huge sphere that crowned Josef Maria Olbrich's Secession Gallery of 1899, in Vienna. Josef Hoffman also used a globe to crown his Stoclet House built between 1905 and 1911 in

13. See Charles Herbert Moore, "Training for the Practice of Architecture," *Record* 49 (Jan. 1921), 56–61.

14. See William H. Jordy, "PSFS: Its Development and Its Significance in Modern Architecture," *JSAH* 21 (May 1962), 47–83.

Brussels. There is some doubt whether Howe knew all these projects; probable sources for his roofscape can be also found among the entries in the Chicago *Tribune* Tower competition in 1922. Nonetheless, one must recall his insistence in 1932 that his own use of the motif of the spheres in his student project for a post office was influenced by the work of the *Jugendstil*.[15]

The failure of Howe's first attempt to come to terms with the new, essentially European, ideas that were just reaching American shores was one not of intention but of expression. He knew well what needed to be done. He perceived the conflict inherent in steel construction between the architect's desire to reveal the structure and the necessity to sheathe it with fireproofing; he understood the potential for powerful, simple forms made possible by steel; but he was confused. During the negotiation with the Saving Fund Society in 1930, he wrote to James M. Willcox about this difficult time in his career: "I looked about in vain for a precedent that seemed satisfactory from the point of view of architectural expression. Finding none I evolved a design of my own whose chief structural interest lay in an emphasis on the possibilities of steel, in the bold recognition of a great mass of masonry standing on stilts and in the elimination of meaningless mouldings. For its external beauty the design depended on purely decorative elements, such as the great globe at the summit of the tower, and the use of set-backs."[16]

His caution and confusion prevented Howe from fulfilling the potential of the scheme.[17] Howe approached the problem of making architecture in steel through the back door: he conceived a building that was so big as to be possible only in steel and then detailed it in masonry. In his words, engineering was, in this scheme, still a "shameful secret of the architectural family." Howe's search for a new order in architecture began with this first scheme for PSFS. The remaining schemes all would be concerned with his search for a way of building in which engineering, "material order," could be reconciled to architecture, "emotional intensity in the field of structural design."[18]

In 1927 the Saving Fund Society, still uncertain about the programmatic requirements for its building at the corner of Twelfth and Market Streets,

15. "George Howe, An Architectural Biography," *T-Square* 2 (Jan. 1932). As late as 1946 Howe reiterated his belief that even his early efforts at the Ecole des Beaux-Arts were colored by "a touch of the Jugend Stil in my final projet[sic]." Letter to Creese, 12 Aug. 1946.
16. Howe, letter to Willcox, 25 July 1932, published in *JSAH* 21 (May 1962), 98–99.
17. "Save for the stilts," Jordy has pointed out, his "timid expression of the metal frame derived from the suspended masonry veneer instead of the visibility of skeletal support." "PSFS."
18. Howe, "Why I Became a Functionalist," p. 1.

decided to erect a temporary banking office on part of the site at 8 South Twelfth Street to ascertain the need for such a facility at this location (*fig. 49*). Throughout the development of this prominent corner in Center City, it should be noted, the advisability of constructing office space was never really doubted.

The challenge of designing a temporary structure that would be economical to build and at the same time sufficiently dignified so as to be comparable with the other branch offices fell in line with Howe's own dissatisfaction with traditional architecture, a dissatisfaction that was growing more noticeable daily. The restricted budget provided him with an excellent opportunity to justify to the bank officials the use of simple materials in an unadorned fashion. At the same time, the need to convey the bank's image and the desire to harmonize with the matter-of-fact colonial Georgian forms of the Friends' Meeting House next door were sufficient reasons to prevent Howe from exploiting any of the more radical European forms that were becoming known in America (see discussion below). There is no reason to believe that Howe was in any way inclined to use these forms or, indeed, that he felt himself able to do so. This was still very much a time of transition for him, although it does seem clear that he had made up his mind to abandon the excesses of his early work. He had visited the Paris Exposition des Arts Décoratifs in 1925, where he was impressed and confused by Le Corbusier's Pavilion de l'Esprit Nouveau. It is probably just as well that he chose to follow a neutral course, one as near to being free from eclecticism of any kind as he had ever pursued, rather than attempting to foist upon the Society what could only have been, at this early stage of his involvement with modern forms, little more than a superficial application of clichés.

The temporary branch bank of 1927 was an impressive attempt toward an architecture based on the direct use of ordinary construction materials and techniques. Unlike the buildings of the contemporary European Machine Style, it grew out of Howe's concern for the processes of building and not for the potential symbolic expression and formal invention inherent in the machines themselves. It is timid, hesitant, and somewhat eclectic in its formal configuration. In its expression of construction, however, it is clarity itself. A series of triangular iron trusses are carried on walls built of the brick salvaged from an old building which formerly stood on the site. These walls rest, in turn, on a base of rough concrete, cast to resemble masonry. A large window announces the entrance on South Twelfth Street. Below this, doors lead to a vestibule and then up a short flight of stairs to the banking room which is flooded with light from windows on the south and skylights on the north. There is, especially in the interior, a sense of the potential power of the **PSFS**

Building that he and Lescaze were to build. If in the bank and office project of 1926 as well as in the twin branch offices of the same year, Howe extended Beaux-Arts forms as far as he was able (as far, perhaps, as they were capable of going), the 1927 branch bank brought him to the limits of his abilities to handle materials frankly and inventively without stepping outside accepted canons of traditional form.

Howe himself was not yet able to embrace the forms of modern architecture; nor were his clients prepared to subject themselves to the hazards of formal experimentation. The last two houses he designed with Mellor and Meigs show no particular advance over earlier work. The first, a house for Mr. and Mrs. Orville Bullitt in Fort Washington not far from Chestnut Hill, was completed in 1927 (*figs. 50, 51*). It is an imposing house—very much in the spirit of the Newbold Estate; it was never published. An amusing and characteristic story is told by Bullitt in connection with its design. In a letter to Helen Howe West, he wrote:

> We had a wonderful time building our house with your father. When I first went to him, I asked if we would have to deal at all with Arthur Meigs (Susy's [Mrs. Bullitt's] cousin) and he assured me we would not.
>
> As you know, we have a magnificent flying staircase to the third floor. The slope of our roof is very steep and when the staircase was in the rough, Susy and I discovered that we could only get to the third floor on our hands and knees as the roof cut off the stairs. I called your father about this and we had a violent argument, in fact, I remember at one point saying to him, "George, please don't talk that way, you will regret it later," but he kept right on. He told me that we had initialed the plans and that therefore he had no further responsibility and would not do anything about it. The result was that instead of the stairs going along the wall, we had to have a steel frame made moving it out and that gave it a very handsome curve.[19]

The second of these houses was for Robert F. McLean, the publisher of the Philadelphia *Bulletin*. It is more obviously eclectic and was, in fact, Meigs's design, which Howe completed after his resignation from the firm. A rambling Tudor manor house, it is in the style that Wilson Eyre made popular for Phila-

19. Quoted in Helen Howe West, *George Howe, Architect,* p. 30.

delphians twenty years before.[20] Thus, at the brink of a momentus decision, Howe remained as yet without a clear vision of the future.

The early commissions from the Philadelphia Saving Fund Society were unquestionably decisive factors in Howe's growing dissatisfaction with the easy romanticism of his past. As he wrote, "the seas of life are stormy, and our Romantic bark broke at last on the rock of American business."[21] No longer could he "look with satisfaction on . . . Wall Street pastoral country places, their lowing pure-bred kine and moaning doves."[22] But the roots of his dissatisfaction lay deeper than his difficulties with the design for the PSFS tower and, although the scheme for an office tower and bank was temporarily abandoned by the client, he did not allow himself to backslide and indulge his longstanding romantic predilections. Instead he moved cautiously toward a more mature architectural point of view.

Howe's uneasiness was noticeable as he celebrated his fortieth birthday in 1926. Forty is often a critical age in a man's life; the French call it the *crise à quarante ans*. It was especially so for Howe, whose wife, children, and home seemed unable to provide the stimulation that his cultivated intelligence, constantly seeking replenishment with new ideas, demanded. The practice of architecture itself had become routine, his commissions almost exclusively residential, his clients almost exclusively his friends. Taking stock of his accomplishments at this critical age, Howe began to wonder if he had indeed fulfilled his potential as an architect.[23]

A number of factors other than the malaise of middle age and the demands of the Saving Fund Society contributed to Howe's introspection. One was his memory of the war, which served to make him feel "singularly remote from the comfortable philosophy of Romanticism" and propelled him almost impulsively "towards a clearer, more austere, and if you like, more democratic architecture. The poor shreds of aristocratic principle we were perpetuating

20. See Robert McLean, "A Few Recollections of George Howe," in ibid., p. 35.

21. "George Howe," in Harvard University, *Class of 1908, Secretary's Sixth Report* (Cambridge, Mass., 1933).

22. Howe, "Some Experiences and Observations of an Elderly Architect," *Perspecta* 2 (1953), 2–5.

23. See Bruno Zevi, "George Howe, An Aristocratic Architect," *A.I.A. Journal* 24 (Oct. 1955), 176–79. Of course, this was not an overnight realization. Helen Howe West writes that her father returned from the war in 1919 "a changed man. He seemed more mature and reserved. I suspect that this is when his and Mother's relationship began to come unstuck. They were impatient with each other, tempers flared with some frequency, and altogether it was not the happiest stage for my sister and me. Many was the Sunday lunch that I left in tears over their squabbles." *George Howe*, p. 27.

looked to me pretty tawdry."[24] Howe remembered the drama of nations struggling for their individuality, the "fragile foundations of states uprooted and in the laborious process of reconstruction." He had only to reflect on the Europe he had left and the America to which he had returned to understand the artificiality of his "romantic and middle-class" existence. Slowly he came to realize that the "modern art which he had laughed at, in a smug Edwardian fashion, was not the empty expression of a dying civilization which he had thought it to be but really the inevitable result and expression of the upheaval from which Europe was just beginning to emerge."[25] Even as late as 1926, recalls R. Sturgis Ingersoll, a close friend and an astute collector of twentieth-century painting and sculpture, Howe "was in a mood of condemning everything 'modern,' [but] a year or so later I believe he became enamored by Le Corbusier and he jumped on the band wagon and applied his extraordinary talents in that direction."[26]

Late in 1926 a friend gave Howe a copy of the first volume of the English translation of Oswald Spengler's *The Decline of the West*. This was a "major event" in his life, and much later he recalled its impact upon him: "In the might of my confusion about modern art and architecture (for having had no part in their origin I could see no justification for proclaiming myself a high-priest of the new faith, an act of dedication pre-requisite to converting my clients) a single luminous statement shone out from Spengler's pages."[27] This statement, the famous comparison of the Temple of Poseidon at Pæstum with the Minister of Ulm, deserves quotation:

> The Temple of Poseidon at Pæstum and the Minster at Ulm, works of the ripest Doric and the ripest Gothic, differ precisely as the Euclidean Geometry of bodily-bounding surfaces differs from the analytical geometry of the position of points in space referred to spatial axes. All Classic building begins from the outside, all Western from the inside. The Arabian also begins with the inside, but it stays there. There is one and only one soul, the Faustian, that craves for a style which drives through walls into the limitless universe of space and makes both the exterior and the interior of the building complementary images of one and the same world-feeling. . . . Now, as soon as the Germanic spirit takes possession of the basilical type, there begins a wondrous mutation of all structural

24. "George Howe," in Harvard University, *Class of 1908, Secretary's Sixth Report.*
25. Ibid.
26. Ingersoll, letter to author, 10 July 1963.
27. Howe, untitled talk, Harvard, 1954.

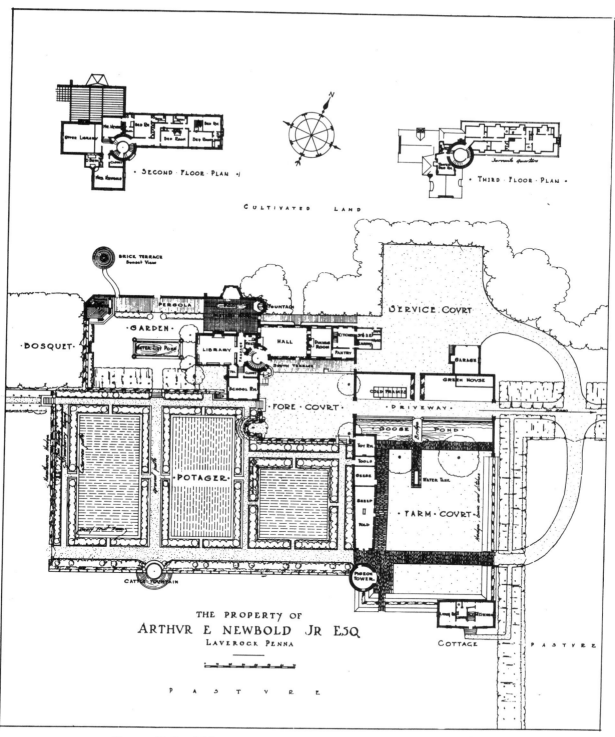

Fig. 31. Mellor, Meigs and Howe. Arthur E. Newbold Estate, Laverock, Pa., 1921–24, property plan.

Fig. 32. Newbold Estate, farm court.

Fig. 33. Newbold Estate, cottage.

Fig. 34. Newbold Estate, tower from forecourt.

Fig. 35. Newbold Estate, stair tower and entrance to owner's apartments.

Fig. 36. Newbold Estate, chessman on door to owner's apartments.

Fig. 37. Newbold Estate, sheep fold, longitudinal section, west elevation, and loft plan.

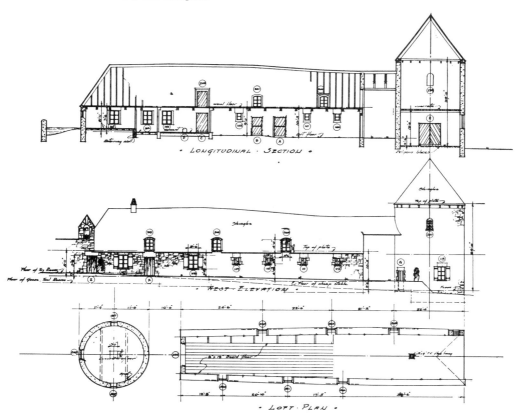

· LONGITUDINAL · SECTION ·

· WEST · ELEVATION ·

· LOFT · PLAN ·

Fig. 38. Mellor, Meigs and Howe. Newbold Estate,
swimming pool, 1928.

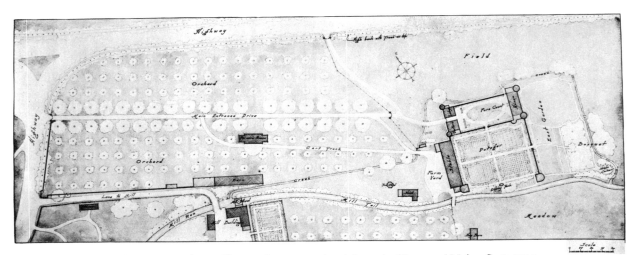

Fig. 39. Manoir d'Archelles, near Dieppe, Normandy, measured and drawn by Howe and Meigs, Sept. 1920

Fig. 40. Manoir d'Archelles, photo from Howe's files.

Fig. 41. Manoir d'Archelles, photo
from Howe's files.

GUT GARKAU

Fig. 42. Hugo Häring, Gut Gärkau, near Lübeck, Germany, 1924, hand drawing of aerial view.

Fig. 43. Robert F. Holden House, Haverford, Pa., 1926, plan.

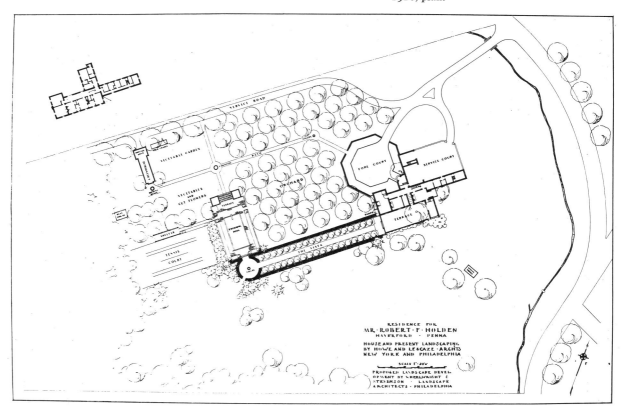

Fig. 44. Holden House, entrance court.

Fig. 45. Holden House.

Fig. 46. Philadelphia Saving Fund Society (PSFS), branch office, 1924.

Fig. 47. PSFS, branch office (West Office), 1926, at night.

Fig. 48. PSFS, branch office and office tower, 1926, project.

Fig. 49. PSFS, Central City temporary branch office, 1927.

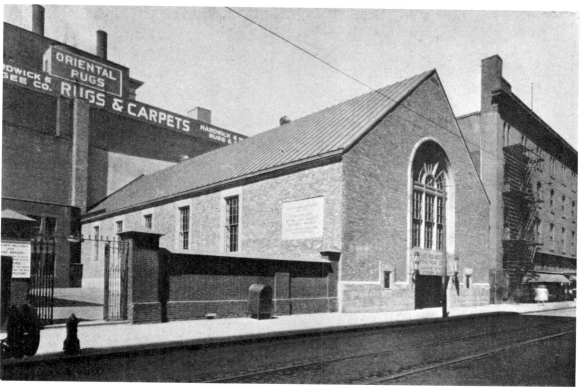

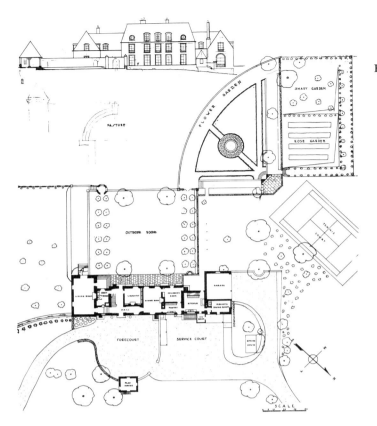

Fig. 50. Mellor, Meigs and Howe. Orville H. Bullitt House, Fort Washington, Pa., 1927, plan and south elevation.

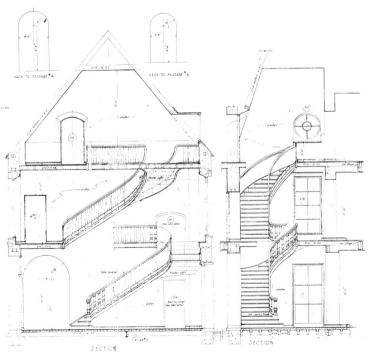

Fig. 51. Bullitt House, section through stair ha[

Fig. 52. Walter Mellor and Arthur I. Meigs. Goodhart Hall, Bryn Mawr College, Bryn Mawr, Pa., 1926–28.

Fig. 53. George P. Tyler House, Elkins Park, Pa., 1928, renovation.

Fig. 54. Monument in honor of the 27th and 30th Divisions, A.E.F., near Ypres, Belgium, 1929.

Fig. 55. Piranesi, view of a tomb, from Howe's files.

Fig. 56. U.S. Coast Guard Memorial, Arlington
National Cemetery, Arlington, Va., 1924–
28, drawing perhaps by Howe.

Fig. 57. U.S. Coast Guard Memorial as built.

Fig. 58. Howe and Lescaze. James M. R. Sinkler House, Westchester, Pa., 1928.

Fig. 59. Sinkler House, living room.

parts, as to both position and significance. Here in the Faustian North the outer form of the building, be it cathedral or mere dwelling-house, begins to be brought into relation with the meaning that governs the arrangement of the interior, a meaning undisclosed in the mosque and non-existent in the temple. The Faustian building has a *visage* and not merely a facade (whereas the front of a peripteros is, after all, only one of four sides and the contredomed building in principle has not even a front) and with this visage, this head, is associated an articulated trunk that draws itself out through the broad plain like the Cathedral at Speyer, or erects itself to the heavens like the innumerable spires of the original design of Rheims. The *motive of the facade,* which greets the beholder and tells him the inner meaning of the house, dominates not only individual major buildings but also the whole aspect of our streets, squares and towns with their characteristic wealth of windows.[28]

This passage, Howe recalled,

produced an immediate and violent impact on my life. Having discovered, through the interpretation of the past, an intimate relationship between mathematics and science on the one hand and architecture on the other, a relationship of form and spiritual content, not of dry technology, I decided, undeterred by Spengler's contempt for all modern art, to seek out the same sort of relationship in the architecture of the present, representing the continuation, or revival of the Gothic craving "for a style which drives through walls into the limitless universe of space and makes both the exterior and the interior of the building complementary images of one and the same world-feeling." Following Goethe's injunction to artists to the effect that, if they would fill their minds and hearts with the thoughts and feelings of their day, the work would come, I read innumerable books (the shelves of booksellers were loaded with excellent new semi-popular disquisitions by the most eminent specialists of the day) on the evolution of geometry, of number, of space-time concepts, of speculative science, of philosophy and history. Immediately it became apparent to me that what we call modern architecture was no mere stylistic whim, or even a new microcosm by the Gods of the late nineteenth and early twentieth centuries . . . but an integral part of a world-feeling which had sprung up in the earliest days of Western thought and had been only

28. Oswald Spengler, *The Decline of the West,* trans. by Charles Francis Atkinson, 2 vols. (New York: Knopf, 1926), 1:224.

momentarily interrupted by the classic twist of the renaissance and classic revival of so-called Enlightenment. In the propagation of this world-feeling I decided, I had as legitimate, if less distinguished, a role to play as the Gods before mentioned.[29]

The Spenglerian division between "Form and Actuality" and "World Historical Perspectives" appealed to the duality of Howe's own thought. Spengler states in the first part of *The Decline of the West:* " 'Form and Actuality' starts from the form-language of the great Cultures, and attempts to penetrate to the deepest roots of their origin in order to provide itself with a basis for a science of the Symbolic. The second part, 'World Historical Perspectives,' starts from the *facts of actual life,* and from the historical practice of higher mankind seeks to obtain a quintessence of historical experience that we can set to work upon the formation of our future."[30] Howe found in the pages of Spengler the basis for an architectural philosophy that would take into account both the traditional principles of architecture as a constructive and space-making art, which he had learned at the Ecole, and the technological and spiritual demands of the present.

Wrested out of the security of familiar solutions, Howe put aside a superficially estimable world in order to begin again at the beginning. His period of self-assessment can be said to have extended from his fortieth birthday in 1926 to 1928. Unquestionably, it was a time of severe mental crisis for him. Another American architect, Frank Lloyd Wright, had experienced a similar ordeal as he approached his fortieth birthday.[31] Both Howe and Wright were unhappy in their marriages but, more importantly, their discontent grew out of their work: Wright's out of the failure of his architecture to gain the social acceptance he believed necessary for its complete success, Howe's out of his inability to transcend the superficial aesthetic prejudices of his socially prominent clients.[32] Howe's confrontation with the commercial world, with its special demands, pronounced the death knell to the romantic ideals of his youth. Maturity, with all its responsibilities, was at hand.

Howe's mother died on 9 May 1926. The death of this redoubtable woman, who had dominated her son's first forty years, freed him for the first time,

29. Howe, untitled talk, Harvard, 1954.

30. Spengler, *Decline of the West,* 1:50.

31. Frank Lloyd Wright, *An Autobiography* (New York: Duell, Sloan and Pearce, 1932), esp. pp. 164–70.

32. See Grant C. Manson, *Frank Lloyd Wright to 1910: The First Golden Age* (New York: Van Nostrand Reinhold, 1958), p. 211.

really, to make his own decisions. This was difficult; he was under a great strain, and he was experiencing the loneliness and sense of emptiness that seemed to affect many sensitive Americans at the time. Finding the materialism of the twenties unsatisfactory as a philosophy of life, he, like others, found success hollow and vapid. There, beneath the surface glitter of the twenties, a core of sickness and fear corroded American life. By 1927 it had eaten its way to the surface. Scott Fitzgerald wrote pointedly of this in his essay of 1931, "Echoes of the Jazz Age":

> By 1927 a wide spread neurosis began to be evident, faintly signalled, like a nervous beating of the feet, by the popularity of cross-word puzzles. I remember a fellow-expatriate opening a letter from a mutual friend of ours, urging him to come home and be revitalized by the bracing qualities of the native soils. It was a strong letter and it affected us both deeply, until we noticed that it was headed from a nerve sanitarium in Pennsylvania.
>
> By this time contemporaries of mine had begun to disappear into the dark maw of violence. A classmate killed his wife and himself on Long Island, another tumbled accidentally from a skyscraper in New York. One was killed in a speak-easy in Chicago; another was beaten to death in a speak-easy in New York and crawled home to the Princeton Club to die. . . . These are not catastrophes that I went out of my way to look for—these were my friends; moreover, these things happened not during the depression but during the boom.[33]

Fitzgerald's "mutual friend" may well have been one of Howe's Harvard classmates, Van Wyck Brooks, whose self-disgust led to a nervous breakdown. A "season in hell," he called it, "when my own bubble burst, when the dome under which I lived crumbled into ruin, when I was consumed with a sense of failure, a feeling that my work had all gone wrong and that I was mistaken in all I had said or thought."[34]

Howe's own close circle of friends seethed with discontent. Francis Biddle felt himself wasted on the conventional law practice he was pursuing. In 1927, at the very time when Howe was haunted by indecision, Biddle published a

33. F. Scott Fitzgerald, "Echoes of the Jazz Age," in Edmund Wilson, ed., *The Crack-Up* (New York: New Directions, 1945), pp. 19–20.

34. Van Wyck Brooks, *Days of the Phoenix. The Nineteen-Twenties I Remember* (New York: Dutton, 1957), p. 187. He goes on to write, "The nadir of common depressions was the peak of mine. Nine-tenths of all my energy was involved in a neurosis and barely one-tenth was left for living. In my *crise à quarante ans* I shrank from all human relations."

novel, *The Llanfear Pattern,* which scrutinized Philadelphia values.[35] Llanfear, a young man of principle determined to reform politics in Philadelphia, thinks himself "resolute . . . in his determination never to give up, never to compromise." But, despite his high-sounding principles, he is a "prig, afraid to go through with anything tough, and timorous of acting on his instincts," and finally, compromising with family and "position," he accepts an appointment as district attorney "from the hands of the Senator whose political machine he set out to destroy." *The Llanfear Pattern* was razor sharp in its indictment; its picture of life "without gaiety and without earnestness, mechanical, content, indifferent," reflected Biddle's own "sense of past frustration."[36] Soon he too was to leave Philadelphia, and his account of his departure suggests some of the attitudes that must also have been Howe's:

> When the chance came, I eagerly turned to public work largely because, without admitting it to myself, I was not satisfied with practice. Its variety was diverting up to a point. But cases came and went; and in rare intervals of self-examination I wondered where I was going, and why. It was good to make a comfortable income and put something away; but after twenty years the output of work and the intake of money proved less satisfying. The practice of law was becoming like any business. There was little dedication to ends beyond monetary rewards for the narrow needs of self. What had at first appeared so exciting and so various in the new adventure of law had fallen into the familiar and the commonplace.[37]

Francis Biddle's brother George was also experiencing serious conflicts within himself during these years. After the war he had sought escape in Tahiti.[38] He returned in 1922, and after much personal unhappiness and a marriage ending in divorce, he determined to build for himself a house that would be "so heavy, so solid—in the time, the intent, the emotion involved, as much as in the broad footings, the stone foundations and the concrete walls of the structure—that [he] could never desert it."[39] Influenced by Howe, Biddle

---

35. Francis Biddle, *The Llanfear Pattern* (New York: Scribner's, 1927). The passages quoted in the text are from Biddle's recapitulation of the novel's plot in *A Casual Past* (Garden City: Doubleday, 1961), p. 333. See also Nathaniel Burt's evaluation of the novel in *The Perennial Philadelphians* (Boston: Little, Brown, 1963), p. 393.

36. Biddle, *A Casual Past,* p. 333.

37. Ibid., p. 398.

38. George Biddle, *An American Artist's Story* (Boston: Little, Brown, 1939), pp. 183–84. See also Biddle's affectionate account of his years in Tahiti, *Green Island* (New York: Coward McCann, 1930).

39. Biddle, *An American Artist's Story,* p. 243.

turned to the "solid masonry of the Pennsylvania Dutch barns, perhaps the pueblos of the southwest or the peasant houses of Europe." An amusing exchange between Biddle and Howe grew out of this, which Biddle relates in his autobiography:

> When I purchased my land I had the choice between a three acre lot, with a view to the north of Bear Mountain and to the south, at night, of the lights of Spuyten Duyvil, or of thirteen acres of wooded swamp land. Hesitating, I asked George Howe, the architect. He said:
>
> "For God's sake take the swamp. It is true that from the open hilltop you have an incomparable and unimpaired view of from twenty to forty miles in every direction, but that in America is not always an unmixed blessing. We are a young and consequently a growing country; nor do we always expand in elements of sheer beauty. You cannot tell what will be added to your view, perhaps some crenelated Scotch baronial manse or Gothic French château at your very gate. In the years to come you will be grateful, if the countryside for twenty to forty miles cannot view you. Nor should one ever build on that particular spot which gives us what the smelling German tourists call *eine wunderschoenste prachtvolle aussicht.* Little by little, as with every new love, you will grow immune to the dramatic novelty of the landscape. After a while you will not look at it at all. Why not, then, have something in reserve; which is not always at your feet; to which you can make—even a five-minute—pilgrimage with some Sunday guest, for whom you are reserving the opiate of your Croton hills and lakes and rivers. Quite from the *Liber Studiorum,* too. That is the palliative of your Croton landscape. It is eighteenth-century rather than American. It drugs with its loveliness instead of shocking one by a sordid, chaotic American challenge."
>
> George's taste is as infallible as his ratiocination is tortuous. I have never regretted his preference for woodlands over hilltops.[40]

If the years between World War I and the inauguration of Roosevelt constitute a period when nineteenth-century principles and ideals were cast aside in favor of those more appropriate to the facts of the twentieth century, then the year 1927 may be regarded as the fulcrum on which the balance between the old and the new tipped with irrevocable finality in favor of the latter. In his first important discussion of the state of American architecture, Henry-Russell

40. Ibid., pp. 247–48.

Hitchcock wrote with appropriate Spenglerian gloom in 1927, "America stands beyond the downslope of the nineteenth century and the apparent gap of the war, and regarding our architecture, we are led to demand whether the time of its discard is at hand or whether, after the superficially historical wastes of the last century, it may be reintegrated as a sound organ in an aging body."[41]

It is difficult to recapture the special spirit of "modernity" that suddenly came to form in 1927.[42] In that year, particularly at the Weissenhof exhibition in Stuttgart, the "mainstream of Modern architecture . . . found its International Style."[43] So it was that in 1927 the leading form-givers of the period to come produced their first significant works: Mies van der Rohe's apartment building at Stuttgart, a far cry from his more expressionistic apartments on the Afrikaanischestrasse or his monument to Rosa Luxemburg, was his first experiment with the structural steel cage; Le Corbusier's double house at Stuttgart culminated his development from the Citrohan projects of 1920–22 while his Villa Stein at Garches, also completed in 1927, was unquestionably his first masterpiece, though it in turn can be traced back to his work at La Chaux-de-Fonds and the Maison La Roche; Aalvar Aalto, a comparative newcomer, was already pointing to the future with his preliminary designs for the Viipuri Library. In 1927 the League of Nations competition brought the monumental possibilities of the new architecture face to face with the established forces of the old guard.[44] Similarly, Gropius's Total Theatre project for Erwin Piscator and his Civic Center project for the town of Halle, both of 1927, are the first of a series of projects for mass-democratic programs that were to become a central preoccupation of this period. In Stuttgart, Gropius began to experiment in earnest with prefabrication—another major interest in the following years and at present still a principal concern of architects.

41. Henry-Russell Hitchcock, "The Decline of Architecture," *Hound & Horn* 1 (Sept. 1927), 28–35.

42. Allen Churchill has written a book about 1927: *The Year the World Went Mad* (New York: Crowell, 1960). See also Robert A. M. Stern, "Relevance of the Decade," *JSAH* 24 (March 1965), 6–10.

43. Banham, *Theory and Design,* p. 305. Gropius was also aware of the importance of 1927 to the evolution and establishment of the International Style. In the preface to the second edition of his book, *Internationale Architektur,* he wrote: "Since the appearance of the first edition [in 1925] the modern architecture of the various lands of western culture has followed the line of development indicated by this book with a surprisingly rapid tempo. Then but an idea, it is today a solid fact." Quoted from Henry-Russell Hitchcock's review in "The Architect's Library," *Record* 66 (Aug. 1929), 191.

44. See John Ritter, "World Parliament. The League of Nations Competition, 1926," *Review* 136 (July 1964), 17–28. Ironically, it was Baron Victor Horta, the pioneering architect of Art Nouveau, who presided over the jury which was to veto Le Corbusier's scheme on a technicality.

Before turning to architectural events in America, consider some other remarkable developments in 1927. It was a year when Calvin Coolidge did not seek reelection to the presidency; when Professor James T. Shotwell of Columbia lobbied to have the nations of the world declare war illegal as a means for solving disputes; when Sacco and Vanzetti were tried and executed. It was a year of tremendous technological progress: radio-telephone service was established between New York and London, and San Francisco and Manila; the first national radio networks were established; television was given its first public demonstration; the movies began to "talk"; the Holland Tunnel—the first underwater vehicular tunnel in the world—was opened to carry automobiles under the Hudson River; Henry Ford, after producing his fifteen-millionth car, ceased production of the Model T and brought out the consumer-oriented, highly styled Model A.[45] It was also the year when the incredible boom of the twenties began to crest, giving way to a decline that would culminate in the stock market crash of 1929.

It was the year in which the stage designer Norman Bel Geddes, having conceived the first "streamlined" train and the first "streamlined" automobile, established himself as an artistic consultant to industry.[46] Calling himself an industrial designer, Geddes invented the profession that was to challenge seriously the position of architects throughout the next twenty years and, in a number of key instances, set the pace. The most provocative technological challenge to architecture during this period was the work of Buckminster Fuller, whose Dymaxion House in 1927 hurled the first volley of his extended polemic against the International Style.[47]

45. For a discussion of the significance of Ford's decision, see William Leuchtenburg's excellent survey of the 1920s in America, *The Perils of Prosperity* (Chicago: Chicago, 1958), pp. 200–01. On the basis of Leuchtenburg's evaluation, there is good reason to claim that Ford's Model A was the first car put into production to embody the principles and techniques of industrial design. This rules out much of Banham's elaborate treatment of automobile design at the end of *Theory and Design in the First Machine Age*. Sheldon and Martha Cheney have also written about the importance of Ford's transition from the Model T to the Model A; see *Art and the Machine* (New York: McGraw-Hill, 1936), pp. 26–30.

46. See Norman Bel Geddes, *Miracle in the Evening* (New York: Doubleday, 1960), ed. by William Kelley, p. 344. The underlying spirit of the industrial design movement in the late twenties is suggested by Ernest Elmo Calkins in "Beauty, The New Business Tool," *Atlantic Monthly* 140 (Aug. 1927), 145–56. Buckminster Fuller has a good deal to say about "The Myth of Industrial Design" in his "spontaneous autobiographical disclosure," *Ideas and Integrities* (Englewood Cliffs: Prentice-Hall, 1963), pp. 76–78.

47. The year 1927 is a key date, often repeated, in *Ideas and Integrities*, in which Fuller devotes a considerable amount of energy to criticizing the Bauhaus and the International Style (see esp. p. 9). Perhaps the most eloquent and influential exponent of Fuller's position in this matter is Reyner Banham (*Theory and Design*, pp. 320–30). Robert W. Marks in *The*

In 1927 America began for the first time to sense her cultural independence from Europe—and, indeed, to feel that Europe, broken by the war and the economic chaos of the twenties, was no longer able to lead. America's new role was probably articulated first by a French writer, André Siegfried, who wrote in 1927 that America had evolved an "entirely original social structure . . . [which] may even be a new age, an age in which Europe is no longer the driving force of the world."[48] Our own writers, especially our critics and historians, reinforced this sense of cultural independence. Vernon L. Parrington's *Main Currents in American Thought* was posited on a belief that American literature was not merely a provincial reflection of English thought but a full-blooded literature in its own right, while Charles and Mary Beard's book of the same year, *The Rise of American Civilization,* asserted that there was not only civilization in America but an American civilization. At the same time that these events were bespeaking a kind of nationalism, Charles Lindbergh's solo flight across the Atlantic on the night of 21 May 1927 may be said to have announced a new international age.

The year 1927 saw the establishment of the first museum devoted to modern art, Albert Gallatin's Gallery of Living Art at New York University. It was an important year for American painters, many of whom, after ten years of wrestling with European cubism, finally acknowledged their inability to accept either the analytic or synthetic approach, and insisted on the direct representation of recognizable objects. A new and thoroughly American kind of "modernism" emerged, which can be best described as precisionism although many other terms have been employed.[49] Charles Demuth's enigmatic painting of 1927, *My Egypt,* reflects the American artistic temper at this decisive moment. Although Demuth was aware of the inherent beauty of industrial structures, he was not completely enchanted by them, and his typically American concern for the recognizable image—in this case two grain elevators—and for the material object prevented him from attempting a reorganization of the shapes into a new pictorial order similar to the attempts of the cubists and their

---

Dymaxion World of Buckminster Fuller (New York: Reinhold, 1960) emphasizes the importance 1927 had in Fuller's career (pp. 18, 21, 24–25, 27–28). The year 1927 was also one of crisis for Fuller. It was the year he became completely disenchanted with business, and, as Marks describes it, "a lower depths period. . . . He felt himself close to suicide" (p. 18). It was also the year of his critical publication *4D,* which eventually led to the "Dymaxion" concept, a term coined in 1929 (p. 21).

48. André Siegfried, *America Comes of Age: A French Analysis,* trans. by H. H. and Doris Hemming (New York: Harcourt, Brace, 1927).

49. See Andrew C. Ritchie, *Charles Demuth* (New York: Museum of Modern Art, 1950), esp. p. 15.

descendants, the purists. Instead, *My Egypt* is a depiction of "twin commercial colossi," an unmistakably "wry comment on the nonexistence of an American past."[50]

Stuart Davis's *Eggbeater* series of 1927-28 and Charles Sheeler's photographs of the Ford plant at River Rouge, also of 1927 (Sheeler was the first American photographer to use the forms of industrial buildings and processes as landscape subjects), announced that American machine art had come to maturity. Indeed, Sheeler's development away from the cubistic abstraction and manipulation of his early work to the precise realism of such important canvases as *Upper Deck* of 1929 may be seen as the principal example of American unwillingness to romanticize the machine; American architects, lagging behind the painters, would not come to a similar point until about 1932.

The architectural scene in America in 1927 was electric with the spirit of "modernism," although it was in no way clear which way the profession would go.[51] While Howe contemplated, with wavering commitment, the new architectural styles—ranging from what is now called Art Deco through the more advanced and radical approach generally called the International Style but really a variety of attitudes relating such movements in painting as cubism, purism, and expressionism, to such architectural issues as functionalism and technology, even the most hidebound conservatives among American architects were just beginning to realize that the best European architects had shed the neoclassic forms of Beaux-Arts academicism once and for all. A most perceptive American reaction to this was that of Samuel Chamberlain, who, after an extensive trip to Europe "in search of modernism," reported that "out of the wilderness of wails of discontented modernists, chafing at the artificiality of the academic and calling loudly for a new vision, a new impulse, there comes a strong and sonorous and uncompromising voice, setting forth the case of modern with unexpected logic, the voice of the pensive and earnest Le Corbusier."[52] In addition to such word-of-mouth reports, there was Le Corbusier's

---

50. John McCoubrey, *American Tradition in Painting* (New York: Braziller, 1963), pp. 47–48.

51. For example, see Oliver M. Sayler, *Revolt in the Arts* (New York: Brentano's, 1930), esp. chap. 1; see also Sheldon Cheney, *The New World Architecture* (New York: Longmans, Green, 1930), pp. 73–118, esp. pp. 140, 144; Ella S. Sipley's review of Edwin Avery Park's *New Backgrounds for a New Age* (New York: Harcourt, Brace, 1927) in *The Arts* 13 (March 1928), 203. In fact, the relatively conservative Architectural League of New York had already in 1926 devoted 300 lineal feet of wall space to an exhibition of materials culled from the displays at the 1925 Paris Exposition; see "Forty-First Annual Exhibition of the Architectural League of New York," *Amer. Architect* 129 (20 Feb. 1926), 261–71.

52. Samuel Chamberlain, "In Search of Modernism. Concerning the Dearth of Material in France for the Inquiring Reporter," *Amer. Architect* 131 (20 Jan. 1927), 71–74.

polemic of 1923, *Vers une Architecture,* which had just been translated by Frederick Etchells. Its awesome challenge—"Architecture or Revolution"—could not be ignored.[53] The mood of the national convention of the American Institute of Architects in 1927 was one of some uneasiness,[54] but it was generally felt that hope lay in the stripped classicized forms of Bertram Goodhue and Paul Cret or in the Art Deco manner of Ralph Walker, Ely Jacques Kahn, and Raymond Hood.[55] Walker's Barclay-Vesey Telephone Building in New York, completed in 1926, had captured the imagination of architects, critics, and the public,[56] as would Joseph Urban's Ziegfeld Theatre[57] and James

53. For example, Le Corbusier's book was reviewed anonymously late in 1927: "We enthusiastically recommend to all students of our ever-moving architecture a book translated from the French of M. Le Corbusier, who according to the foreword, is an 'eminent architect' in his own land. We must admit that his name has heretofore been unknown to us but his book is certainly an awakening and stimulating treatise. He sees the greatness of our future in a scientific expression of the possibilities of steel beams, mass-production units, bare concrete walls and a complete avoidance of all unnecessary detail. In a word, we must consider the *function* of a building and that *only* if we are to arrive at a truly *new* and beautiful architecture." "On Our Library Table," *The Architect* 9 (Dec. 1927), 287–88.

See also George S. Chappell ["T-Square"], "The Sky-Line: Luxurious Boxes, Empty Niches," *The New Yorker,* 12 Nov. 1927, pp. 95–97. (*The New Yorker* inaugurated regular architectural criticism, its famous "The Sky-Line" column, in one of its first issues [11 April 1925, p. 8, signed RWS]. In October 1926 Chapell, a New York architect, took over, under the pseudonym of "T-Square." After 12 Dec. 1931 he was succeeded by Lewis Mumford, who remains at the post at this writing, although he has written little in recent years for the magazine.) See also Douglas Haskell, "Review," *Creative Art* 2 (March 1925), xxv; C. H. Blackall, "Review," *Amer. Architecture* 133 (20 May 1928), 712; Claude Bragdon, "Towards a New Architecture," *The Outlook* 148 (15 Feb. 1928), 243.

54. In his speech, A.I.A. president Milton B. Medary reflected the apprehension with which the old guard greeted the spirit of modernism. See A.I.A., *Proceedings of the Sixtieth Annual Convention* (Washington, D.C., 1927), pp. 5–8.

55. Walker, Kahn, and Hood, who were close friends and sympathetic to each other's work, were grouped together and dubbed by Frank Lloyd Wright the "Three Functioneers" of New York architecture. According to Allene Talmey, in "Profiles: Man Against the Sky," *The New Yorker,* 11 April 1931, pp. 24–27: "They are three little men who build tall buildings, and who probably rake into their offices more business than any other architects in the city."

56. This building established Walker at the forefront of the profession. See, e.g., Lewis Mumford, "The Barclay-Vesey Building," *The New Republic* 51 (6 June 1927), 176–77. Walker was very careful always to separate himself from International Style modernism. Though Le Corbusier admired the Barclay-Vesey Building enough to permit its inclusion as an illustration in the English translation of *Vers une Architecture,* Walker was at some pains to declare that "the new architecture will not be a thing of slab-sided cubes or spheres, built up of plane and solid geometry in which there is no element of time (something absolutely lacking in either primary forms or colors), but will have an infinite variety of complex form and an intricate meaning that will be comprehensive to minds that are able to project through beyond infinity." "A New Architecture," *Forum* 48 (Jan. 1928), 1–4.

57. See A. R. Shurleff, "Architectural Notes—The Ziegfeld Theatre by Joseph Urban and Thomas Lamb," *The Arts* 11 (March 1927), 148; "The Ziegfeld Theatre, NY," *Forum* 46

Gamble Rogers's Medical Center for Columbia later in 1927.[58] Frank Lloyd Wright was at the nadir of his influence and prestige. Relegated by Thomas E. Tallmadge to the limbo of lost causes along with Sullivan,[59] he was virtually without work, beseiged by bill collectors and lawyers, and thought to be dead by some of the younger exponents of what would come to be called the International Style. Toward the end of the year, however, things began to look up. Wright was occupied with a resort project that was never to materialize, called San Marcos-in-the-Desert, and Michael Mikkelson, editor of *Architectural Record,* offered him $10,000 for a series of articles, "In the Cause of Architecture," which were to go a long way toward his architectural comeback.[60]

In 1927 there was, as Sheldon and Martha Cheney wrote, "a spreading machine age consciousness."[61] It was the year of the Machine Age Exposition in New York which, more than any other single event, opened American eyes to the wealth of new forms at their disposal. The exposition was the brainchild of Jane Heap, coeditor with Margaret Anderson of one of the most influential of the so-called little magazines, *The Little Review.*[62] For the first time, the American public was asked to look at machines, machine parts, and machine products, and to recognize in their purely utilitarian shapes significant artistic form. In addition, models and photographs of many important European buildings, as well as many examples of Russian constructivist art, set designs, and architecture, were shown. Because of the novel Russian art, the exposition received considerable attention in the daily press and was well attended.[63] It

(May 1927), 414–16 and pls.; [Chapell], "The Sky-Line," *The New Yorker,* 27 Nov. 1926, p. 80.

58. See Lawrence Moore, "The Medical Center," *The Arts* 14 (Nov. 1928), 284–86; [Chapell], "The Sky-Line," *The New Yorker,* 6 Nov. 1926, p. 74.

59. Thomas E. Tallmadge, *The Story of Architecture in America* (New York: Norton, 1927), chap. 9, "Louis Sullivan and the Lost Cause." By 1936, when Tallmadge brought out a second edition of his book, the resurgence of Wright's career and Sullivan's reputation was reflected not only in the text but in the new chapter title, "Louis Sullivan, Parent and Prophet."

60. *Architectural Record* was unquestionably the most innovative among the American professional journals and, under the direction of Mikkelsen and A. Lawrence Kocher (who became managing editor late in 1927), the format was modernized and the magazine transformed into a sounding board for new ideas. Kocher's career, especially his pioneering efforts as journalist-architect during his ten years with the *Record,* deserves careful study.

61. Cheney, *Art and the Machine,* pp. 7–8. See also Stuart Chase, *Men and Machines* (New York: Macmillan, 1929), esp. pp. 247–51.

62. See Herbert Lippman, "The Machine Age Exposition," *The Arts* 11 (June 1927), 324; *The Little Review* (Winter 1925); Jane Heap, "Machine Age Exposition," *The Little Review* (Spring 1925).

63. See "Machine Age Exposition," *New York Times,* 22 May 1927, sec. 12, p. 23; "Russian Night," *New York Times,* 29 May 1927, sec. 2, p. 1.

can surely be regarded as the first major event of the modern movement in America.

Added to this intellectual agitation were some serious American attempts at building in the most advanced forms of European modernism. In New York, William Lescaze built the Capital Bus Terminal, and in California, where Rudolph Schindler had erected his constructivist Lovell Beach House the year before, Richard Neutra built the more conventional Jardinette garden apartments with strip windows (as superficially conceived as those of Hood's McGraw-Hill Building of 1930-31), white walls, and other trademarks of the new style.[64] Neutra's book *Wie Baut Amerika?*, published in 1927, presented, besides a discussion of technology, the author's futurist urban vision, "Rush City Reformed." The projected office tower in Rush City—more constructivist than futurist, however—was to influence Howe's final designs of PSFS (see chapter five). Neutra long claimed that the "Health House" for Dr. Lovell was also conceived in 1927.[65] Clarence Stein and Henry Wright's "City of the Motor Age" at Radburn, New Jersey,[66] the first section of which was completed in 1927, was perhaps more humane in its separation of pedestrian and motor traffic than Neutra's Rush City but was surely less exciting in its architectural forms. Stalled by the Depression, Radburn never grew to its full size; yet its principles dominated new-town planning in America throughout the thirties and early forties and are potent to this day.

Howe was acutely aware of the revolution that was taking form everywhere about him. As early as 1925, when he visited the Exposition des Arts Décoratifs in Paris, he had become alerted to modernism. He "read *Towards a New Architecture* but saw no escape from . . . his world."[67] In the spring of 1928, he was still uncommitted to any of the numerous modern "styles." Inhibited by an inner compulsion to avoid decisive action, he awkwardly teetered between a complete break with the past and a variety of possible compromises. By about April, in a Spenglerian mood, he had made up his mind, as he told an audience of architecture students at Harvard twenty-five years later, that he must do his part "to propagate the Western world-feeling through architecture. As a pre-

64. See David Gebhard, *Rudolph Schindler* (New York: Viking, 1972). Especially important are Gebhard's claims for Schindler's Lovell House in the context of Hitchcock and Johnson's canonical definitions of an International Style; for the Jardinette apartments, see Esther McCoy, *Richard Neutra* (New York: Braziller, 1960).

65. Stern, "Relevance of the Decade."

66. See "A New City," *The Architect* 9 (March 1928), 681-82; "Radburn, New Jersey. A Town of Modern Plan," *Architecture* (New York) 57 (March 1928), 135-36.

67. Howe, untitled talk, Harvard, 1954. He may also have read Frederick Etchells, "Le Corbusier: A Pioneer of Modern European Architecture," *Creative Art* 3 (Sept. 1928), 156-63.

liminary step, I resigned from my firm, sold my house, the badge of my servitude to romantic-classicism, . . . moved into an innocuous non-stylistic relic of evolution, and set myself up, with two draftsmen, as a priest of the Modern Faith."[68] This brief recounting of events long past, though correct in outline, makes the process of Howe's transformation seem far simpler and less painful than it actually was.

For one thing, Howe did not want to disrupt the smooth working relationship of his partnership. He knew that neither Mellor nor Meigs thought as he did and that Meigs, whose conservatism was as notorious as his temper and who regarded all talk of modernism as nonsense, would not allow the arrangement to terminate amicably.[69] Howe waited for the right moment; finally, in the spring of 1928, a number of matters brought things to a head. Howe, through his partnership, had been commissioned to prepare designs for an airport for Camden, New Jersey. According to a paper about Howe written by Eleanor Madeira in 1940 (one in which Howe cooperated in the preparation), this commission caused him once again to question "the irrational and current practice of using steel merely as the invisible support of a false and meaningless sub-divided screen-work had prejudiced him against [steel], but now it became unavoidable." According to Madeira, Howe "is now [1940] very much ashamed of this airport, however, because lack of funds and outside influence led his original plans astray."[70] At the same time, Meigs insisted on designing for the Newbold Estate a swimming pool whose general profile and detail derived from his own highly stylized design for Bryn Mawr College's acoustically improbable auditorium, Goodhart Hall, which was nearing completion at about this time (*fig. 52*).[71] The Newbold pool was a splendid piece of set

68. Howe, ibid. The house into which Howe moved, on Bell's Mill Road in Chestnut Hill, was, however, moderately altered by him.

69. It should be noted, though, that Meigs was not complacent or without ideas of his own. In 1927 he defined architecture as "an arrangement of cubical elements whereby their juxtaposition and relativity produce *esthetic* emotion. It is not four walls and enclosed space, it is a turn in the spiral of infinity." Anticipating Howe's ideas of the thirties and later, he concluded that "what a piece of architecture really is, one may learn if one walks in a wide circle around it keeping one's eye fixed always upon it." "The Architecture of Houses Discussed by A. I. Meigs," *Country Life* (U.S.) 53 (Nov. 1927), 58–59. See discussion of Howe's ideas about architectural space in chaps. 7 and 8.

70. Eleanor Madeira's paper is reprinted in West, *George Howe*, pp. 12–26.

71. For Goodhart Hall, see Arthur I. Meigs, "Goodhart Hall," *Record* 65 (Feb. 1929), 105–56. The nature of Meigs's own particular commitment to a functionally expressive architecture is nowhere more clearly stated than here: "What does architectural design boil down to but to have a want, to find an idea to fit it, to clothe and build the idea in materials, and to seek to make the materials harmonize, to apportion to each material the job that it is fitted to do, and to try and leave the materials comfortable and happy in the end."

design, a Gothic-style ruin conceived in the spirit of Beckford's Fonthill Abbey (*fig. 38*). But to Howe it seemed an altogether unfortunate departure from the principles of the firm's earlier work, when the partners were not without ideals. He and Meigs had an enormous row; Howe quit the firm (a serious blow to it, since he had been responsible for the Saving Fund Society commission, the economic mainstay of the organization), and Meigs never spoke to him again. Meigs's partnership with Mellor continued until Mellor's death in 1940.

Although Howe was not yet completely free of the aesthetic values that had shaped his thought in the years before the war and that he perpetuated for a decade after its conclusion, he was determined to begin anew. His break with the past would be of significance only if he could back his new attitudes with a body of work equal in quality to that of his romantic country house days.

This was more easily said than done. It was difficult to establish which direction of the so-called modern movement in architecture was the most suitable to his sense of freedom and release—and indeed, which offered the most profound principles by which he could guide his architectural career. Although on the surface there seemed to be a clear-cut choice between "traditionalism" and "modernism," there was a whole middle ground of what might best be described as proto-modernism ranging from the stripped classicism of Paul Cret as manifested in his design for the Folger Shakespeare Library, to the particularly beguiling Art Deco Style (as it is now called) that was being given spectacular visibility in this country by Kahn, Walker, and Hood. Howe was well aware of the limitations of Art Deco which, more than any other direction within modernism, seemed to catch the fancy of the satiated café society that was becoming so influential in the late twenties.[72] He questioned its superficiality and in his inaugural address as a modernist, "Modern Decoration," delivered on 20 April 1929 at the newly opened art museum in Fairmount Park, he took the opportunity to deprecate it as the commercialized veneer that it often was.

72. T. H. Robsjohn-Gibbings in his *Homes of the Brave* (New York: Knopf, 1954), pp. 41–42, provides a somewhat snide characterization of the "seamier" side of Art Deco taste. See also Russell Lynes, *The Tastemakers* (New York: Harper, 1954), pp. 243–47; Bevis Hillier, *Art Deco of the 20s and 30s* (New York: Dutton, 1968), esp. pp. 10–13. Hillier's use of the term Art Deco has come to supplant the name Jazz Modern, popular from the late fifties through the sixties. E.g., Vincent Scully uses it in discussing Raymond Hood's McGraw-Hill Building in his *American Architecture and Urbanism* (New York: Praeger, 1969), p. 154. A good brief discussion, with particular reference to the architecture of Rockefeller Center, and by extension American commercial architecture of the late 1920s in general, can be found in William H. Jordy, *American Buildings and Their Architects: The Impact of European Modernism in the Mid-Twentieth Century* (Garden City: Doubleday, 1972), pp. 79–82.

To what must have been, at best, a confused and ever so politely hostile audience, Howe attempted to distinguish the "sound traditionalism" of modern forms from the applied decoration of Art Deco. "To those whose impression of modern decoration has been gained from the department stores and nick-nack shops," the insistence on the "simplification and elimination of ornament" in the design of decorative, i.e. everyday objects, may not seem to square with the facts. Unfortunately the more eccentric twists and turns of a few talented extremists have been seized on for exploitation by sensational imitators, whose work has received wide publicity, and has obscured to the public mind the depth and extent of the modern movement. As opposed to the purveyors of lightning zig-zags and floral monstrosities, Francis Jourdain urges that "ornament delights only the primitive element in us. Civilized man alone delights in the stark form that arises from a happy expression of a purpose. It is the great achievement of the best modern architects and decorators to have correlated all the mechanical, architectural and decorative elements of today, and evolved an organic growth, which promises to be fruitful, as opposed to the dry artificialities of the recent past, which have led us yearly from one fad to another, each as sterile as the last. A beginning only has been made."[73]

The extreme functionalism of the Neue Sachlichkeit was another modernist approach. This was often mistakenly assumed to be the Bauhaus point of view, primarily because, by the time American architects became aware of that influential and misunderstood institution, its directorship had passed from the relatively flexible Gropius to the dogmatic Swiss architect Hannes Meyer. Howe knew well enough the dangers of this oversimplified approach: because it was more an attitude toward program than a fully developed vocabulary of forms, and because it insisted that the forms of buildings could and should develop solely from a pragmatic diagrammatization of their functional areas and structural systems, it produced an extensive body of pretentious socio-logical, economic, and technological theory, and almost no important architecture.[74]

For Howe, then, the most promising future definitely lay in the direction of what Henry-Russell Hitchcock and Philip Johnson were, in 1930–32, to

73. Howe, "Modern Decoration," lecture delivered at the Philadelphia Art Museum, 20 April 1929.

74. A rather interesting description of the Bauhaus under Hannes Meyer is to be found in a review of an exhibition of Bauhaus work held at the John Becker Gallery in Jan.-Feb. 1931. See "A Review of the Field in Art Education: the Bauhaus," *Art Digest* 5 (15 Jan. 1931), 27–28. See also Lewis Mumford, "Form in Modern Architecture. Part V. The Wavy Line vs. the Cube," *Architecture* (New York) 62 (Dec. 1930), 315–18.

isolate and term—perhaps too categorically—the International Style. Howe was at first attracted to what Jordy has described as the first or European phase of the International Style, and what I would prefer to describe as the Machine Phase (of the International Style). The Machine Phase had developed during the 1920s in Europe and had just come to maturity in 1927, as we have seen. The forms of the Machine Phase, though cubist in their origin, were intended to relate, at least symbolically, to the forms of machines and to the hardware of a machine culture, such as smokestacks, pipe rails, and steel ship's ladders. These forms were the result of what Banham has described as the "selective and classicizing" taste of the pioneer masters of the modern movement; the desired qualities of "simplicity of form and smoothness of finish . . . are conditional attributes of engineering and to postulate them as necessary consequences and intentions."[75]

It is important to emphasize that another, and perhaps more philosophically sound, formalist position existed simultaneously with those already mentioned. Supported by such architects as Hans Scharoun, Gerrit Rietveld, Johannes Duiker, the brothers Max and Bruno Taut, and Hugo Häring, it rejected the classicizing modes of Le Corbusier and Mies, in favor of a very distinct philosophical and aesthetic point of view, which may very well have taken the *principles* of the International Style (and, indeed, even some of those of the Neue Sachlichkeit) far more seriously in building design than did either of those styles' proponents, and informed their shape-making with a rigorous expressionism. The strength of this approach, which I have elsewhere termed Rational Expressionism,[76] is often underestimated, especially in America, which, coming to modernism late, received its message of reform in a highly edited version. That is to say, as a result of an apparent ruthless suppression of its principal spokesmen by the leaders of CIAM at its first meeting at La Sarraz in 1928, and the subsequent political events in Germany, the

75. Reyner Banham, "Machine Aesthetic," *Review* 117 (April 1955), 225–28. Later, as we shall see in chap. 5, Banham describes this classicizing preference as one of "abstract idealism." See his *The Architecture of the Well-tempered Environment* (London: Architectural Press, 1969), p. 204; see also Jordy's discussion of the "machine style" in his *The Impact of European Modernism*, pp. 118–19, 127.

76. See Robert A. M. Stern, "Beaux-Arts Theory and Rational Expressionism," *JSAH* 21 (May 1962), 84–95. Rietveld is particularly interesting in this regard, for he quickly overcomes what Banham describes as the "abstraction" of the Schroeder House in favor of a splendidly integral combination of steel frame and concrete planks in his chauffeur's quarters of 1927, that is, as Theodore Brown points out, "exceptional . . . within the context of Rietveld's work . . . decades ahead of its time and appropriately regarded as a prefiguration of Mies van der Rohe's work at I.I.T." See *The Work of G. Rietveld, Architect* (Cambridge, Mass.: M.I.T., 1958), p. 88.

leading "rationalist-expressionist" architects were never given the opportunities to enter the hallowed halls of canonical modernity. Yet in Europe they were a very powerful force and their monuments, many of which seem far less dated today than those of the Machine Phase, may be studied with profit.[77] Moreover, as I shall attempt to demonstrate, its attitudes triumphed in American practice, shifting from the symbolic abstractions of the mechanomorphological or Machine Phase of the International Style to the more developed integration between construction and its expression, which marks what has been called by Jordy the second phase of the International Style and which I prefer to describe as the Technological Phase of that style.

At any rate, it was the Machine Phase (that is, the first phase of the International Style) which, under the spell of Hitchcock's growing authority and later under that of the more polemical Johnson, rapidly became the accepted avant-garde architectural vocabulary. Howe recognized the propagandistic nature of Hitchcock and Johnson's book, *The International Style.* He wrote that although it was in no sense intended as a defense against or answer to "the attack of Wright and others on the International Style, it constitutes in fact both. It is an admirable and scholarly work which brings out with great clarity the distinction between mere good planning and buildings, or bare 'functionalism,' and imaginative structural design. The analysis of the significance of volume as opposed to mass, and of the support, defining plane, and subdividing screen, as differentiated from the continuous wall and sloping roof, is "skilful and clear." Howe objected to the "didactic brevity" of the text and he found "the criticism incorporated in the captions . . . unnecessarily irritating . . . since they are more often than not personal aesthetic judgements."[78] He objected to the polemics of many of the leading European Internationalists as well. "He was repelled in the writings of these men by the burial of that which was purely architectural under an emotional mass of what seemed to him doubtful sociology, economics and archaeological analogy."[79]

Based on a set of definite aesthetic criteria, the Machine Phase of the Inter-

---

77. For a recent discussion of the effects of the "purist" purge at the 1928 meeting at La Sarraz, see Walter Segal, "The Neo-Purist School of Architecture," *Architectural Design* 42 (June 1972), 344–45. See also Charles Jencks, *Architecture 2000* (New York: Praeger, 1971), pp. 35–41; Peter Cook, *Architecture, Action and Plan* (New York: Van Nostrand Reinhold, 1967), esp. chaps. 2 and 3. See also chap. 3 of this book, nn. 63–66. Julius Posener views this same codification process of the International Style from the perspective of the German experience, in *From Schinkel to the Bauhaus,* p. 9.

78. Howe, "Creation and Criticism," two book reviews, *Shelter* 2 (April 1932), 27.

79. Ibid.

national Style came to be focused primarily upon a purity of building shape, with special reference to the pristine envelope and its skin. Among its principles was an insistence upon volumes rather than mass and upon the elimination of ornament, and, most importantly, a preference for pure geometry, which was held to be the highest form of expression. These formal principles were demonstrated in a corpus of works that comprise, for most architects and critics today, the leading monuments of the modern movement. Their relationship to machine culture was purely symbolic. Structure was regularized in order to be ignored and was considered independent of space and facade. Space was conceived almost exclusively in terms of interlocked volumes, more or less in movement, or in what Siegfried Giedion came later to insist upon as "flow." Largely because of the power of Hitchcock and Johnson's polemics and the authority lent them by the support of Howe, it was the Machine Phase, with its clearly perceptible set of modern formal images, that had the greatest influence on those men who were to shape modern architecture in America at the end of the 1920s.[80]

The critical nature of Howe's support in bringing the ideas and forms of the International Style in architecture before the lay and professional public cannot be overstated: in 1932 he was forty-six years old, with all the right social, intellectual, and professional credentials. He was, in addition, the co-architect of a preeminent work of design in the new vocabulary, the PSFS. Hitchcock was twenty-nine years old, and, although he had written critical articles and reviews as well as *Modern Architecture,* in 1932 he had neither the force of a major academic institution behind him nor the recognition bestowed upon him which his enormous scholarship now supports. Johnson, who has since become an international figure in architecture, was twenty-six years old. He would not choose to go to architecture school for another eight years, and his first major work, his own so-called Glass House in New Canaan, would not be built until 1949. And finally, the very institution which was seeking to launch this new movement, the Museum of Modern Art, was only three years old and operating in temporary quarters in an office building on Fifty-Seventh Street in New York.

While the influence of the Machine Style was a salutary one, at last breaking down the barrier of historic precedent that obstructed American architectural practice, it marked in some ways—especially in the integration of technology and architecture—a retrogression, one that many American archi-

80. Philip Johnson's almost poignant struggle to free himself as an architect from these narrow constrictions is documented in his contribution to Heinrich Klotz and John W. Cook, eds., *Conversations with Architects* (New York: Praeger, 1973), pp. 11–50.

tects found peculiar in a style that purported to be modern. Beginning probably with Sullivan and certain of Wright's early large-scale works, and leading to Schindler's Lovell Beach House, Neutra's Lovell Health House, and Howe and Lescaze's PSFS Building, a distinctly different set of images had evolved in America. These were based on the use of structural cages and an exploitation of the possibilities of compositional types similar to, when not actually derived from, the formal researches of Mondrian rather than Ozenfant.[81] The next chapter will develop this theme, but here it is important to point out that this particular set of circumstances combining with the shift from Europe to America of the leaders of the new architecture led to the second or American phase of the International Style, which I would prefer to call the Technology Phase. For in America, in place of the platonic, rather arbitrary rendered stucco volumes of Le Corbusier's Villa Savoye, a pioneering architect like Neutra, in designing the Lovell Health House, worked with an articulated steel cage infilled with light-weight concrete panels—a system of construction and formal expression years ahead of Le Corbusier in its actual relationship to available technology at the scale of a house. This second or technological phase of the International Style had its formal origins in such German buildings as Gropius and Meyer's Chicago *Tribune* Tower competition entry of 1922; Max Taut's entry in the same competition and in his splendid exhibition building of 1926 for the German Manufacturers Association at Düsseldorf, whose wood frame and tile panel construction predicts the forms of the finest product of the Technology Style—Mies van der Rohe's buildings of 1939–45 at the Illinois Institute of Technology; and in Rietveld's chauffeur's house of 1927.[82] Similarly, the origins of Mies's handling of concrete at the Promontory Apartments in Chicago can be found in Taut's building of 1928 for the German Publishing Association in Berlin. Thus, in the work of Mies, who had been their compatriot in the days of the "ring" and the magazine *G*, the rational-expressionist architects, defeated at La Sarraz, enjoyed a somewhat Pyrrhic victory. It was not until after World War II that one of them, Hans Scharoun, would be able to build at a scale appropriate to the seriousness of his ideas.[83]

Certainly matters were never as simple as Hitchcock and Johnson made

81. See chap. 5, p. 124.

82. For Taut's building see Bruno Taut, *Modern Architecture* (London: *The Studio*, 1929), p. 188. Many of the buildings which may have influenced Howe and Lescaze, such as Döcker's hospital at Waiblingen (see chap. 5, n. 37), are illustrated in this book.

83. The "ring" consisted of Hugo Häring, Eric Mendelsohn, Ludwig Mies van der Rohe, Walter Gropius, Bruno Taut, Max Taut, Otto Bartning, and Ludwig Hilbersheimer. For Scharoun's postwar work, see Margit Staber, "Hans Scharoun. Ein Beitrag zum organischen Bauen," *Zodiac* 10 (1952), 52–93, and 195–200; Posener, *From Schinkel to the Bauhaus*.

them out to be in 1932 and, indeed, if the term International Style is to have
any meaning, its scope must be broadened and the marked divergence between the forms of its first phase and those of its second must be accounted for.

Having chosen the general direction of the Machine Phase, though, as we
shall see, quickly moving beyond them in the formation of the Technology
Phase, Howe, together with George Daub and Louis E. McAllister, two draftsmen who remained loyal to him after his break with Mellor and Meigs, set up a
small office on South Nineteenth Street and tried to become a modern architect. His first commissions as a modernist did not encourage wild artistic spec-
ulation. In remodeling George Tyler's house at Elkins Park, he was restricted
by Tyler's conservatism and, more importantly, by the high-shouldered neo-
Georgian profile of the existing house (*fig. 53*). Howe could not see his way
safely beyond the once revolutionary forms of the neoclassicist John Soane,
and he produced a sharply outlined, precisely detailed red-brick box that might
well have pleased the architect of 23 Lincoln Inn's Fields. As a mantelpiece
decoration for Mrs. Tyler's bedroom, Howe commissioned his friend Gaston
Lachaise to design one of those craggy, tough-skinned eagles with which he
was beginning to establish his reputation as a sculptor.

Howe was awarded three commissions by the American Battle Monuments
Commission. The first, a chapel at Bony, France, on which the sculptor Sidney
Waugh collaborated, and the second, a monument at Ypres, Belgium (*fig. 54*),
also a collaborative effort with Waugh, though simple in their massing and
detail, are still very traditional in character. Both are of 1928–30. The third,
a simple pyramid at Arlington National Cemetery honoring the U.S. Marines,
adorned with one of Lachaise's most gracefully modeled eagles, is a more
successful piece of neoclassic design (*figs. 56, 57*). Probably based on a drawing of Piranesi's, a photographic negative of which was among Howe's office
files when he died, Howe's design with its fluidly curving base has a sculptural
power and lift that the Böcklin-like rendering prepared by Howe's office does
not suggest.[84] Possibly designed as early as 1924, it was built in 1928. A photo
negative in Howe's files suggests its source in Piranesi (*fig. 55*).

84. The chapel at Bony, Madeira writes, "is the most significant. Of white granite and
blocky in shape, it is not designed in any traditional style. . . . the most unusual and original
feature is a cross of light made by open slits in the wall facing the entrance door. By this
cross Howe tries to express his belief that, as space in a house is a relationship between
indoors and outdoors, in a religious building it is a relationship between temporal finite space
and eternal, infinite space. It becomes symbolic even more than physical." "George Howe,"
in West, *George Howe*. For a discussion of Meigs's and Howe's relationship to Lachaise, see
Lincoln Kirstein, *Gaston Lachaise* (New York: Museum of Modern Art, 1935), p. 12.

Only with the house for Mr. and Mrs. James M. R. Sinkler, at Westchester, Pennsylvania, of 1928–30, did Howe begin to hit his stride as a modernist (*figs. 58, 59*). The Sinkler House is a transitional work, a kind of combination of High Hollow and the Holden House but stylistically and compositionally freer than either. The masonry is coarsely laid up to emphasize the pattern of the joinery in a manner anticipating the rough-dressed stone walls favored by Le Corbusier and Breuer in the 1930s; the house itself sits on a high podium with big openings, recalling those at High Hollow, giving out from the principal living spaces to small projecting semicircular balconies. The balcony rails are delicate strands of iron similar to those developed for the cages at the school banking department of the main office of PSFS.[85] Inside the living room low, rounded furniture, quite Art Deco in profile and in the patterns of the upholstery fabrics, was casually arranged around an enormous divan piled high with pillows.

In March 1929 Howe was asked by the Philadelphia Saving Fund Society to prepare new drawings for the bank and office tower at Twelfth and Market Streets. This project had been delayed since 1926, during which time the Society tested the site with the temporary branch bank already discussed. Meigs was also asked to submit drawings for a traditional scheme, probably merely as a formality. James Willcox, the Society's president, always preferred to work with Howe, and according to Isaac Roberts, a member of the original building committee, had decided in all likelihood that he would be the architect and perhaps, even, that the building would be "modern"—that is, "progressive."[86]

Howe submitted four schemes, dated 20 March and 29 March 1929. All were surprisingly modern, and Howe received the commission. Schemes one and two were variations of each other as were schemes three and four. These last two had almost no influence on the final design but are interesting in themselves. In them, at the client's request, Howe designed an office building in which a five-story garage was placed above the ground-floor banking chamber; a U-shaped office tower was placed above the garage podium and opened into a light court on the Twelfth Street side. Despite the unusual inclusion of a

85. See A.I.A., Philadephia Chapter, *Yearbook of the Annual Architectural Exhibition* (Philadelphia, 1929). Howe relegated the Sinkler House, the Holden House, the branch banks for PSFS, and some "unimportant" interiors to a period in his work that he described as "composite modernized traditionalism." Letter to Walter Creese, 28 June 1946. (See p. 4 above.) An elevational study for the Sinkler House, which was not adopted, was drawn by Lescaze in June 1929, probably when the house was already under construction.
The cages in the school banking room are illustrated in Jordy, "PSFS."
86. Isaac Roberts, quoted in Jordy, "PSFS," p. 59.

garage (with all its attendant complications), the scheme is rather offhand, and it seems clear that it did not especially interest Howe.

Schemes one and two are more developed. Scheme one represents a fuller coverage of the site than two. Dated 20 March 1929, scheme two is significant in its freestanding tower slab, set back from the street and property lines, and in its skin composed of alternating horizontal masonry bands and window layers (*fig. 60*). These, although continuous around the corners, are interrupted at column points. The interplay between columns and horizontal masonry bands and "strip" windows is carried out on three sides of the tower; the pattern of support and supported is thus clearly established. The south wall with its peculiar systems of setbacks, employed no doubt to express the decreasing number of elevators in the upper floors of the tower, is not yet the separate element it would become in the final design. The banking room, at street level as in the Beaux-Arts project of 1926, is a cage of glass and steel encased by columns. The scheme is definitely transitional, hesitant, and not especially modern. Nonetheless, the changes in fenestration patterns, the use of setbacks and cantilevered planes, and the bold treatment of the air-conditioning grilles and chimney make, at least at the rooftop, for an exciting effect.

Scheme two, drawn up early in 1929, represents Howe's first mature essay as a modern architect. It received the most elaboration of any of the PSFS schemes of this period and probably was his favorite. A major breakthrough from the forms of the past, it still testifies to his inability, despite his passionate desire to be modern, to abandon certain of his traditional convictions about the proper expression of structure, construction, and space. His compositional instincts, still attuned to formal precepts of Beaux-Arts design, fell back on an automatic symmetry when faced with the problem of elevators. Confused by his desire to articulate structure and at the same time to have that structure help to define the interior spaces, Howe moved the columns at the north wall (over Market Street) near the center. This breaks the rhythm of the structure, although it does make the end space, in many ways the choicest, usable. He then placed a stairway in the narrow space between the two columns and lit it with a continuous vertical window. This stairway was allowed to descend behind the plate-glass window wall directly into the banking room. Thus the integrity of a separation between service space in the form of vertical circulation and rentable space in the form of lofts is compromised, and a rather too simple solution is substituted.

In terms of previous American skyscraper design, this project stands as a synthesis between Sullivan's concern for horizontal and vertical interplay, best seen in the Bayard and Guaranty Buildings, and the design—not so refined structurally but more concerned with a statement of power—produced by Frank Lloyd Wright for the San Francisco *Call* in 1912. Howe's project represents an advance over these in its careful composition not only of structural but also of functional elements as seen in the careful articulation of the truss bridging, the distinction made between the nature of the slab of offices and the vertical circulation core, and the sophisticated treatment of mechanical elements in the roof. Its forced symmetry, its impractical arrangements of elevators, and the overwrought articulation of the core as well as the vertical window strip on the north elevation, are less successful. In its external effects, it resembles most closely the scheme drawn up (but never submitted) by the Danish architect Knud Lönberg-Holm for the Chicago *Tribune* Tower competition. That scheme, referred to by Hitchcock in *Modern Architecture* and widely illustrated in European publications, consisted of a rectilinear tower with a central service core and offices around on three sides.[87] Poorly worked out from a functional and structural point of view, its elegant skin of contrastingly colored facing materials now seems merely a twodimensional exercise in De Stijl planar composition. The use of dark and light colors framing the windows and indicating the structure compares with Howe's more direct, if less dazzling, attempts at such expression. Even the awkward symmetry of the end elevation predicts Howe's scheme—so much so that one is tempted to stress a relationship between the two. The inconsistencies of Howe's scheme two—urbane, self-contained, and carefully composed—can be attributed to a lingering mental habit of symmetry. This scheme for PSFS needs no illuminated spheres to proclaim its quality.

87. Henry-Russell Hitchcock, *Modern Architecture: Romanticism and Reintegration* (New York: Payson and Clarke, 1929), p. 200. Hitchcock writes of the *Tribune* competition that except for Lönberg-Holm's project there were no submissions that made significant formal advances over the proto-modernism of what he called "The New Tradition."

5. Howe and Lescaze

> There are things that intelligence alone is able to seek, but which, by
> itself, it will never find. These things instinct alone could find; but it will
> never seek them.
>
> Henri Bergson, *Creative Evolution*

Despite the merits of the early schemes for PSFS, Howe was not satisfied with
his progress as a "modern" architect. Where today we are able to see more
positive qualities in his work, he could see only lingering traditionalism. So
desperately did he want to be modern that in 1929 he began to look around
for a partner who would bring to the firm some experience with the design
principles of the International Style. William Lescaze was such a man, and
they became partners on 1 May 1929.

Lescaze, just beginning to gain recognition as an architect and designer,
had been considering a partnership with Eugene Schoen, a successful architect
and interior designer working in the style of Josef Hoffman and the Vienna
Secession.[1] One afternoon in April, while Lescaze was still thinking over
Schoen's offer, William Stix Wasserman, a young stockbroker with connections
in Philadelphia and New York who knew both Howe and Lescaze well, introduced them. His introduction "took place as the result of a friendship that had
sprung up between [Wasserman's] wife and Jeanne de Lanux. Lescaze was a
friend of hers, and one weekend she brought him to Philadelphia where he met
George."[2] It was Howe who suggested the partnership, holding out to Lescaze
the probability of a commission from the Saving Fund Society for a large office
building in the heart of Philadelphia. Naturally enough, Lescaze considered
the offer favorably and an agreement was draw up.

The role assigned to each of the partners was as follows: "Howe undertakes, in a general way, to assume the responsibility of establishing ad-

1. For Schoen, see Walter Creese, "American Architecture from 1918 to 1933, with Special
Emphasis on European Influence" (Ph.D. diss., Harvard, 1949), pt. 2, p. 17; C. Adolph Glassgold, "The Decorative Arts," *The Arts* 14 (Oct. 1928), 215–17. Examples of Schoen's office
furniture may be seen in *Record* 64 (Sept. 1928), 248, and in Paul T. Frankl, *New Dimensions*
(New York: Payson and Clarke, 1928), pls. 39–41.
2. William Stix Wasserman, letter to author, 8 January 1974.

vantageous business connections, attending meetings and conferences, and conducting negotiations connected with the inception and execution of partnership business. Lescaze undertakes, in a general way, the responsibility for architectural designs, the conduct of the office or offices, and the supervision of building construction."[3]

It was agreed that each partner would retain his personal staff and office and that the firm would be known as Howe and Lescaze.

William Lescaze, ten years Howe's junior, was born in Geneva, Switzerland, in 1896.[4] He studied with Karl Moser in the Zurich Technische Hochschule. Moser, Lescaze's great inspiration, was, to use Howe's phrase, one of the "secondary luminaries" in the development of modern architecture. Howe, disregarding Perret's church at Raincy, considered Moser's enormous Church of Saint Anthony of 1923 at Basel as "the most striking religious [edifice] of recent times."[5] After working in the devastated areas of France in 1919 and 1920, and in the office of Henri Sauvage in Paris,[6] Lescaze emigrated to New York in 1923, followed shortly by Moser's son Werner. The elder Moser had suggested that Lescaze's interest in monumental architecture might find its opportunity for fulfillment in America. Unable to gain employment in New York, Lescaze headed to Cleveland to work for the tradition-bound firm of Hubbell and Benes for about six months.[7] He returned to New York in November 1923 when commissioned to remodel a town house on Sutton Place for Mr. and Mrs. Simeon Ford.

In New York, despite the vigorous support of the Swiss consul, commissions were hard to find for a young modernist architect, especially one who not only fancied himself a spokesman for the avant-garde but also possessed visions

3. Reprinted in William Jordy, "PSFS: Its Development and Its Significance in Modern Architecture," *JSAH* 21 (May 1962), 47–83.

4. For biographical data, see Lescaze, *On Being an Architect* (New York: Putnam's 1942), esp. pp. 241–43. See also Robert M. Coates, "Profiles: Modern," *The New Yorker*, 12 Dec. 1936, 44–50; Henry-Russell Hitchcock, "Howe and Lescaze," in Alfred Barr et al., *Modern Architecture. International Exhibition* (New York: Museum of Modern Art, 1932), p. 144.

5. Howe, "Modern Architecture," *U.S.A.* 1 (Spring 1930), 19, 20, 23.

6. Sauvage, a pioneer modernist, wavered between the varying modern modes. His "Galerie des Boutiques Françaises" at the Paris Exposition of 1925, e.g., is overrun with insistently curvilinear Art Deco ornament, while his apartments at 24 rue des Amiraux, Paris, show important futurist influence. For the former, see René Herbst, *Les Devantures, Virtrines, Installations de Magasins à l'Exposition International des Arts Décoratifs* (Paris: Moreau, 1925), pl. 35. For a discussion of the latter in terms of the assimilation of futurism into the International Style, see Reyner Banham, *Theory and Design in the First Machine Age* (New York: Praeger, 1960), esp. sec. 2. See also n. 35 below.

7. Hubbell and Benes designed in 1916 the strongly eclectic art museum in Cleveland; see G. H. Edgell, *The American Architecture of Today* (New York: Scribner's, 1928), p. 248.

of the monumental. Lescaze, however, seemed willing to compromise with established eclectic taste. Thus a commission for a boy's dormitory at the Edgewood School in Greenwich, Connecticut, which was erected during the summer of 1925, was, with its gabled roofs, dormers, picturesque asymmetrical composition, and Collegiate Gothic details, more closely related to the kind of work Howe was doing at that time than it was to advanced European modernism.[8]

Although Lescaze has enjoyed the reputation of a lifelong practitioner in the International Style, his commitment to modernist architecture in these early years was ambivalent. During the twenties he appears to have pursued an even narrower eclecticism than Howe and his partners, and without the restraint and respect for materials that gave their work dignity. His own duplex apartment, for instance, was filled with Spanish antiques—something no self-respecting modernist would have dared to do at that time. The bedroom, with its vibrant yellow rough plaster walls, heavily carved furniture, and elaborate hangings, was bold bordering on the theatrical. Entering the bathroom—raised three steps from the bedroom so that the tub might be "sunken"—was likened by *Arts and Decoration* to "stepping into a pool in the heart of a jungle." This effect was enhanced by the mural painted by Lescaze in "bright, tropical colors"; besides the stylized plant and animal forms that entirely covered the walls, a waterfall was depicted seemingly cascading into the slate-covered tub below.[9]

Most of Lescaze's commissions were for commercial and residential interiors.[10] They did not reflect the thought or forms of the International Style but grew out of the Art Deco style that in 1927 was becoming extremely fashionable in New York.[11] Le Corbusier's remarks in *Towards a New Architecture* are pertinent to this growing interest in the decorative arts which acted as a wedge to open the minds of Americans toward the possibilities of a new archi-

8. "Boys' Dormitory," *Architecture* (New York) 55 (April 1927), 207–08.

9. "A Bit of Old Spain in New York," *Arts and Decoration* 28 (Nov. 1927), 50–51. See also Lescaze's showroom for "Foo-Kei—Chinese Importer," in Architectural League of New York, *Yearbook, 1925*; also his "Mural Painting for a Candy Store," in Architectural League of New York, *Yearbook, 1926.*

10. See Lescaze, *On Being an Architect,* p. 134.

11. For a contemporaneous discussion of the growing importance of the Art Deco style in the late twenties, see Henry-Russell Hitchcock, "Some American Interiors in the Modern Style," *Record* 64 (Sept. 1928), 235–43. Hitchcock writes, "In 1927, although in some cases they had been at work quietly for many years, there began to appear in America designers capable of producing modern design more suitable for wide American use than the imported objects which find ready sale only when they are incidental, inexpensive and gay, such as wall papers and lamp-shades."

tecture. "Decorative art," he said, "at least provided a good opportunity to unload the past and feel our way to the spirit of architecture."[12]

A typical design by Lescaze of the period is the display room for Nudelman and Conti.[13] Visual interest is centered on an overly clever treatment of the door and display cases, which employ mirrors and plaques of brass and blue and white glass. Treated in a flat and insistently asymmetrical manner, the detail lacks the measured restraint of the finest De Stijl work to which it otherwise owes a great deal; it is best described, stylistically, as Art Deco.

Lescaze was commissioned by Frederick Loesser and Company, a Brooklyn department store, to design, as a permanent exhibition, an apartment interior consisting of a living room and a man's study.[14] Probably Lescaze's most successful interior of the period, it is admirably restrained, using a limited palette of colors: oyster white and warm gray walls with silver trim. The furniture is upholstered in gray tweed. Red, black, and blue color accents are scattered about the room. Certainly not traditional, the Loesser rooms' conservative modernism hardly prepares one for the experimentation that Lescaze indulged in when commissioned by the R. H. Macy Company to design a penthouse studio for its International Exhibition of Art in Industry of 1928.

In the Macy's scheme the space is dominated by the treatment of the floor with its overlapping circles of color. The steps seem too big for the room, especially in their solidity and lack of articulation where they join the wall and floor planes. The curvilinear forms of the chromium and white leather furniture are not in harmony with the rectangular planes of the constructivist chair. The walls, though treated simply, suffer from the inclusion of various small objects placed at random and out of scale with the bold planar treatment. Although startling, on close inspection the design fails for lack of a unifying idea. It suffers also from its two-dimensional quality, which is more closely related to graphic design than to architecture.[15]

12. Le Corbusier, *Towards a New Architecture*, trans. by Frederick Etchells (New York: Payson and Clarke, 1927), p. 90. It is often forgotten that Le Corbusier's interest in the decorative arts preceded his concerns for either painting or architecture. His first publication was a pamphlet, *Etude sur le Mouvement d'Art décoratif en Allemagne* (La Chaux-de-Fonds, 1912). See also his *L'Art decoratif d'Aujourd'hui* (Paris: Crès, 1926).

13. See Glassgold, "The Decorative Arts." Also illustrated in this article is an office by Lescaze for the Amos Parrish Company.

14. Illustrated in Hitchcock, "Some American Interiors," and in "A Modernistic Apartment," *Architecture* (New York) 58 (Aug. 1928), 89–92. See also "Glimpse of New York Modernistic Apartments," *Arts and Decoration* 29 (Sept. 1928), 64; C. Adolph Glassgold, "Decorative Art Notes," *The Arts* 13 (May 1928), 296.

15. See C. Adolph Glassgold, "Art in Industry," *The Arts* 13 (June 1928), 375–79; "The Macy Exposition of Art in Industry," *Record* 64 (Aug. 1928), 137–39; "Interior Architecture," *Amer. Architect* 133 (20 June 1928), 823–27; *House and Garden* 57 (April 1930), 82.

In 1928 Lescaze designed a hunting lodge at Mount Kisco, New York, for Count Jean de Sieyes.[16] He also submitted an entry in the League of Nations competition and prepared a project for "The Future American Country House."[17] Lescaze's only other executed architectural commission before joining Howe was a small bus terminal in New York City, built in 1927 and destroyed before 1932 (fig. 61).[18] This design's ambivalence between a structure suspended from cables and walls that appear to be load bearing is symptomatic of the lack of formal precision that antagonized many architects and potential clients still wavering in their commitment to the ideals of the new architecture. More importantly, the crudity of detailing in this and other buildings engendered an obvious distrust in the technical competence of modern architects and in the technological relevance of modern design; the shoddy materials earned for the International Style a reputation as a "poor man's style." While this label was of some use as a palliative in the economically depressed thirties, as a polemical tool it was so closely related to the principles of utilitarian functionalism that it became, in the long run, an obstacle to the intelligent comprehension by Americans of the *strictly symbolic* ideals of modern architecture.[19]

Relatively inexperienced in the art of building, Lescaze brought to his partnership with Howe a lively, fairly vigorous, but unconsidered vocabulary of modern forms. Indeed, if one examines his work before the spring of 1929, there is less relationship to the International Style than one might have expected. Aside from the lapses into purely traditional forms, the work seems to resemble more that of Mallet-Stevens than that of Le Corbusier. Cubistic rather than volumetric, it is more *moderne* than modern. Surely there is little to predict the high quality of design that PSFS has led critics to associate with Lescaze. One is inclined to agree with Hitchcock's impressive evaluation of 1929: "The work of the Swiss Lescaze in New York has been chiefly restricted to interiors in which he had shown perhaps more virtuosity than integrity. But the difficulty of receiving effective cooperation in a city whose 'modernism' consists in copying the poorest French models of the New Tradition excuses much, as does also the inherent difficulty of installing completely coherent New Pioneer rooms in old buildings."[20]

16. See Hitchcock, "Howe and Lescaze," p. 144.

17. Lescaze, "The Future American Country House," *Record* 64 (Nov. 1928), 417–22. See also Jordy, "PSFS."

18. Hitchcock, "Howe and Lescaze," p. 144.

19. For a discussion of this subject from the viewpoint of a critic seeking to expand the scope of influence of the modern movement at the end of the 1930s, see John McAndrew, ed., *Guide to Modern Architecture: Northeast States* (New York: Museum of Modern Art, 1940), pp. 9–18.

20. Henry-Russell Hitchcock, *Modern Architecture: Romanticism and Reintegration* (New York: Payson and Clarke, 1929), p. 205.

George Howe's second scheme for PSFS, of March, 1929, had been the product of a long, lonely year of introspection and search. Its forms were crude but, with the exception of some lingering symmetry, they were not arbitrary. Although based on a profound concern for the elements of architectural construction, they were not sufficiently lyric in their expression of that concern to satisfy Howe. He understood that although his break with the past was clean and clear it would never be complete; that the unconscious residue of twenty years of thought and practice could never really be wiped out. Some of it, the stylistic mannerisms, hindered his development as they had done in the 1929 scheme for PSFS and in the Sinkler House, but others—the wonderful grasp of structure and space, the instinctive compositional skills and sure sense of style —would always serve him in good stead. For the moment, Howe wanted no part of any of these. He wanted, desperately, to be modern. His search for a system of architectural expression consonant with modern needs had been, so far as he was concerned, a failure, and he was terribly discouraged. As he later wrote to James Willcox:

> I felt I had failed either to evolve or discover such an expression until I became conscious of the meaning of the so-called modern system of design to the west in America and to the east in Europe. It was then I entered into my present partnership with a man who had long been studying and practising the new system. I feel it is fundamentally an architectural rediscovery of the meaning of the past and above the mere whim of individual taste. On that basis I shall defend it without personal bias since it is not my own discovery but that of many other men seeking a technically and expressively satisfactory solution of modern architectural problems.[21]

Together, he and Lescaze set out to arrive at modern forms through hard work, a painful search, a "penetration of the meaning of things."[22] Their search for modern forms can be documented in two ways: a corpus of works and projects emanating from the offices of Howe and Lescaze, and a series of speeches, letters, and articles written by Howe.

The terms of the partnership agreement seem clear enough on the surface, but close consideration of the buildings designed by the firm leads one to reflect on the actual working relationship which existed in day-to-day practice be-

21. Letter, Howe to Willcox, 26 May 1930, published in *JSAH* 21 (May 1962), 96–97. It is interesting to note Howe's homage not only to European modernism but also to its offshoot in the "west"—presumably the work of Wright and Neutra and Schindler.
22. Howe, "Modern Architecture."

tween these very different men who were often ninety miles apart—one in New York, the other in Philadelphia. The intense loyalties of certain of the draftsmen and office assistants make it very difficult to unravel after forty years the real nature of the partnership, which even during its very existence was a matter of mystery to knowledgeable outsiders like Philip Johnson, who, though long a close friend of Howe, was never certain of his contribution to the firm or of his ability as a designer within the canonized vocabulary of the International Style. Just before the partnership was dissolved on 1 March 1935, an agreement was drawn up by the partners allocating the responsibility for all the executed work and some of the projects handled during the partnership.[23]

In this chapter I will discuss those works which in accord with this agreement are to be considered joint efforts and in which, because of reasons of geography or personal relationship, Howe is likely to have played an important part in the overall design process. I will also discuss related, unbuilt work, for which no specific agreements dealing with attribution were made. A more detailed discussion of this agreement and an explanation of the manner by which certain works, though apparently the product of the partnership, are actually to be credited to one or the other of the partners follows in chapter seven.

Lescaze brought the first important commission to the firm, and he was surely responsible for its design.[24] Mr. and Mrs. Leopold Stokowski had donated the funds for a nursery school building at the Oak Lane Country Day School and suggested Lescaze, a personal friend, as architect. The headmaster,

23. Lescaze sent a copy of this document, which bears the date 15 Feb. 1935, to A. Lawrence Kocher, editor of *Architectural Record*, on 12 Aug. 1935, after certain erroneous attributions had been made in the magazine.
    Despite this allocation, it is only fair to note that Lescaze specifically stated in later years that he actually designed all the work attributed to Howe and Lescaze. About PSFS he stated: "The simple truth is that I designed PSFS and nobody else" (Jordy, "PSFS"). It is clear that Howe did not agree. He wrote Lescaze on 29 Oct. 1934: "It is impossible to have a succession of jobs like the P.S.F.S. in which quite effectively and in a very real sense we both participated in the design." At the time of the dissolution of the partnership, he offered Lescaze full design credit for all works by the firm save PSFS and its garage. Lescaze wrote Howe on 25 Feb. 1935: "For sentimental reasons, Oak Lane, Field, Hessian Hills School, Curry and Wilbour Library should continue to be known as joint undertakings." For details of the partners' lengthy and acrimonious correspondence, see chap. 7.
    24. Lescaze wrote that Stokowski "told me of a school near Philadelphia to which he and his wife wanted to donate a little nursery building. He said that it made no sense to him unless it was a modern building since it was to be for two- and three-year old children, and when they grew up he thought most everything would be modern." *On Being an Architect*, p. 243.

William Burnlee Curry, had advanced ideas about education but not about architecture. Lescaze took him on as a pupil, and a long and mutually profitable friendship began.[25]

The Oak Lane School was designed by Lescaze in the spring and built during the summer of 1929 (figs. 62-64). A pioneering venture in many respects, it was both the first school in the International Style to be built in the United States, and the first executed work of the new firm of Howe and Lescaze. The building was intended to consist of three units: two classrooms connected by a hall unit which contained a kitchenette and a washroom as well as a teacher's office. Due to a limited budget of around $10,000, only half of the original plan could be constructed. Thus were built one classroom as well as the adjacent wall of the other, which was necessary so that the end of the porch could be closed in. The porch consists of two levels: a lower deck covered over for rainy weather by the upper, reached by a stair and used in good weather as a sunroom and outdoor play area. This upper porch level is sheltered by the walls of the building itself on two sides and by a high, protective parapet on the others. The central hall area, though a perfect square in plan and completely self-contained, is made to interlock in elevation in accordance with prevalent notions about asymmetrical massing and interlocking cubes of space.

The Oak Lane School is sited at the top of a slight hill in suburban Philadelphia. Built of concrete block and stuccoed over, the walls facing south, west, and north were painted white; those facing east, blue. Keeping in mind the school's experimental program, which was intended to "suggest freedom rather than to imply restrictions," and the ages of the children (two to four years), the architects attempted to reduce the scale of the building wherever possible in order to accommodate the children. Thus doors, stair risers, and other details are low, so that "the children may feel an intimacy with their surroundings instead of being compelled to make the visual adjustment to an adult world constructed for an adult size."[26] The furniture designed for the children is simple and completely devoid of the bric-a-brac then considered necessary to amuse them.

25. Curry returned to England in the early thirties to become headmaster of the Dartington School at Totnes, for which Lescaze designed the principal buildings. See Gerald Heard, "The Dartington Experiment," *Review* 75 (April 1934), 119; "House, Totnes, South Devon," *Review* 77 (March 1935), 108; "Churston Development," *Record* 81 (May 1937), 31–33. These buildings, except the house at Totnes, are erroneously credited to Howe and Lescaze.

26. "The Three R's—Contemporary Version," *Creative Art* 7 (Nov. 1930), 372–73.

The Oak Lane School was published extensively here and abroad, and was probably the first American example of the International Style to achieve any degree of fame. The response to its daring design was remarkably favorable, and it established the firm of Howe and Lescaze as the best known of the new modernists practicing in America. The crudeness and boldness of the exterior seemed, ironically, to express perfectly the new no-nonsense attitude to education and design that the Depression was to make seem not only fashionable but almost imperative.[27]

Hitchcock found the school "not particularly advanced" in its construction. "Impressive as it was at the time," he wrote in 1932, less than three years after its completion, "it appears now to have had value chiefly as a manifesto to turning American attention to new architectural possibilities."[28] Howe and Lescaze were aware of the publicity value of the school from the first. Realizing that much was at stake, they considered every aspect of the construction in detail. As Lescaze recalled, "We wanted it as perfect as possible. A decision had to be made immediately about the kind of flooring. We were convinced that the best material was cork, but cork cost five or six hundred dollars in addition to the budget. Frantic telephone calls and wires. All of the trustees were away on vacation. We couldn't let our building, our creation, suffer, so my partner and I decided it would be cork even if we had to pay for it. Which we did. That itching carries one away."[29]

The Oak Lane School is surely more important as a marker in history than as a work of architecture. It is an interesting though unsuccessful experiment in the manipulation of scale through the adjustment of the sizes of standard elements: the jump in scale between children-sized and adult-sized doorways and windows strikes a jarring note. Nonetheless, the positive plastic and spatial qualities which are achieved in the treatment of the wall and through the use of the roof as a play space make it an impressive first step in the development of the firm's work.

Like the Oak Lane School, the Hessian Hills School, built at Croton-on-Hudson, New York, in 1931, was highly progressive in its educational philosophy (*figs. 65–68*). Its trustees and sponsors, almost all distinguished

27. Talbot Hamlin resented the school's crude power, writing that "with its dry and academic use of starkly 'modernist' forms of the Le Corbusier type [it] seems, however interesting, forced and out of place. . . . [It] gives the impression of being theoretical and doctrinaire." "Architecture," in Herbert Treadwell Wade, ed., *The New International Yearbook*. (New York: Dodd, Mead, 1931).

28. Hitchcock, "Howe and Lescaze."

29. Lescaze, *On Being an Architect*, p. 13.

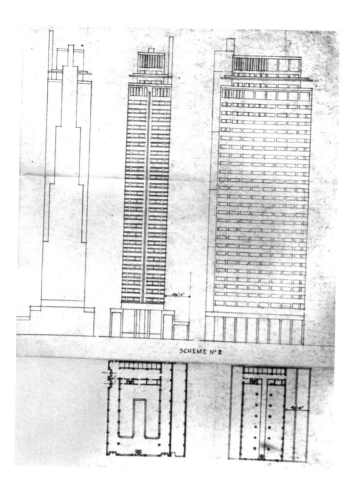

Fig. 60. PSFS, projected scheme two, drawing dated 20 March 1929.

SCHEME N° 2

Fig. 61. William Lescaze. Capital Bus Terminal, New York, N.Y., 1927.

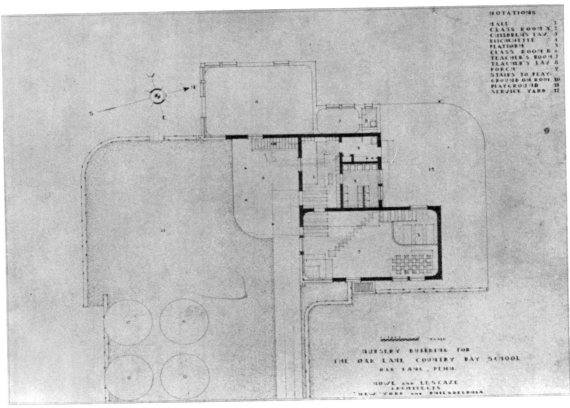

Fig. 62. Howe and Lescaze. Oak Lane Country Day School, nursery building, Philadelphia, Pa., 1929, plan.

Fig. 63. Oak Lane Country Day School.

Fig. 64. Oak Lane Country Day School, interior of main classroom, nursery building.

Fig. 65 Howe and Lescaze. Hessian Hills School, Croton-on-Hudson, N.Y., 1931, model of scheme one, rear view.

Fig. 66. Hessian Hills School, model of scheme one, aerial view.

Fig. 67. Hessian Hills School, scheme two, view of classroom wing, 1931–32.

Fig. 68. Hessian Hills School, scheme two, interior of typical classroom.

Fig. 69. Howe and Lescaze. Housing development for Chrystie-Forsyth Sts., New York, N.Y., 1931–32, project.

Fig. 70. Chrystie-Forsyth development, view of park areas from under apartment slabs.

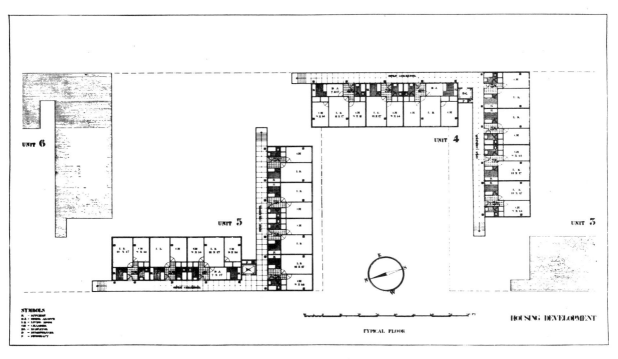

Fig. 71. Chrystie-Forsyth development, plan of typical floor.

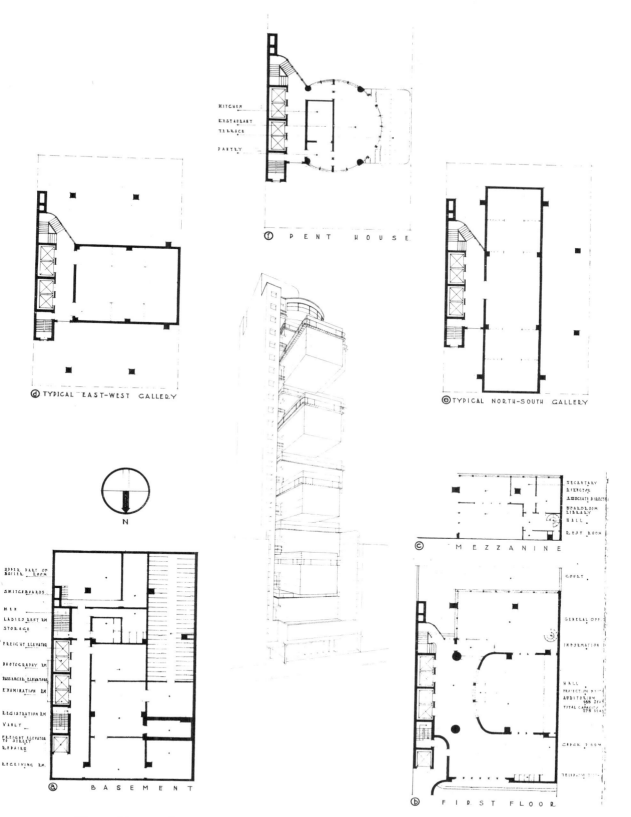

KITCHEN
RESTAURANT
TERRACE
PANTRY

ⓕ P E N T H O U S E

ⓓ TYPICAL EAST-WEST GALLERY

ⓔ TYPICAL NORTH-SOUTH GALLERY

N

SECRETARY
DIRECTOR
ASSOCIATE DIRECTOR
BOARD ROOM
LIBRARY
HALL
REST ROOM

ⓒ M E Z Z A N I N E

UPPER PART OF
BOILER ROOM
SWITCHBOARDS
MEN
LADIES REST RM
STORAGE
FREIGHT ELEVATOR
PHOTOGRAPHY RM
PASSENGER ELEVATORS
EXAMINATION RM
REGISTRATION RM
VAULT
FREIGHT ELEVATOR
TO STREET
REPAIRS
RECEIVING RM

ⓐ B A S E M E N T

COURT
GENERAL OFF.
INFORMATION
HALL
PROJECTION BOOTH
AUDITORIUM
168 SEAT
TOTAL CAPACITY
275 SEATS
CHECK ROOM
TELEPHONE

ⓑ F I R S T F L O O R

Fig. 73. Museum of Modern Art, isometric drawing and plan of first variation of scheme four.

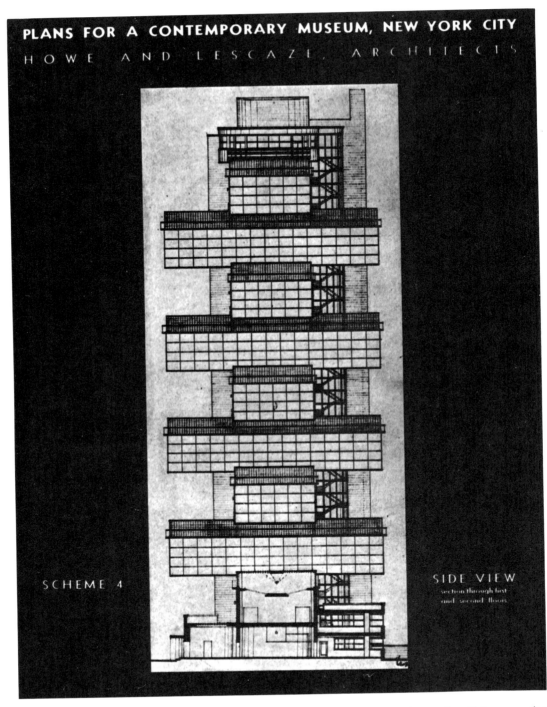

SCHEME 4

SIDE VIEW
section through first
and second floors

Fig. 74. Museum of Modern Art, drawing of first variation of scheme four, side view, and partial cross section.

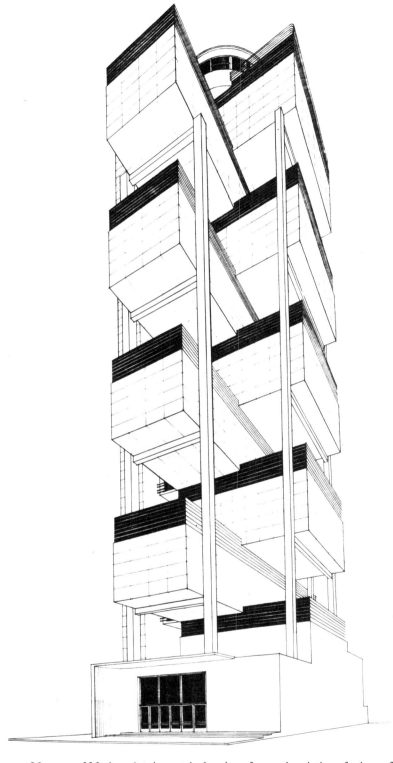

Fig. 75. Museum of Modern Art, isometric drawing of second variation of scheme four.

Fig. 76. Museum of Modern Art, second variation of scheme four, model.

Fig. 77. Museum of Modern Art, plans and perspective of scheme five, Aug. 1931.

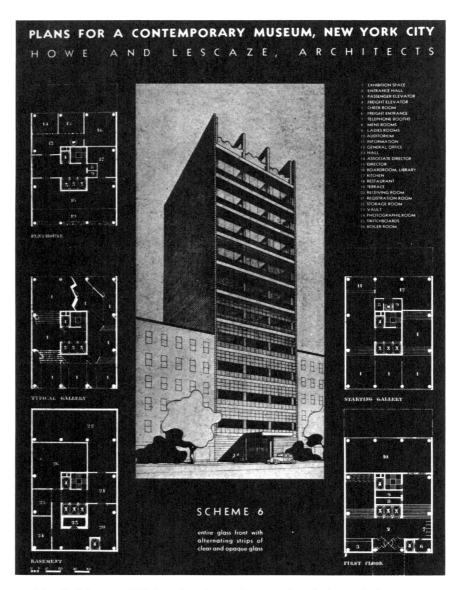

Fig. 78. Museum of Modern Art, plans and perspective of scheme six, Sept. 1931.

Fig. 79. Museum for R. Sturgis Ingersoll, Pennlyn, Pa., 1929, project.

Fig. 80. Howe and Lescaze. Frederick V. Field
House, New Hartford, Conn., 1931–32.

Fig. 81. Field House.

liberals, included Howe's old friend George Biddle, who had just completed his masonry house nearby.[30] The new school buildings were to replace the original facilities which had burned.[31] At first it was thought that a local architect, Harvey Stevenson, should be awarded the commission, but it soon became apparent that his conservative outlook was not in keeping with the program of the school. Biddle, naturally enough, suggested Howe; Mumford and others seconded the choice. But progressive ideas in education were one matter; in school design, another. During the building process Biddle had to champion his architect on many occasions against those who feared that the school would turn into a grim functionalist exercise.[32]

Two schemes were proposed for the school, which was to occupy a beautiful though difficult site on the slope of a gently rolling but quite rough hill. In the first scheme, abandoned because of the estimated cost of $100,000, advantage was taken of the change in level to provide a building three stories high, two floors of which would be entered directly on grade. Howe described this scheme: "A ground plan, bent at an obtuse angle, fits a curving and sloping hillside. The construction is to be primarily of steel and concrete. Contrasting with the white washed outer walls will be the banded windows and black lines of the terrace railways and posts. The inner walls of the porch and the protected walls will be green."[33] The plans called for nine classrooms and several workshops as well as a library, an art studio, music room, a teachers' room, and some offices. Howe and Lescaze's design, possibly derived from Richard Döcker's Krankenhaus Waiblingen built at Stuttgart between 1926 and 1928, provided that each of the upper stories was made to step back to allow for wide terraces for the floor above.[34]

30. In addition to Biddle, the trustees and sponsors included Heywood Broun, Millicent Carey, Stuart Chase, John Dewey, Theodore Dreiser, Hugh Ferriss, Waldo Frank, Mrs. R. P. Kepell, Lewis Mumford, Mrs. A. R. E. Pinchot, Mrs. Eugene Savage, Edward J. Steichen, Prof. E. L. Thorndike, Oswald G. Villard, and many others. See "Ultra-Modern Design Accepted for School," *New York Times*, 30 April 1931, p. 26.

31. Elizabeth Moos, "Statement," 14 Nov. 1931, prepared for *The American School and University Yearbook* but not published; copy among the Howe papers. Miss Moos was the school's director.

32. See "Will Erect Functionalist Building," *Art Digest* 5 (1 June 1931), 10, in which Howe attempted to dispel the trustees' fears.

33. Ibid.

34. For Richard Döcker's little-known hospital at Waiblingen, see his book, *Terrasen Typ* (Stuttgart, 1929). The origins of this type of masonry in modern architecture can be traced to many of Sant' Elia's drawings and to Sauvage's flats at the rue des Amiraux, Paris, of 1924. Lescaze was surely familiar with Sauvage's apartment building, and it is not unlikely that he or Howe might have had the drawings of Sant' Elia in mind, although they were not to enjoy

The use of step-back massing is unusual. Of the many schemes to use this compositional device, only that of the Hessian Hills School derives its section from the sloping contours of the site; its use affords a possibility for monumental scale on one side—where uninterrupted verticals can be expressed, as in the covered entry—and for a smaller scale on the other, as in the terraces stepping up the hill, where individual floors and their component units are clearly defined.

The second scheme, which was accepted, was never completed for financial reasons, though what was built cost only $47,000. Only two stories high, it consisted of an auditorium-gymnasium block connected to a two-story classroom unit sited atop an earth platform held back by a curved retaining wall built of concrete. Shop facilities were in a small wing to the rear. The second story of the classroom wing was to have been set back although it was not to extend over the first floor at the rear of the building. Only the first floor of classrooms and the shop wing were constructed initially; the auditorium-gymnasium block came a little later; the second-floor classrooms never at all.[35]

As finally constructed, Hessian Hills is simple almost to the point of bareness. All artistry is concentrated in the siting, the elegant proportions of the openings, and the concern for the direct expression of materials and construction techniques. The walls of the classroom buildings are treated as a woven fabric of reinforced concrete columns, infill panels of concrete, steel casement windows, and standard doors, these last two painted blue. The interior treatment is equally simple, with no decoration except for the exposed radiators, which are painted black for contrast. Flooring is gray asphalt tile except in the carpentry and textile shops where maple is used, and in the forge, clay rooms, and labs where it is finished cement. The shop wing is of gray brick with factory sash and wooden roof, a decision made for reasons of economy and justified by the separation from the main building. The school

wide circulation until Alberto Sartoris's book, *Gli elementi deli' Architettura funzionale* (Milan) was published in 1932. Aside from Marcel Breuer's use of this device in a project for a hospital in 1929, I know of no other project that exploits it so thoroughly until Le Corbusier's project for apartments at Durand, Algeria, in 1933 and his law courts, planned for Algiers, of 1935. Lescaze wrote of Sauvage's use of "setback terraces"; see *On Being an Architect,* p. 232. They may also be seen in Agnoldomenica Pica, *Nuova Architettura* (Milan, 1936).

35. In her unpublished statement, Elizabeth Moos pointed out that the "financial limit was $65,000.00. In addition, we felt it would probably be impossible to raise sufficient funds to erect the entire building immediately, so the plan had to permit a part to be constructed later. The amount of building we now have cost us $40,000.00. Our physical requirements are met. Our building is beautiful, satisfying, peaceful, harmonious. It has no purposeless decoration, within or without. Its white walls and grey floors make a perfect background for the children and their colorful work. Its beauty is a beauty of proportion and unity."

marks, as Hitchcock noted in 1932, "an enormous advance" over Oak Lane "in frankness of construction and simplicity of design."[36] Chafing at its exposed concrete surfaces (adopted because of the stringent budget and not from any formal preferences) and finding them lacking in "lightness and grace," he was able to compare the building favorably with such leading European examples as Hannes Meyer's school at Beroun, Germany, and André Lurçat's school outside Paris.

The plan Howe and Lescaze prepared for the Chrystie-Forsyth housing development was the most serious attempt made to that date in America in the direction of a sociologically comprehensive and formalistically modern solution to the vexing problems—acute by 1931—of large-scale urban housing (*figs. 69–71*). To be located on a recently cleared site between Chrystie and Forsyth Streets in the teeming slum district of New York's Lower East Side, the project was never built, and no American scheme for a similar program was erected which even began to rival it in scope, formalistic ambition, and quality until that for Lake Meadows, designed by Skidmore, Owings and Merrill in 1950. The site, now a public park of the most workaday type, is 2,450 feet long and 125 feet wide, and it is crossed by a number of streets dense with automobiles and people. On this extremely valuable piece of land, Howe and Lescaze, mindful of the necessity for economy and the appropriateness of high population densities in this particular section of the city, proposed to erect 24 nine-story apartment slabs raised on columns, leaving the ground floor free to serve for the most part as a public park and recreation area. Parking for cars was not considered a requirement.

These 24 apartment slabs are set at right angles to each other, to insure light and air as well as to maintain a reasonable distance between the buildings. This "cranked" arrangement of the building units is ingenious, and the variation achieved by the simple device of pairing two slabs at right angles to each other and locating the outdoor corridors on opposite sides of the slabs goes a long way toward relieving what might have been a grimly repetitious design. The existing grid plan of the area's streets is continued without interruption throughout the project. This is made possible by the use of columns or pilotis and the placement of buildings over the streets themselves. The 85 stores distributed throughout the site serve as focal points without seriously interfering with the open space devoted to parks and playgrounds.

The apartment plans are simply organized, with a minimum of space taken over by circulation and with generous amounts of natural light provided by

36. Hitchcock, "Howe and Lescaze," p. 144. Elsewhere Hitchcock was rather more critical; see "Architecture Chronicle," *Hound & Horn* 5 (Jan.-March 1932), 272-77.

the continuous windows. The steel skeleton construction allows for the use of nonbearing interior partitions that would permit flexibility within the apartment as well as expansion of apartment size by a recombination of the dwelling units.

The buildings are treated as simple volumes defining open space. North-south units are 170 to 195 feet from existing buildings while the distance between the east-west buildings is 80 to 90 feet, about 30 feet wider than an average New York street. This is still narrow enough to maintain a real sense of spatial enclosure.

Howe and Lescaze's suggestion for Chrystie-Forsyth grew naturally out of Le Corbusier's investigations during the previous ten years.[37] The arrangement of the slabs, which are plain almost to the point of monotony, is derived from the continuous low multiple-dwelling units that Le Corbusier used as space definers in his La Ville Radieuse project of the late twenties and that he was to develop in his plans for Algiers during the 1930s. In many of these projects, Le Corbusier was working toward a rigidly cellular scheme in which the living unit was expressed on the facade; this profoundly humanistic conception was at last brought to realization in rather compromised form at the Unité d'Habitation at Marseilles in 1948. Howe and Lescaze's project goes in the opposite direction, seeking to develop the possibilities of flexible planning within a structural skeleton. It is a series of stacked floors that do not reveal on the facade anything of the nature of the enclosed space. The stressed horizontals are insistent but are kept in check by the relatively short length of the individual slabs, their juxtaposition, and the use of exposed stairways at the ends.

On 9 February 1932 the architects presented their plan at a luncheon at the Ritz Tower Hotel, to which were invited housing experts and builders.[38] The project, whose apartments were designed to rent for $10.95 per room, was estimated to cost $5,750,000. This seemed very attractive to the East Side

37. The extraordinary diagrammatic clarity of the Chrystie-Forsyth scheme may in part be explained by the presence in the Howe and Lescaze office of the Swiss-trained architect Albert Frey, whose work in association with Albert Kocher ranks among the most distinguished examples of International Style in America, probably the best of which was the Aluminaire House of 1931. See "Aluminaire: A House for Contemporary Life," *Shelter* 2 (May 1932), 56–58. The house was exhibited at the Architectural and Allied Arts Exposition at the Grand Central Palace, New York, April 1931, and re-erected at Syosset, Long Island, by the architect Wallace K. Harrison. See chap. 6, n. 35.

38. See "Explain Houses on Stilts," *New York Times,* 10 Feb. 1932, p. 43; "Backs Housing Plan for Chrystie-Forsyth Area," *New York Times,* 3 May 1932, p. 21.

Chamber of Commerce which, on 3 March 1932, endorsed the project and set out to finance it. The *New York Times,* after commenting on the "somewhat startling" architecture of the project, also commended it, stating that the proposed plan "seems to meet the social requirements."[39] On 10 March, Lescaze conferred with city officials in the hope of receiving support. None was forthcoming and, as the national economic situation worsened, hope for the project was diminished and finally abandoned. New York was thereby deprived of a project that possessed, in the somewhat curiously phrased opinion of Hitchcock, "an architectural conscientiousness comparable to that of the best European housing. . . . The lightness, straightforwardness, and skillful construction of necessarily inexpensive material leads to as much of architectural distinction as can be hoped for in building of sociological significance."[40]

The regularity and unassertiveness of Howe and Lescaze's scheme were its strengths. By raising the buildings above ground, by allowing the existing street pattern to continue, by encouraging the free movement of people within the project, and by judiciously interspersing the green areas with shops, they did not create an isolated sector but a new, vital part of the community. Although the project rejects the street as an organizational factor, its recognition of the ingredients of urban life—small spaces, variety of choice for the moving pedestrian, mixture of uses—appears to go well beyond the limited and rather standoffish sociological attitudes of Le Corbusier's work at that time. At the same time, the anonymity of the Chrystie-Forsyth design is regret-

39. Editorial, "Model Housing," *New York Times,* 4 March 1932, p. 18. Two other firms submitted proposals for the site: Holden, McLaughlin and Associates, and Sloan and Robertson. For the first, see Arthur Holden, "Facing Realities in Slum Clearance," *Record* 71 (Feb. 1932), 75–82; for the second, see "New York Architects Apply for Federal Loan on Housing Project," *Record* 74 (July 1933), 13, and *Amer. Architect* 142 (Nov. 1932), 30. Two other contemporary urban housing projects, although intended for other sites, deserve mention here. See "Garden Apartment Schemes Developed by Clauss and Daub," *Record* 71 (March 1932), 196–97: "Carl Mackley Houses, Philadelphia," *Record* 75 (Feb. 1934), 120. The Carl Mackley Houses, often referred to as the Juniata Park Project, is the only one of those thus far mentioned to have been built; indeed, in terms of style, it is the first modern public housing project in America. Designed by Alfred Kastner and Oscar Stonorov in association with W. Pope Barney, this bold, clever scheme is an outstanding contribution to the solution of the problem of housing design. Richard Pommer, Vassar College, is currently researching the role of Philadelphia architects in the housing movement of the 1930s. See also chap. 8, n. 12.

40. Hitchcock, "Howe and Lescaze," p. 146. In reviewing the Museum of Modern Art's international exhibition of modern architecture, Lewis Mumford found "the model for a series of low-rental apartment houses by Howe and Lescaze much more convincing as pure architecture than their Philadelphia skyscraper." "The Sky Line. Organic Architecture," *The New Yorker,* 27 Feb. 1932, 49–50.

table and, ultimately, a far less potent contribution to the urban landscape than Le Corbusier's great and humane achievements.

In May 1930, the trustees of the newly organized Museum of Modern Art asked Howe and Lescaze to prepare preliminary schemes for a new building for the museum, whose rented gallery space in the Hecksher Building at 730 Fifth Avenue was rapidly becoming inadequate.[41] Because the trustees had no specific site in mind, the architects assumed a typical city plot on the south side of a street, 100 feet deep and approximately 60 feet wide (*figs. 72–78*).

Each of the three preliminary schemes devised by Howe and Lescaze offered a different solution for getting natural light into the galleries. A number of sketch perspectives resembling some of Lescaze's early drawings for PSFS remain to document these early suggestions. Scheme one provides continuous topside lighting through ribbon windows. A clearly expressed service tower rises at one side of the site. The exhibition floors rise uninterrupted for six floors, where there is a setback, above which are three more floors. Scheme two is identical except that its facade is completely glazed. The rendering suggests that glass block, or even glass tubing, was envisioned. The glazed facade is treated not as a curtain but as infill with floor levels clearly expressed. In the third scheme, which marks a considerable departure, light is brought into the galleries through skylights located at the setback of each floor.

In June Howe and Lescaze were asked to develop a scheme more completely. The trustees had in mind two possible sites, both similar to that

41. See A. Conger Goodyear, *The Museum of Modern Art: The First Ten Years* (New York, 1943). In 1930 Howe was serving as the first chairman of the museum's junior advisory committee; see Russell Lynes, *Good Old Modern* (New York: Atheneum, 1973), p. 75.

Howe and Lescaze had once before worked on a museum problem. In 1929 R. Sturgis Ingersoll asked Howe to submit a proposal for a small gallery. A perspective rendering of the firm's proposal shows a gently curved structure set in the garden of the Ingersolls' house—a subdued design in the manner of the Oak Lane School (*fig. 79*). In a letter to the author dated 10 July 1963, Ingersoll wrote: "We have all made mistakes in our lives but my mistake with respect to the proposed museum is one that I will always regret. By the Spring of 1929 Mrs. Ingersoll and I had a considerable collection of twentieth century paintings and sculptures. George Howe was a close friend of mine—I asked him to design a small 'art gallery' for placement on our lawn at our present home at Penllyn, Montgomery County. It was just to be a one-room affair with a balcony for music, i.e. dance music. I think Lescaze played a good deal a part [sic] in the design. By the Fall of 1929 all was ready to go and the estimated cost was $10,000. As I recall, just before we asked for the bids the stock market crash came along and I was scared to death and we cancelled the project and deeply to my regret we never revived it. As I now look back on the incident I feel sure that I could somehow or other [have] raised the $10,000 and proceeded with the venture. . . . It would really have been a gem of a building and would have been a perfect frame for our collection of art. I think it fair to say it would [have] been the first modern building in Philadelphia. I believe George was just starting the plans of the Philadelphia Saving Fund."

hypothesized in the preparation of the earlier schemes. In scheme four the architects imaginatively explored possibilities for lighting. By ingeniously combining artificial lighting with skylighting in a multifaceted light-mixing chamber, they made it possible for each gallery to be illuminated from many directions. The base of this glazed chamber is the continuous diffusing sash that constitutes the ceiling of the gallery. For the regulation of intensity, the chamber is equipped with light-controlling blades and reflectors operated by photoelectric cells. This system was tested by the architects who had a one-quarter-scale model built by the Structural Glass Corporation. These light boxes were also intended to house mechanical equipment such as ducts, pipes, and electrical conduits. The galleries have no conventional windows, but gallery fatigue is counteracted by the outlook from the glass-enclosed staircase and from the windows in the lobby of each floor.

The unique functional and spatial organization is derived from the limitations of the site and from the system of natural lighting. Each gallery is a self-contained spatial unit with its own entrance and exit leading to the elevators and staircase, which are housed in a separate service tower. Nine boxes of space—Howe called them "horizontal blocks"—are placed one above another and at right angles to each other. Five short ones extend east to west; four long ones extend north to south. At the rooftop there are a restaurant and terrace; at the ground floor, an auditorium. A mezzanine houses the administrative offices while the two basements house mechanical equipment and storage space.

The exterior walls were to be faced with marble or white glazed brick (materials chosen for their "smooth and refracting surface").[42] The finish of the interior walls was to be a smooth plaster painted a flat dark color. The structural system was a simple and dramatic one of support and supported, even more meticulously articulated than at PSFS. Two sets of columns, tied by beams at each gallery level, rise uninterrupted for the height of the building. Slid in between the columns are the gallery boxes, which rest on the beams and not on the gallery below. Though this scheme is not completely worked out, it seems a logical extension of those constructivist influences within the Technology Phase of the International Style as well as a precursor to current efforts in the direction of composition using pre-formed spatial units set within a structural frame or grid.[43]

42. "A Proposed Museum of Contemporary Art for New York City," *Record* 80 (July 1936), 43–50.

43. See, for example, Vittorio Vigano's Istituto Marchiondi and Atbat-Afrique's "Housing" at Algiers in Banham, *The New Brutalism*, passim. See also Moshe Safdie, *Beyond Habitat* (Cambridge, Mass.: M.I.T., 1971), passim.

In the autumn of 1931, the museum's trustees renewed their interest in building a permanent home. Howe and Lescaze prepared two new schemes. In scheme five they adopted a system of staggered light chambers that received light from two sides only; this loss of lighting flexibility was compensated for by an increase in gallery space. Scheme six is in a sense a return to scheme two with its all-glass front of alternating clear and opaque glass. It is probably the most handsome of the sequence. Formally, it is an elegant solution in its clear separation of structure from bounding walls, the simple entrance symmetrically disposed, and the treatment of the round concrete columns at the penthouse level (predicting Le Corbusier's Visual Arts Center at Harvard in 1963). The clear separation of service tower from gallery space is sacrificed to what the architects regarded as a "novel solution of the traffic problem: visitors would be taken up to the uppermost floor and would go down through the galleries by means of a quarter of a flight of stairs at every exhibition room."[44] It is interesting to speculate on the relationship among this scheme, published in *Architectural Record* in 1936, Wright's Guggenheim Museum, first conceived in 1943, and Edward D. Stone's much later design for Huntington Hartford's Gallery of Modern Art, completed in 1964. It is especially tantalizing to reflect on since scheme six came very close to being constructed. Had not John D. Rockefeller, Jr., donated the house on West Fifty-Third Street, which served as the museum's headquarters between 1932 and 1938, some variant of scheme six or one of its predecessors would most likely have become the first Museum of Modern Art.[45]

A number of commissions for interior remodelings sustained the firm during the difficult early years of the Depression. Designed for the most part by Lescaze in the New York office, they need not be discussed in detail. By and large, they are marked by insistent asymmetrical composition, extensive use of white and gray painted surfaces, blond wood finishes, and tubular metal furni-

---

44. "Proposed Museum of Contemporary Art."

45. One might add that the building designed and built for the museum in 1938-39 by Philip Goodwin and Edward D. Stone is far less advanced and daring than the best of the Howe and Lescaze proposals. Certainly one of Stone's most important works, credit for extraordinary refinement of the proportioning of the facades, which fit so easily into New York's streetscape, must be shared by Goodwin, probably the only other Beaux-Arts romanticist besides Howe to make the step into the International Style with success. Never so good a designer of romantic country houses as Howe, it is understandable that Goodwin's International Style work is also less interesting. To Stone remains, no doubt, the general conception: especially the audacious scooped entry with its curving glass flow-defining wall derived from Mies's Tugendhat House, the excellent lettering of the jutting end wall visible from the east, and the nautical roof terrace and club room at the top.

ture that was often designed by Lescaze and sold through a retail business he ran during this period called the Lescord Shop.[46]

These early years, though charged with polemical fire, were not very productive for the few American designers working in the International Style, who were forced to confine their practices to interiors or even to individual houses —hardly appropriate Machine Age commissions. The American public in general, quite naturally far more concerned with the economic crisis than with anything else, was more than a little impatient with the claims of the propagandists for the new architecture, who talked so much and built so little. Time has surely justified our national impatience, as I have tried to suggest; the vision of a new technological architecture, so eloquently outlined by Le Corbusier and his American disciples, seemed more than a little naive and anticlimactic when held up to the day-to-day technological achievements of American skyscraper construction, still booming as late as 1931, when the Empire State Building was completed.

In the first year or so of their partnership, Howe and Lescaze designed a number of interesting proposals for houses which never materialized. The cost for the first one, a house for Arthur Peck at Paoli, Pennsylvania, was estimated at $147,000. Had the house been constructed, it would have proved, if only by dint of volume and budget, an important milestone of the International Style in America. Only slightly less expensive was the proposed house for Maurice Wertheim at Cos Cob, Connecticut. Finally, there was the far more modest house for Mrs. G. F. Porter at Ojai, California, which is the prototype for the Field House.

The first house to see construction was built for Frederick V. Field (*figs. 80, 81*). Completed in 1931 at New Hartford, Connecticut, at a cost of about $50,000, it was essentially a refinement of the design direction begun in the Oak Lane School and developed in the Porter House project. It points up the similarity in approach between Lescaze and the French architect Robert Mallet-Stevens, whose massively cubistic designs differ noticeably from the weightless volumes of Le Corbusier's *prisme pur*. The Field House is awkwardly conceived: the combination of structural systems robs it of a sense of lightness just as the ubiquitous curved corner destroys the volume of the principal room. The interiors are consistently handled, however, and smoothly finished to set off the ample curves of tubular furniture to advantage.[47]

46. For a general discussion of International Style interior design in America in these years, see Philip Johnson, "The Modern Room," in Holger Cahill and Alfred Barr, eds., *Art in America in Modern Times* (New York: Museum of Modern Art, 1934), pp. 72–74.

47. For a further discussion of the relationship between the Field House and purism in terms

The Field House is of much less interest than projects by other American modernists fortunate enough to be able to build during those hard and unsympathetic times. It in no way compares with Wright's pavilion-like project, House on the Mesa, or even the small house he succeeded in building for Malcolm Willey; Neutra's innovative Lovell Health House or his V. D. L. Research House; Schindler's Lovell Beach House; or Kocher and Frey's Aluminaire House. Even Raymond Hood's house for Joseph M. Patterson at Ossining, New York, designed in association with John Mead Howells in 1930, although related in plan and massing to Howe's later Square Shadows, is only slightly less advanced than the Field House in its attempt, as Hitchcock described it, "to assimilate many of the features of contemporary European domestic design such as roof terraces, large windows and uncapped walls."[48] The desire for solidity, more directly and consistently stated in the Patterson House through the use of chamfered corners, is compromised by the camouflage of colored paint covering the walls in a manner reminiscent of German "romantic-expressionist" experiments of ten years before.[49]

Without question the most important building designed by the firm was the thirty-two-story combination bank and office building erected by the Philadelphia Saving Fund Society at the corner of Twelfth and Market Streets in the heart of the city (figs. 83–97).[50] PSFS, as the red neon lights proclaim, is a

of current practice, see Robert A. M. Stern, "Stompin' at the Savoye," Forum 138 (May 1973), 46–48.

48. Henry-Russell Hitchcock, "Raymond Hood," in Barr et al., Modern Architecture, p. 130. See also "A Country House, Ossining, New York," Architecture (New York) 65 (Jan. 1932), 31–36.

49. See David Gebhard, Rudolph Schindler (New York: Viking, 1972), for an interesting discussion in terms of house design of the relationship between varying forms of European modernism in America at this period.

50. This discussion of PSFS, in part an outgrowth of my article, "PSFS: Beaux-Arts Theory and Rational Expressionism," JSAH 21 (May 1962), 84–95, also includes material first put forth by W. H. Jordy in his "PSFS," an article which, together with my own and an appendix of documents, constituted an entire issue of JSAH. Although we worked independently and from different points of view—Jordy's concern being with the role of PSFS in the history of the commercial office tower, mine being more centered around Howe's career—the preparation of these articles was marked by what I believe was a mutually beneficial close collaboration. Nonetheless, each of us is wholly responsible for his own contributions as I am for the synthetic version in this book. Comparison with Jordy's original article will, however, reveal how dependent this discussion is on his and on the abbreviated, revised version that he and Henry Wright later published: "PSFS," Forum 120 (May 1964), 124–29, 143. It is also dependent on

leading monument in the modern movement as well as a memorial to the remarkable president of the Saving Fund Society, James M. Willcox.

The idea of an office building tower surmounting a banking room at the corner of Twelfth and Market Streets had been under consideration by the Saving Fund Society since 1926, as we have already seen. The suitability of the site for a branch bank had been established in 1927; of its suitability for a commercial office tower there had never been any doubt. One block away from City Hall, in a high-volume middle-class shopping district near all major department stores, across from the Reading Rail Terminal and just a few blocks from the Suburban Station, the proposed location was ideal for such a venture. Yet obviously none of these factors in any logical way predicted a great architectural monument. James M. Willcox, as bank president and chairman of the building committee and its most forceful member, is the pivotal figure in the story of the construction of PSFS.

Willcox was a man of rare qualities. Without his support the conservative board members might never have considered the notion of a modern building. This esteemed Philadelphian was "outwardly aloof," Jordy has written, "so much so that Howe always referred to him as 'Mr. Willcox.' "[51] Because Willcox was autocratic and preferred to work alone, he rarely consulted his committee. Most of the decisions about the building were made in private meetings with Howe, for which no records remain. We will never completely understand why this conservative Philadelphian supported this radical project. Certainly he was no innovator himself. Jordy writes:

> He was a connoisseur of tradition, although not apparently of the visual arts to any marked degree. He was, however, much traveled and so well educated that he must have been among the few American bank presidents of the twentieth century who was fluent in Latin. His portrait in the Board Room reveals something of his complex nature. Thin, elegant, with the long tapered fingers of an aesthete, and seated with a certain indolence of posture strange to corporate portraiture, the painting also reveals steel-blue eyes, implacably penetrating, and, on second glance, the apparent indolence may rather represent the act of settling back for keener observation.[52]

Jordy's *American Buildings and Their Architects: The Impact of European Modernism in the Mid-Twentieth Century* (Garden City: Doubleday, 1972), pp. 87–164.

51. Jordy, "PSFS," p. 48.

52. Ibid.

With remarkable patience Howe, in a series of letters, set out in the late spring of 1930 to convince Willcox of the merits of his case. This was to be no harangue, but one of the most civilized conversations between architect and client about the art of architecture ever recorded (though not completely). Willcox was an intelligent and responsive but not exactly eager student; Howe a patient, if somewhat detached, teacher, and at the peak of his persuasive powers. The restlessness of the previous five or six years seemed to have been channeled at last into his concern for the future of architecture, and his preference for indolence to have been swept aside in the immediacy of his involvement. The philosophic struggle of the past few years had deepened his understanding immeasurably, and his veneer of urbane charm seemed to be developing into a more profound urbanity of manner and thought. There was much to learn on both sides. And when the dialogue was complete, Howe realized, with fitting humility, the magnitude of Willcox's contribution. So it was, when Philadelphians praised PSFS to Howe, he waved aside the compliments with "It's Mr. Willcox's building."[53]

Indeed, the task of getting the radical design past the board of directors was as herculean as that of overcoming tremendous public resistance to it, particularly in Philadelphia where, as Howe pointed out in a letter to Walter Creese:

> Every pressure of society is brought to bear on the owner to convince him that if he allows himself to be influenced by a mad artist's ideas, he is fit only for Kirkbride's. The least step in the direction of modern thought therefore resolves itself into a tug-of-war between the wills of the public and the architect, with the client taking the place of the usual rope. The stresses thus engendered in the person of the President of the Philadelphia Saving Fund Society had not a little to do, I believe, with his nervous collapse and ultimate demise [he died in 1935]. The architect and the public meanwhile continue to enjoy excellent health.[54]

Willcox was a demanding client, and his dialogue with Howe constantly tested the architect's ideas to the fullest extent. At the same time, he trusted Howe, as well he might. Both men had much in common, not only in social position but in their mutual respect for the tradition of humanistic investigation that had characterized the education of American gentlemen for many years. Moreover, Willcox recognized Howe's sincerity. Howe was no wild revolutionary; his conversion to modernism had been a slow, painful, and cautious proc-

53. Quoted in ibid., p. 50.
54. Letter to Walter Creese, 12 Aug. 1946.

ess. It is reliably reported that Willcox frankly asked him whether he would pledge his word "as a gentleman" that he was providing the Society with a respectable building and not simply seeking for himself the publicity that comes with novelty.[55] Responsibility of this kind brings out the greatness in a man as it tries his patience to the breaking point. "As a gentleman," Howe gave his word.

Willcox was concerned, above all, with building not just a commercial office block but a monument worthy of the tradition of the Society, which is the oldest savings bank in the United States. PSFS had to be a sound investment in the profoundest sense of that word. He wished to have a building with a future, one that would be capable of competition with newer buildings decades later. In this Willcox has been justified, as the rental records attest. Even during the Depression, PSFS has always remained over ninety per cent rented.

PSFS is far more complex in its massing than the average skyscraper of today or, for that matter, any other notable tall building from the first Chicago School onward. Its complexity of form mirrors its complexity of program. It is, in the best sense of the word, a functional building. As Jordy relates, "It was built, substantially as originally presented, with James M. Willcox . . . leading his committee toward its eventual acceptance. He did so, as he later assured the press (and reassured his Board and the general public), not because the building was 'ultra-modern'—a quality he distrusted—but because he believed it to be 'ultra-Practical.' "[56]

At the moment when final negotiations for PSFS got under way in the spring of 1930, Howe wrote an essay, "Modern Architecture," for a short-lived though excellent magazine, *U.S.A.*, published in Philadelphia. In it he outlined a four-stage program that he believed to be suitable both in the design of an individual building and in the development of a coherent architecture in general:

> The first stage involves the formulation of a program by the community, that is to say, a tabulation of its physical and spiritual requirements, to-

55. Jordy, "PSFS," p. 48.

56. Ibid. Howe's version of Willcox's program was the following: "The problem as presented to the architect is, can dignified and beautiful banking quarters be designed between stores below and office space above without sacrificing any one of the three? The answer of the functional architect is—yes. The fact that the president of the savings bank looks on himself as a trustee rather than as the master of millions is in itself both dignified and beautiful. All the designer has to do is to give form to the executive's conception without fear or concealment in order to achieve the desired architectural end." "Modern Architecture, the Universal Language. A Synthesis of Economics and Aesthetics," speech delivered at the University Club, Philadelphia, 4 Dec. 1931.

gether with the order of their interrelation. In other words, the community must learn to know what it wants. The second stage involves the provision by the engineer of the material means to fulfill the community's program. The third stage involves the assimilation of the spiritual significance of the program in terms of its material fulfillment, and the ordering of its elements, with due emphasis on the important and subordination of the unimportant, in such a way as to produce a work of art, or, as Clive Bell has comprehensively expressed it, "significant form." This is the duty of the architects, who, at the fourth or decorative stage, must also direct the activities of painters, sculptors, and ornamentalists, the same time giving the widest possible scope to the individual collaborators.[57]

Using this four-stage program as a foundation, any analysis of PSFS must begin with the most important functional consideration, the decision to locate the banking room on the second floor. This left the ground floor free for stores, which could generate the kind of shopping traffic from which the bank drew its clientele.[58] Urbanistically, it was the wisest of decisions as well: PSFS stimulates life in the street where most ground-floor banks, somber in design with restricted hours of use, do the opposite.

Once the banking room was located on the second floor, the organization of the base of the building seemed determined: the low shops at street level as well as the elevators, escalators, and stairs to the banking floor giving entrance at the side. Above the banking hall, the next three floors are devoted to banking offices. The lowest, somewhat larger in plan and more lavish in exterior treatment, contains the executive offices. The upper two house the bank's general offices and are in exact conformity with the slab that rises above except that they do not cantilever out beyond the last row of columns at the Market Street end. Together, the three banking-office floors form a kind of notch which softens the transition between the base and office slab above, which is placed asymmetrically on the site in an effort to insure proper light and air on three sides and in all the offices. No office space is more than twenty-nine feet from

57. Howe, "Modern Architecture," pp. 19, 20, 23.
58. Jordy has carefully searched for examples in Detroit and Montreal which are said to have influenced the placement of the banking room on the second floor, which in turn was very influential in the designing of the International Building at Rockefeller Center in New York. But second-floor banking rooms are not without precedent in Philadelphia. Good Quaker notions of thrift probably lie behind these designs and, although there is no reference to Howe's having in mind this particular Philadelphia custom, one can assume that he, or perhaps Willcox, was aware of it.

the windows.[59] The service spine, placed across the rear of the site and perpendicular to the office slab, contains elevators, stairways, a fire tower, and toilet facilities as well as a comparatively small amount of office space. Turning an almost blank facade to the south, it acts as a buffer against possible development on adjacent property.

The rooftop is an intricate complex of platforms and terraces surrounding an executive suite. An observation platform (now a television relay station) and the giant red neon sign which surrounds the cooling towers necessary for the air conditioning complete the roofscape. The massing, for all its complexities and picturesque asymmetries, was not determined solely by formal considerations, although they were very important, but was the result of a carefully studied effort to give each variation in form a basis in necessity.

If we consider the cross section, the structural organization of the building, so carefully related to the functional division of spaces, is easily comprehended. A complex rooftop, composed of small spaces, is fundamentally load bearing. Below, the weight of each tower floor is carried downward on four files of steel columns, the outermost being set flush with the interior face of the wall plane and projecting beyond at the outside. A 16-½-foot-deep truss bridges the banking floor in a clear span of 63 feet. This makes possible the column and side aisle arrangement of the room, which, along with the entrance from the side at the midpoint of the long axis, is reminiscent of Wright's Larkin Building. The smaller trusses at the first and second floor levels brace the two rows of columns under their enormous load. Thus the section, with its numerous small spaces at the top giving way gradually to larger spaces and finally to an enormous great hall, is conceivable only in steel. Later Howe made reference to this seeming reversal of the normal order of things, so logical in steel, when he remarked, "The true sculptural quality of an organic design arises from the moulding of internal space and the shaping of the skeleton to contain it. The functional architect delights [in the] huge torso [of the building]

59. Later the slab configuration of the RCA Building in New York was given great attention by architects and the press. This is surprising since the RCA Building is not only less innovative than PSFS but also less pure from the point of view of functional and structural expression, and less potent visually as a modern image. Howe commented on Rockefeller Center as follows: "I understand the towers of Radio City are to be designed in the current vertical style, which is no more than a derivative of Gothic, even though its true nature be masked by modernistic ornament. It seems regrettable that this should be so, for I am convinced that certain well-defined principles of modern design called functionalism . . . are certain to prevail before long over traditionalism and patternism. The most important building project in the country should not be doomed to early obsolescence." "George Howe . . . Says," undated press release, ca. 1931.

swaying on tendoned ankles. He would no more attach false stone pedestals on them than we would put lead shoes on Pegasus."[60]

PSFS embodied numerous technological innovations. It was the second sky-scraper in the United States to be completely air conditioned (the twenty-one-story Milam Building in San Antonio, completed in 1928, had been the first). The architects had recommended air conditioning from the beginning but the building committee was reluctant and originally decided to air condition only the first four floors (stores, banking room, and executive offices) and the roof-top executive suite. But the desire to make PSFS more attractive to prospective tenants than its competition and an excruciatingly hot summer in 1931, when building operations were well under way, are said to have influenced the trus-tees' decisions—but only after the steel had been erected to the twentieth floor. The air-conditioning ducts for the bank were integrated as much as possible with the giant trusses over the banking room while the twentieth floor was given over to the air-conditioning equipment for the offices. Another innova-tion was the installation in the bank's office space of acoustic ceiling tiles, slipped onto a metal framework in a manner which has since become standard practice.[61]

PSFS is an "ultra-Practical" building and an economical building, as well, if by that term one does not mean cheap but rather precise, direct, and unorna-mented. It is well known that one of the viable interpretations of Mies's well-known dictum, "less is more," is "less costs more." Fortunately, PSFS was built on an inflationary budget in a deflationary period when building costs were remarkably low. Wisely deciding to take advantage of reduced prices, the Society increased its expenditure for materials and encouraged experimenta-tion with new processes and techniques, especially in the use of metal. But the architects were thwarted by restrictions in the local building code. The use of metal spandrels, for example, was prohibited, and they were forced to settle for brick. Thus in its exterior detailing PSFS is fundamentally a masonry building.

It is one thing to make a building possible and another to make an expressive work of art out of the act of building itself. It is, as Howe stated, at this stage that the architect enters. He had produced five schemes for PSFS since 1926. The first, presented in 1926, had been traditional. The other four, presented in

---

60. Howe, "Abstract Design in Modern Architecture," *Parnassus* 8 (Oct. 1936), 29–31.

61. Le Corbusier, on his visit to Philadelphia in 1935, was shown PSFS—"C'est magnifique!" he pronounced—and was impressed by the attention to detail and especially by the vault which is air conditioned in the daytime by means of an enormous round pipe that curves into it. At night, the pipe swings away on a track to allow the vault to close.

the last days of March 1929, had been self-consciously, if not successfully, "modern." In May of that year, Howe had joined with Lescaze, although it was not until early December that the project for PSFS was reactivated. The stock market crash in the autumn of 1929 had delayed the project and had brought it dangerously near to being shelved once again, perhaps permanently. But the tremendous drop in prices seemed to make the early days of the Depression remarkably favorable for building; besides, the very act of building itself would aid the economy by making jobs as well as inducing confidence in the minds of depositors and the public in general. On 2 December 1929 the first drawing for PSFS emerged from the office of Howe and Lescaze—a rough pencil sketch by Lescaze which established the general form of the base of the building. Its boldness and its confident handling of asymmetrical massing testify to the rigor of Lescaze's approach. At the same time, despite the lifting of the banking floor to the second level and the introduction of a curtain wall of ribbon windows on three sides—cantilevers were not considered until later—the general massing of the tower, with the services articulated at the rear and the use of separate entrances for the banking room and offices at the extremities of the site, is essentially Howe's. What is most important is the dynamism of the drawing, the almost brutal confidence with which Lescaze suggests the insistent horizontals, the sleekness of the corner, the overwrought interlockings of the base, spine, and slab.

A second sketch, also by Lescaze, is somewhat more detailed and refined. Done in wash, it is dated Christmas Day 1929. Here, as Jordy has pointed out, we are permitted to sense more than in any other drawings for the building "something of the excitement of the aesthetic at the time. Bathed in a mysterious luminescence, the building appears particularly weightless as it rises effortlessly in the night above its scrubby competition. So dynamic is the cubist opposition and especially the thrust of the cantilevered window ribbons against the outwardly tilted edges of the building—so much more so than the inert cars scattered about on the wet pavement—that it appears to burst its seams. Such ebullience contrasts markedly with the classicistic restraint of Howe's scheme. Despite the long ribbon windows that apparently imply a cantilever, Lescaze has stated that no cantilevering was envisioned at this time."[62] The signs, the ovoid supports, the meaningless cantilever below the office slab hardly improve that scheme, which was presented in model form in July 1930 to the building committee of the Society. Significant changes in it include the development of a cantilevered structure to justify the drawing of Christmas

62. Jordy, "PSFS," p. 53.

Day as well as the use of a cantilever at the Market Street elevation. The model also reveals a rather complex rooftop silhouette including a kind of cockpit placed symmetrically atop the Market Street elevation, and an illuminated sign using only the initials PSFS.

With regard to the difficult question of authorship in the firm of Howe and Lescaze, PSFS is a special case. It is their most carefully documented completed building and, more importantly, it is their only building on which Howe worked independently before the partnership. Not only was PSFS initiated by Howe, but it was developed by him to an extent which, as we have seen, approximates the final result. Of equal importance is the fact that Howe retained control of the design and of the relations with the client throughout the three and one-half years of design and construction.

Howe was much more an intellectual than an imaginative architect; before joining Lescaze, he realized that he had carried the forms as far as he could. Undoubtedly in the final scheme it was Lescaze's imagination which led Howe on, especially in the conception of the dramatic skin that envelops the building. But from Howe's scheme two it can be safely inferred that the decisive contribution, the building's structural and functional organization, was Howe's.

Perhaps the clearest statement of the separate attitudes of the two partners toward design were those quoted by *Architectural Forum* in its December 1932 issue. Lescaze stated, "The phenomenon of creating a *plastic image* is each time an equally *exciting adventure* [italics added]. . . . People argue: 'steel, glass, functionalism, post functionalism,' I say 'yes, but architecture please.' Or they pile up boxes on top of boxes. I say, 'no, please, architecture.' . . . First, you put your brain on the program of requirements, then something clicks in your heart. . . . You push a T-Square on some tracing paper, and work and work to make it architecture." Howe said, "Architectural beauty is the result of the successful *interpretation of a human problem in terms of a structural technique* [italics added]. . . . No external mass which does not express an internal function can have any organic significance as beauty. It follows also that the potentialities of the structural technique must be expressed in the visible structural members and their outer shell, and not concealed behind a false screen or loaded with meaningless . . . masses."[63]

For Lescaze, PSFS was a rare opportunity to shape the "monumental" architecture that he longed for. Here was a commission of greater magnitude than any other building ever conceived by the practitioners of the International

63. Howe, "Statement," *Forum* 57 (Dec. 1932), 484.

Style. As a skyscraper, it was the symbolic commission of the times; as a *modern* skyscraper, it was a challenge to the times. None like it had been built, and only rarely, as in the Chicago *Tribune* Tower competition of 1922 and the projects for tall buildings by Mies and Le Corbusier, had anything near its size even been imagined in the vocabularies of either the first or second phase of the International Style.[64] But for Howe PSFS was even more important. It was a daring expression of deep personal conviction, an intellectual and aesthetic breakthrough unprecedented in American architecture. No other architect of his generation and his Beaux-Arts training manifested anything like his combination of intellect, imagination, and deep personal courage. No other architect had so much to lose in terms of career and personal standing in the profession in an effort to extract greater meaning from his art. "Only he could do it," Bruno Zevi has written. "He had gained professional and personal prestige that permitted him to avoid direct polemics and to overcome obstacles with a witty epigram, with an elegant phrase. . . . His name signified a *security* that infused faith. The arrival of rationalism in the United States was made possible only by the mediation of a personality revolutionary in architecture while traditionally aristocratic in his temperament and make-up."[65] Howe's romantic work had been to the generation of architects just younger than he a kind of revelation and a beacon: it had shown them that sincerity and simplicity were more important goals in design than originality for its own sake. For this reason, he had earned from his peers an enviable reputation. This he cast aside. Howe, in other words, staked all.

Yet it should be reiterated that over the years Lescaze, as his influence in the profession waned, came increasingly to insist on full credit for the design of PSFS. In his autobiography, *On Being an Architect,* he referred to Howe as his "business partner," and in 1962, seven years before his death, he reasserted his claim for consideration as the sole designer of PSFS[66]—both these despite the detailed allocation of responsibility prepared at the breakup of the partnership in 1935 (see chapter seven). Recently Earle W. Bolton, Jr., for many years an associate of Howe and at the time of the design of PSFS a draftsman in the New York office of Howe and Lescaze, shared with Todd Cooke, Jr., of PSFS, some recollections. Despite their partisanship, they serve to remind us that architecture, particularly of complex projects, is at best a cooperative

64. For a discussion of the *Tribune* competition in relation to PSFS, see chap. 4.
65. Bruno Zevi, "George Howe, An Aristocratic Architect," *A.I.A. Journal* 24 (Oct. 1955), 176–79.
66. Lescaze, letter to William Jordy, 25 Jan. 1962. See Stern, "PSFS," n. 39.

effort and that Lescaze's claims, though perhaps justified in certain respects, seem on the whole inflated.[67]

The great success of PSFS came from its resolution of the horizontal floor slab with the vertical support. It is ironic that this demonstration of structural expression did not grow directly out of the architects' desire for an expression of vertical support but rather at the insistence of James Willcox. While it is true that Howe had established such a relationship in his scheme two of March 1929, it was not incorporated into the early Howe and Lescaze proposals. Influenced by the insistent horizontality of European designs, Howe and Lescaze produced a scheme composed of a slab of unrelieved horizontals which appeared to be cantilevered from a vertical service core. Visually this was dis-

67. See Lescaze, *On Being an Architect*, p. 133; see also Stern, "PSFS," n. 39. The PSFS memo of Bolton's recollections states: "While George Howe maintained a small office of the partnership here in Philadelphia, the PSFS job was run out of the New York office where Mr. Bolton was stationed. The then-President of the Society, James Willcox, apparently conceived a distinct distaste for Mr. Lescaze and, according to Bolton, asked or demanded that Lescaze be kept out of his (Willcox's) office. Accordingly, Mr. Bolton often found himself as emissary of the New York office in its dealings with PSFS and, in consequence, was privileged to sit in on conferences and other meetings which normally would not have been open to someone of his relatively junior rank. Mr. Bolton remarked that, from the outset, Mr. Willcox and the Society's Managers were insistent that the building be of highest quality. In fact, Mr. Bolton noted that the PSFS Building is virtually the only project on which he can recall working where cost represented no particular limitation. The low price levels prevailing during the depression days when the building was constructed of course assisted the Society in taking this handsome attitude.

"Mr. Bolton characterized William Lescaze as essentially a designer and interior decorator rather than an architect. Accordingly, he is inclined to ascribe the credit for the PSFS Building, as an architectural and structural concept, to George Howe. However, Bolton was frank to confess some slight dislike for Lescaze and equal fondness for George Howe, who, incidentally, Bolton believes could have been the United States' greatest architect of the 30's and 40's had he not been so lazy. Bolton also emphasized that the Howe and Lescaze partnership was a combination which produced more than the sum of its parts. While many of Lescaze's design ideas, according to Mr. Bolton, were deplorable, Howe apparently had the facility for seizing on them and extracting their good features or modifying them into something successful.

"I asked Mr. Bolton how he accounted for the high level of detailing and finish in the PSFS Building in view of George Howe's legendary impatience with detail work. Bolton confirmed this idiosyncrasy of Mr. Howe's and ascribed credit for considerable of the details to secondary figures in the Howe and Lescaze office, presumably including Bolton. He also mentioned that a young, middle-European architect, whose name Bolton could not recall but which is, he believes, mentioned in the Jordy article [Walter Baerman?] was largely responsible for the detailing and finish on the 33rd floor. Bolton emphasized, however, that Mr. Willcox and the Building Committee were themselves active and meticulous in selecting woods and fixtures from samples suggested by the architect. . . .

"Mr. Bolton agreed that it was remarkable that, having previously handled only such small commissions as the Oak Lane Country Day School and several houses, the Howe and Lescaze partnership could proceed without intervening steps to produce a landmark design for a major office building. Perhaps this creative and productive effort in a sense over-taxed the partnership." Memo of April 1969, published in West, *George Howe*, pp. 30–32.

astrous, as Jordy points out.[68] The unrelieved horizontals were given their theoretic justification by Howe in a letter to Willcox, dated 26 May 1929 and the first of a series which survives. Here he returned to a position essentially the same as that of 1926 when, apparently influenced by Moore's writings, he had first engaged in this particular form of architectural rationalization. After remarking about the necessity today, as in the past, for architects to give "practical and formal expression" to their "imaginative conceptions within the limits of laws which [they] may help to expound and extend but which [they] cannot make," he went on to write that he would

> consider only that portion of the architectural law which in our opinion imposes an external recognition of the horizontal subdivisions of the building. . . . Today men extend the area of their buildings by superposing a great number of horizontal spaces for their cooperative convenience in attaining the modern ideal of the greatest good for the greatest number. The inevitable external expression of their intention is a series of alternating horizontals of masonry and glass to express the horizontal spaces and give a maximum of light and air to workers. . . . Structural logic also imposes a horizontal expression. . . . In the steel form of the skyscraper the actual supports of the external casing are not the vertical columns but the continuous horizontal brackets which run around the building at each floor. . . .
>
> Aspect also imposes a horizontal treatment. . . . Since it is necessary to treat the base of the skyscraper visibly as a glass shell around a steel frame (for store windows), the entire casing of the building must be treated as a light veil supported in horizontal banks on successive brackets attached to the steel structure. . . . The horizonal treatment therefore seems to be imposed by human intention, construction and aspect alike.[69]

Howe was pushing the crutch of structure, as Philip Johnson was later to call it, to its ultimate limits and, in his enthusiasm for the stressed horizontal, which he felt to be modern, he convinced himself that what was important was not the expression of the space and the structure that made the space, but rather the space and the envelope that bounded it.[70] He was aware, though, that even the horizontal brackets, not to mention the floor slabs, had to transmit their forces, visually at least, to the ground in some fashion. To this end he wrote to Willcox:

68. Jordy, "PSFS," p. 65.

69. Howe, letter to Willcox, 26 May 1930.

70. Johnson's phrase comes from his article, "Seven Crutches of Modern Architecture," *Perspecta* 3 (1957), 40–44.

> There is an element of the skyscraper, however, which is intentionally vertical and inseparable from the idea of great height and accessibility. The elevator, stairway and fire tower are vertical communications and must be expressed as such. In designing the building of the Saving Fund Society we have developed these elements to the south as a strong spine to which the horizontal office floors are attached as a sort of ribs. This arrangement produces we believe a sense of organic unity in a visible combination of intention, structure, and expression.[71]

Fortunately, Willcox was not impressed. Howe was able to convince him of the logic of horizontal spaces visually cantilevered from a vertical spine which contained the circulation, but Willcox remained intractable in his desire for some expression of vertical support in the slab. "The way of the innovator is hard," he wrote on 3 June 1930, "and although my sympathies are generally with him he is not always right."[72] The vertical or horizontal effect is merely a matter of emphasis, since the tower itself is unimportant; the object, the perpendicular mass, is achieved in both cases. Willcox found Howe's strongest point to be that concerning the use of glass at the base, and he suggested the introduction of verticals as decoration. This Philadelphian was ready to concede that a banking room did not need to be surrounded by a colonnade in order to be dignified, but he would not accept the possibilities of a thirty-two story-tower that looked as structured as a layer cake. In his demand for such vertical structural expression, Willcox was asking no more than Charles Herbert Moore had always demanded. That is, he was demanding an expression of the facts of structure as they were known to be in masonry construction. Howe was willing, in these schemes, to depart from his accepted belief in a particular kind of structural expression, but not from the principle of structural expression itself. To this end, he was able to convince himself that the horizontality of the design was an expression of the structural nature of the exterior sheathing.

Willcox was in the hospital during most of June 1930, and during his absence nothing more could be done, but the architects prepared the model according to Lescaze's revision of December 1929 and Howe's more recent philosophic justifications. When the model was presented in early July, it was accompanied by another long discourse from Howe, in which he carefully discussed the issue of the cantilevered skin and the unbroken horizontals, pri-

71. Howe, letter to Willcox, 26 May 1930.
72. Willcox, letter to Howe, 3 June 1930, published in *JSAH* 21 (May 1962).

marily on the basis of functional considerations. But Willcox remained firm.

A letter from Howe to Willcox dated 25 July 1930 reviews the architect's position concerning the new architecture, going on to explain in detail the reasons for the architectural features employed and discussing in terms of economics and mechanical efficiency each point advanced in the May 1930 letter: the separation of entrances and the location of the banking room on the second floor, and the blank wall above the great banking space which not only expresses the 18-foot-deep trusses but also "the fact that steel and economics have reversed the order of masonry construction and that the heavy mass, no longer necessary or even desirable, belongs at the base of the building, which must be dedicated to revenue producing or useful spaces encased in glass.[73] This area also provides space for ventilating equipment required for the ground-floor stores and banking rooms. The 1930 design provides over 200,000 more square feet and 60 percent more floor area than the 1926 design. And this was available at an increase of only $930,000, about 20 percent more than the first design. The building was "to cost in round figures $12,500,000 including land, architects', engineers', and builders' commissions, a fully furnished banking room with safe deposit vaults and other banking space for present and future requirements, 50% of office partitions and a fund for advertising and accounting expenses, but not floor covering and bank furniture."[74] The Fuller Construction Company was called in for estimates in late July.

Willcox's demands for verticals in the tower presented the architects with the problem of making "a significant unity" out of two elements conceived in two distinct architectural vocabularies. It probably would have been "safer" to restudy the cubism of the base to achieve greater conformity with the constructivism of the tower. Instead it was decided to integrate the two elements by means of a third, which in the series of schemes submitted in the autumn usually took the form of a three-story unit of more square footage than the tower but not covering the whole plot.[75]

Each scheme represented some important concession on the part of the

73. Howe, letter to Willcox, 25 July 1930, published in *JSAH* 21 (May 1962), 98–99.

74. Minutes of the meeting of the building committee, PSFS, 8 Nov. 1930. The total cost of the building itself, when complete, was $7,420,942.37. See West, *George Howe*, p. 10.

75. Bruno Zevi has recorded Howe's own version of the bitter and difficult sessions which he had to endure with Willcox and the building committee in the summer and fall of 1930. Often they would send for him, alarmed by some feature of the plans. They would refuse to accept the scheme; Howe would laugh, talk of "this and that," and then add some offhand phrase such as, "It doesn't matter." Thus he "played on his skepticism, convinced no one, but calmed everyone." Zevi, "George Howe"; see also Zevi, "George Howe," *Metron* 25 (1948), 10–11.

architects to what the board thought a bank and office building should be like. Each, in its inclusion of an inappropriate detail, looks so ridiculous as to make the logic of the original conception even more apparent. The scheme prepared in November and December 1930 emphasized the structure. They vary from thoroughly retrogressive buildings sheathed in masonry in semimodern fashion, very much like that proposed by Howe in 1926 (now submitted, no doubt, more in sorrow than in anger and probably intended to serve as a warning rather than as a recommendation), to scheme seven, which is close to the final design save that the banking room is surrounded by engaged columns, clearly nonsupporting (and probably included to remind the building committee of the folly of the past, which had considered a colonnaded building as the chief symbol in America for a bank). But the board objected strenuously to the lack of columns on the exterior of the banking room. These were included and remained there, obviously nonstructural and decorative, until the building was under construction in 1931.

The conception of the slab was altered at Willcox's insistence, then, in the last months of 1930. Although it is ironic that neither Howe nor Lescaze was responsible for so significant a contribution as the column-spandrel relationship, it is also noteworthy that Howe, in scheme two of 1929, had already established this interplay between support and supported. With the adoption of this structural device, problems such as the location of office partitions were solved and, more importantly from Howe's point of view, all was at once brought to order: significant form once again was the product of a structural and spatial integration.

With the acceptance of the columniated scheme seven on 10 December 1930, all the elements began to fall into place. Difficulties were ironed out in the course of preparing the working drawings, and all except the rooftop had been designed when drawings were filed in January 1931. Excavation was begun in February, and in the following months, the scheme was refined to its present aspect. The significant change from the symmetrical rooftop complex to the now familiar asymmetrical arrangement was brought about by the need to locate air-conditioning equipment on the roof and the desire to bring the composition of the roof in line with that of the rest of the building.

Because of the complicated sequence of development between 1926 and 1932 and because of Lescaze's unwillingness to acknowledge any debt to the work of his contemporaries, much less his partner, it is difficult to evaluate the degree to which the design of PSFS is consciously derived from the architecture of the twenties. One fact is certain, as Jordy has proved: "The search for literal duplication of form between PSFS and European buildings only reinforces one's awareness of its originality."[76] Although the facade of PSFS, in its fenestration and its use of the cantilever, definitely relates to the street facade of Osswald's Stuttgart Tagblatt Building (which in its overall massing also begins to suggest the T-shape of PSFS' design)[77], only Richard Neutra's office building project for Rush City Reformed bears a significant conceptual resemblance to PSFS.[78] Walter Creese, who was probably the first to point out this similarity, observed, "Insofar as the free expression of engineering potentialities is concerned, the Neutra scheme is certainly more advanced."[79] This is true as it applies to the expression of the decreased weight carried by the cantilevered floor slabs as they extend beyond the last columns, a device exploited by Johannes Duiker in his Open Air School and later by Louis I. Kahn in his Richards Medical Research Building.[80] On the other hand, Creese, writing from a viewpoint inspired by Gropian structural determinism, fails to note that Neutra's scheme, hiding all its mechanical equipment within, is, as Jordy has suggested, much less advanced as a total expression of the modern office building than PSFS. Indeed, it is precisely the combination of sophisticated structural and functional expression that distinguishes PSFS from its contemporaries.

Lescaze claimed not to have been influenced by the Rush City Reformed project, although he was likely to have known it either from its publication in Neutra's *Wie Baut Amerika?* (1927) or in its republication in Henry-Russell

76. Jordy, "PSFS," p. 75.

77. The Tagblatt Building was illustrated in a number of important publications. See Maurice Casteels, *The New Style: Architecture and Decorative Design* (London: Batsford, 1931), p. 144; Francis Keally's sketch, incorrectly labeled as "A Seventeen-Story Apartment Building," *Record* 65 (Feb. 1929), 175. It is almost certain that Howe knew this drawing, which followed the coverage of Mellor and Meigs's Goodhart Hall at Bryn Mawr. In fact, the plate on the page opposite Keally's sketch is a drawing of a detail of the main entrance door at Goodhart Hall and bears the credit line: Mellor, Meigs and Howe. The issue also contains an extensive article on automobile garages which Howe may well have consulted in preparing his scheme two for PSFS. The Tagblatt Building was also published in S. Chermayeff, "Film Shots in Germany," *Review* 70 (Nov. 1931), 131–33. See also H. Allen Brooks, "PSFS: A Source for Its Design," *JSAH* 27 (Dec. 1968), 299–302, and Scully's comparison of PSFS with Knud Lönberg-Holm's submission to the Chicago *Tribune* Building competition, in *American Architecture and Urbanism* (New York: Praeger, 1969), pp. 151, 154.

78. The Rush City Reformed project also served as an illustration for an article by Neutra, "Architecture Conditioned by Engineering and Industry," *Record* 66 (Sept. 1929), 272–74, which in many ways outlines the need for a shift from the Machine Phase to the Technology Phase of the International Style.

79. Creese, "American Architecture from 1918 to 1933," pt. 1, p. 33.

80. For Duiker's Open Air School, see E. J. Jelles and C. A. Alberts, *Duiker 1890-1935* (Amsterdam, ca. 1972), pp. 52–69. For Kahn's Richards Medical Research Building, see Vincent Scully, *Louis I. Kahn* (New York: Braziller, 1962).

Hitchcock's *Modern Architecture* (1929). Perhaps it was the more widely read Howe who recognized, in this tower of horizontal layers slung between columns and cantilevered at the end, the logical expression of the structural ideas with which he had been grappling for so long.

The relationship between the Neutra scheme and PSFS is far more profound than what one would expect from what may only be an accidental physical resemblance. Both buildings share an attitude toward the expression of structure and technology (though not of function) that was to become during the next fifteen years of the International Style a distinctly American concern. The volumetrics of the International Style are equally applicable to its first, European phase, the Machine Phase, and to its second, American phase, the Technology Phase. As we have seen, what distinguishes the phases, an indication of the growing maturity of the modern movement, is an increasing dissatisfaction with the quality of Machine Phase buildings as constructed objects and a greater use of steel construction and its cagelike organization, instead of the more plastic reinforced concrete.[81] The architects of the Technology Phase were not concerned so much with the shapes or processes of machines but with the assembling processes of building construction. From the art-for-art's-sake aestheticism of the "free facade," the growing use of steel in the thirties brought with it a concern for repeated, prefabricated unit construction and for skin-and-bones articulation of the building frame. Thus in its concern for "processes," PSFS, departing from Machine Phase precedent in its opposition of columns and floor slab, marks an important change of emphasis within the International Style.

Similarly, the discrete expression of functions is an important innovation. While the idea of functional legibility is essential to Beaux-Arts theory, two notable projects of the twenties prefigure this development in the modern movement. Gerrit Rietveld's "Core System" was intended for low-rise mass housing schemes and is therefore not specifically analogous.[82] The other, Werner Moser's project for a skyscraper, is closely related programmatically and derives from the work of Frank Lloyd Wright, especially his project for the National Insurance Company of 1924.[83] Moser, the son of Lescaze's mentor, had been working for Wright since 1923. One day Wright left the office for a

81. See Stern, "PSFS;" William Jordy, "The Symbolic Essence of Modern European Architecture of the Twenties and Its Continuing Influence," *JSAH* 22 (Oct. 1963), 177–87; Jordy's "The International Style in the 1930's," *JSAH* 24 (March 1965), 10–14.
82. See Theodore M. Brown, *The Work of G. Rietveld, Architect* (Cambridge, Mass.: M.I.T., 1958), p. 89.
83. See Frank Lloyd Wright, "In the Cause of Architecture: Sheet Metal and a Modern

week and told "his boys" that each of them should prepare a competitive design for the National Insurance Building. Moser's solution, subsequently published widely,[84] grew out of his fascination with the "aspect" of "steel framework and the transport elevators [used] during construction of the skyscrapers." Moser "made several variants of that theme in spatial and functional expression" which differ from Wright not so much in the final appearance, although they are far less ornamental, as in the philosophic premises that substantiate their forms.[85] Wright based his scheme on the possibilities inherent in the cantilever while Moser, although exploiting cantilevered steel construction, concentrated instead on the relationship of vertical services, housed in separate towers, to the office slab. "The building is easily read," *Architectural Record* noted in December 1930. "Separate functions are separated in space, material and construction, permitting a rational solution of each individual problem."[86] The influence of Moser's project—especially in the context of its presentation in the *Record* during the very month when the final form of PSFS was being determined—is difficult to estimate. Lescaze surely knew this project of his old friend.[87] Howe, who had been working toward such a separation of services from usable space—his concern growing as much from Beaux-Arts theory as from modern theory—could not have helped but be interested in it. But although it may have been of inestimable value as a confirmation of Howe and Lescaze's thoughts, its influence on the actual form of the building is not certain.

It was at the time of publication of Moser's building in the *Record,* 28 November 1930 to be exact, that the architects reluctantly surrendered to the client's demand for expressed verticals. The article, which concerns itself with just

---

Instance," *Record* 64 (Oct. 1928), 334–42. Wright's own experiments with the tall building during the 1920s and early 1930s, e.g. the National Life Insurance Company project, though almost definitely of no influence on Howe or Lescaze, also relate quite closely to PSFS. See also Henry-Russell Hitchcock's comparison of Wright's project and PSFS *In the Nature of Materials* (New York: Duell, Sloan and Pearce, 1942), p. 81.

84. See Ludwig Hilbersheimer, *Internationale Neue Baukunst* (Stuttgart, 1927), pl. 36; Erich Mendelsohn, *Russland, Europa, Amerika* (Berlin, 1929), pl. 142; "Design for Office Building," *Record* 68 (Dec. 1930), 489.

85. Werner Moser, letter to author, 25 July 1963.

86. "Notes on Drafting and Design," *Record* 68 (Dec. 1930), 485–88.

87. Moser writes: "I do not remember the detailed discussions I have had with Lescaze during our encounters in Chicago and New York. Certainly the problem of how the high rise buildings might express their structural character and their functions in terms of human scale was one of the themes, about which we talked intensively, during my stay in the U.S.A., 1923–1926. Probably he had seen the European publications of my design later on." Letter to author, 25 July 1963.

this problem, illustrates numerous industrial buildings, all of which give credence to the then startling observation that "the masonry wall serves two functions: support and protection. Frame construction leads to segregation of supporting members and enclosing walls and beginning of spatial separation. Use of steel and reinforced concrete reduces size and number of vertical supports. In the building shown . . . no attempts were made by the designers to disguise the specific character of the construction by emphasizing the vertical supports to suggest masonry construction."[88] Conversely, the article goes on to note that "vertical obstructions" can "become architectural features." This unquestionably fell in line with the advice of the real estate men, who argued that the interruption of the continuous window band in the design of PSFS would be a boon in the placement of the office partitions.[89]

The success of PSFS is directly related to the calculated use of contrasts. In the tower this can be seen in the contrast of horizontal floor slab and vertical support; the hardness of form caused by these oppositions of column and spandrel is set off by the richly textured smoky-gray brick spandrels which in turn contrast with the glass. The materials of the exterior were chosen to "carry out," according to Howe, "the structural articulations. . . . This sober yet significant color scheme in which each color is assigned a distinct functional subdivision of the composition, expresses by its purposeful order all that is best in the quiet dignity of American business building.[90] The banking room, with its mutually responsive curves at the corners, is composed of a series of contrasting wall planes executed in gray and white marble, glass, and nubble curtains. Yellow siena marble was used to face the two executive balconies, although Howe had originally preferred a more subdued pink. The columns of the banking room were treated, according to John Harbeson, simply as a "piece of the wall moved out." The sides parallel to the dark gray wall are of dark gray marble, while the other two sides are of white marble. Harbeson has shown the similarity between Howe's use of this device and the treat-

88. "Notes on Drafting and Design."

89. See Jordy, "PSFS," n. 66. The brochure prepared by the rental agent, Richard J. Seltzer, proclaims that PSFS "offers you a decidedly greater amount of daylight than that offered by any other office building in the city today. It is the result of careful planning and the architectural appreciation of the relation of daylight to efficient work. The building was *designed* to be day lighted!" *A Few Outstanding Reasons Why Intelligent Business and Professional Men Are Leasing Office Space in the Philadelphia Saving Fund Building,* 8-page brochure (Philadelphia, n.d.). This point is also stressed in a more lavish 20-page brochure produced by Seltzer (n.d.). Both brochures on deposit at Avery Library, Columbia.

90. Quoted in Howe and Lescaze, "Planning, Engineering, Equipment. The PSFS," *Forum* 57 (Dec. 1932), 543-46.

ment of the mouldings on the columns in Frank Furness's Broad Street Station in Philadelphia.[91] The floors are dark gray granite, the counter fronts Belgian black. The chrome furniture, all of which was designed by the architects, is upholstered in blue leather. Howe was probably responsible for the subdued richness of materials and colors that characterized the main banking room. These are not the stark contrasts employed so frequently and effectively in many early International Style buildings; rather, these are the subtle opposi-tions of structure, materials, and texture which enhance the total image and aim at a synthesis. With the ceiling bathed in an even luminescence and with local light at the counters only, the effect was one of shadowy splendor with patches of reflection and glare spotted here and there on the shiny marble surfaces. Here indeed was an architecture according to Howe's own understanding of the International Style, addressing "itself directly to the imagination and the intellect, using the eye only as a recording instrument," throwing the mind "back from its polished planes into pure space."[92] One cannot help but agree with the editors of *Architectural Review,* when they heralded the room in 1934 for a "simple and impressive grandeur which is unique in modern archi-tecture."[93]

The equally impressive treatment of the thirty-second floor is probably without parallel in the history of modern architecture in America.[94] It is the most lavish and carefully detailed suite of rooms ever executed in a modern commercial building. Although in part it is the result of the generous budget, more importantly, the high quality and the superb execution of the materials as well as Howe's magnificent taste are responsible for the unique character of the suite. For the Philadelphia bankers' own use, Howe set out to capture the effect of restrained luxury, which they expected in traditional designs and which must have been a delightful surprise to them in a wholly modern work. Dark tones of woods and fabrics are contrasted with the uninterrupted pano-rama of sky, and the progression of spaces from light to dark again is bril-liantly handled as one is led from the dim elevator hall through a corridor—paneled on one side, flooded with light from continuous windows on the other

91. John Harbeson, "Philadelphia's Victorian Architecture, 1860–1890," *Pennsylvania Maga-zine of History and Biography* 67 (1943), 269–70. For a more detailed presentation of Furness's work, esp. the Broad Street Station, see James F. O'Gorman et al., *The Architecture of Frank Furness* (Philadelphia: Museum of Art, 1973), p. 180.

92. Howe, "Abstract Design in Modern Architecture."

93. "The Philadelphia Savings [*sic*] Fund Society Building," *Review* 73 (March 1933), 101–06.

94. The closest prototype one can find for the detailing of this suite is Gabriel Guevrekian's Villa Heim at Neuilly-sur-Seine, France, of 1928. See *Moderne Bauforme* 28 (May 1928), 11.

—to a small dining alcove, the mellow atmosphere of which is a result of a careful blending of natural and artificial illumination. Beyond this is the dark board room, hung with the formal portraits of past presidents of the Society. The dining room leads directly to an enclosed solarium, reminiscent of a promenade deck on a luxury liner. The dining room's own air of ponderous luxury seems to be suffused with the heavy scent of expensive cigars. Dark browns and rich blues predominate in the imposing and simple furniture. This was Howe's pride and joy: a room of elegance, yet one of considerable masculinity. Here men could talk.

PSFS is architecture reduced to its most simple and serviceable form, combining "rugged strength approaching ugliness" with an incredible richness and refinement.[95] Every element is reduced to its barest essential so that it might, in Howe's words, "lay bare the abstract space-time ideal in all its clarity."[96] The whole is conceived in terms of line, point, and plane; gone is the display and the materialistic ostentation that obscured Beaux-Arts principles. Yet PSFS, propaganda to the contrary, is no functionalist exercise. Its greatness is in part an outgrowth of the quality of its materials and the craftsmanship of its construction. It is an expensive building—the architects and the client well understood the foolishness of tightfistedness—but in no way extravagant. Luxurious materials are employed with austere economy. As such, it embodies to this day James Willcox's desire for a working monument.

The architects and the client agreed that the design of an office building did not end with the building itself or with its more important interior spaces, but that it included every item of hardware, piece of furniture, and fixture down to the ashtrays on the desks. In the case of PSFS, so little modern furniture and so few modern objects were available in this country—and what were, were usually Art Deco—that it seemed necessary to have all interior fittings designed especially for the building. Moreover, the Depression had made custom design much less a luxury, especially in the light of the bank's generous pre-Crash building budget, than would ever again be the case. Manufacturers themselves were anxious to experiment with new metals such as stainless steel in any way suggested to them. Because of this curious turn of events, PSFS comes closer to being a total design statement than any other skyscraper ever built. Not even the Seagram Building, conceived as much as a monument to

95. Frederick Gutheim, "The Philadelphia Saving Fund Society Building: A Re-Appraisal," *Record* 106 (Oct. 1949), 88–95, 180, 182.

96. Howe, "Abstract Design in Modern Architecture." Howe also wrote a poem in 1932 titled "Space, Time and Delancey Place." See "Confusion of an Architect on First Reading About Space and Time," *Architectural Record* 109 (May 1951), 14.

quality in architecture as to quality in gin, can rival PSFS in this respect.[97]

A wisecrack contemporary with the construction of PSFS went: "Yes, but will it make a good ruin?" Fine materials—marble, copper, stainless steel, and bronze—combined with expert maintenance seem to have answered that question for a while, at least. Some critics, such as Frederick Gutheim, have pointed out that "what has aged is not the building but the style. Without even entering you see the enormous curved corner, the building's principal label of association with the modern movement of the late '20's and early '30's."[98] Although critics such as Hitchcock pointed out that the corner destroyed the sense of volume while at the same time making the transition between the tower and base extremely difficult,[99] they have neglected to point out that, urbanistically, the curved corner at PSFS works magnificently well. Like every other feature of the massing, it is conceived in careful relationship to the pressures of functions. The curved corner, expressing the sweep of sidewalk life, impinges on the spaces of the banking floor, a strong reminder of the activities of commerce upon which the institution so much depends.[100]

The subdued indirect lighting used as overall illumination, highlighted by pools of brighter lights which also date the building, have given way to uniform fluorescent lighting in the office tower. The improved illumination enhances the effect of the simple, precisely detailed corridors executed in blacks, whites, and grays, and accented with judiciously located areas of primary color. In the main banking room, where local light from desk lamps was relied on almost exclusively for illumination, a series of high intensity incandescent fixtures has been recessed into the ceiling. This does considerable damage to the composition of the planes and creates annoying reflections as well.

The executive suite at the top of the tower remains virtually unchanged, and its restrained design has thus far proved itself durable. It has become the unofficial reception room, through the generosity of the Society, for the city

97. Howe discussed the experimental nature of the technology and finishes used in PSFS in "Private and Public Administration Buildings," in Paul Zucker, ed., *New Architecture and City Planning* (New York: Philosophical Library, 1944), pp. 37–44. The comparison between PSFS and the Seagram Building is based on a conversation with Philip Johnson, New Canaan, Ct., April 1961. See also Jordy and Wright, "PSFS."

98. Gutheim, "The Philadelphia Saving Fund Society Building: A Re-Appraisal."

99. Hitchcock, "Howe and Lescaze."

100. Robert Venturi stresses "the curved base, rectangular shaft, and angled top as manifestations of multiple functions contained within the building. . . . One exceptional Modern building, the P.S.F.S., gives positive expression to the variety and complexity of its program. . . . [Its] varieties of functions and scales (including the enormous advertising sign at the top) work within a compact whole. Its curving facade, which contrasts with the rectangularity of the rest of the building, is not just a cliche of the '30's, because it has an urban function. At the lower pedestrian level it directs space around the corner." *Complexity and Contradiction in Architecture* (New York: Museum of Modern Art, 1966), pp. 75, 39.

government. It was the view over the city from this room that took the breath of the United Nations Headquarters Site Commission when they visited Philadelphia after the war, and made them consider "Penn's Greene Countrie Towne" as a possible site for the organization's headquarters. From these rooms one can look out beyond the harbor, eastward as George Howe might have, and muse on his achievement: he had, for the second time in his life, been a docile student at the feet of his beloved Europe. Absorbing its lessons, he had achieved a structure that might stand proudly alongside the works of foreign masters: the one American skyscraper which, as Hitchcock wrote in 1932, "is worth discussing in the same terms as the work of the leading architects of Europe."[101]

PSFS, along with Neutra's Lovell Health House, marks the turning point within the International Style from the Machine Phase of the twenties to the Technology Phase of the thirties and forties (see note 50). It was also the fulfillment of what Howe had been seeking since the war.[102]

Built at a unique time in American history, it exemplifies the perennial schizophrenia in American architecture: the unresolved conflicts between the search for classicistic perfection, and the recognition of the expediencies of function and the moment. It is a reply to two problems: the meticulously particulated complex of shapes now in their middle age and thriving at the corner of Twelfth and Market Streets, and the soaring symbol of modern Philadelphia, the magnificent tower seen down the Parkway from the Schuylkill, ageless in its classic solution of the classic modern problem.

Public reaction to PSFS was immediate and generally favorable. Crank letters to the Society were remarkably few and patently absurd.[103] Leopold Stokowski, in a letter to Howe dated 24 November 1931, referred to "a marvelous pile of architecture" encountered on one of his infrequent trips to Center City, which "looked so much like you that I knew you must be the creator of it."[104] This from a friend of Lescaze!

101. Hitchcock, "Howe and Lescaze."

102. See "George Howe, An Architectural Biography," *T-Square* 2 (Jan. 1932), 20–23.

103. One letter was reprinted at Howe's suggestion and without the author's signature in the Philadelphia *Evening Bulletin* for 28 Jan. 1932. It attacks the building as "an awful abortion" and expresses sympathy for the architects "because, no doubt, it must have been with a good heart that you smothered the artist in you to design such a structure." Howe, still trying to resolve his own conflict between rationalism and romanticism, replied: "Functionalism, mechanistic as it may sound, is in reality only another way of getting at romance. The feeling of its advocates is only that the romance of steel and business is different from the romance of the farm and the cathedral."

104. Stokowski, letter to Howe, 21 Nov. 1931, quoted in part in "Philadelphia's Fancy," *Fortune* 6 (Dec. 1932), 65–69, 130–31.

On opening day, 1 August 1932, men stationed in the banking room to listen to the conversation of the visitors found the public reaction highly favorable. Most people seemed to see in this new departure in design something that inspired confidence: this was an institution that planned ahead, a safe place for money. Newspapers were not so favorable. The Philadelphia *Sunday Dispatch* for 10 October 1932 saw PSFS as a "mute but eloquent warning that there are boundaries beyond which the mania for originality that disregards established canons of taste may not go without courting the gods of disaster. What a hideous thing that building is, utterly destitute of the faintest claim to comeliness, an affront to public taste and an eyesore to the shopping community. . . . It's barbaric, repellent, epically stupid." The *Sunday Transcript* of 27 December 1931 was more succinct: "Never has such an ugly building been perpetrated. . . . That it will ever pay real profits is not at all likely."

The opinions of fellow professionals mattered greatly to Howe. Albert Kelsey, the well-known Philadelphia architect and former associate of Paul Cret, in a letter to the editor of the *T-Square Club Journal,* avoided discussing the building as a work of art, choosing instead a sociological tack and lambasting its relationships to the urban surroundings, "to the difficulties of municipal housekeeping," and to street traffic.[105] His references to the glare of plate glass in the eye of the passerby and to the effect of the design on the "mental health" of the pedestrian must have hurt Howe deeply. Paul Cret, with characteristic intelligence, understood PSFS from the start. Indeed, he claimed to see in the horizontality of the design a fulfillment of his teachings of the previous decade. In a simple letter to Howe, dated 28 March 1931, he wrote:

> I have just seen in the *T-Square Club Journal* the studies for the building at Market Street. It is excellent, and I have an idea it will establish an epoch in Philadelphia.
>
> I hope these are the final studies and that not too many changes have been imposed on you. With well chosen materials (and they will be) it will be a very beautiful work.
>
> With compliments to Lescaze and yourself,
>
> Your friend,
Paul Cret

Howe was deeply moved by this letter from his old friend, whose opinion he valued highly. On 1 April 1931, he wrote to Cret of his deep conviction of the rightness of the direction he was following: "But, as you can imagine, the weight of external criticism has been very hard to combat, not only when it comes from those in power, but also from your own colleagues. It is therefore

105. Albert Kelsey, letter, *T-Square Club Journal* 1 (April 1931), 30.

a great source of strength and encouragement to be assured of a good opinion which I prize so highly."

Almost ten years after its completion, PSFS was awarded the Gold Medal of the Philadelphia Chapter of the American Institute of Architects. I conclude this chapter with a characteristic exchange of letters between Howe and Lescaze, then no longer partners and not on the most cordial terms. Lescaze to Howe, 10 May 1939:

> Dear George:
>
> Thank you very much for your telephone call and later your letters telling me that our P.S.F.S. building has been awarded the Philadelphia Chapter medal for the year 1939. It was extremely thoughtful of you to phone me so quickly about it and it indeed made me very happy.
>
> The failure of the newspapers to make it a joint award did, naturally, spoil to some extent the pleasure at first felt. But I should have remembered that Philadelphia never forgave me altogether for having as they used to say "spoiled George's good taste." As you know, I never thought I did. Did I?
>
> I'll be delighted to see the medal when it has been inscribed. What is it made of if it's no longer gold?

Howe to Lescaze, 15 May 1939:

> Dear Bill:
>
> Thanks for your letter of May 10th. It was fun to see you in New York. As to Philadelphia's opinion of my taste I have always found it to be of the lowest at any given moment.[106] If you had not been so obvious a target for disapproval as a stranger in our midst either my own waywardness or some outward circumstance would have been blamed for the supposed decline in my esthetic judgment. Now that P.S.F.S. has been accepted, I suppose it is necessary to Philadelphia's own self esteem that it should be attributed to a native son.
>
> The medal is now made of bronze and a very ugly bronze at that, as you will see.

106. The intensity of established Philadelphia's resentment against Howe was considerable throughout the 1930s. His break with his former partners and their values, his relationship with Lescaze, and unfortunately the sudden international prominence of their work, especially PSFS, were all causes for this hostility. In 1933 Maxwell Levinson attempted to secure the coveted Philadelphia Award for Howe. Despite a well-organized campaign with letters and endorsements from leading personalities in art and architecture, including Philip Johnson, Alfred Barr, Norman Bel Geddes, Howard Robertson, and Norman N. Rice, and the logic of the choice (previous winners had included Samuel Yellin, Paul Cret, and Connie Mack), Howe failed to receive the award, which carried with it a gold medal and a $10,000 stipend.

6. In the Cause of a Modern Architecture

> The test of a first-rate intelligence is the ability to hold two opposite
> ideas in the mind at the same time, and still retain the ability to function.
> F. Scott Fitzgerald, *The Crack-Up*

Substantial though the oeuvre of Howe and Lescaze was, considering its venturesome formalisms and the stultified economy of the period, building design by no means constituted the firm's sole contribution to the development of modern architecture in America. Howe, following the example of the European leaders of the modern movement, recognized that its success was dependent upon the establishment of a sympathetic and informed climate of opinion. More than Lescaze, he was suited to the role of polemicist: his apparent reticence shielded a caustic tongue; his blasé demeanor, intense convictions. With a superb command of language and an agile and engaging wit, he made a splendid advocate for the cause of modernism. His age and his unusual background gave him an aura of respectability lacking in the other leading modernists (who were, as a rule, very young or foreign-born, or both). He brought to the cause the dignity of his standing in the profession as well as something almost as useful, his social position. Like Roosevelt (to whom he felt no special affinity), Howe was regarded with suspicion by his peers. And like Roosevelt he enjoyed so secure a social position that few would call him down publicly.[1]

Howe's polemic writings are characterized by candor and by a reluctance—derived, in part, from his innate skepticism—to discuss questions of architectural form. Preferring to have the work of his firm stand for his own point of view, he chose to explore in his writings the larger question of the relationship between architecture and the modern world. Almost never using the term International Style (until the early 1950s, when he was forced into it by Frank Lloyd Wright and when it had begun to achieve the status of a historical fact), Howe saw modern architecture in a much more fluid context which, he wrote in the spring of 1930,

---

1. Others of Howe's "radical" Philadelphia friends faced similar abuse. See George Biddle, *An American Artist's Story* (Boston: Little, Brown, 1939), esp. pp. 252–95; Francis Biddle, *A Casual Past* (Garden City: Doubleday, 1961), p. 352. See also Francis Biddle, *In Brief Authority* (Garden City: Doubleday, 1962), p. 148. Helen Howe West relates that Howe "loathed" Roosevelt and states that her mother believed the origin of this intensely negative feeling extended back to school days at Groton. Letter to author, 13 June 1973.

includes properly all those buildings in which an effort is apparent to return to sound tradition, as opposed to stylistic tradition, that is to say, to the interpretation of function, spiritual as well as material, logically and imaginatively, in terms of modern materials, internally structural as well as visible. Modern architecture is not produced by the mere application of startling superficial ornament, but represents a fundamental and organic change in point of view toward the problems of life, brought about by the economic, sociological and philosophic modifications in our outlook which have accompanied the development of science, and its mechanistic and humane applications to daily life. It follows that modern architecture has very little to do with what is generally understood as modern decoration, which is for the moment the product of individual fancy, untrammeled by basic restraints, and as variable and unimportant as the length of a woman's skirt. Fashion may change with the quarterly dividend, but the fundamental principles of architecture remain unalterable.[2]

Later Howe was to state his position more succinctly, in an address to the sixty-third convention of the American Institute of Architects in 1930: "Modernism is not a style. It is an attitude of mind. Greek and Gothic are immutable only because they are mere images of realities that no longer exist. Modernism is as changing as daily life. It is also as inevitable."[3] It is evident, he said, "that the fundamental principles of mechanics, form and construction which we have inherited constitute the basis of modern design, even when applied to radically new problems and materials." Though the principles may remain reasonably unchanged, these new problems and materials are bound to bring about totally new architectural forms.

Howe felt that technological progress had long enough gone unchallenged by new architectural forms.

Today the great mass of building is a sprawling mass. Good architecture . . . has lost touch with the everyday needs of men except in their most conspicuous and fundamental manifestation. The efforts of architects to guide the democratic tide of construction have proved futile because

2. Howe, "Modern Architecture," *U.S.A.* 1 (Spring 1930), 19–20, 23. According to Helen Howe West, Howe "was instrumental in starting that short lived magazine *U.S.A.*" Letter to author, 13 June 1973.

3. A.I.A., *Proceedings of the Sixty-Third Annual Convention* (Washington, D.C., 1930), pp. 25–28.

traditionalism is personal and exclusive. Traditionalism has failed, not in the eyes of the public but in the eyes of the architects. The road has come to a dead end. The pioneers of the modern movement have pointed the way out.

Having abandoned technology, the traditionalist has also abandoned the privilege of exercising the technical competence which made the client turn to the architect in the past as a final court of appeal. Thus, without realizing it, the traditionalist "has willfully resigned his post as judge in matters of contemporary architectural expression. In order to maintain his authority, he has set up the bench of taste based on archaeological erudition. Unfortunately, taste is not subject to codification. As a result every man, lay as well as professional, can claim as great a knowledge of its vague laws as his neighbor."

Continuing, Howe insisted that modern architecture is concerned not with "personal technique" directed toward astounding originality but with the development of a technique "that every man connected with the building industry today could understand and use. . . . Seizing with imagination and courage the opportunity offered by the elimination of the rules of design imposed by gravitational stability, [the modern architect] has suspended about his skeleton framework a gossamer veil of glass and light building materials, reformulated to meet modern needs in the light of modern economic and engineering genius."

Howe used the term "functionalism" sparingly, as we have seen in the case of the Hessian Hills School. He developed his attitudes toward this ambivalent term in an address delivered on 13 November 1931 before the Department of Architecture of the College of Fine Arts of New York University.[4] Howe began by stating his

> conviction that only by meeting economic and technical conditions squarely can we architects be *artists* today. The architect must be primarily a designer and only secondarily an economist and engineer. . . .

4. The talk, "Architectural Deflation or the Practical and the Aesthetic in Modern Architecture," was privately printed (New York, 1931). The *New York Times,* in its coverage on 14 Nov. 1931, chose to emphasize Howe's more casual remarks about economics, especially real estate. The *Times* reported in part: "Mr. Howe . . . said that 'architecture, along with other economic activities, has gone through an orgy of inflation and is now suffering the consequences. When the deflation is complete, three normal types of client will remain: disappointed owners who have missed the market, desperate owners who have paid more for their land than revenues can possibly justify, and disgruntled owners who have obtained possession by foreclosure.'" "Bids Architects Find Use for Idle Land," p. 19.

[Engineering and economics] are the plastic medium of the architect out of which his work must grow. . . . There must be no more talk of ugly necessities. A modern necessity is neither beautiful nor ugly except as we make it so. [Functionalism, as a term, is only applicable when it covers] every human aspiration and achievement. In the narrow practical and structural sense in which it is often used it has little or no meaning. The conscious intention of the functional architect is to interpret the ideals of civilization, religious, political, social and economic, that is to say the inclusive function of modern life, in a common medium of structural expression based on the special function of contemporary industrial technology.

Later Howe wrote of the need to bring "out anew the fact that functionalism is essentially an aesthetic movement. . . . To quote from Le Corbusier from memory—'I am, in the final analysis, interested only in beauty.' "[5]

He further stated his beliefs in an address, "Organic or Ornamental?," delivered at the Town Hall Club on 14 November 1930. Believing that architecture could be divided into two schools, the "ornamental" and the "organic," he said, "Within the organic school there are roughly three tendencies, distinguished by differences of emphasis rather than of fundamental thought. These three are the mechanical, the functional and the stylistic."

The first tendency manifests itself in Buckminster Fuller's Dymaxion House, which is "an attempt to move forward at one step to the ultimate application of the most scientific knowledge to human comfort, going far beyond any existing public demands." Fuller's work, "radical" and "experimental," is the line of "inevitable development of the future." But it implies "a state of social and industrial organization which may be long in taking shape."

The functional tendency, which grew out of contemporary developments, is concerned with the use and adaptation of "existing technical means" and the analysis of "existing wants." Its "aim is to produce a minimum of wasted effort, approximating the methods of the engineer, though with a greater emphasis on human welfare as opposed to efficiency." In a far more outspoken manner than any of his previous articles betrayed, Howe stated that both tendencies, the mechanical and the functional, "generally disregard aesthetics as an end in themselves, the first entirely, the second almost so. The func-

5. Howe, "Functional Aesthetics and the Social Ideal," *Pencil Points* 13 (April 1932), 251–18. See also Robert L. Anderson's reply, "Dogmatic Functionalism," *Pencil Points* 13 (July 1932), 505–07.

tionalists never go further than to say that what is perfectly useful must be beautiful, and many of them deny that there is any such thing as beauty in the accepted meaning of the term."

The stylists, Howe continues, referring to the last of the three "organic" tendencies, believe that

> the business of the architect in cooperating with the engineer is to produce beauty over and above utility. They differ from the ornamentalist only in claiming that beauty is more than skin deep, and that superficial decoration unrelated to organic structure is as passing and unimportant as fashions in cosmetics or the length of skirts. They strip their buildings bare to expose an athletic and well-conditioned body. . . . On the other hand, they mould these bare forms with disciplined care, and unlike the mechanists and the functionalists, hold beauty always in view as their objective.
>
> It is evident that this organic architecture, however emphasized, is in fact a projection of the engineer's ideal. It is the engineer who has converted the amoebic cellular building into an elaborate skeletal structure with a complicated organic system of circulation, breathing, hearing, nerves, and so forth, and it is consciously and gratefully on the foundation of engineering progress that the organic school of architects proposes to raise its structure.

Like so many of Howe's polemic statements of the early 1930s, this one reflects a classic moment of idealism: a new world, almost without precedent, without a past, seemed to lie open before American architects. But even within the ranks of modernists—ranks that were never so solid as Hitchcock, Johnson, and Barr led people to believe—there was serious dissension. Although there were a number of arenas for this intramural debate, none was as influential or as stimulating as the pages of *T-Square,* a Philadelphia journal of architectural opinion to which Howe lent considerable moral and financial support.

In 1930 Howe became president of the T-Square Club in Philadelphia, which conducted an evening atelier for the study of architecture. The atelier had in former years published a journal, and it was now suggested that publication be resumed. Maxwell Levinson, a young student, was made editor. Going about his task with enthusiasm, he secured numerous advertisements at favorable rates. But as the publication date approached it became apparent to

Levinson and John S. Carver, *massier*[6] of the atelier, that the other members had no intention of cooperating, although various commitments had been made and contracts signed. This was reported by Carver to Howe, who summoned Levinson to his office. Outraged by the lack of cooperation on the part of the atelier that had originally suggested publishing the journal, Howe's sense of fair play was also deeply affected by the treatment accorded Levinson. Howe decided that the journal bear the name of the T-Square Club and that the club, not the atelier, should be responsible for its publication. Levinson would remain as editor.[7] Thus began an extraordinary episode in American architectural literature, a debate that for the first time brought the great questions of organic versus International Style architecture, social versus personal concern, and designer versus engineer into focus in the United States. And the key figure was Howe.

Knowledge of the history of the *T-Square Club Journal* and its successors, *T-Square* and *Shelter,* is basic to an understanding of the architectural climate of the years 1930–32. In its pages appear virtually all the important architectural ideas of the time. Quickly outgrowing its origins as a local magazine, it reflected the three distinct phases that marked the architectural upheaval following the Crash in 1929: the rejection of Beaux-Arts design forms, the sudden acceptance of the Machine Phase of the International Style, and the almost immediate challenge to the validity of that style on the part of a technologically oriented avant-garde. Howe, in his preface to the first issue, set the character for the first year of the magazine's life as an open forum for architectural debate among men representing all phases of contemporary architectural thought. In a rather flowery introduction he wrote that whereas a "generation devoted to illusion bequeathed to us a notion of Truth, not as a lovely naked maiden men had pictured from ancient times but . . . an elderly spinster aunt never stripped of her decorous bustle, bombazine and adjustable curls," he sees her now left

in the midst of her rich lands subjected to a series of lightning metamorphoses by the lack of an agreement among a sufficient number of men to justify her assuming a definite form for an appreciable instant.

We of the middle generation have called on her in vain to show herself as Ultimate Truth for we have no notion what Ultimate Truth is like. The younger generation takes a more realistic view . . . and is trying to select among her unnumbered roles the one they would wish her to play

6. An elected office in the Beaux-Arts atelier system, roughly equal to president of the student body or "student-in-charge."

7. Interview with Levinson, Philadelphia, Aug. 1961.

for this night only. Discussion, recrimination and blows are a necessary
preliminary to agreement among many. . . . Good luck in the battle
royal.[8]

In the early months of 1931 most of the contributions to the *Journal* were
from Philadelphia architects. This, in a city whose architecture was dominated
by the humane French academicism of Jacques Grèber and Paul Cret, meant
that all comments were tempered by the prevailing respect for architecture
considered neither as a scientific nor as a technical pursuit but primarily as an
art—a concept already under attack in Europe—and furthermore, considered
as a sovereign art with its own immutable laws. The distinction, also crum-
bling in Europe, between style in architecture and architectural excellence as
such, was maintained by such diverse contributors as Howell Louis Shay and
Norman N. Rice. Shay, deeply imbued with the Beaux-Arts tradition, stated,
"It is not so important a matter whether a design be modernistic, traditional or
stylistic. It is either good or bad architecture and will survive and perish as
such."[9] Rice, one of the first Americans to study with Le Corbusier, argued
ardently and logically for the new architecture, writing, "The tradition of
architecture—architecture itself—has been and always will be this: to build as
well, as solidly and in as fitting a manner as the materials and technical knowledge of the times allow. . . . The *raison d'être* of architecture is the provision
of spaces."[10]

Howe contributed two articles to the *T-Square Club Journal* in its first year.
One, a discussion of PSFS, did much to explain the design in terms of "the
human intention of the building and . . . its structural technique."[11] This
article aroused considerable comment among Howe's contemporaries. Albert
Kelsey's and Paul Cret's letters to him have been mentioned in chapter five.
Howe's other article, less enthusiastic in tone, reflects his fundamental skepticism.[12] With deep conviction but characteristic understatement, Howe tried to
establish his basic tenets while remaining reluctant to commit himself to the
dogmatic claims of the Internationalists. Functionalism seemed too simplistic:

8. Howe, "A Fair Future to the T-Square Club Journal!," *T-Square Club Journal* 1 (Dec.
1930), 3.
9. Howell Lewis Shay, "Modern Architecture and Tradition," *T-Square Club Journal* 1
(Jan. 1931), 12.
10. Norman N. Rice, "The New Architecture," *T-Square Club Journal* 1 (March 1931),
14–19.
11. Howe, "A Design for a Savings Bank and Office Building," *T-Square Club Journal* 1
(March 1931), 10–13.
12. Howe, "A Further Vague Pursuit of Truth in Architecture," *T-Square Club Journal* 1
(Feb. 1931), 13–28.

"the mere solution of practical problems." Structure, on the other hand, held within it the potential for a "human symbol." The functionalists did their job well in discarding "all the complicated combinations of the past and . . . [reducing] architectural expression to its elements. [But] these elements . . . are first human, and second structural. The mechanical elements affect the final result only secondarily insofar as they make certain forms possible and in purely industrial problems."

The early history of the *T-Square Club Journal* is marked by a widening influence in the profession and by a diversification and increased sophistication of the arguments presented. Contributions originally had to be coaxed out of local architects, but the *Journal's* expanded circulation made it a highly sought forum for architectural discussion. These developments can be attributed to a variety of causes. Commercial trade publications such as *American Architect, Architectural Record,* and *Architectural Forum* were suffering as a result of the Depression and of their ambiguous philosophic commitments. Efforts to please subscribers and advertisers of all architectural persuasions meant repeated editorial compromises pleasing no one. Enthusiasm for the graphic presentation of contemporary architectural work in periodicals was at its peak. The early *Pencil Points* with its elaborate treatment of the work of Samuel Chamberlain, Hugh Ferris, and others, remains the prime example of this dangerous tendency. Habits of imitative architecture and eclecticism were not easily broken; illustrations and details of the work of Le Corbusier and Mallet-Stevens merely replaced those of Bertram Goodhue and John Russell Pope. Words and ideas were scarce. Levinson offered the pages of the *T-Square Club Journal,* on the other hand, to anyone who was able to present an idea logically and articulately. In addition to Shay and Rice, Dwight James Baum, Arthur I. Meigs, Louis I. Kahn, Harvey M. Watts, Louis Skidmore, Lee Lawrie, Wilson Eyre, and others took advantage of the *Journal* to air their diverse and often carefully thought-out views. But it is important to state that a balance was preserved and that the magazine itself maintained a reasonably neutral position.

The majority of the club members had little sympathy with the modern movement and in time preferred to sever relationships with the *Journal*. Its circulation grew steadily outside Philadelphia, reaching the surprisingly high figure of 4,000 in 1932, but, in Philadelphia itself, it plummeted to a handful of subscriptions.[13] Yet in the first year of publication it had performed a mag-

13. Interview with Levinson, Aug. 1961. The official resolution severing the connection between the magazine and the T-Square Club is included in "A Letter from the President . . ,"*T-Square* 2 (Feb. 1932), 5.

nificent service to architecture. Without the pressure of economic necessity, it was able to avoid the quest for "completeness" that has always been the *bête noire* of the commercial publications. Avoiding the peripheral features concerning the ethics and the economics of professional practice, this was truly a magazine of architecture as art. The disapproval of the club members toward the magazine reflects less on the daring publication than on the timidity of the traditionalists.

In January 1932 the magazine's title was shorted to *T-Square;* Levinson remained editor. No longer sponsored by the T-Square Club of Philadelphia, it derived considerable financial support from Howe, who played more than ever a key role.[14] With amazing clairvoyance he postulated the central concerns of the coming years in his editorial in the January issue: "There has never been a time when necessity has not stimulated interest in the formulation of architectural ideas. Architecture no longer gilds only the tips of a prosperity but touches the depths of our social and economic existence. An examination of its place in life is inevitable."[15]

The editorial commitment of *T-Square* to Internationalism in architecture marked the growing success of the style's aggressive spokesmen, as well as the liberal financial support provided by Howe who, along with Lescaze, already was the movement's leading American practitioner. Contributors to *T-Square* included such pioneers as Richard Neutra, Philip Johnson, Norman N. Rice, Le Corbusier, and Rudolph Schindler. Interpreting the idea of a new architecture in the broadest manner, the magazine accepted contributions as well from that group of modernists who for a variety of reasons and in varying degrees rejected not only Art Deco but also the Machine Phase of the International Style. These men, Irving Bowman, Norman Bel Geddes, Henry Churchill, and Buckminster Fuller, had little in common save a peculiar variety of anti-intellectualism, a love of engineering and engineering techniques, and a distrust for the aesthetic side of architectural design. It was typical for Howe to include such contributors, whose extreme positions seemed to many to be outside the realm of architecture.

The famous debate between Frank Lloyd Wright and Howe, published in *T-Square,* was the single most important clash of the early days of Internationalism in American architecture, although only a few of Wright's catch phrases and not the underlying seriousness of the discussion have remained in our memories. This was not simply an encounter between two men representing

14. Interview with Levinson, Aug. 1961; R. Buckminster Fuller, letter to Richard Pommer, 5 June 1973.

15. Howe, "The T-Square," *T-Square* 2 (Jan. 1932), 5.

two philosophies of architecture but a passage of arms between two leading modernists, both sworn enemies of the conservatives. With the benefit of hindsight, it can be claimed with only slight exaggeration that the stake was the direction of the new architecture in America itself.

Levinson had been corresponding with Wright, already engaged in his personal war with the International Style, in an effort to secure a critical statement about the Philadelphia Saving Fund Society Building, then under construction. Claiming not to have seen enough of the building to write knowledgeably about it, Wright asked permission to submit an article of his own choosing, which turned out to be an exceedingly personal attack upon Internationalism in architecture and, in particular, upon its practitioners in America. These last were seen as super salesmen, purveyors of a "culture weed" which contained in the abstraction of "straight-line, and flat-plane, . . . and the single-curved surface" the "expedient" modern formula. Internationalism in America was another manifestation of eclecticism, which as "a form of self-abuse too long practiced, has rendered us impotent. Such architecture as we have, we got that way. We are prostitute to any formula because we are prostitute to the machine." Remarking on the embarrassment he offered to disciples by still being alive, Wright cited the now-classic remark said to have been made by Philip Johnson: "We always come to the realization that Wright is alive with a kind of shock." To this he countered, devastatingly as always:

> [The] predatory "internationalist" . . . elects a formula derived from an architecture living, or just beginning to live, and kills the architecture.
> Any man's art is dishonored by imitation.
> Any nation's life is dishonored by seizing formula instead of perceiving principles.
> If only our country would *"raise the flowers, now that we all have got the seed,"* from seed: principle, the seed, transplanting not preferred . . . what a country![16]

Howe, enraged when he read this piece before its publication, submitted a reply to be published in the same issue, pending Wright's approval. Called "Moses Turns Pharaoh," it marked the first time that Wright was debated and attacked as an equal by a leading supporter of the International Style. Howe succeeded in matching Wright's bombastic brilliance with impassioned intellectual precision and moral indignation. His pride and integrity, not to men-

16. Wright, "For All May Raise the Flowers Now/For All Have Got the Seed," *T-Square* 2 (Feb. 1932), 6–8.

tion his professional ethics, were considerably wounded. "Mr. Frank Lloyd Wright, abandoning the part of Moses, is suddenly turned Pharoah in the architectural theatre. With tragi-comic gesture he has cast into the river all new born male children of the tribe 'Internationalists.' Though his stage waters are neither deep nor swift enough to be mortal it is his obvious intention to wash away the good name of his victims. Such an ill-meant ducking of the innocent even in play cannot pass without protest."

Howe attacked Wright's architectural nationalism and his lack of interest in the "international ideal" of a "humanized . . . industrial civilization. Since Wright uses the terms interchangeably, it must also be assumed that all 'Internatonalists' are to him 'New Eclectics' or common cheats." Praising internationalism in politics as well as in architecture, Howe called for a "free exchange of ideas" in order to provide a "richer soil in which to grow." He went on to question Wright's derisive use of the term "eclecticism" and mused on the possibilities of a healthy manifestation of that phenomenon, suited to the majority of architects, "men of common clay, untouched by creative genius," who may, by pursuing "personal eclecticism even though they do not subscribe to eclecticism as a philosophy," produce competent architecture. Observing the perennial conflict between Wright and his disciples, he questioned the nature of eclecticism and style: were we to have a similarity of architectural expression rooted in sound principles or "a traditionless chaos such as has existed for a century that a genius like Mr. Wright can appear to impose a first order on amorphous matter."[17]

So we find Howe, a hesitant Internationalist, placed in the awkward position of defending a style of which he was not absolutely certain himself. He is self-conscious about his own somewhat eclectic approach to the International Style; and his reserve, his measured indignation as contrasted with Wright's personal and sarcastic polemic, is interesting as an insight into the growth of his understanding of the new attitudes in design. Such dignity on Howe's part was not lost on Wright, who stated in a letter of 1 February 1932 to Levinson: "Mr. Howe is a man whose quality and sincerity I do not question. He pleads the perennial cause of eclecticism eternal. And, sometime, I will take him on his own ground and answer him as he deserves. I wish I had him for a partner, myself." In the same letter Wright attempted to distinguish between "the high faith of internationalism" and the "predatory internationalist"; between "transplanting" and "importation." "We have imported everything we have—even our citizens. National pride is no factor in my judgement for no-one has more freely opened his heart, home, work or his mind to the Tom, Dick, and Harry

17. Howe, "Moses Turns Pharaoh," *T-Square* 2 (Feb. 1932), 9.

of the architectural wide-world."[18] Yet the syncretistic melting pot of American culture, which modifies the original Anglo-Saxon ingredients as much as it modifies other racial and cultural strains, was incomprehensible to Wright, who was narrowly brought up at a time when such an influence was unapparent. Howe, by contrast, was a man of broad international culture, by education as well as by choice.

Nonetheless, a most unusual friendship grew up between these two men who shared so little common ground save their own high standards, innate snobbishness, and profound affection for architecture. This friendship was triggered no doubt by Wright's provocative and laconic note to Howe, so often misquoted, concerning their verbal duel. The note is now lost, but Howe often quoted its substance as follows: "Dear George: This is just to tell you that in the present story I am not Moses, I am God. F. Ll. W." Howe was never a subscriber to the image of Wright as God, but he did see in this great architect, whom he felt to be the greatest since Michelangelo, "one of those strange vital giants our country brings forth at intervals who seem to embody in their single persons the whole frustrated impulse of the nation."[19] Indeed, it is as a con-

18. Wright, letter to Maxwell Levinson, 1 Feb. 1932.

19. Howe quoted the note and compared Wright to Michelangelo in his speech, "Why Then?—Why Now?" delivered on 15 May 1953 at the opening of the exhibition "Philadelphia Architecture in the Nineteenth Century" at the Philadelphia Art Alliance. It is included in West, *George Howe*, pp. 66–79. Wright's letter to Howe is quoted by Howe in "Some Experiences and Observations of an Elderly Architect," *Perspecta* 2 (1953), 2–5. By 1936 Howe and Wright were on good enough terms for the former to introduce the latter to an audience. But his remarks are laced with caution: "Anyone who is assigned the task of introducing a speaker as well known as Frank Lloyd Wright must appear slightly ludicrous in his own eyes. This is a great and glorious if somewhat disorderly country in which we live and anyone who believes that it makes any real difference who is President enjoys an enviable simplicity of mind. In the same way . . . Frank Lloyd Wright is a fine and upstanding if somewhat turbulent individual and anyone who thinks it makes any difference who introduces him is laboring under an amiable delusion. . . . I cannot help remembering that Frank Lloyd Wright and I have had words before now—he speaking from Olympian heights and I from the earthly footstool—but finding myself lately in a pacific mood, I have been led to wonder whether we could not, all of us, progress more quietly in the accomplishment of our legitimate ends. The answer, I think, is no . . . Frank Lloyd Wright seems to me . . . the ideal rebel, always consistent and intellectually honest. He is well aware that for him organization spells death. . . . While the academicians ride the storm in their great ships, and little groups of frightened revolutionaries improvise rafts for their safety, Frank Lloyd Wright swims alone. No one can estimate the power of so fearless and independent an individual."

By 1939, as West writes, correspondence between the two "seems to be warm and friendly as they discuss trying to save the Robie House in Chicago. April 14, 1939—F. L. Wright to G. Howe: 'Thank you for your help. Wish I could see more of you this summer—somehow—Why not Taliesin?' To which Howe responds: 'I hope my small contribution may prove to have been useful. I would also like to see you. I need oxygen treatment. Working for the Government, as I am now doing, burns up a lot of tissue' " (p. 53).

versation across the years that the Howe–Wright debate remains fascinating to us today. The robustness of the fully developed individualism of the late nineteenth century—confident, brash, and courageous—encounters in the pages of *T-Square* the sophisticated self-consciousness of a century that had not found its own social or architectural expression and was just outgrowing its literary birth pangs. It can be said that in the pages of *T-Square* Wright came to grips intellectually with twentieth-century America for the first time since 1914, perhaps even for the first time at all, while Howe, in his reply, faced for the first time a problem that, for younger architects (so-called second generation modernists), became quite obsessive as the modern movement gained acceptance in the following decades and as architects sought to extend its vocabulary of forms: in an architectural culture dominated by three great form-givers, Wright, Mies, and Le Corbusier, is not everything after them a form of eclecticism? Howe's architecture in the following years can be seen as an effort to integrate, creatively rather than derivatively, the lessons of these modern masters with native building functions and modern technological demands.

In April 1932 *T-Square*'s title changed once again, this time into *Shelter, A Magazine of Modern Architecture*. The title was coined by Buckminster Fuller, and its not very subtle change of emphasis from *T-Square*, a strict and traditional architectural reference, to *Shelter*, a term that evokes a progressive image and is concerned with the role of architects in an economic, technological, and sociological context, established another marker in the transition of the International Style from that of a Machine Style to that of a Technology Style. Fuller explained the shift of emphasis:

> George Howe's interests were changing rapidly at that time, and discouraged at the need for a new name [to replace *T-Square* which it turned out was held under copyright by Charles Scribner's] he decided to discontinue financial backing of the . . . magazine. The men who did the actual publishing work were the two Levinson boys of Philadelphia . . . [who] came to me in New York hoping that I could help them out and I decided to take over the magazine, giving it the name *Shelter*. In order to be able to carry it, I sold a considerable amount of my life insurance policies. The Levinsons had already been promised some financial help from Philip Johnson so the first issue of *Shelter* embraced a packet of items entitled International Architecture, which Johnson wished to publish.[20]

20. Fuller, letter to Richard Pommer, 5 June 1973.

The April issue was devoted to the newly founded Museum of Modern Art's first exhibition of architecture: "Modern Architecture: International Exhibition," held in March 1932. The editorial board comprised Maxwell Levinson as editor and George Howe, Henry-Russell Hitchcock, Alfred H. Barr, Jr., and Philip Johnson as associate editors. The issue was a compendium of explication and criticism of the new architecture and a polemic, although not in a narrow sense. The criticism ranged from the conservative viewpoint of the unreconstructed traditionalists to a fulmination by Wright entitled "Of Thee I Sing." Five of the talks presented at the symposium on the exhibition which the museum had recently sponsored were included. As a document of the International Style in America, this issue of *Shelter* is equalled only by the catalogue of the exhibition itself, prepared by Hitchcock and Johnson, which has achieved preeminence among the documents pertaining to the introduction of European modernism into the mainstream of American architecture.

As with the International Style as a whole, the editorial policy of *Shelter* was swept up in the almost pathological desire of the time for architecture to become a kind of "automatic reflection" of the forces that form the basis of economic and social behavior. Thus the title of the magazine was changed once again—still under the influence of Fuller, now made guest editor—into *Shelter, A Correlating Medium for the Forces of Architecture*. The technologically biased wing of the modern movement was in full control: Fuller, Henry Churchill, and Knud Lönberg-Holm were the principal contributors. With the publication in the May 1932 issue of Fuller's three essays on "Universal Architecture," the functional and structural determinism of his building conceptions found their first full statement.[21]

Shelter appeared once again and for the last time in November 1932.[22] Levinson, who had become an ardent convert to Fuller's architectural philosophy, remained as titular editor but the issue was almost exclusively Fuller's, whose criticisms of the International Style are well known and have been

21. This issue seems to mark a critical turning point, perhaps inaugurating the Technological phase of the style. For the first time, issues of technology and social planning, particularly as related to the architecture of low-cost dwellings, achieve a dominance over issues of symbolic form. Typical of the shift in emphasis is Roger Sherman's essay "Transition," in which it is claimed that the new architecture will emerge from the economic chaos of the depression, that "the early work of Oud, Gropius, Le Corbusier . . . was clear, courageous, splendid and intuitively true. Today their work is called 'international' and the exhibits of their imitators at the MOMA become merely exponential indices of an integrated purpose. That purpose is the best-for-least shelter developed industrially in terms of mechanical adequacy for survival and development." *Shelter* 2 (May 1932), 29.

22. The *Shelter* of 1938–39 was strictly a Fuller affair.

sympathetically discussed by Reyner Banham.[23] As Fuller stated it recently:

> The issues following Johnson's issue of *Shelter* are entirely of my own writing or my own selection. I was still at this time confident that new important ideas were not being accepted in the professional world of designers, if the ideas emanated from non-professionals, and particularly if those ideas challenged the ethics and economic validity of the system within which the patrons of those professionals prospered. I was committed to ideas and not to money. . . . You can assume that all illustrations as well as a number of the articles were written by me or represent my viewpoint and initiative. The articles on ecology and environment and pictures on pollution and so forth were my own.[24]

Fuller offered a form of architectural criticism which, although it was non-architectural in content, was beginning to exert a tremendous influence on architects. The architect-engineer and the big multifaceted architectural office, both presumably capable of producing technologically valid solutions to building problems, seemed particularly potent in light of the Depression whose economic privations gave the statistically "demonstrable" claims of the technologist a tinge of reality and a luster of tangibility completely lacking in the empty promises of politicians and architects, modernist or otherwise who, though they talked about function and efficiency, appeared to be in practice devoted to meaningful extravagance. Against the economic and social chaos of the early 1930s, Fuller, who is not strictly either an architect or an engineer but a philosopher whose focus is turned to those disciplines, came to be regarded by some as possessed of unique insights into architecture. His Dymaxion House, despite its questionable technology and its fundamentally antiurban qualities, began to appeal as an architectural solution to the problem of mass housing. To understand this sudden acceptance of Fuller, one must look backward to World War I, when architects, finding themselves cast in the mold of engineers in order to aid in the mobilization of resources, seemed to be receiving an inordinate amount of public recognition. Cass Gilbert, the architect of the Woolworth Building, was highly praised for the structurally stark concrete warehouse he designed in Brooklyn for the U.S. Army, and Bertram Goodhue for the new town at Tyrone, New Mexico. This desire on the part of many architects to create an illusion of ruthless efficiency

23. Reyner Banham, *Theory and Design in the First Machine Age* (New York: Praeger, 1960). Banham's decision to include Fuller in a book about the "First Machine Age" (which I prefer to label the "Machine Phase") is a little unclear to me.

24. Fuller, letter to Pommer, 5 June 1973.

in their office practice and in the functioning of their buildings was aided by a publicity campaign conducted by the American Institute of Architects.

The commercial magazines fanned the flames, so to speak, filling their pages with legal, financial, and engineering advice, much of it secondhand and thereby only emphasizing the fundamental superficiality of the profession's grasp of these issues. Talbot Hamlin, pronouncing post mortems on this form of architectural madness—the wild pursuit by architects of the forces behind architecture—described the boom years as a period when "architects, particularly the larger offices, became imbued with the psychology of their clients. All the Hooverian dogmas of individualism, salesmanship, profit-making, were swallowed unquestionably. . . . As he became immersed in financial schemes and details, his professional position weakened; the architect was merely one of several cogs in the machine of corporate and individual profit chasing." After the Crash "the profit chasers sought other fields; the architect was forgotten. He learned bitterly of the gratitude of wealth."[25]

Fifteen years later Howe expressed it differently, recalling that "the rigidity of American architecture" in the 1920s gave way, at least in the area of housing design, to a concern for "efficiency and economy, emphasized during the Depression, and that only where these have been demonstrated as realities in modern design, in industry, and to some degree in commerce, has [modern architecture] taken hold. We are still materialists rather than socialists."[26] These "financial architects," having no strong architectural tradition to return to, and no real position in the world of finance where they were never more than guests, then explored a conception of an architecture related to technology. Seeking to understand the roots of the economic holocaust about them, they attempted an analysis of what came to be known as "real wealth," which, according to Fuller, is "nothing more than the extent to which man, at a given moment, has harnessed forms of universal energy and, in the process, has developed a re-employable experience." For Fuller, essential human experiences consisted of "survival, fabricating with tools, and the turning of hazards into advantages."[27]

25. Talbot Hamlin was quoted by Charles A. and Mary R. Beard in *America in Mid-Passage* (New York: Macmillan, 1939), p. 773. In Nov. 1929 the publishers of *Amer. Architect* stated these ideas rather more baldly: "The architect has been termed a professional man. So he is. *But in this year of 1929 he is nearer to being a business man than ever before in the history of his craft . . . the day when a good designer is enough has passed.*" Editorial: "The 'New Architecture' and the New 'American Architect'," *Amer. Architect* 136 (Nov. 1929), 20–21. See also Michael A. Mikkelsen, "Editorial: Expansion of the Architectural Record for 1930," *Record* 66 (Nov. 1929), 501–02.

26. Howe, letter to Walter Creese, 28 June 1946.

27. Fuller, "Universal Architecture," *Shelter* 2 (May 1932), 33–42.

That Howe was not interested in vituperative, innuendo-laden criticism has been illustrated in his debate with Wright. But in that skirmish the issue had been one of architectural interpretation. Here the issue was deeper: architecture itself seemed at stake. Caught in the embarrassing situation of being associate editor and almost sole financial supporter of a magazine whose editorial policy was completely at odds with his personal philosophy, Howe withdrew his support from *Shelter* in an exchange of letters with Levinson and Fuller which brought the issues of architecture versus technology sharply into focus in an influential and widely circulated journal.[28]

In a letter to Levinson dated 13 July 1932, Howe wrote, "However interested I am in the potential good to be extracted from a mechanical civilization, I am at the present time so strongly opposed to the extension of the mechanical principle that I should prefer to have my name removed from *Shelter* as associate editor." Stating his preference for the ideals of *Erewhon,* he asserted that "aesthetics and social reform have in my mind nothing to do with each other. As a designer it is a matter of indifference to me whether the mechanical civilization be moral or immoral. If, on the other hand, you ask me to join a movement of social reform, then, I say the mechanical civilization is spinach." Again we see how deeply rooted this American pioneer designer was in the aesthetic tradition of the past; his was the voice of an architect-designer who traditionally sought to *give* architectural form to the best thought of his time, not merely to reflect this thought. The commitment was to architecture primarily; to the times, only secondarily.

Fuller had stated his position as a search for "new form—not re-form." Writing to Howe on 1 August 1932, he expressed regret over the former's departure "inasmuch as this was much more your venture than mine." Citing the magnitude of social, economic, and political changes, he became almost desperate in tone, relating the successive desertions of colleagues and supporters he had suffered.

Howe replied on 29 August 1932. He stated his conviction that the "mechanistic principle is self-destructive" and that as a "humble artisan . . . I take man's social and economic vagaries as my subject matter and depict them architecturally, implying neither praise nor blame, as a writer may take lust, rapacity, homicide or any other human failing without constituting himself its advocate or judge. I do not choose, on the other hand, in my capacity as a private citizen to promote the practise of what seems to me to be mechanistic vices, though in my public capacity—as an architect—I find it amusing to

28. The exchange can be found in *Shelter* 2 (Nov. 1932), esp. 125–28.

portray them." One may note the word "amusing." It was this somewhat detached position of aristocratic aloofness that made Howe's commentaries on architectural enthusiasm so valuable, so eminently sensible, and, at the same time, so self-undercut. Howe was not an enthusiast. Rather he was a man confronted by a world bent on a particular course, a mechanically oriented civilization. But his own commitment was to life, to civilization, to architecture, and not to the times. The times for him were merely one of the many tools which made up architecture; they did not dictate, they contributed.

Howe at this period submitted for publication in *Shelter* some thesis drawings done by students at the Princeton University School of Architecture. These were rejected by Levinson, then at the zenith of his enthusiasm for Fuller. This action was explained by Fuller in a letter to Howe dated 6 September 1932, in which he stated that *Shelter*'s policy in the immediate future would be "confined to the publication of only the most scientific rendition of structure; with not the slightest regard for theories of aesthetics."[29]

Lest all this sound like a tempest in a teapot, it should be noted that *T-Square* and *Shelter* enjoyed enormous success and appeared to satisfy a deep-seated need among design professionals for articulate disclosure. In terms of circulation, the journals gave the so-called major publications a run for their money, although the amount of advertising, the real source of income, was negligible. Fuller's first act after taking over *T-Square* and renaming it was

> to notify all advertisers with which *T-Square* had continuing contracts that I was discontinuing all advertising as it called for deadline commitments. I did so because I was determined that the magazine would be published only when we had something we felt humanity needed to know and to publish only when we felt it was timely.
>
> *Fortune* magazine was inaugurated also in 1930 and sold for an unheard of price of one dollar. I notified subscribers that with each edition and increased popularity the subscription rate would be increased according to our needs. Some copies sold for as much as two dollars. It was amazing how swiftly subscriptions increased.[30]

29. Attacking Howe's faith in *Erewhon*, Fuller remarked that "a confusion as to essential relationship of 'mechanistic' to its emergent era exists in your mind . . . [which] is borne out by your citation of Butler's *Erewhon*, appropriately protesting the fatalistic presumption of causality and its closed-book aspect in Butler's day, which the scientific world has so relatively recently, and completely, dismissed from its cosmology." It is interesting to note that in 1927 Lewis Mumford wrote a rather desperate introduction to Butler's novel, fearing just such a boundless mechanistic world, a world of no human values such as Fuller seems to advocate as a reality.

30. Fuller, letter to Pommer, 5 June 1973.

The polemic extended itself beyond the printed word. Three events—the Rejected Architects show in April 1931, Howe and Lescaze's resignation from the Architectural League in February 1932, and the "Modern Architecture: International Exhibition" at the Museum of Modern Art in February 1932— marked a kind of turning point in the campaign for the acceptance of modern or, more precisely, International Style architecture in the United States.

The Rejected Architects show was a protest on the part of the young Internationalist architects against the important exhibitions of the Architectural League of New York. These were held, as a rule, in the cavernous gloom of the Grand Central Palace. The League's exhibition for 1931 was especially ambitious in conception because it was the fiftieth such show. The selection committee, "in its wisdom," as Philip Johnson has said,

> had refused a great many modern designs, had refused works by people who were well-known to all of us at the time, but were especially proteges of George Howe in Philadelphia. Actually, the PSFS was included in the exhibition, but so many were left out that George Howe and Bill Lescaze came to the defense of the younger, omitted men. It seems humorous now, but it was deadly serious at that time. . . . So angry did we get at this, that some of us, Alfred Barr of the Museum of Modern Art, and I, the Director-to-be of the Department of Architecture, set up an exhibition in a storefront on Sixth Avenue which we called 'Rejected Architects,' after the famous Salon des Refusés of Paris a hundred years ago. We showed men like Alfred Clauss and Oscar Stonorov, who are now such well-known Philadelphia architects, and we made a lot of noise by having sandwichmen parade up and down Lexington Avenue in front of the Grand Central Palace, to call attention to the unfairness of the League. The League was to us the Establishment that needed doing away with.[31]

31. Philip Johnson, speech at the annual meeting of the Architectural League of New York, 26 May 1965, printed in the League's *News Bulletin* (ca. Sept. 1965), pp. 1–4. In the full text of the speech, Johnson got his dates wrong—the League's exhibition was in April 1931, not 1930. Barr, also, confuses the dates in Russell Lynes, *Good Old Modern* (New York: Atheneum, 1973), p. 107, in this case postponing the event to 1933.

The "Rejected Architects" were Stonorov and Morgan, Hazen Size, William Muschenheim, Walter Baerman, Elroy Webber, and Richard Wood. (Alfred Claus's name does not appear in any of the publications concerning the show.) They issued a statement to the press justifying their action, asserting that "in 1931 a Salon des Refusés is still useful" and that the enemy was not so much the traditionalist architects as those "modernistic" architects "who have recently won popularity in America" and whose work they felt to be "capricious and illogical." Johnson also appears to have gotten the address wrong: the sandwich man's poster read, "See Really Modern Architecture, Rejected by the League, at 903 Seventh Avenue."

Time has mellowed Johnson's memory of the League's show. The exhibition techniques were a disgrace, and the reaction of the League was less jovial and timid than Johnson implies.[32] The League was more than angry; it was embarrassed. Ely Jacques Kahn stated to the press the day after the "Rejected Architects" opened their salon that "no models had been refused by the League because they were too modern. . . . The number of exhibits submitted was so much greater than we had anticipated that the Committee selected what they considered the best work."[33] Nonetheless, as Johnson pointed out at the time, although the League show "contained work as modern as that displayed in the Fifty-seventh Street Show, the official explanation smacks of the smug rejection slip."[34]

The League's selections were not so much reactionary as uninformed, obvious, and a trifle vulgar. PSFS and the first scheme for the Hessian Hills School were displayed, though not very prominently, and A. Lawrence Kocher and Albert Frey's full-scale project for an aluminum house was shown. But, as Douglas Haskell wrote, "fifty years, and the Architectural League has become a habit. How accustomed it all seems. Columns and gables, gables and columns, the pictures scattered higgledy-piggledy over the big walls; a few skyscrapers in between . . . and a couple of Dianas. . . . Then upstairs among the booths the man who wanted to sell an overhead garage door."[35]

32. The League officials were enraged by the picketing and a number of times attempted to have the sandwich man apprehended as he paraded up and down before the doors of the Grand Central Palace. See "Rejected," *Art Digest* 5 (1 May 1931), 16–17; Ralph Flint, "Architects Show Fine Work . . .," *Art News* 29 (25 April 1931), 3, 5.
Helen Appleton Reed noted in the Brooklyn *Eagle,* "The present exhibition definitely establishes one fact, the unfortunate absence of any sense of exhibition techniques and discipline—the more noticeable in the exhibition dedicated to architecture where sound structural principles are the ones involved." Quoted in *Art Digest* 5 (May 1931), 17. See also James Johnson Sweeney, "Around the Galleries," *Creative Art* 8 (June 1931), 445–47.
33. Quoted in "Rejected," p. 16.
34. Johnson, "Rejected Architects," *Creative Art* 8 (June 1931), 433–35.
35. Douglas Haskell, "The Column, the Gable and the Box," *The Arts* 17 (June 1931), pp. 636–39. Significantly, as Haskell points out, "Mr. Kocher's aluminum box . . . was sponsored not by the architectural committee but by a group of manufacturers and industrial contractors." And Philip Johnson remarks on "the [painful] disillusionment of one League Member" when he was finally convinced that Kocher's Aluminum House was actually a part of the Exhibition sponsored by the League." "Rejected Architects." See chap. 5, n. 38.
The award of the coveted Gold Medal to Shreve, Lamb and Harmon for their Empire State Building was not inappropriate. This edifice was accurately described by Haskell who saw it "caught at the exact moment of a transition—caught between metal and stone, between the ideal of 'monumental mass' and that of airy volume, between handicraft and machine design, and on the swing from what was essentially handicraft to what will be essentially industrial methods of fabrication. No building has been so basically progressive, or half so fascinating a problem." Douglas Haskell, "The Empire State Building," *Creative Art* 8 (April 1931), 242–44.

Johnson, who masterminded the succession of events, assessed their significance shortly afterwards in an article in which he claimed that "the public
found a new thrill in the Rejected Architects. Here was the chance to witness
an unusual fight. Not everyday does the orderly profession of architecture
dramatize itself in a blaze of controversy. The hullabaloo was initiated by the
critics who, bored with the external monotony of the League's offerings,
jumped at the chance to support a rival group. . . . So universal today is the
romantic love of youth in revolt, especially in the realm of art, that one by
one the other writers climbed on the 'Rejected Architects' bandwagon."

But he was quick to point out that

> [the] critics of both the Rejected Architects and the League Show have
> been uncritical. None considered the Salon des Refusés as representing a
> new style of architecture, ignoring the catalogue which listed the elements
> of the International Style. Not only have they not recognized the style
> but they have not even remarked on the chaos in contemporary build-
> ing. . . . So, a Salon des Refusés has once again served to announce a
> new departure. The International Style comes to New York. Of course,
> there have been pioneers. Mr. George Howe's courageous decision to
> leave a conventional practice to join with the young Lescaze; Lawrence
> Kocher's and Lönberg-Holm's impressive work on the *Architectural
> Record* have started the ball rolling. The trips of Norman Bel Geddes
> and Joseph Urban to Europe have made ribbon windows the mode, even
> if these men themselves have never fully understood the new architecture.
> But it remained for the Rejected Architects to give the International
> Style what might be called its first formal introduction to this country.[36]

All this was but a prelude to the events of February and March 1932. The
Museum of Modern Art opened its international exhibition of modern archi-

---

At least one critic was pleased with the League show. The redoubtable and reactionary Royal
Cortissoz of the New York *Herald Tribune,* wrote, "Perhaps the most significant thing about
the exhibition is the intimation it unmistakably conveys that the disciples of tradition are as
numerous as ever, proceeding happily about their tasks, all unconscious of the doom that the
modernistic propagandists pronounce over them as they dip into the historical styles." Quoted
in "The League," *Art Digest* 5 (1 May 1931), 17. But Helen Appleton Reed spoke for the
informed minority when she wrote in the Brooklyn *Eagle,* "The exhibition is an accurate cross
section of prevailing standards in American architecture—these irrelevant sentimental sculptures and reliefs, these cornices and false façades and dwelling houses which superimpose upon
their functionalistic interiors fitted with electric refrigerators and incinerators, any traditional
style which the owner happens to fancy." Quoted in ibid.

36. Johnson, "Rejected Achitects."

tecture in February 1932; Howe and Lescaze was one of the few American firms invited to exhibit.[37] PSFS, then nearing completion, was the principal modern work of architecture in the country, and, in terms of Alfred Barr's emphasis on the technology of skyscraper design as a uniquely American contribution to modern design, it represented the key work by American architects in the show. "The new skyscraper in Philadelphia by Howe and Lescaze," Barr wrote, "is a monument to the true persistence and artistic integrity of a firm which has only recently, after years of discouragement, persuaded clients, real estate brokers, and renting agents that the International Style may not be a commercial liability."[38] Hitchcock furthered the contention that in the work of Howe and Lescaze lay a positive direction toward the application

> with full regard for all our conditions, [of] the technical and the aesthetic ideas of modern architecture as they have been developed in the last decade in Europe. They are not nationalists nor are they importers. They recognize that since the nineteenth century, techniques and design have developed differently in America than in Europe. They aim to bring these developments together and to work as a firm of American architects respectful of, but not dominated by, the concepts of the rationalists and the functionalists. Theirs is the direction in which our better architecture may be expected to advance."[39]

The museum, inaugurating one of its most persistent informational ploys, held a symposium in connection with the exhibition on 19 February 1932. The proceedings and an accompanying editorial were published in *Shelter* in April 1932.[40] Much of what was said is not germane to our subject, though Raymond Hood's account of the evolution of his career is witty, wise, and an inter-

37. Although it was not publicly known at the time, the Trustees of the Museum of Modern Art demanded that "an exact balance be preserved between the number of American and foreign architects featured in the exhibition." Johnson got around this by dividing the exhibition into two parts. The first, dealing with the "extent of modern architecture," was quantitative in its approach. In this section work by the following architects was shown: Clauss and Daub; R. G. and William Cory; Frederick Kiesler; Kocher and Frey; Thompson and Churchill; and Oscar Stonorov (with Tucker and Howell). The second part was qualitative, devoted to the exhibition of individual architects. Five Americans were included: Frank Lloyd Wright, Raymond Hood, Howe and Lescaze, Richard Neutra, and the Bowman Brothers. See A. Conger Goodyear, *The Museum of Modern Art: The First Ten Years* (New York, 1943); Lewis Mumford, "The Sky Line. Organic Architecture," *The New Yorker*, 27 Feb. 1932, pp. 49–50.

38. Barr, "Foreword," in Alfred Barr, et al., *Modern Architecture: International Exhibition* (New York: Museum of Modern Art, 1932), p. 16.

39. Hitchcock, "Howe and Lescaze," p. 145.

40. "Symposium: The International Architecture Exhibition," *Shelter* 2 (April 1932), 3–9.

esting contrast to Howe's, whose own statement at the symposium seems more deeply felt. Perhaps giddy with a sense of the adventure of the occasion, and caught up in the earliest anticipations of a New Deal (Roosevelt had not yet taken office), Howe spoke out in stronger terms than ever before:

> Our cities change their aspect without sense or sequence or any real relation to the significance of our lives. New York, which looked for a long time like a solemn exhibition of mausoleum art, is now taking on the aspect of vernissage day at a competition for apprentice pastry cooks. Those who have been responsible for these phenomena refuse to face the realities of existence. One of the most prominent group of the pastrycook school (whom Frank Lloyd Wright calls the Three Functioneers) said the other day in a public address that functional housing was bad because it made people tenement conscious. Such a judgment is pure nonsense. It is a pity, he says in effect, that people live in tenements when the country is so beautiful, but since they must, let us at least stand by our honored President and make an architectural pretense that they don't. Out of such muddle-headed thinking can come only soft and muddle-headed architecture, and beauty is . . . the child of order and intensity.[41]

The immediate impact of the museum's exhibition is difficult to measure. It was well attended while on view in New York from 10 February to 23 March, and it traveled nationally, but coverage in the press was not extensive, although some interesting reviews did appear before the exhibition closed in New York.[42] What did catch the public fancy and emerge into a cause célèbre of even greater proportions than the Rejected Architects show was Howe's and Lescaze's decision to quit the Architectural League of New York. The League had mounted yet another of its mammoth exhibitions, tastelessly installed and belligerently mediocre. Howe and Lescaze had submitted three works, none of

---

41. Ibid.

42. Ralph Flint, in "A Conservative Spirit Rules in Architects Show," *Art News* 30 (5 March 1932), 5–6, reported that attendance at the museum's show was nearly twice that at the League's. Russell Lynes reports that 33,000 people saw the show, though he states that this was "not a large number, as attendance went for other shows at the Museum that season"; see *Good Old Modern*, p. 87. See also Flint, "Present Trends in Architecture in Fine Exhibit," *Art News* 13 (Feb. 1932); Catherine K. Bauer, "Exhibition of Modern Architecture," *Creative Art* 10 (March 1932), 201–06. More extensive evaluations did not appear until later. See, e.g., "Architecture Chronicle. International Architectural Style," *Hound & Horn* 5 (April-June 1932), 452–60; John Wheelwright, "The Grand Manner in Contemporary Lintel Construction," *Hound & Horn* 5 (July-Sept. 1932), 702–08.

which was accepted for display. They were a project for a skyscraper in New York, a project for a house for Arthur Peck at Paoli, Pennsylvania, and a house subsequently built for William Burnlee Curry, the former headmaster of the Oak Lane School. Miffed, and assuming that the League's rejection of their work was a gesture of retaliation for their participation in the previous year's Rejected Architects show, Howe and Lescaze decided to make the most of the situation. The League's action, Philip Johnson recalls, was just the opportunity they had been waiting for to "strike a blow for progress against reaction."[43] Howe resigned from the League on 25 February 1932, Lescaze two days later. Because PSFS was the principal ornament to the American section of the International Exhibition, the Museum of Modern Art hired the noted publicist Edward L. Bernays, who succeeded in having the event reported on the front page of the *New York Times* on Sunday, 28 February 1932, and the item received wide coverage in other American cities as well as abroad. Howe and Lescaze received scores of congratulating messages. Lescaze's statement to the press was bold and idealistic: "We stand for clarification of architectural principle. We are perfectly willing to fight alone rather than make compromises with the crowd. The issue is too serious to be treated lightly. An architect must be able to practice his profession according to his individual convictions rather than the convictions of the group."[44]

The League was completely unprepared for this high-powered attack. Its president, Julian Clarence Levi, replied on Monday: "As I understand it, there are two reasons why Mr. Howe and Mr. Lescaze resigned, the first being that the rejection of their exhibits proved that the League was not in sympathy with their artistic principles and, secondly, that if these artistic principles were at variance with the League's principles membership in the League became inadvisable." Levi went on to say that the League, because its "membership comprises many schools of thought," does not interfere with the "artistic principles of its members" and that Howe and Lescaze's work was rejected along with about sixty percent of the material sent in.[45]

On 20 March 1932, Howe, exploiting the polemical possibilities of the occa-

43. Johnson, speech, Architectural League, 26 May 1965.

44. Lescaze, quoted in *New York Times,* 28 Feb. 1932, pp. 1, 22.

45. "Denies League Curbed Architects Who Quit," *New York Times,* 1 March 1932, p. 43. A typical reaction to Howe's resignation, symptomatic of the general state of confusion prevailing in the profession, was Henry Saylor's, who wrote, "the [League's] show this year, and for some years past, has contained work no less radical [than Howe and Lescaze's]. The League, as a matter of fact, has a hard time these days, what with the resignation of the extreme left wing members and the extreme right wing members, many of whom are fully convinced that the League has abandoned everything worthwhile in life and made itself unsuitable for the presence of these gentlemen." "The Editor's Diary," *Architecture* (New York) 65 (May 1932), 291.

sion, made the following statement about the League's jury: "They are false modernists of the most dangerous kind, mere opportunists and fashion mongers, who have made the modern movement a sort of circus sideshow of their own wares. The League's shows are completely lacking in architectural interest. They are in reality largely trade exhibits and the League takes no attitude at all toward architecture in theory."[46]

Howe recalled,

> the embarrassment of the League was intense. They sent emissaries to beg us to withdraw our resignations and call off our pickets. Needless to say, we stood firm on our resolution to mortify them to the limit of endurance.
>
> This was a valuable experience and a complete answer to Hillaire Belloc's sardonic moral, "Decisive action in the hour of need/Devotes the hero but does not succeed." At the same time I learned another lesson. After this evidence of the news value of resignations I decided to resign from everything to protest against everything. No one paid the least attention. Moral: Never attack except from prepared positions.
>
> Of course I could not but realize that the League had slapped my wrist because they considered me an unfaithful Romantic, an opportunist, and a renegade.[47]

Regrettably, little of immediate consequence came of all of this. The realities of economic depression, affecting architecture more directly than probably any other profession, made even the most rigorous functionalist line sound suspiciously fey. Johnson quit the Museum of Modern Art in 1934, entering a strange political and journalistic career and not returning to architecture until 1940;[48] Hitchcock concentrated on his career in the universities; and Howe and Lescaze, within two years, terminated their partnership and went their separate ways.

---

46. Howe quoted in Philadelphia *Public Ledger,* 30 March 1932. Hitchcock wrote that the exclusion of the work of Howe and Lescaze "is a symbol that the League as a barometer of American architecture has ceased altogether to give correct or even intelligible readings," "Architecture," *Arts Weekly* 1 (11 March 1932), 12–13. See also Harold Steiner, "The Architectural League," idem., 18 March 1932, p. 27; "Architectural Tiff," *Art Digest* 6 (15 March 1932), 13; Mumford, "The Sky Line. Organic Architecture."

47. Howe, "Some Experiences and Observations of an Elderly Architect," *Perspecta* 2 (1953), 2–5.

48. For discussions of Johnson's political career in the 1930s, see Arthur M. Schlesinger, Jr., *The Age of Roosevelt,* 3 vols. (Boston: Houghton Mifflin, 1960), 3:72, 630; William L. Shirer, *Berlin Diary* (New York: Knopf, 1941), p. 213; Lynes, *Good Old Modern,* pp. 92–93. See also Johnson's "Architecture in the Third Reich," *Hound & Horn* 7 (Dec. 1933), 137–39.

7. Toward a Modern American Architecture

The arts, literary, plastic, musical, reveal two facts: the enormous energy of American life does not infuse them, and the American traditions do not inform them. . . . We stand between two worlds, one of which cast us off so that it is no longer ours; the other of which is yet unborn so that it, too, although within us, is outside our control.

Waldo Frank, *Rediscovery of America*

The story of the breakup of the partnership between Howe and Lescaze is an unpleasant one even as these things go. To begin with, the collaboration had never been of the most intimate kind. The partners differed in age, personal style, and interests; throughout the firm's existence they maintained separate offices, Lescaze in New York, Howe in Philadelphia. By 1933 there was very little work for either of them. Howe's personal finances were at a low ebb, and Lescaze was earning his way as much through the proceeds of the Lescord shop, which he had established to market his and others' designs for decorative objects and furniture as through the practice of architecture itself.[1]

What existed from 1 December 1932 to 1 March 1935 was a corporation, Howe and Lescaze, Inc. Under this agreement, Howe became exclusive architect for the residences of William Stix Wasserman, at Whitemarsh, Pennsylvania, and Robert F. Welsh at Laverock, Pennsylvania. At the same time, all work done by Lescaze after 21 July 1933, under the name of Howe and Lescaze or under his own name, was the sole responsibility of Lescaze.

So it was that the partnership was retained as a legal fiction, it appears, as much to advance Lescaze's career as for any other reason. Howe claimed to want to retire from architecture; he closed his office in Philadelphia, though he listed his home as an office address on the Howe and Lescaze stationery. And, if he believed in the merits of a project Lescaze was interested in, he was will-

---

1. That the partnership was rumored to have already broken up is confirmed in a letter from Howe to Aymar Embury II, dated 20 Aug. 1934, concerning the possibility of work at the Brooklyn Museum. The letter is interesting as an early example of the struggle between public officialdom, with its traditionalist architectural preferences, and the growing ranks of so-called modernist architects, usually of a younger generation.

ing to lend the prestige of his name as well as to put in appearances at parties and meetings.

This arrangement, which may have been promising on paper, did not work out well in practice. Howe was concerned about lending his name to projects he did not support, in particular a housing development in Philadelphia for which Lescaze wished to become architect. As Howe wrote to Lescaze on 29 October 1934,

> You told me that your interest in the undertaking would depend on how much interest I took in it . . . I have, however, reconsidered. Not only do I feel lukewarm about the government housing program—I feel violently antagonistic. Under the circumstances my advocacy would be ineffective, if not possibly detrimental, for it is impossible to act contrary to one's convictions without letting some indication appear in one's acts and works, even consciously. . . . [It must be] impossible when, as in our case, both members of the firm are known to the outside world as designers and each one, without any will on his part, has a following of vociferous partisans. Whether all the work is done in the New York office or not, I shall be unable to avoid situations like Wasserman where a client comes to me and asks me personally to design a house for him [see below]. His obvious purpose in asking me to do this being to obtain something else than he would obtain from you, the finished result would necessarily differ from your work and raise the question of individual authorship.

Howe, it seems, just wanted out. He was not certain what his future course of action would be, but he assured Lescaze that he was "not prepared . . . to abandon the status of architect at the present time."

Howe's decision no doubt came as a blow to Lescaze. In a letter, now missing, he apparently wrote Howe that he wanted all work done between 1929 and 1934 to remain credited to Howe and Lescaze, independent of the actualities of the commissions. Howe, although he agreed "in theory" in a letter of 5 November 1934, felt that "in practice" such a fiction "was impossible to maintain." Apparently Lescaze had made a suggestion about the attribution of the Welsh House, according to Howe "avowedly not much to boast of," which would leave Howe as its architect of record while, presumably, the Wasserman House, a major piece of work, would be credited to Howe and Lescaze.

Lescaze countered with a brief and bitter reply dated 13 November 1934:

> All right, George, if you must break completely, good luck be with you always. But that is no reason for us not to behave like well-bred

human beings. If you will not be in town to discuss our announcement, make a draft of what you would suggest and send it to me for my opinion.

You really do not know how much I hope you find a way out for you.

A letter from Howe to Lescaze of 3 December 1934 makes clear how much Lescaze felt he needed Howe's name to support his career and how unwilling Howe was to misrepresent his actual participation in the firm. In referring to an accounting irregularity, which became "the basis of my present stand," Howe concluded:

Small as it is, I regret that I cannot take it lightly. Even if I accept your explanation, in regard to the money question, that your chartered accountant would automatically have credited my accountant with the money due me, the fact remains that you concealed from me, not by oversight or silence—but by a deliberately misleading statement in writing—a transaction in which my responsibility was involved and of which you knew I would disapprove. You did no wrong to Purdy & Henderson, I know that you disagree with me in my attitude about such things, but even so I cannot admit the right of one partner without further consultation, to substitute his judgment for the other's in a joint transaction, and to act contrary to the other's wishes, immediately after implicitly, if not explicitly, agreeing to follow a certain course. We have had open disagreements about financial questions before, but concealment under any circumstances, even if intended to be only temporary, is indefensible, and is sufficient evidence to me that there can be no "meeting of the minds," and therefore no satisfactory business relation between us.

I am sorry that the ship of a staunch and adventurous crew should break on so small a reef. Unfortunately this tiny projecting peak is the summit of a mountain of possible misunderstanding which may be exposed at any time by wind and tide.

I wish you and Mary all happiness and good fortune. May you build innumerable monuments to the glory of modern architecture.

I shall have a form of agreement terminating our association, as well as a release for each of us from financial responsibility for the other's work, drawn up for you to submit to Mr. Isaac for suggestions or approval. I know you will agree with the feeling I have expressed that our present anomalous position must be clarified at once, and see that if any situation arises requiring either of us to speak of our prospective separation he must be at liberty to do so.

By 1 March 1935 the partnership of Howe and Lescaze as well as the firm of Howe and Lescaze, Inc., had been dissolved.[2] Howe's career lacked direction. An elaborately conceived partnership with Norman Bel Geddes rapidly aborted when it turned out that Howe was legally unable to become a partner of Geddes, who was not a licensed architect. His reasons for joining Geddes remain unclear, but it is possible to surmise that his concern with the forces that shape design led him to feel that industrial designers, with their eyes cast in the directions of both the marketplace and aesthetics, were going to play an increasingly important role in the future.

Geddes was the most spectacular of this new breed of industrial designers, having, in fact, invented the term in 1927. His career began in the theater and its razzle dazzle never left him in anything he set out to do. In 1929 he designed a series of display windows for the Franklin Simon department store in New York which are said to have stopped traffic on Fifth Avenue, and, along with Frederick Kiesler's displays of the same year for Saks and Company, immediately revolutionized display techniques across the country.[3] His book of 1932, *Horizons,* was as dramatic and flashy a prophecy of the commercial architectural expression of the new age as, ironically enough, Hugh Ferriss's book, *The Metropolis of Tomorrow* (1929), had been a re-cap of the old. *Horizons* was tremendously influential; the dynamic drawings of sleek form on its pages established the acceptable form for modernity during the thirties while the text made "streamlining" a household word.[4]

Geddes, who often seemed a popular counterpart of Buckminster Fuller, substituted for the engineer's brilliant verbal and technical skills, showmanship and an unforgettable drawing style; instead of Fuller's compulsive intellect, he offered a remarkable sense of design—an ability to capture the public's fancy with beguiling images of a fantastic world just beyond tomorrow.[5] Fuller's passionate belief in utilitarian functionalism led him to try to give the American people just what he thought they needed; Bel Geddes's unbounded imagination offered them, in a time of economic privation, a vision of what they craved.

2. Lescaze continued to practice on his own until his death in 1969. Among his better-known works are the Unity House retreat in the Pocono Mountains of Pennsylvania, and the Longfellow office building in Washington, D.C. Neither in any way approaches the diagrammatic clarity and formal rigor of PSFS. See Gilles Barbey, "William Lescaze: Sa carrière et son oeuvre de 1915–1939," *Werk* 58 (Aug. 1971), 559–63.

3. See Frederick J. Kiesler, *Contemporary Art Applied to the Store and its Display* (New York: Brentano's, 1930), p. 134; "Shop Window Displays," *Record* 68 (Sept. 1930), 215–19.

4. Norman Bel Geddes, *Horizons* (Boston: Little, Brown, 1932). See also Douglas Haskell's review, "A 'Stylist's' Prospectus," *Creative Art* 12 (Feb. 1933), 126–33.

5. See "City 1960," *Forum* 67 (July 1937), 57–62.

Howe entered into partnership with Geddes in June 1935.[6] Their ideals were lofty though tinged with that commercialism and flagrant disregard for practicality that always underlay Geddes's projects. According to *Architectural Record,* the partners intended to "provide domestic or commercial building owners with a broad survey of mechanical and architectural trends for their own consideration and use."[7] Every aspect of design was within their scope— from set design through merchandising display, railway equipment, landscape, illumination, and even architecture.

Since Geddes was not a licensed architect and his ability for spending money was well known and of rather little use in getting clients, Howe's role in the partnership was probably to have been a diplomatic one; his air of eminent respectability was to counterbalance Geddes's reputation for flamboyance. In any case, things did not work out satisfactorily and Howe returned to Philadelphia and reopened his small office with Louis McAllister and Earle W. Bolton, Jr., his trusted lieutenants in this period, as associates.[8]

Howe's first major work after the dissolution of his partnership with Lescaze, but within the time-frame of Howe and Lescaze, Inc., was Square Shadows, the house he designed for William Stix Wasserman. Before 1929, and quite likely even as early as 1927 or 1928, while still in partnership with Mellor and Meigs, Howe had prepared designs for what Wasserman described as "a typically Georgian mansion." This scheme, now lost, may have resembled that for the George Tyler House, previously discussed. According to Wasserman,

> Upon forming his partnership with Lescaze, [Howe] destroyed the original plans and presented me with an entirely new set of plans and drawings which almost completely reflected Lescaze's devotion to Le Corbusier. I was presented with a concrete structure which resembled a modern fac-

6. See "New Partnership: George Howe and Norman Bel Geddes," *Record* 78 (July 1935), 47; "Partnership," *Forum* 63 (July, 1935), supp. 13; "Old Friends Plan to Soar on Building Boom," *Newsweek,* 8 June 1935, p. 18. Interestingly enough, Geddes makes no mention of the partnership in his autobiography, *Miracle in the Evening* (New York: Doubleday, 1960). The partnership lasted long enough for Howe to send a prospectus to Franklin D. Roosevelt, with a personal note, dated 29 May 1935, which, though he addressed the President "Dear Franklin," he signed with his own name in full.

7. "New Partnership," p. 47.

8. Helen Howe West writes: "When it was established that Norman, while a brilliant designer, theatrical and commercial, wasn't a registered architect, this union was illegal and forthwith disbanded. However, I think this venture cost G. Howe in the neighborhood of $25,000." *George Howe, Architect* (Philadelphia: William Nunn, 1973), pp. 54–55.

Fig. 82. George Howe, portrait photograph at time of completion of PSFS.

Fig. 83. PSFS, rough preliminary sketch of the base of the final building, 2 Dec. 1929, sketch by Lescaze.

Fig. 84. PSFS, model of the design as presented July 1930.

Fig. 85. PSFS, 12th and Market Sts., ca. 1931, under construction.

Fig. 86. PSFS, diagonal view from Market St., showing north and east elevations.

Fig. 87. PSFS, wide-angle view of curved corner of banking room.

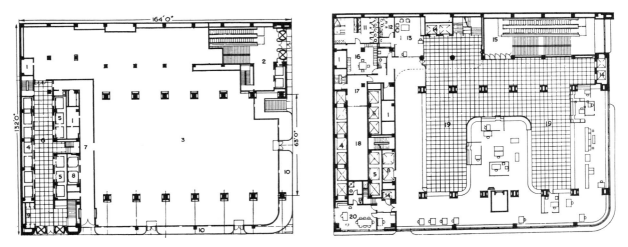

Fig. 88. PSFS, (a) plan of ground floor showing lobbies and commercial space and (b) plan of main banking hall on second floor.

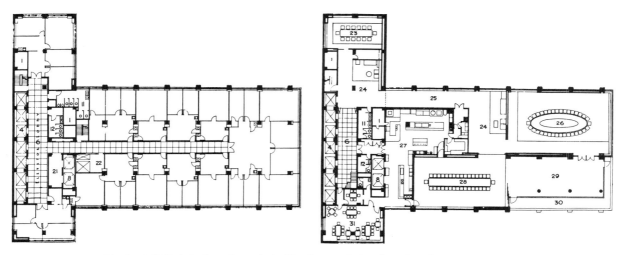

Fig. 89. PSFS, (a) plan of a typical office floor and (b) plan of rooftop executive suite.

Fig. 90. PSFS, entrance to banking hall.

Fig. 91. PSFS, banking hall, viewed from above.

Fig. 92. PSFS, banking hall, view toward balconies.

Fig. 93. PSFS, safety deposit boxes.

Fig. 94. PSFS, view toward vault.

Fig. 95. PSFS, clock.

Fig. 96. PSFS, solarium.

Fig. 97. PSFS, reception area with dining room beyond.

Fig. 98. Square Shadows, William Stix Wasserman House, Whitemarsh, Pa., 1932–34, presentation collage showing a model of scheme two (1929).

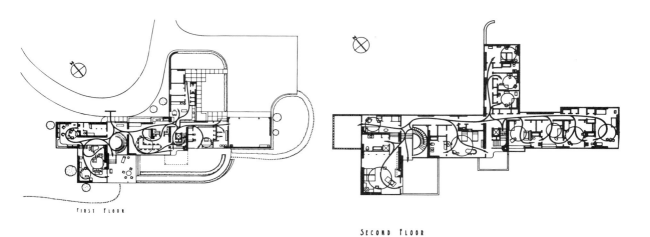

FIRST FLOOR

SECOND FLOOR

Fig. 99. Square Shadows, (a) and (b) plans showing spatial flow diagrams.

Fig. 100. Square Shadows, view of northwest elevation.

Fig. 101. Square Shadows, view from the west.

Fig. 102. Square Shadows, stairway.

Fig. 103. Square Shadows, living room.

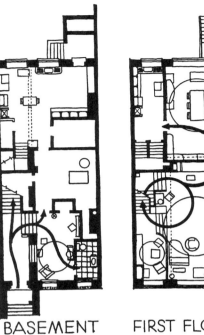 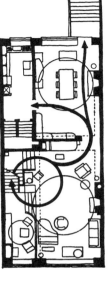 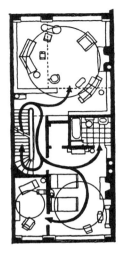 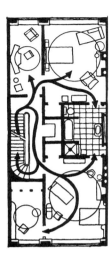

BASEMENT   FIRST FLOOR   SECOND FLOOR ,   THIRD FLOOR

Fig. 104. Maurice J. Speiser House,
Philadelphia, Pa., 1935,
plans showing spatial flow
diagrams.

Fig. 105. Speiser House.

tory. Some of the interiors replete with marble walls and stainless steel reminded me of a bank, while other rooms looked like a modern brothel, and some resembled what you would expect to find in a beauty parlor, such as that conducted by Elizabeth Arden. I remarked at the time that all that was needed to make the room complete was a series of chairs on which were attached hair drying apparatuses.[9]

The drawings for this scheme of 1929 reveal a highly complicated, fundamentally traditional, plan and a ponderous cubistic massing of elements which reflects an applied modernism (*fig. 98*). A pencil rendering by Lescaze, dated June 1929, shows the entrance side of the house and suggests, in an impressionistic way, a wide range of materials including concrete, horizontal wood siding, brick, and local stone. This concern for materials that were on the whole natural, solid, and weighty was in definite contradiction to accepted Machine Phase ideals.

In August 1930, after the project had been abandoned as a result of the stock market crash, Talbot Hamlin described the design as "an attempt to give a purely Le Corbusier abstract modern exterior to a conventional plan."[10] In 1932 Wasserman's interest in building a country house was renewed; but the original scheme by Lescaze was abandoned for reasons of cost, and Howe was retained to prepare new designs. Square Shadows is the first building he designed without a partner since the timid efforts of the difficult year 1928. It is his most original scheme and in many ways his most traditional. Paradoxically, today it is his least well known and least appreciated.[11]

The prophetic design of Square Shadows was based on the plan and massing of the 1929–30 scheme—which probably was Lescaze's contribution (*figs. 99–103*). In its sophisticated combination of brick, local stone, and reinforced concrete, it carries forward the confused suggestions of the 1929 scheme as well as those experiments in the expressive use of materials made at the Sinkler House—but without the gloss of Lescaze's Machine Phase vocabulary. Wasserman, inclined more than many potential clients toward experimentation,

9. Wasserman, letter to author, 8 Jan. 1974.

10. Talbot Hamlin, "Architecture," in Herbert Treadwell Wade, ed., *The New International Yearbook* (New York: Dodd, Mead, 1931). See also C. Adolph Glassgold, "House of William Stix Wasserman," *Forum* 53 (Aug. 1930), 227–30. A slightly different version of this proposal for the Wasserman House was published in A. I. A., Philadelphia Chapter, *Yearbook of the Annual Architectural Exhibition* (Philadelphia, 1929).

11. Square Shadows has been published in a significant manner only twice: "Square Shadows," *Forum* 62 (March 1935), 195–205; James Ford and Katherine Morrow Ford, *The Modern House in America* (New York: Architectural Book Publishing Co., 1940), pp. 61–62.

wanted a house that would be modern, but one that would have the gracious air of the traditional country houses for which Howe had long been known. Willing to do away with the overt historicism that had marked traditional house design, he was nevertheless not prepared to spend his days in a "cardboard box." It is said that he told his architect that he would not build a "white elephant" in the Whitemarsh Valley. So it was that from the first the solution lay in building a modern house using traditional materials.[12]

The plan is baronial in size. In it Howe applied to the new aesthetic of asymmetrical movement, which Siegfried Giedion was to call "flow," an attitude toward spatial composition that, though superficially quite different from most Beaux-Arts techniques, which were confined to static groupings, was in fundamental ways dependent on them.[13] Spaces are defined by walls, which are considered as planes of contact between them. Their length or the size of their openings measures the openness of the spatial relationships between the various rooms. Thus, as the pattern of movement drawn in the plans indicate, individual spaces, conceived in a static fashion, are related to each other dynamically. As Howe wrote, "The lines of human circulation in the plans are curvilinear axes of actual movement which replace the old rectangular axes of theoretical movement."[14]

The most interesting interior space at Square Shadows is the entrance hall. Concluding that the essential characteristic of such a room is a "sense of passing through," Howe envisioned it as a point of transition not only between the first and second floors but also between the indoors and the outdoors.[15] Using a

12. For a discussion of Wasserman's attitudes to Square Shadows, see "Off the Record," *Fortune* 12 (Oct. 1935), 34. Earle W. Bolton provides us with some insights, perhaps a little blurred and romanticized by time, into Howe's method: "Howe sketched the . . . Wasserman House . . . on yellow paper in ¹⁄₁₆ in. scale. He handed these sketches to Bolton and Louis McAllister, and left for Europe. The house was completed before his return." William Jordy, "PSFS: Its Development and Its Significance in Modern Architecture," *JSAH* 21 (May 1962), 47–83.
A rather more down-to-earth aspect of the working relations between client and architect is provided by Howe's letter of 14 Dec. 1934 to Wasserman. In this letter, which deals largely with problems related to fees, he wrote: "I want to tell you how courageous I think you were to build at all at a time like this, how much I enjoyed working with you and Marian, in spite or perhaps because of our little disagreements, which were after all only an expression of our joint efforts to achieve a satisfactory result, and what an extraordinary thing I know it to be for an architect to be allowed to express his ideas as completely as you allowed me to express mine."
13. See Siegfried Giedion, *Space, Time and Architecture,* 4th ed. (Cambridge, Mass.: Harvard, 1962), esp. pp. 594–95. Howe also used the phrase "flow," as in his discussion of the Speiser House (see n. 31 below.)
14. Howe, quoted in Ford and Ford, *Modern House,* p. 61.
15. Ibid.

flying semicircular stairway that comes in contact with the walls only once, he hoped to keep the spatial flow free and to convey a sense of walls extending beyond the stairs without interruption. The construction of the stairs was extremely complex: closed flush veneered railings form built-up bent girders which carry the entire load; treads and risers are cut between these and carry only themselves. This stairway was built in sections by connecting short turnbuckles on the inside of the carriages before the support was plastered.

The stairway and the entrance hall have never been photographed well. Pictures have always made the dark, solid railings seem out of keeping with the essential lightness of the form. Actually, the veneered surfaces are very sleek—streamlined, to use the vocabulary of the day—and enhance the sense of movement within the space. Howe was able to take the graceful spiral form associated with traditional country houses and apply it to a structural system so new as to be almost unique. (Only one other stair of this type was known to exist at the time of construction, that in Antonin Raymond's Kawasaki residence in Tokyo in 1933.)[16] Howe was always proud of the entrance hall, and there is little doubt that the warm teak wood, the sand-colored walls, and the light streaming through the Venetian blinds produce a rich, arresting, and modern, if somewhat glossy, statement.

The interiors generally display the same richness and imagination that characterized the executive floors at PSFS. Working closely with the decorator Jeanne de Lanux, Howe exercised great care in the selection of fine woods and marbles. The use of color is extremely subtle, although now and again sharp contrasts are employed. For example, the fireplace mantel in the living room combines travertine, ebony, and a rich blue. In the treatment of the room itself, muted colors, including sand, grayed robin's-egg blue, ebony, taupe, and sienna are all combined to provide an unusually harmonious effect.

But it is the exterior of Square Shadows with its wonderful scale and expressive use of materials that is most revolutionary. Expansive, with all load-bearing walls built of Chestnut Hill limestone in Howe's customary manner, it is grand without being in the slightest way pompous. Non-load-bearing walls, supported by steel or concrete lintels, are built of red brick laid in a bonding pattern which emphasizes their nonstructural character. Concrete floor slabs are extended to form hoods and balconies which, where necessary, are supported by tall steel pipe columns painted black and by concrete girders cast integrally with the slab. The massing of the house is complex yet direct and unforced. The organization of the plan—a long rectangle with two wings—is

16. See Siegfried Giedion, "The Status of Contemporary Architecture," *Record* 75 (May 1934), 378–79.

emphasized by the balconies and terraces. The chimneys and mechanical risers are pushed beyond the plane of the wall and made round in shape to enrich the composition.

The importance of Square Shadows lies in two directions: first, as a protest against the skin-deep formalism of the Machine Style; second, as the first important exploration on the part of a modern architect in America of the possibilities inherent in the materials rather than the forms of vernacular architecture, and, in particular, of the traditional masonry construction of the Philadelphia region.[17]

As a protest against the Machine Style, Square Shadows can be compared with the most elaborate house in that style then to be erected in this country: the house for Richard H. Mandel at Mount Kisco, New York, designed by Edward D. Stone in association with Donald Deskey.[18] Also of 1934, the Man-

17. Elizabeth Mock wrote that interest of "young intellectuals of the 'twenties" in the "peasant geometry of Aegean and Hopi villages as well as the perfect white cylinders of grain elevators" had shifted by the thirties to "a new interest in more specifically native folk architecture. Stimulated, perhaps, by Wright and Le Corbusier's experiments with natural materials in the de Mandrot House (1930–31) and the Swiss Dormitory at the Cité Universitaire in Paris (1932–33), Americans looked again at the stone and wood barns of Pennsylvania, the white clapboard walls of New England, the low, rambling ranch houses of the West, and found them good. They were not interested in the picturesque detail of these buildings, but in their straightforward use of material and their subtle adaptation to climate and topography." Mock cited as a "traditional example of the differentiated use of material" the Pennsylvania barn, choosing to illustrate her remarks with Charles Sheeler's well-known photograph of 1915, *Bucks County Barn.* Mock, *Built in U.S.A.* (New York: Museum of Modern Art, 1944), pp. 9–25. See also John McAndrew, ed., *Guide to Modern Architecture: Northeast States* (New York: Museum of Modern Art, 1940), esp. pp. 11, 13.

18. See "Residence of Richard Mandel," *Forum* 60 (March 1934), 185–86; "House of Richard H. Mandel, Mt. Kisco, New York," *Forum* 63 (Aug. 1935), 78–88. The Mandel House was likened to "a giant airplane [which] seems to partake of the openness of the landscape and the sky. Harmony is successfully accomplished with nature's setting by means of contrast rather than blending with the soil (as, for instance, in George Howe's 'Square Shadows')." Not surprisingly, the Mandel House and Square Shadows were published together in *Fortune;* see "The House that Works. I," *Fortune* 12 (Oct. 1935), 59ff. See also, in the same issue, p. 34, "Off the Record," for profiles of Wasserman and Mandel.

See also Edward D. Stone, *The Evolution of an Architect* (New York: Horizon, 1962), pp. 32, 42–45. Stone erroneously states that the Mandel House was "the first modern house in the East." It was actually preceded by a number of "modern" houses, including A. Lawrence Kocher's house for Rex Stout in Connecticut, designed with Gerhard Ziegler. See McAndrew, *Guide to Modern Architecture,* p. 20; "House of Rex Stout," *Record* 73 (April 1933), 288; *Record* 74 (July 1933), 45–49. For Kocher and Frey's Aluminaire House, see chap. 5, n. 38, and chap. 6, n. 35.

Most ambitious of the pre-Mandel "modern" houses to be built were Howe and Lescaze's Frederick V. Field House and Lescaze's own town house in New York. Stone also erroneously claims the first American use of glass block; the distinction belongs in all probability to Lescaze. Square Shadows should also be compared to Frederick Kiesler's Space House. See Kiesler, "Notes on Architecture. The Space House. Annotations at Random," *Hound & Horn* 7 (Jan.-March

del House demonstrates Stone's lack of interest in the rational expression of construction. Stone was merely typical of Machine Phase designers in his willingness to ignore the demands of his discontinuous concrete block structure in favor of an applied aesthetic of sleek continuous stuccoed surfaces painted white, whereas at Square Shadows Howe, acknowledging the facts of a complexly organized structure, sought to express them in a direct fashion, not to gloss over them. Stone's geometry is skin deep while Howe's is a reflection of the way the building is put together.

The blunt rectangularity and elegant fenestration of Square Shadows does bear comparison with Mies van der Rohe's brick country houses of the twenties and early thirties, especially the Herman Lange House of 1928 at Krefeld, Germany. But, although Mies respected every detail and calculated the construction of his buildings down to the last brick, in the Lange House he was only marginally concerned with the expressive potential of the building fabric, suggesting that the brick was a skin rather than a bearing wall.[19] Howe, like Mies, turned to natural materials as a result of the demands of his client, just as he and Lescaze were goaded into the expression of the verticals in PSFS by James Willcox. But, unlike Mies in the Lange House, Howe accepted this request with enthusiasm and produced a work at once indigenous to its locale and thoroughly modern, and one, in this sense, closer to the work of Hugo Häring. Square Shadows is the result of Howe's conscious intention to americanize the International Style. His early work in masonry and his understanding of the local Philadelphia vernacular with its tradition of "differentiated use of material" in construction stood him in good stead. His return to that vernacular was a manifesto in the movement away from the Machine Phase toward the Technology Phase, which had begun almost immediately upon the importation of the European movement to this country in 1927. Square Shadows is an important marker as a step toward the use of natural materials and the articulation of forms on the basis of the actual construction of the building (no more the "free facade") within the framework of the International Style. Stone, brick, concrete were all expressed frankly, and textured, massive, weighty

1934), 292–93. It should also be compared, along with Howe's Fortune Rock (discussed below), with Neutra's house for John Nicholas Brown. See Willy Boesiger, ed., *Richard Neutra, Buildings and Projects* (Zurich: Girsberger 1951), pp. 42–47.

19. It is interesting to compare Philip Johnson's two evaluations of the Lange House, written twenty-five years apart. In the first there is only reluctant acceptance while in the second there is a complete shift to an enthusiastic recognition of the house as a constructed object in brick. See "Ludwig Mies Van Der Rohe" in Alfred Barr et all, *Modern Architecture: International Exhibition* (New York: Museum of Modern Art, 1932), p. 174; *Mies Van Der Rohe* (New York: Museum of Modern Art, 1947) p. 35.

materials used in an acceptable modern context, thereby pointing the way to other architects, suggesting to them that wood and steel and other metals could be handled in a more complex manner than the vocabulary of the Machine Phase of that style had hitherto suggested.

Square Shadows was overlooked during the late 1930s and the 1940s as American architects, in their search for a useful vernacular tradition, restricted themselves to wood both for economic reasons and because of a lingering belief in the primacy of "lightness" in the canon of both phases of the International Style. But it was inevitable that architects should seek again the massive, permanent qualities of traditional building. Le Corbusier led the way. The frequently cited curving random masonry wall at the Swiss Pavilion and the de Mandrot House no doubt served as prototypes for the Wasserman House. But it was not until after World War II that Square Shadows found its proper descendant in his Jaoul Houses at Neuilly, where a comparable structural system combining brick bearing-walls and arched concrete floor slabs produces a composition of tremendous force, one which, even more than the Unité d'Habitation at Marseilles, serves notice on the inherent limitations within the canonical International Style. Le Corbusier's own integration of passionate romanticism and rigorous logic—an integration more complete and more intense than Howe's—at last seems to have brought to maturity that highly expressive way of building with simple materials first explored in 1923 by Häring at Garkau and developed by him in an apartment house in Berlin in a way that prefigures Square Shadows. In a fundamental sense, Howe's work had always been part of this movement which, for many architects today, appears to hold within it the possibility for an architecture at once modern, articulate, and linked to society and its traditions—a true vernacular.[20]

Square Shadows is fully air conditioned, and it is the first residence to use a high-velocity system for cooling. Enormous care was given to every detail of the interior in an effort not so much to deny the existence of the mechanical system but to prevent it from intruding on the house itself. In turning from

20. For the many critical attitudes toward the de Mandrot House—probably the most important exploration of vernacular techniques in the International Style to precede Square Shadows, see: Henry-Russell Hitchcock, in Barr et al., *Modern Architects,* p. 76; Lewis Mumford, "The Sky Line," *The New Yorker,* 9 Nov. 1935, pp. 66–70; *Mock, Built in U.S.A.,* p. 14. For the Jaoul Houses and Le Corbusier's postwar work in general, see Vincent Scully, *Modern Architecture* (New York: Braziller, 1961); Reyner Banham, *The New Brutalism* (London: Architectural Publishing Co., 1966). For Häring's apartment houses at Berlin, see Luigi Fillia, *La Nuova Architectura* (Turn, 1931), p. 230. Jürgen Joedicke, ed., *Hugo Häring* (Stuttgart: Kramer, 1965), pp. 110–13, contains Häring's Berlin apartment houses as well as a similar scheme for Charlottenburg.

the "symbolism" of the Machine Phase to the "realism" of the Technology Phase, Howe was quick to see new possibilities in a developed technology, but characteristically he never allowed himself to consider technology as more than a tool in architectural design. In contrast, Lescaze designed a house at Tuxedo Park, New York, in 1937 for Arthur Loomis as an effort largely to "verify certain air-conditioning theories."[21]

Howe realized that the mechanical miracles of our day were no longer news. By about 1935 it became clear that the machine as a romantic symbol, except in certain areas such as automobiles, was no longer (if, indeed, it has ever been) an issue.[22] The almost fetishistic brilliance of Philip Johnson's Machine Art exhibition of 1934 came as the high watermark of the period rather than as the clarion of a new age. For Americans, the machine was not regarded as an object to be revered but rather the opposite, a household object, an extension of everyday life. Indeed, throughout the thirties, Americans found it more difficult to understand the mechanolatry of European architects who to this

21. See "House for A. L. Loomis," *Forum* 71 (July 1939), 36–41; "Tuxedo Park House," *Architectural Review* 86 (Nov. 1939), 197–200; Ford and Ford, *Modern House,* pp. 71–73.

22. That the "machine age" had become an obsessive issue in American life in the late 1920s is nowhere more clearly stated than by the historian Charles A. Beard, in his introduction to the book he edited, *Toward Civilization* (New York: Longmans, Green, 1930). Beard wrote that "the battle over the meaning and course of machines grows apace, with resounding blows along the whole front. What appeared to be a few years ago a tempest in a teapot, a quarrel among mere 'literary persons,' has become a topic of major interest among hard-headed men of affairs. . . . No theme, not even religion, engages more attention among those who take thought about life as well as living." See also Ralph Flint, "The New Age and the New Man," in ibid.; Charles A. and Mary R. Beard, *America in Midpassage* (New York: Macmillan, 1939), pp. 762–75, 814–21.

The realization that the "engineered" work of architecture did not satisfy fundamental human needs, particularly in the area of domestic architecture, was clearly articulated as early as 1931 by Douglas Haskell in his "Utilitarian Design," *Creative Art* 9 (Dec. 1931), 375–79, and his "Is It Functional," *Creative Art* 10 (May 1932), 373–78. Perhaps the fullest statement of these issues in terms of house design is Joseph Hudnut's "The Post-Modern House," *Record* 97 (May 1945), 70–75, an elaborately annotated reprint of which was among Howe's papers. Howe quoted from it in his incomplete book, "Of Houses and Human Bondage." Hudnut, who as Dean of Harvard's Graduate School of Design in the late 1930s and 1940s, was responsible for bringing Gropius and Breuer to the United States, decried the distortion of the architecture of the 1920s into a "cold and uncompromising functionalism," the "excuse for an arid materialism wholly alien to its intention." He continued: "A 'fearless affirmation' of the functions of nutrition, dormition, education, procreation, and garbage disposal is quite as false a premise for design as that clatter of rambling roofs, huge chimneys, quaint dormers, that false symmetry of shuttered window and overdoor fanlight, which forms the more decorous disguise of Bronxville and Wellesley Hills. . . . When I think of all these elements, so varied, so impressible, so unhackeyed, which lie at our hand . . . I am astounded that architects should have need of a science to sustain their role in the life of our houses. . . . Our forfeit is that we must look (and think) like an engineer. We must have—God forgive us—an engineered house."

day still seem to regard the machine with special awe and still castigate Americans for not following suit.[23] By the middle thirties, the excitement of the Machine Age seemed over. In the 1920s, it may have been no more in actuality than a side issue, one of stylistic rather than social reform, a reaction to the superfluity forced on us all by a reckless prosperity. In the economically depressed thirties, those same intellectuals who had seen the machine in almost cult terms during the late twenties turned to other issues of a more pragmatic and social nature, leaving the machine age in the limbo of forgotten causes.[24] This, then, was accompanied by the shift of emphasis within the International Style from that of a machine formalism symbolically evoking the shapes of machines to a technological formalism, concerned with the expression of the way a building is built.

By the end of the decade, Howe and others were willing to go much further. In a radio interview in 1939 Howe said:

> I think everybody agrees that comfort and convenience are the essentials of a modern house, but there *is* something else, and . . . that something is style. . . . I feel that the modern style *is* in the best American tradition, the tradition we are building and have been building from earliest colonial days, the tradition of achievement and technical competence in the material field, the tradition of willingness to try any reasonable experiment to attain the better life in the spiritual field. . . . I feel that, in principle, the modern style house is tailored to modern man's exact measure, to his physical needs and mental requirements, and that any unpleasant wrinkles of stylized fashion . . . will be ironed out, given time and a sufficiently broad field of experiment. Tremendous progress has already been made in humanizing what has been called "the machine for living."[25]

Howe's feeling for the innate characteristics of materials, especially for the mass and weight of masonry, was built into his architectural personality. As a traditional architect, he had been content to compose the *parti,* then to give it romantic form with reference to geometric configurations evocative of the

---

23. See, e.g., Douglas Haskell, "Utilitarian Design," *Creative Art* 9 (Oct. 1931), 375–79.

24. See, e.g., Lewis Mumford, "Machine Art," *American Mercury* 3 (Sept. 1924), 77–80; and his contribution to "Fairs," *Forum* 65 (Sept. 1936), 170–91. See also Sheldon and Martha Cheney, *Art and the Machine* (New York: McGraw-Hill, 1936), esp. p. 173.

25. Howe, "The Modern House: The Architect's Point of View," preliminary draft script, 18 Dec. 1939, to be broadcast on radio as part of the CBS–Museum of Modern Art series, "What Does Modern Art Mean to You?".

past, and finally to build those configurations in a rational and expressive manner. At Square Shadows he abandoned half of his romanticism, the direct evocation of the past, in favor of the other half, a strong geometry based on the facts of a building as a constructed object. In so doing, he began at the beginning—going forward, reuniting the *parti* with the construction to yield form.[26]

In 1935 Howe remodeled a town house for Maurice J. Speiser in Philadelphia (*figs. 104, 105*). Lescaze, before the breakup of the firm, had remodeled for himself a house at 211 East Forty-Eighth Street in the Turtle Bay area of New York.[27] The contrast between these houses reveals to a great extent the differences between the two architects.

The Lescaze town house is characterized by an extremely elegant interior.[28] By virtue of its air conditioning, it is a sealed refuge against the city; by virtue of its design it turns its back on its immediate environment. The exterior is significant for the introduction to America of high-style architecture of glass brick—a material which, even more than concrete, came to symbolize modernism in the thirties. The facade is significant also, for its appalling assertiveness. The stuccoed house, painted white for maximum contrast, is just a little taller, just a little farther forward on the street and, because of the glass brick, when lit, more than a little brighter and showier than its neighbors. It is almost a kind of billboard for its architect and, alas, for its particular kind of modernism as well.[29]

26. It is very likely that Howe regarded the house a failure. Eleanor Madeira writes: "The house, however, does show the effects of Howe's absorption in commercial building during the years just previous [to Square Shadows], and the architect himself believes now that it has too much of the commercial atmosphere. Another of its faults is the flat roof which has not worked out because the air in the insulation under the roof condensed in time and caused many leaks." "George Howe," in West, *George Howe,* pp. 12–26.

27. See Lewis Mumford, "The Sky Line," *The New Yorker,* 15 Sept. 1934, pp. 99–101; "City House of William Lescaze," *Forum* 61 (Dec. 1934), 388–98; "City House of William Lescaze," *House and Garden* 66 (Dec. 1934), 31–33; "William Lescaze, Interior Architect," *The London Studio* 16 (Dec. 1938), 304–07; Herbert Williams, "The Home of an Uncompromising Modernist," *Arts and Decoration* 51 (April 1940), 5–7; "Casa Lescaze a New York," *Metron* 9 (1946), 44; Ada Louise Huxtable, *Four Walking Tours of Modern Architecture in New York* (New York: Doubleday, 1961), p. 49.

28. To appreciate the interior's restraint, one need only compare it with the gaucherie displayed at the exhibition of modern design held at the Metropolitan Museum of Art in 1934. See "Contemporary Quinquennial," *Forum* 61 (Dec. 1934), 408–20.

29. Lescaze reworked the scheme somewhat in two other houses he designed in New York. See "House for Mrs. R. C. Kramer," *Record* 81 (Feb. 1937), 30–36; and for the Edward A. Norman House, 125 East Seventieth Street, Mock, *Built in U.S.A.,* pp. 50–51. The influence of the Lescaze House may be seen in Morris B. Sanders's house of 1936 at 219 East Forty-ninth Street; see "House for Morris B. Sanders," *Forum* 64 (March 1936), 157–66.

Howe's design for the Speiser House stands out as an example of adjustment to an established urban context. In this most beautiful setting on Delancey Place just off Rittenhouse Square, Howe sought to recapture in modern terms the scale of the existing row houses. Although the fenestration is increased nearly one hundred percent over the existing prototype, the size of the panes in the new windows is deliberately kept small. The disposition of the openings is carefully adjusted to those of the neighboring houses. Similarly, the broad band of limestone serves to emphasize what is still the main living floor, despite the relocation of the entrance to street level. All projections from the facade were removed, but the cornice and the mansard roof, although radically altered, were kept to maintain the continuity of the row.

Inside, the plan is considerably open, given the narrow confines of the row house. Howe's description of the interior makes clear the new spatial synthesis which he was seeking and which, in part, he attained: "The most remarkable contribution to the amenities of everyday life is undoubtedly the new sense of space. This has been achieved by intelligent understanding of the relation between communications—such as halls, stairs and vestibules—and the spaces devoted to conversation, reading, eating and recreation." Although he went on to argue for an open plan in which "every space flows naturally into the next," he suggested that "openings, partitions, and furniture [be] so disposed that quiet and privacy can be found wherever it is needed, without the necessity of closing doors."[30]

At the Speiser House an old double sliding door between the living room and the dining room was replaced by a doorless opening at one side of the room. This was so planned that the setting and clearing of the dining room table and other services are at all times invisible to the occupants of the living room, while the sense of space is never interrupted by closed doors. Katherine Morrow Ford, probably basing her remarks on a statement of Howe's, wrote:

> By . . . simple devices of modern space design, a narrow, constricted and restless system of isolated cells has been converted into a continuous flowing space. Within this space are places for quiet tasks, and ornaments are so related to necessary lines of movement that the two never conflict. Rather, they work together to create an atmosphere of tranquility. It also allows full development of the modern technique of living, with its mechanical complexities, in a way that a traditional structure never does.[31]

30. Quoted in Katherine Morrow Ford, "An Old Town House Can Lead Itself to Modern Living," *Christian Science Monitor,* 23 July 1940, p. 6.
31. Ibid.

Throughout the thirties and forties Howe continued to develop his own variation on the notion of spatial flow. Building very little of real distinction except for some housing projects of the early 1940s (discussed in chapter eight) and Fortune Rock, he had few opportunities to implement his ideas. A number of statements remain, however, which indicate the direction of his thought. Finding the accepted categories of traditionalists versus modernists useless in the "post-revolutionary" period, Howe substituted two descriptions of his own coining, "internalists" and "externalists," which, in their references to architectural principles rather than styles, have considerable merit. The concern of the internalists, he wrote, is with "Space as Void, as Cosmic Emptiness, to which . . . [the architect] gives monumental purpose and meaning by the addition of an architectural expression." The concern of the externalists, on the other hand, is with the "moulded matter" that encloses space.[32]

In 1948, to an audience at Princeton, Howe made his most explicit statement in this regard. Speaking in a vein very much influenced by the teachings of Wright, who was in the audience, and making a reasonably explicit criticism of Corbusian attitudes, Howe said:

Since we find real space is now almost as flowing in fact as ideal space in imagination, we must of necessity give up old timeless ways of thinking about space. Flowing space can be neither enclosed nor excluded—not even limited, by thought or fact. It can only be directed. It is easy to understand, in the sense that they are variables, dependent on the values of current thought and action, and turn out to be, not objects to be looked at in the light, but aggregates of planes of references defining the movements, whether in or out or through, of certain portions of universal curvilinear space. To one who has looked at modern building in this way, all the traditional concepts of scale, proportion, facade, grouping, and so forth, become meaningless.[33]

In 1949, when Howe was a Resident Fellow at the American Academy in Rome, he renewed the acquaintance of Bruno Zevi, whom he had met occasionally in the previous two or three years.[34] Though he had recently returned

32. Howe, "Monuments, Memorials and Modern Design," *Magazine of Art* 37 (Oct. 1944), 202–07.

33. Howe, "Flowing Space: The Concept in Our Time," in Thomas H. Creighton, ed., *Building for Modern Man: A Symposium* (Princeton: Princeton, 1949), pp. 164–69.

34. Howe was the first Resident Fellow to be appointed in the revitalized program instituted by the Academy's new director, Laurance Roberts. He was also the first modernist architect to be installed in an official capacity in the once-sacred stamping ground of the American Beaux-Arts establishment.

from Harvard, Zevi, a young Italian architect, was quite critical of Le Corbusier and very much influenced by Frank Lloyd Wright.[34] At this time Howe
was anxious to test his new theories about the internal and the external against
the great buildings of the past, and, together with Zevi and American architectural students at the Academy, he explored the city and nearby sites with as
much enthusiasm as had marked his extensive travels forty years before, and
with far more wisdom. It is interesting to reflect on the degree to which Howe's
ideas may have influenced Zevi, whose book *Architecture as Space* is surely
one of the first important modern critical evaluations of traditional buildings
according to that special, and necessarily, post-Wrightian, criterion.[35]

With the exception of the Thomas House (Fortune Rock), Howe's work of
1935–39 is not very significant. In all likelihood this can be attributed as much
to the economic conditions of the period as to Howe's probable lack of interest
in architectural practice.[36] One house, that designed in 1937 for Isaac D. Levy
in Germantown, was, at the client's insistence, Georgian in style, though decidedly "modernized." The most complex commission of this lean period was
a remodeling of the headquarters of the Philadelphia *Evening Bulletin,* carried
out from 1936 to 1941 (*figs. 106, 107*). Howe employed black granite, plate
glass, and glass block to form a new base in striking juxtaposition to the
masonry-clad office building above. Inside are some interesting features, including a circular counter and desk arrangement devised for the classified ad
takers, and the circular copy desks in the newsrooms. Howe's refined sense for
detail can be seen throughout, even to the purpose-designed built-in fire ladders. But the project is most notable for its organizational implications: the
remodeling continued for five years without hindering the existing facility's
operations. Louis McAllister is credited with orchestrating this most complex
feat.[37]

In 1938 Howe entered the ill-fated Wheaton College arts center competition, sponsored jointly by the Museum of Modern Art and *Architectural*

35. Bruno Zevi, *Architecture as Space* trans. by Milton Gendel (New York: Horizon, 1957).
The American edition was edited by Joseph A. Barry of *House Beautiful* (see n. 65 below).

36. Helen Howe West refers to two minor projects which I have been unable to locate. One
is a remodeling for Richard W. Hale in Dover, Mass., and the other is an "embellished Hodgson
House in Maine." *George Howe*, p. 53.

37. The *Bulletin* remodeling was cited in the Pittsburgh Glass competition in 1938. The jury,
whose members included Lescaze, Raymond Loewy, Gardiner Dailey, and Albert Kahn, stated:
"From the point of view of the requirements of the problem, this is an effective dramatization
obtained in the combined use of different kinds of glass. Has the double function of giving light
by day and advertising by night." "Pittsburgh Glass Competition," *Forum* 70 (Jan. 1939), 37–54.

Forum. This was the first time that an established American institution of higher learning was willing to experiment with modern architecture outside of the classroom; for the first time, a competition was organized with the intent of producing a modern building.[38] The college selected certain architects and invited them to compete: Walter Gropius and Marcel Breuer, William Lescaze, Lyndon and Smith, and Richard Neutra. The winning schemes were given considerable attention in the press and the drawings were circulated nationally. The standard of judgment seemed to be a functional one; of the program's five "criteria," only one, concerning the "suitability of the building in size and character to a small college in a rural community," did not grow out of strictly utilitarian considerations. On that basis, one can hardly object to the award of first prize to the efficiently planned entry of Caleb Hornbostel and Richard Bennett. Neither it nor the handsome second-place entry of Gropius and Breuer continues to hold as much interest today as those of Eero Saarinen or Neutra.[39]

Howe, dividing the program into two separate buildings, produced a scheme that equals Neutra's for refinement and sophistication of structural expression. At first glance, one is impressed by his bold use of exposed roof trusses on the stage house, almost fifteen years in anticipation of Mies's design for Crown Hall at the Illinois Institute of Technology, while closer inspection reveals a skillful interplay between structure and fenestration. Nonetheless, the overall conception, partially because of the division into two buildings, seems somewhat hesitant. The scheme shared fifth position with those of Saarinen, Percival Goodman, and the firm of Lyndon and Smith.

In 1938 Howe, assisted by Oscar Stonorov and Cornelius Bogert, designed "Children's World," the children's amusement area for the World's Fair at Flushing Meadows, New York (*fig. 108*).[40] The program was a difficult one and Howe's solution is outstanding. The entire area was unified by a wooden boardwalk, along which a series of wooden shelters were built to give shade

38. The jury consisted of Walter Curt Behrendt, John Wellborn Root, Edward D. Stone, Roland A. Wank, Stanley R. McCandless, Esther Isabel Seaver, and John McAndrew. George Nelson was the professional adviser.

39. Saarinen's scheme predicts the more famous prizewinning design of 1939 for the Smithsonian Institution. Howe served on the jury for the Smithsonian competition, along with John A. Holabird, Henry R. Shepley, Walter Gropius, and Frederic A. Delano. See "Smithsonian Competition," *Forum* 70 (June 1939), 28 supp; Mock, *Built in U.S.A.*, pp. 44–45. Neutra's entry, an elegant one deriving much of its strength from its clear expression of structure and treatment of windows, also seems appropriate in scale and character.

40. Harassed by child guidance experts and countless other specialists, Cornelius Bogert produced a delightful, satiric list of "Required Reading" for designers of children's architecture,

and pattern. The rides and amusements, elegantly conceived without sacrificing the spirit of the occasion, constitute a mild spoof on the revered monuments of the past: a windmill, a baronial castle, Venice—complete with
gondola—the Roman Forum, Pisa; all were made to exist in a sophisticated
landscape traversed by a steam locomotive. On the other hand, certain rides
were treated almost as sacred found-objects. As Eleanor Madeira writes, "In
supervising the general tone of the Amusement Area, Howe shows good judgment, for no one but a carpenter designed the roller-coaster, no architect had
a hand in the bob-sled design, and so the fun-structures were kept down to the
simple and accepted traditional tastes of children who wouldn't and couldn't
enjoy a mechanized and futuristic adaption of their country fair amusements."[41]

The administration building for the Amusement Section, which bears
Stonorov's mark, was so neatly detailed that it intruded in no way on the
festive spirit of the place. A large sign—for which the only conceptual sketch
drawn by Howe remains—provides fitting punctuation to the project. All in
all, it is a delight, combining economy through the use of the then relatively
new plywood technology, great wit in the handling of signs and necessary outdoor furniture such as kiosks and ticket booths, and genuine humaneness in its
introduction of plywood "shutters" which, in addition to unifying the design
provide necessary closure after hours and shade to the walkways in the daytime. Unlike the majority of the buildings at the Fair, it seems what it should
be: light, festive, impermanent, and never honky-tonk.

Howe also contributed to the "America at Home" feature, a new addition to
the fair when it reopened in 1940. In addition to designing a room, he provided text and captions for the coverage given by *Architectural Forum* to the
entire display. "Modern living" exhibits of this kind, especially those at the
Metropolitan Museum of Art during the late 1920s and early 1930s, and those
at the World's Fair in New York in 1964, are usually suffused with a wholly
meretricious glamour. "America at Home" was only somewhat different. In-

---

which was among Howe's papers. The entries included: A. H. Van Keuren, F.A.H., *The Patho-
logical Approach to Exposition Architecture; Where Angels Fear to Tread: An Analysis of the
Children's World;* Frank W. Darling, M. E., S. OF ARCH., *Standard Amusement Park Practice—
The Rise and Fall of the Scenic Railway with Tables;* William Exton, Jr., *The Compendium of
Facts and Phrases—Everyman's Guide to Lubricatory Oratory;* George Howe, "Plastic Forms
Resulting from a Contemplation of the Child Mind," *Harper's Bazaar,* October 1938; Herbert
Spiegel, F.E.C., *A. S. T. M. Standard Specifications* (D-39802-C, Decibel Equivalents of the
Yodel; K-4983-M, Physical Properties of Geysers; X-2187-A, Factors in the Tintinabulation of
Temple Bells); A. C. Brady, *An Evaluation of the Child as a Potential Profit.*

41. Madeira, "George Howe," in West, *George Howe,* pp. 12–25.

stead of making an "appeal to cafe society," Howe wrote, it was designed by Shepard Vogelgesang to appeal to "the prosperous Sunday drivers seeking escape." Though the exhibition was for this reason "more realistic," it tended to "be rather remote from life" in its emphasis on "escape" rather than "participation."[42]

Howe's own contribution, a room in a "Pennsylvania Hill House," was little more than a backdrop for the unusual and highly organic wooden furniture of Wharton Esherick. Howe wrote that the "plan of the room is conceived by the architect as a setting for Mr. Esherick's spiral stair (which is taken bodily from his workshop) and furnishings rather than as a simulation of reality." Esherick's organic, curvilinear shapes and his ability to bring out the tensile qualities in wood result from "his personal sense of the direction of the grain and natural color value of the [material] . . . —every form is a surface determined by his feeling for the infinite variety of the sense of touch."[43]

Howe once told a group of students that "architecture, . . . though produced by man, resembles more a natural phenomenon than an artifact."[44] This would seem to be the case with what is, at this writing, probably Howe's best known house, the summer and weekend cottage called Fortune Rock, which he designed and built for Mrs. Clara Fargo Thomas at Somes Sound, Mount Desert Island, in 1937–39 (*figs. 109–20*). With two wings gracefully perched on the rocks and the main living space thrust out on giant cantilevers, Fortune Rock is both romantic and rational; its boldly proportioned simple rectangular masses with their pitched roofs seem quite at home in the rugged Maine landscape. Fortune Rock was, as Bruno Zevi wrote, Howe's "farewell to architecture and he put all his love in it. He indicated a road; he opened to rationalist language the direction indicated by Wright."[45] For a whole generation, this house was, after Wright's Falling Water, perhaps the most persuasive image of American domestic architecture. For the English architect Sir Charles

42. Howe, "New York World's Fair, 1940," *Forum* 73 (July 1940), 31–42. Howe's commentary is brief, in turn appreciative, scathing, mocking, but always well mannered. Often it tells less about the exhibit than about his own preferences, as when he deprecated the "mechanistic quality" of Muschenheim's "Parents' Retreat" or when he praised Gilbert Rhode's "Unit for Living," which, "though perhaps necessarily the least interesting of the designs as personal invention, probably presents the closest approach to the requirements of the industrial application of 'Design for Luxury' in America."

43. This virtuosity was brought into play again in a house in Chestnut Hill designed by Louis Kahn for Esherick's sister Margaret. Photographs of its exterior can be found in Vincent Scully, *Louis I. Kahn* (New York: Braziller, 1962).

44. Howe, "Architecture and 'Creative Evolution,'" *Perspecta* 2 (1953), 1.

45. Bruno Zevi, "George Howe, An Aristocratic Architect," *A.I.A. Journal* 24 (Oct. 1955), 176–78.

Reilly, it was a "Frank Lloyd Wrightish, Peter Pan kind of playhouse for those who want to enjoy the sun and air to the utmost," a house which seemed "to have caught the modern spirit of week-end adventure extraordinarily well."[46]

Fortune Rock was to have been part of a complex of three buildings intended to serve as a summer camp for Mrs. Thomas and her family. Preliminary drawings, dated January 1938, indicate a "Main House,"—insistently cross-axial in plan, comprising a kitchen, two servant's bedrooms, a coatroom, and dining and living rooms—which though less dramatic, predicts Fortune Rock in a general way. The second building was a dormitory of two equal wings set at right angles and half levels to each other, housing the young guests of Mrs. Thomas in small cubicles, with the long corridors containing desks and storage. The third building, a small cottage for the owner and her husband, consisted of a sitting room, bedroom, and bath.

Unfortunately, this ambitious project had to be abandoned for financial reasons. The program and design of the Main House underwent considerable transformation, emerging in the drawings of September 1938 as the final version which was built: the living room wing became two bedrooms, the servants' rooms gave way to the kitchen which in turn became the dining room, the coatroom became a changing room, and so on. The original, basically cross-axial organization was maintained. A long wing, parallel to the shore, contains dining and kitchen facilities at one end, sleeping quarters at the other. Between these, it is intersected by two small appendages, offset from each other, one containing the dressing rooms, the other a two-story-high hallway that contains a steeply pitched stairway which plunges dramatically past an intimate cave of seating into the forty-foot-long living room with its five-mile vista down the length of Somes Sound.

The house is sited at the water's edge on a rocky headland between two shaly beaches. The contours and native growth have been left undisturbed. The long, low horizontals of the main block of the house were designed, to "recall the broad surfaces of Somes Sound and to form a link between land and seascape. The overhang of the living room beyond the cliff accentuates the idea not only in aspect, but in giving the observer standing on the balcony the impression of being on the deck of a ship."[47]

Just as at PSFS, where the clients forced the adoption of the column-spandrel relationship that is the key organizing element of the design, so too

46. Sir Charles Reilly, "Some Contemporary American Building," *Architects' Yearbook* I (London: Elek, 1945), 120–31.
47. Madeira, "George Howe." As beautiful as Fortune Rock is, it is also a maddeningly ro-

at Fortune Rock the distinctive feature, the unusual double cantilever beams which support the living room wing, were reluctantly designed by the architect to satisfy Mrs. Thomas's vision of a room that would ride above the waters of Somes Sound at high tide, one which would project itself out over the land and into the enveloping panorama of sea and sky. The drawings of September 1938 indicate that Howe, with his Beaux-Arts sense of static shapes, had intended to support the living room on a tapered stone wall. This was in one sense correct—so far as Howe's training was concerned—for the dramatic thrust of the living room wing was to do more to enrage his academic contemporaries than any other feature of the house. (It inspired the eminently Beaux-Arts dean of the School of Fine Arts at Yale, Everett Meeks, to exclaim in a lecture: "This, gentlemen, is an example of the cantilever gone mad!") Indeed, the use of such large structural members in residential design is unusual. Wright made extensive use of the cantilever at Falling Water in 1936, but there is little structure visible because his concern for horizontal spatial continuity is made to triumph over an expression of vertical support. In addition, the cantilevered decks are simple extensions of the interior spaces, while at Fortune Rock it is the living room—indeed, the whole volume of this wing of the house—that is lifted above the void. There is also an echo here of Sullivan's more hesitant use of a similar device in the Bradley House of 1907 at Madison, Wisconsin.[48]

The forms and the materials both make Fortune Rock an authentic essay in regionalism. The house is almost entirely the product of Maine craftsmen; even the concrete cantilevers were made by a local bridge builder. The colors

---

mantic response to particulars of the summer climate in Maine. Madeira wrote that "it is amusing to note a few flaws of this house, because they are so expressive of Howe's personality and character. The high shallow fireplace that doesn't draw well dates back to his earliest houses, for he is oblivious to all complaints. Added to this is the lack of screens, on the theory that the south breeze keeps the mosquitoes away, and they hinder the view anyway. What a romanticist! Here is our functionalist carried away on Wagnerian wings." To this Howe replied: "Your kindly gibes at my romanticism I take in the spirit in which I believe they are meant. Actually, if you had ever heard me discuss realistically with my clients the necessity of choosing between romance (large windows, clear view, free movement of air, no fly-screens, no curtains, spiritual comfort, bodily discomfort) and practicality (small windows, shades, curtains, fly-screens, restricted passage of air, freedom from flies, mosquitoes, bodily comfort, spiritual extinction) you would realize that I am aware of the proportion of sense and nonsense in what I choose to issue for publication." Letter to Madeira, 10 July 1940, published in West, *George Howe*, pp. 26–27.

48. Bruno Zevi, *Storia dell'Architettura Moderna* (Turin: Einaudi, 1950), p. 490, suggests that Fortune Rock is a fusion of Wrightian and European developments. The discussion of spatial continuity in Wright's architecture is taken from Vincent Scully, *Frank Lloyd Wright* (New York: Braziller, 1959). For Sullivan's Bradley House, see Hugh Morrison, *Louis Sullivan* (New York: Peter Smith, 1952), pp. 204–05, pls. 67–68.

and textures also belong to the sea and to the Maine landscape: the granite foundations, oiled cedar clapboards, silver-gray shingles, and atmospheric painted gray-blue undersides of the eaves (extensions of the interior planked ceiling).

Fortune Rock exemplifies the best of the renewed interest in native building forms and construction techniques that, as we have seen, comprised an important part of American architecture during the late 1930s. Architects, reacting against the white cardboard forms of the Machine Phase, turned to the traditional material of American domestic architecture, wood. Seizing its simplest expression, the frame sheathed by clapboards or flush siding, they achieved surfaces yielding effects almost as precise as those attained in the Machine Phase and with almost as little intrinsic meaning. The simplicity of stressed skin construction and its variants eliminated the difficult aesthetic problems that come with skeleton construction and made for an easy marriage of natural materials and machined finishes. But the resulting forms were as skin deep as those stuccoed boxes against which the architects protested. Typical of this approach was the house at Wayland, Massachusetts, designed for Henry G. Chamberlain by Walter Gropius and Marcel Breuer in 1940. That there is no expression of how the forces are to be transmitted from these surfaces around the openings seems of little importance. That the stressed skin has so little to do with the nature of wood may be confirmed if one revisits such a house as this today—to find it warped, streaked with rain, the applied precision of its forms invalidated by the inherent traits of the material and the effects of time.[49]

Howe had already passed through this stage. As early as 1931 he had begun to experiment with traditional wood forms in designing a cottage for his former clients, Mr. and Mrs. H. F. C. Stikeman, to be erected at Senneville, near Montreal, Quebec (*fig. 121*). Though picturesque in such details as the gable profile, the Stikeman Cottage attests to the freshness of Howe's approach. Nonetheless, in its disregard for the inherent order of the construction, it is as superficial as the house at Wayland. Its configuration, however, inspired by the example of the earlier work of such Swiss modernists as Paul Artaria and predicting Gerrit Rietveld's wooden country houses in Holland at the end of the decade, holds within it the possibilities, if not for a true regionalism based on form, at least for a more logical use of wooden construction.[50]

At Fortune Rock Howe went beyond the work of Artaria and the Stikeman Cottage, his rationalism demanding a clear expression of the construction ac-

---

49. See Mock, Built in U.S.A., pp. 36–37.
50. See Theodore M. Brown, *The Work of G. Rietveld, Architect* (Cambridge, Mass.: M.I.T.,

cording to the requirements of the material. He devised a system of six-inch-
by-six-inch posts ten feet on centers defining bays and dictating the location of
windows. Lintels, placed above the ceiling plane, act as tie beams and, at the
same time, allow the ceilings to continue out flush to the edge of the eaves.
The combination of the abstract clarity of elemental shapes with sensitively
used natural materials makes Fortune Rock an altogether memorable house.
At once modern and American, it brings to the fore the whole question of
regionalism, which dominated American domestic architecture from the late
thirties to the early fifties. The renewed interest in natural materials led to an
interest in the characteristics of specific localities and finally in the local forms
which had been evolved. This concern produced a number of regional movements, the best of which could be found at the geographical extremities of the
continent where native American traditions are most self-consciously cultivated. In New England, Gropius and Breuer cast their vision toward Europe
for shapes and for the precisely machined surfaces that they had come to insist
upon as the true expression of modernity.[51] In so doing, they denied themselves the possibilities of a true regionalism. One needs only to compare Fortune Rock with Breuer's own house at Lincoln, Massachusetts, to sense the
tragedy of the Bauhaus architect in America. They lacked a sense for the solidity of materials, using stone and wood for their surface qualities alone. In
California, William Wilson Wurster's pragmatic informality was more promising. But the increasing Oriental influences in his work tended to lead to a
somewhat fallacious romanticism of wood construction and dominated his
very remarkable understanding of that material. Fortune Rock stands apart
from the work of these men. Comparable to it, however, is the house for
Weston Havens near Berkeley, California, designed by Harwell Hamilton
Harris in 1940, which, in its dramatic siting and bold use of inverted gables,
approaches the spirit of Howe's design.[52]

There is a haunting quality of loneliness about Fortune Rock which recalls
the paintings of Edward Hopper, especially his *Rooms by the Sea,* now in the
Yale University Art Gallery. In Hopper's painting, as at Fortune Rock, there
is a strong tension between the man made and the natural—the hard, clear
lines of the window frames and deep blue waters of the sound below. Here, on
the Maine seacoast, Howe, that lonely Harvard graduate, neither wholly Yankee, European, nor American, fulfilled his architectural search. Photographs

---

1958), figs. 141–45. For Artaria's work, see his *Ferian- und Landhaüser* (Zurich: Verlag für
Architektur, 1947).

   51. See Vincent Scully, "Doldrums in the Suburbs," *Perspecta* 9–10 (1965), 281–90.

   52. See "Hillside House for Weston Havens," *Forum* 79 (Sept. 1943), 77–87.

show him standing on the balcony looking back, we may imagine, toward Europe, from which he had learned so much. Here surely was the man-made complement to Thoreau's love of the Great Beach at Cape Cod, a place, he wrote, where "a man may stand and put all America behind him." For the second time, he had succeeded in dumping overboard the excess baggage of the past without losing sight of the lessons it had to teach. At Fortune Rock the interaction between his romanticism—the memory of the past expressed geometrically—and his rationalism—the action of the present expressed structurally—seem at last, twenty-five years after High Hollow, to have transcended the syncretism of Bergson and to have become a synthesis.[53]

In 1941 Howe designed a house for Mr. and Mrs. Beaumont Newhall, who had admired Fortune Rock and owned a small parcel of rolling hillside in Scarsdale, New York. Newhall was librarian at the Museum of Modern Art and was just then beginning his pioneering career as a historian of photography. The house was Howe's last design for a private dwelling. If asked to design a house in later years, he would say, "I will not design residences. Too difficult—Average house is hotel, restaurant, factory, utility plant and club house all in one ruinative package with a price limit on it. That's too tough."[54] Such was the case when his own daughter Helen and her husband set out to build a house in Chestnut Hill in 1948.

Looking back, Newhall has described his and his wife's attitude of mind in 1941 as that of "loyal, dedicated, Museum of Modern Art people," a bit shocked when their belief "in the gospel of the International Style" was confronted by the local zoning ordinance which did not permit flat roofs. Howe, on the other hand, "took it superbly in stride" and was "delighted" as well by

53. Howe, "Preface and 'Creative Evolution.'" *Perspecta* 2 (1953), 1. Vincent Scully writes in 1974: "It is inconceivable to me that when I came to write about the new Shingle Style [*The Shingle Style Today, or The Historian's Revenge* (New York: Braziller, 1974)], I omitted mention of this house, even though I had always discussed it in class, and you [Stern] and other young architects failed to catch the omission. But somehow—this house—despite considerable publication—doesn't seem ever really to have had much effect upon anybody. It was as if encapsulated in the curious limbo of its period—just as Howe in general has hitherto remained." Yet in his *American Architecture and Urbanism* (New York: Praeger, 1969), p. 178, his assessment of the Thomas House is exact. In the Thomas House, Scully wrote, "the flat roof and rendered stucco of the International Style were both abandoned in favor of forms no less sharply, even ironically, defined but more natural than those of the International Style to local techniques and conditions. It was a tautened Shingle Style. Here, rather than in Wright's wooden houses of the period, much of the domestic work in wood of the 1960s was prefigured."

54. Handwritten note found among Howe's papers.

the challenge of the Newhall's budget of $5,000 as well.[55] Indeed, all the restrictions seemed to fall in with his own growing concern for low-cost domestic construction. Together with Robert Montgomery Brown, he had already designed for *Life* magazine a prototypical low-cost house, a variation of which was later built in a Long Island suburb. Even the cost of Fortune Rock, except for the foundation work, had been only around $18,000.[56]

In the Newhall House, Howe developed the post-and-beam system first used at Fortune Rock, revealing it on the interior and making it more expressive in terms of the entire design. The house is square in plan. Two files of four-inch-by-four-inch posts, four feet on centers, carry paired three-inch-by-eight-inch joists. These posts form two bays flanking a larger central bay. Thus the structure frankly defines the major living space in the center, the flanking fireplace nook and stairway on one side, and the kitchen, dining and darkroom spaces on the other: once again, as in the Beaux-Arts training of his youth, simple geometric spaces defining distinct functional areas are given definition by structure.[57]

The Newhalls wanted floor-to-ceiling windows to take advantage of the view, but Howe insisted on sill-high windows and a "catwalk," which in its extension beyond the house begins to suggest a pinwheel and provides a proper visual base for the structure, covering the concrete foundation and enhancing the pavilionlike effect. The partitions were to have been made of standard four-by-eight-inch sheets of plywood fitted between and around the posts. As designed, these proved difficult and expensive to build, demanding a precision commanded by cabinetmakers and not carpenters. So, "reluctantly," the Newhalls and Howe parted ways and the house was never built.

The Newhall House, though by no means completely worked out, not only predicted the concern with modular construction which was to obsess architects in the late forties and early fifties but went beyond it. It is not a two-dimensional graph-paper distribution of elements but a regularized composition of

55. Beaumont Newhall, letter to author, 22 July 1963.

56. In a brief statement prepared in 1953 for *L'Architecture d'Aujourd'hui*, Howe claimed that "the cost of the house in 1939 was $18,000.00, of which $10,000 was spent on foundations. Reproduction cost, as of today, would probably be between $50,000 and 60,000." Unpublished information sheet.

57. As such, it may well predict Louis Kahn's Adler and De Vore house projects of the middle 1950s in which a similar *parti* is explored in masonry. Philip Johnson's Boissonas House at New Canaan, Ct., built in 1958, is probably derived in part from these experiments as well, though, interestingly enough, his neoclassic predilections prevent him from varying the bay sizes according to the spatial requirements. See Scully, *Louis I. Kahn.*

building components. Harwell Hamilton Harris's article of 1953, "Rhythmic Integration of Panel Elements," can be said to relate to this direction in Howe's thought, and his presence at Yale during Howe's tenure there as chairman of the Department of Architecture is undoubtedly related to Howe's continuing interest in modular proportioning systems.[58]

In 1953–54 Howe was entangled in a kind of footnote to his career of the 1930s. Elizabeth Gordon, the editor of *House Beautiful,* had just launched an attack on the International Style. Miss Gordon's campaign, which Howe labeled "xenophobic and McCarthyesque,"[59] and which is now almost forgotten, bears scrutiny on two levels: first, as a manifestation of the pervasive effect of McCarthyism even in that presumably resolutely nonpolitical period of American architecture; second, as a manifestation of the growing dissatisfaction with the forms of the International Style as the aesthetic vocabulary of modern architecture.

Gordon, who as early as 1947 had asked in an editorial, "Is Modern Architecture Mature?" delivered her major attack in April 1953 in an article, "The Threat to the Next America," and followed it up in October with "Does Design Have Social Significance?" In the latter editorial she implied that to the degree that American architects subscribed to the principles of the International Style, they were un-American and were giving aid to the cause of totalitarianism in the United States: "The International Style is an ideal of architecture for would-be dictators. It offers the physical structure for total control."[60] Thinking that she would find a sympathizer in Howe, whose longstanding concern for the americanization of European tendencies was well known and whose friendship with Frank Lloyd Wright—the hero of her campaign—was perhaps the closest of any architect's in the country, she wrote asking his opinion. His

58. Harwell Hamilton Harris, "Rhythmic Integration of Panel Elements," *Perspecta* 2 (1953), 36–44.

59. Howe, letter to Mrs. R. S. Christensen, a staff member of the 1954 Boston Arts Festival, 25 May 1954 (see below). A copy of the letter was sent to José Luis Sert, dean of Harvard's Graduate School of Design.

60. See in *House Beautiful:* "Is Modern Architecture Mature?," 88 (Feb. 1947), 59; "The Threat to the Next America," 95 (April 1953), 126–30, 250–51; "Does Design Have Social Significance?," 95 (Oct. 1953), 230, 313–15, 318. See also the reply of thirty West Coast architects, including the leading Bay Area practitioners William Wilson Wurster, Theodore Bernardi, and Donn Emmons, which criticizes Gordon's implications that International Style architects are "subversive" and "protests the evaluation of art works based on political criteria" and recognizes America's "healthy" artistic condition [while finding] "misleading and untrue" the "implication that all 'good' art has its roots in America and all that is European is subversive, perverted or sick." "Letter to the Editor," *House Beautiful* 95 (Oct. 1953), 312.

reply of 27 March 1953 must have been extremely disappointing to Gordon:

"Grandmother, what big teeth you have!"

Here they are, all in a shiny row: "It can't happen here" . . . "self-chosen *elite*" . . . "dictators" . . . "authority beyond themselves" . . . "mass hysteria" . . . "collapse of reason" . . . "social implications" . . . "regimentation" . . . "total control" . . . "self-confidence is shaken" . . . "mysticism of this small but influential clique" . . .

We (if you include me in the Less is More "Party") or they (if you do not) are pleased to learn that the nation trembles at the "Party's" frown. The "Party" had no idea it was doing so well. The "Party's" campaign to overthrow the Women's Government of Good Taste by force has been going on for a quarter of a century (you will find my first rabble-rousing speech in the recorded proceedings of the annual convention of the American Institute of Architects, 1932) but, as you yourself say (in italics), *"in the meantime the home-grown variety of modern design has developed slowly and steadily along sound functional lines for well over 60 years and is in a remarkably healthy and progressive state"*. Now that you have disclosed its true strength to the "Party" it will put an end to that *home-grown* nonsense in short order.

Until you disclosed the cheering facts I did not know how extensively the ideologies of our foreign agents, Mies, Gropius and Le Corbusier, had infiltrated the American consciousness. You mention, as belonging to the "Party" those guilty of "cantilevering things that don't need to be cantilevered". These cannot be Mies or Gropius, who prefer stilts. They must be the traitors F.Ll.W. (whom you mention regretfully elsewhere, along with "Maybeck, Greene and Greene and others" as having produced the "roots of our *good* (italics yours) modern architecture") and G. Howe, I fear, (who once designed a house described by the then Dean of the School of Fine Arts at Yale as an example of the "cantilever gone mad"). And who are they whose "chairs are meant more to be looked at than sat in"? You say "when they get 'practical' they design a molded chair . . ." The traitor Charles Eames is certainly one of these. Last (and worst), editors of "Trade Journals" and directors of "Avant-Garde Museums", have joined the "Party". To whom *can* you refer?

Of course such notorious doctrinaires and expatriates as Eliot and Hemingway have long since imposed the corrupt notion that Less is More on a decadent literary age.

In conclusion, I suggest that the Women's Government of Good Taste, in opposition to "Less is More", adopt as its slogan "More (advertising) is Less (art)". Hail, the Next America!

> Respectfully yours,
> George Howe
> Chairman
> [Department of Architecture,
> Yale University]

Howe was deeply hurt by Miss Gordon's interpretation of his work, although he covered his displeasure with courteous and characteristic good humor. Outwardly amused by her naïveté, he was shocked by the implications of her statements and by their power to do real harm. That she had chosen to read his experiments with local techniques and native forms as a rejection of modern architecture, or at least of the International Style, and not as a reinterpretation, naturally came as a blow; but that she would proceed to make absurd and harmful accusations about the loyalty and integrity of the leaders of the modern movement—whom he respected for their great contributions and whom he had come to regard as his friends, whose companionship and advice he had sought and whose respect he had earned—seemed beyond his ability to cope with, at least publicly. Privately, he made no effort to conceal his anger and disappointment. A mock and rather ribald "symposium" that he wrote for private distribution to friends indicates his truer feelings.[61]

---

61. Howe gave it the title "It Was a Great Symposium":

The Intruder had been informed that the Symposium was to be held that day at the residence of the Lady Editor. On arriving at the door the neat Maid who answered the bell informed him that the Editor was ailing but was receiving guests in Her Chamber. When the Intruder entered the Presence the Editor did not notice his arrival. She was lying in the middle of a modish Triple Bed talking loudly to the Chancellor of the College of Fellows, who was reclining at Her left side under the coverlet.

"What's the matter with Her?" whispered the Intruder to the Acolyte who was swinging a censer by the door.

"She's suffering from painful menstruation incident to the rise and fall of Her circulation," answered the Acolyte in a low voice.

"And is the Chancellor sick too?" inquired the Intruder.

"He's been subject to undulant xenophobia for years," said the Acolyte, "and has to keep his feet off the ground as much as possible."

"So what the hell are *you* doing here?" hissed the Intruder.

"I'm waiting to announce the Coming of the Saviour," murmured the Acolyte mildly.

During this exchange the Intruder had had time to identify several other Symposiacs to whom the Editor and the Chancellor were paying no attention. In a dark corner the avant-garde Director of Architectural Exhibitions and his friend the avant-garde Critic-Historian were throwing dark looks at the bed-ridden pair and murmuring dark words to the Promoters of Retail Sales, while the Observer of the Skyline was practicing Bird-Calls at the window.

Wright took up Gordon's cause with the inflammatory zeal so uniquely his own, producing a vitriolic pamphlet containing, among others, the following claims:

THE INTERNATIONAL STYLE IS NEITHER INTERNATIONAL NOR A STYLE. Internationalism is Totalitarianism.

Already totalitarianism has taken to the short cut. Become proliferous. It is now on the march in a procession called "Modern Architecture." Have these "Knights of the Cliché" ever really studied Architecture? No —nor do they even practice it. They have sold it ready made, over the counters of schools, museums and periodicals.

Organic or truly American architecture emerged as a new IDEA above the confusion of the sudden awakening of Architecture sixty years ago

---

But hardly had the Acolyte explained the reason for his presence to the Intruder when he began to swing his censer convulsively, exclaiming loudly, "He cometh! He cometh!" and indeed, at that moment, the Saviour floated into the chamber, crowned by His Pork Pie Halo and borne aloft on the Wings of His Inverness Cape with the Fur Collar, and settled down under the coverlet on the right side of the Editor away from the Chancellor.

"Is He sick too?" grated the Intruder to the Acolyte.

"Yes," whispered the Acolyte, blushing, "He's in love with the Editor."

As though in answer to the word Love a small man disguised as Cupid ran into the room carrying before him a little tray on which flickered three little Nightlights.

"Who the hell's *that*?" hissed the Intruder.

"That's the Dean," whispered the Acolyte politely, "and those Nightlights are the Three Lamps of Modern Architecture, which he is about to offer to the Saviour, the Editor, and the Chancellor."

"Be off, or I'll kick you downstairs" said the Saviour icily as the Dean offered Him the first Nightlight, and suiting action to word He extended from under the coverlet a neat English boot whose toe projected the Dean backward through the door with a satisfying clatter.

"My Love," said the Saviour, turning tenderly toward the Editor, "you speak with the Voice of God—Mine!" and at this *boutade* the Two smiled at one another knowingly, though the Chancellor was not amused. At that the American Mercury materialized from the air pungent with Editorial Femininity.

"If you will look in my Dictionary of Quotations," said Mercury with classic calm, "you will find an old German Proverb that says *No Bed is Big Enough for Three.*"

"*Less is More!*" screamed the Editor, "the Teutonic Threat is my very Chamber!"

'In my Dictionary of Quotations," resumed Mercury, "under the noun *Bedfellow,* you will find as reference, *see Misery, Politics, Poverty.*"

"No more Misery, no more Poverty, but how I love *Politics!*" cackled the Saviour, hugging the Editor leeringly.

"O, you wonderful Man God!" shrieked the Editor, burying Her face in the Saviour's fur collar.

"If you will look up the noun *Fur* in my Dictionary of Quotations," continued Mercury, "you will find that *The Fur That Warms a Monarch Warmed a Bear.*"

"He's a Teuton Communist!" roared the Chancellor, the Editor and the Saviour with one voice, and as Mercury flapped the wings on his heels in flight through the door the Three leapt out of bed to run after him in hot pursuit. The sound of their pelting feet diminished down the stair until it was swallowed by the bang of the Front Door.

and it now encounters the "tout and scramble" of this occupational pro-creation by the architectural type.[62]

Howe had intended his letter to be his only public contribution to the contro-versy, but Wright's pamphlet seemed to "require more serious consideration." So he told an audience at the Philadelphia Art Alliance:

> I have already pointed out that the Master denies to all men other than himself the privilege of self-determination. This is inevitable since he has declared himself God, even though the declaration that he is God was made with humorous intent. Yet at the same time he does not want the works of his children to be formed in the image of his own creation. Any consistent *style* of design is to him mere *fashion,* even though de-signed in imitation of his own work, and hence is repugnant to him. In fact he leaves no self. Controversy makes strange bedfellows. The Master of magazine *fashion* in branding totalitarian all who oppose the Master's and the Mistress's dictatorship, which is in fact no dictatorship, since its aim is to perpetuate chaos not to establish order.

But, though not yet great, there is definitely a twentieth-century style, one growing out of Wright's Unity Temple and the Prairie Houses and interpreted by the

> European architects in a more generalized form, which may be called "Social-Function-Technological architecture." This is the style Wright is attacking as "Internationalism," only because it has been transplanted to America. It took its present shape in Europe only after World War I, when economic pressure was intense. In the newly rich United States it was considered a "Poor Man's Style" and was despised as such. An im-perial traditionalism was the fashion of the day until the nineteen twen-

---

*   *   *   *

"Let's go have a drink," said the Intruder to the Acolyte, so they left the Director, the His-torian, and the Promoters still darkly whispering in a dark corner and the Observer still prac-ticing Bird Calls at the window.

*   *   *   *

"It was a Great Symposium," said the Acolyte after his third Martini.

62. Frank Lloyd Wright, "Frank Lloyd Wright Speaks Up," *House Beautiful* 95 (July 1953), 86–88, 90. See also "Perspectives," *Record* 113 (June 1953), 9, and in the same issue, p. 12, Wright's letter to the editor, dated Feb. 1953. Vincent Scully's article "Frank Lloyd Wright and the International Style," *Art News* 53 (March 1954), 32–35, took Wright to task; it was a conscious attempt to use history against McCarthyism. See also the ensuing discussion in *Art News* 53 (Sept. 1954), 49.

ties, when the "Moderne" style began to prevail. This in turn was replaced by the "International" or "Modern Style" in the nineteen thirties.

Now it must be admitted, in these fashion-conscious times, that *any* style is properly subject to suspicion as a mere sales device. So I must justify my faith in the "International" style, if that is the name you choose to give our mode of expression, of which, as a matter of fact, I am not a pure exponent.

My faith in this "International Style" is not based on its performance but on the direction it is following. It is, in my opinion, the only direction leading to the possibility of Henry James's "noble congruity." It does not accept Frank Lloyd Wright's individualist philosophy, which can lead only to the death of architecture coincident with the death of the man who produces it, especially if he is God. Architecture is a *collective art* requiring the collaboration of more than one man and his slaves to create a "Great Style." Fifty years ago certain great men asserted that architecture must be founded on a common understanding of an image of nature, of a philosophy and of a science. For their purpose they had to issue manifestoes. For their pains they were mocked as "weight-lifters with cardboard dumbbells." And indeed so they were. Architects alone cannot bear the weight of a "Great Style." To raise so mighty a structure they need the assistance of priests, philosophers and scientists. But these, as I have already quoted Alfred North Whitehead as saying, are not really interested. They are interested only in criticising the efforts of architects from the sidelines, including Frank Lloyd Wright's.

So I call on you, priests, philosophers and scientists, to formulate a unified concept of our world today to be the content of architecture. For a century and a half you have left architecture to be the sport of individualism and mass commercialism, deprived of a concept of a whole reality, however consciously conceived, of which it may be the symbol and the configuration.[63]

But Howe's involvement with "the Gorgon Gordon's hissing head" was not quite done. In 1954, he, Burnham Kelly, and José Luis Sert were appointed members of a committee to judge the architectural section of the Boston Arts Festival.[64] Because the organizing committee for the festival had neglected to

63. Howe, "Why Then?—Why Now?" speech delivered at the opening of the exhibition, "Philadelphia Architecture in the Nineteenth Century," Philadelphia Art Alliance, 15 May 1953.
64. "Boston Arts Festival Exhibit," *Record* 116 (July 1954), 10–12.

send invitations to every New England state, the average quality was low. Unaware that the sponsors of the festival "intended to give it a Grand Award with a blast of drums and trumpets," Howe later wrote to Thomas Creighton, the jury chose a simple, fundamentally traditional seaside house designed by George W. W. Brewster for Mr. and Mrs. J. Gordon Gibbs at Marion, Massachusetts. As a work of architecture, the Gibbs House is tautly elegant but of marginal intellectual interest.[65]

Elizabeth Gordon instructed her chief staff writer, Joseph Barry, to cover the story. Exulting in the house's seductive traditionalism, Barry took polemical advantage of a well-intended but quite ill-advised statement made by Sert in defense of his choice, in which he said that, in adapting "traditional New England architecture to modern use and needs," the Gibbs House avoids "all the tricky clichés of many modern houses which, aiming at the sensational, never benefit the people who live in them."[66]

When asked, Howe refused to make a statement to *House Beautiful*. But it was a futile gesture made too late. Gordon was busily rallying a cause around so obviously weak and noncommittal a work of design that she overplayed her hand, laying it bare in all its absurdity.

Howe shrewdly realized that Gordon's balloon would collapse of its own pretentiousness. Moreover, as he wrote to Thomas Creighton, editor of *Progressive Architecture,* he found it "amusing" and perhaps comforting that "at the judgement the effort to modernize the local idiom" was compared to Fortune Rock, which was just being "discussed again in architectural magazines in France, Germany and Japan." After all, he asked Creighton, "Who am I to throw the last stone?"[67]

65. Howe, letter to Thomas H. Creighton, 23 July 1954.

66. The Gibbs House is another of the many houses designed by Brewster or by architects like him such as Carl Koch and Robert Woods Kennedy that show how slim the line and unguarded the borders were in the late forties between the work of various regionalists and the sentimental eclecticism of the "early American" revivals. See Joseph A. Barry, "What Makes an Award-Winning House?" *House Beautiful* 96 (Aug. 1954), 78–83, 115–16; for an early house of Brewster's, see "Residence of Mr. and Mrs. L. H. H. Johnson, Jr., Marblehead, Massachusetts," *Record* 52 (Nov. 1937), 116–19.

For a contemporaneous parallel to the Howe-Gordon exchange, see the exchange in *Magazine of Art* between Philip Johnson and Peter Blake, and Robert Woods Kennedy: Kennedy, "The Small House in New England," 41 (April 1948), 123–28; Blake and Johnson, "Architectural Freedom and Order: An Answer to Robert W. Kennedy," 41 (Oct. 1948), 228–31; "Letters to the Editor," reply by Kennedy, 41 (Nov. 1948), 276. For a discussion of the regionalist movement, see Lewis Mumford, "The Sky Line: Status Quo," *The New Yorker,* 23 Oct. 1947, pp. 104–06, 109–10.

66. Barry, "What Makes an Award-Winning House?"

67. Howe, letter to Creighton, 23 July 1954.

8. Patron and Educator

An attitude which although triumphant in failure cannot endure success is bound only to be a phase. The modernists were driven back onto traditions and society, as recognition inevitably reconciled them with what they spat on. Moreover, the intensely political nature of the times in which we live makes the role of social outcast almost impossible. So the modernist movement has become absorbed into a new kind of conformity and academicism.

> Stephen Spender, "The Modernist Movement is Dead,"
> *The New York Times Book Review,*
> 3 Aug. 1952 (clipped by Howe for his files)

At the bottom of the heart of every human being . . . there is something that goes on indomitably expecting in the teeth of all experience . . . that good and not evil will be done to them.

> Simone Weil (copied by Howe among his papers)

Howe to Lou Kahn: "Lou, you of all people know I was never much of an architect."
Kahn: "Oh, no, George, you were a superb one."
Howe: "No, Lou, but you know what I should have been?"
Kahn: "What, George?"
Howe: "A patron."

> As remembered by William Huff

Howe had been concerned intermittently with the problems of low-cost mass housing throughout the thirties. As has been discussed, one reason for the breakup of his partnership with Lescaze was his unwillingness to solicit a particular commission for publicly assisted housing in Philadelphia because he did not believe in the wisdom of the then-prevailing (1934) governmental policy. "It is said that [Howe] after the 1932 elections, wrote to . . . [Roosevelt] a very long letter about issues of housing, planning and politics. . . . Roosevelt did not answer."[1]

1. Bruno Zevi, "George Howe, *Metron* 25 (1948), 10–11. No record of this letter was found among Roosevelt's papers at the Presidential Archives, Hyde Park. The correspondence from Howe remaining among Roosevelt's papers pertains to his partnership with Geddes, and his efforts to secure the commission for the design of the United States Pavilion at the Paris Ex-

Howe, in partnership with Lescaze, had designed the Chrystie-Forsyth project of 1932, which was intended for what were then considered middle-income families. In 1939, in partnership with Robert Montgomery Brown, a much younger architect with whom he had become friends in 1930 when the latter was a student at Princeton, and with whom he was associated in name only in the design of a house in 1938,[2] Howe prepared a design for a proto-typical builder's house for a suburban family of average means. This not particularly inspired design, prepared under the auspices of *Life* magazine, was built at Amityville, Long Island.[3] Its simple recall of Downingesque cottage design is marred by too-blatant pseudo-colonial details, probably the result of an effort to work within the prevailing tract-builder's vocabulary and techniques.

Howe's frame of mind with regard to the housing situation during the 1930s was negative and somewhat radical in its belief that political reform must precede a major housing effort. Early in the decade he had written that five "readjustments" ought to be made "within the framework of . . . [our] vague but generally accepted political philosophy."[4] These "readjustments" ranged from government subsidies for housing through government control of industry and of the distribution of land use (with the possibility of government ownership of land and natural resources), to the "rearrangement of political subdivisions along flexible regional lines, permitting zoning and planning on a broad scale." Howe believed that such an "extension of social control" was

position of 1937, a job which ultimately went to Paul Lester Weiner (then married to Alma Morgenthau, sister of Secretary of the Treasury Henry Morgenthau). A letter to "His Excellency, President of the United States," 9 Nov. 1936, included a copy of a letter of the same date to Senator Frederick A. Sterling, Commissioner for the United States Section, Paris Exposition, which Howe apparently wrote at Roosevelt's suggestion. This letter was probably suggested by the President in an effort to get out of an awkward clash between conflicting loyalties.

2. For the origins of the friendship, see Howe, letter to Brown, 7 March 1930. On 10 July 1936 Howe and Brown entered into a somewhat strange agreement by which they would split fees on any commission "arranged by . . . Howe, either in his own name or in the name of . . . Brown." However, the agreement was not to be construed as a partnership between Howe and Brown, nor a joint venture. It really represented a device wherein Howe could accept small commissions and turn them over to Brown for their actual design and the supervision of the construction. Such was the case of the residence for Mrs. Anna H. Donnelly at Saunderstown, R.I., for which Howe received 35% of the fees and agreed to "undertake all negotiations with the owner [and] assume personal responsibility for the work." Letter, Howe to Brown, 10 July 1936. When the Donnelly House was published, full credit was given to Brown.

3. An earlier group of *Life* houses had included work for various income groups designed by Frank Lloyd Wright, William Wilson Wurster, and Edward D. Stone, among others. See *"Life* Houses," *Forum* 69 (Nov. 1938), 312–48.

4. Howe, "Planning Low-Cost Housing," typescript, no date, on deposit in the vertical file of the Museum of Modern Art Library, New York.

necessary before a "complete and rational revamping of urban and other areas may become possible."

By 1939–40, faced with the prospect of a war and its attendant impact on the economy and with a decade of political as well as housing experimentation by all levels of government to look back on, Howe appears to have been sufficiently positive in his attitude to participate in the Defense Housing program as co-architect of a number of key projects and to occupy a number of key positions in the federal government. When he was commissioned by the U.S. Housing Authority to design housing for 450 families at Middletown, Pennsylvania, he was at least cognizant of the limitations implicit in the housing program as it grew out of the American political, social, and economic situation (*figs. 122, 123*). Because Howe did not enjoy working alone, always needing, it would seem, a partner to spur him on, he looked about for someone who might assist him in tackling the formless problem of mass housing. Louis I. Kahn seemed to be just such a person, and Howe offered him a partnership in 1940.

Today Kahn occupies an eminent position among the world's architects. This was not the case in the thirties, for reasons that Vincent Scully has discussed with great understanding in his monograph on Kahn.[5] When Howe took him on in the summer of 1940, Kahn was virtually untried as an architect, although his theoretical work in housing and planning was well known in Philadelphia in the late 1930s. In addition, he was in many important ways Howe's opposite: an odd jumble of a person, he was an architect whose concern with sociological and political matters was an outward manifestation of his as yet inarticulate dissatisfaction with the formal principles of the International Style to which, however reluctantly, he then subscribed. Only a short time before joining Howe, he had proposed, in that recklessly offhand manner which characterized so many International Style planning schemes, to redesign the central part of Philadelphia along lines suggested by Le Corbusier's Ville Radieuse project for a city of towers and parks.[6]

Kahn, honored by Howe's offer of partnership, accepted it immediately.[7] The first task of the new firm was the completion of the drawings for the

5. Vincent Scully, *Louis I. Kahn* (New York: Braziller, 1962), passim.

6. Louis I. Kahn, "Imaginative Study of Philadelphia Done Over on Modernistic Planning Principles," Philadelphia *Evening Bulletin,* 17 May 1941, p. 3.

7. Howe first took Kahn on as a junior partner but, as Kahn stated to the author in an interview in July 1961, Howe soon chose to set things on an equal footing. Later, in 1941, when Howe became quite busy with his consulting work in Washington, Oscar Stonorov, who had assisted him in the design of "Children's World," was brought in as a third partner. With Howe's appointment as Supervising Architect, the firm became Stonorov and Kahn.

Middletown project, or Pine Ford Acres as it came to be known. The project was intended to provide housing for workers at the Middletown Air Technical Service command near Harrisburg. Howe's design, a timid one, is a further simplification of the *Life* prototype of 1938–39. The design of the housing units seems painfully conventional today. Yet Howe's original proposal calling for flat roofs caused so much controversy that he was forced to devise a combination of flat and pitched roofs to answer the objections of the local authorities. A community building, possibly designed a bit later and probably reflecting Kahn's influence, serves as a focal point, and its great sheltering roof comes as a relief after the rather nervous skyline of the dwelling units caused by the arbitrarily shifted roof planes.

Pine Ford Acres does not compare well with other housing developments commissioned by the government as part of the mobilization effort. It does not match, for example, the taut elegance of Hugh Stubbin's houses at Windsor Locks, Connecticut, where individual gabled boxes are set precisely on the flat, sandy landscape with an almost Japanese restraint.[8] Nor does it approach Gropius and Breuer's work at New Kensington, Pennsylvania, in which rectangular boxes—sometimes raised on pipe-column *pilotis,* sometimes tied to the landscape along one side, poised above it at the other side—are set in measured opposition to a difficult hillside site. But, though it is not so formally adventurous as the New Kensington project, Middletown is surely less arbitrary. Particularly irksome was Gropius and Breuer's decision to turn the backs of a great many houses toward the street for the purposes of orientation.[9] It is quite likely, in fact, that Howe had the New Kensington houses in mind when, in association with Kahn and their new partner Oscar Stonorov, he undertook in 1942 an evaluation of the wartime housing program. This evaluation, "a close study . . . of what people want rather than what standards allow," was intended as a serious reexamination "after eight years of 'organized housing' . . . [of the] actual value of plans developed for one-, two-, and three-bedroom units and their relation to actual use, now that many projects have

8. See "Defense Houses at Windsor Locks, Connecticut," *Forum* 75 (Oct. 1941), 212–15; "80 Permanent Units—Rental, Windsor Locks, Connecticut," *Forum* 76 (May 1942), 328–31. Howe found these houses to be the product of "Stubbins' search for domestic charm within the framework of a strict geometrical pattern." Howe, "The Meaning of the Arts Today," *Magazine of Art* 35 (May 1942), 162–67, 190.

9. See "Defense Houses at New Kensington, Pennsylvania," *Forum* 75 (Oct. 1941), 218–20; "Aluminum City Terrace Housing," *Forum* 81 (July 1944), 65–76. The latter article includes an interview with the project's tenants, who questioned with considerable justification every so-called "functional innovation," especially the orientation of the houses. Before its completion, Howe was optimistic about this project, calling it a "brilliant study in topography, orientation and a new approach to the dwelling unit." "Meaning of the Arts Today."

Fig. 106. Howe with Louis McAllister. Philadelphia *Evening Bulletin* office, view of entrance, 1936–41, renovation.

Fig. 107. Philadelphia *Evening Bulletin* office.

Fig. 108. Howe with Oscar Stonorov, Herbert Spiegel, Cornelius Bogert. "Children's World," New York World's Fair, New York, N.Y., 1939, from above.

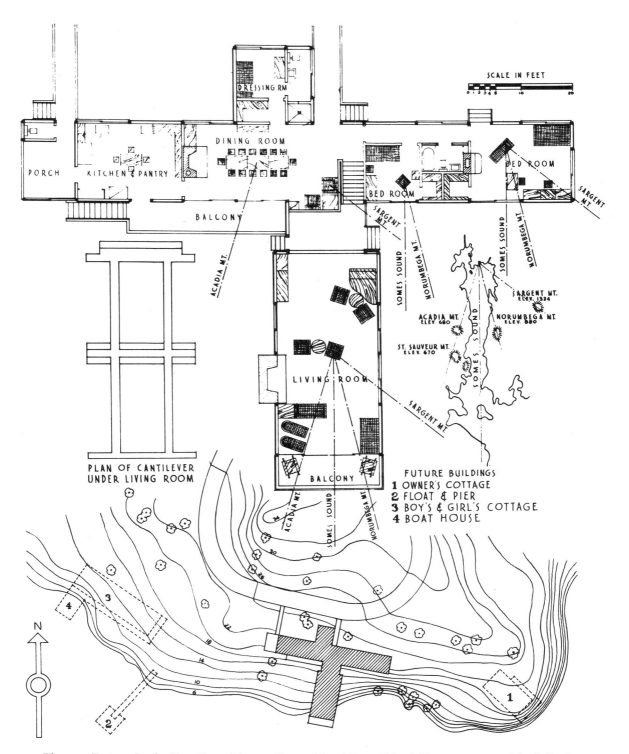

Fig. 109. Fortune Rock, Clara Fargo Thomas House, Mount Desert Island, Me., 1937–39, combined site plan showing built and contemplated work and plan of main house.

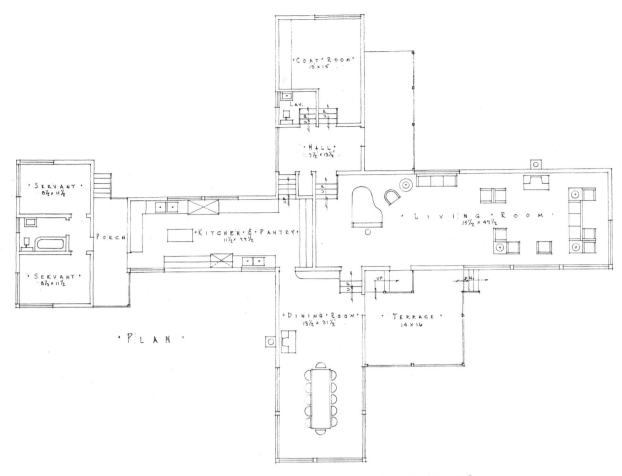

Fig. 110. Fortune Rock, plan for projected main house, Jan. 1938.

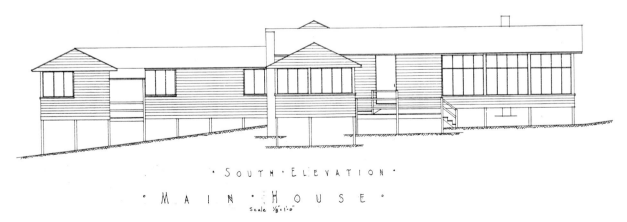

· SOUTH · ELEVATION ·

· MAIN · HOUSE ·

Scale ⅛"=1'-0"

Fig. 111. Fortune Rock, south elevation of projected main house.

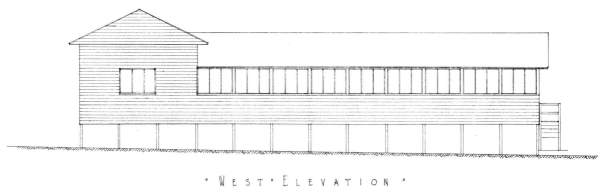

· W E S T · E L E V A T I O N ·

Fig. 112. Fortune Rock, west elevation of projected dormitory building.

Fig. 113. Fortune Rock, south elevation
of projected owner's cottage.

· S O U T H · E L E V A T I O N ·

Fig. 114. Fortune Rock, from the south at high tide.

Fig. 115. Fortune Rock, the two-story connection between the upper wing and the living room.

Fig. 116. Fortune Rock, looking up the stairs from the living room to the upper wing.

Fig. 117. Fortune Rock, living room, looking toward the south.

Fig. 118. Fortune Rock, owner's bedroom.

Fig. 119. Fortune Rock, living-room wing from the east at high tide. Howe is on the balcony.

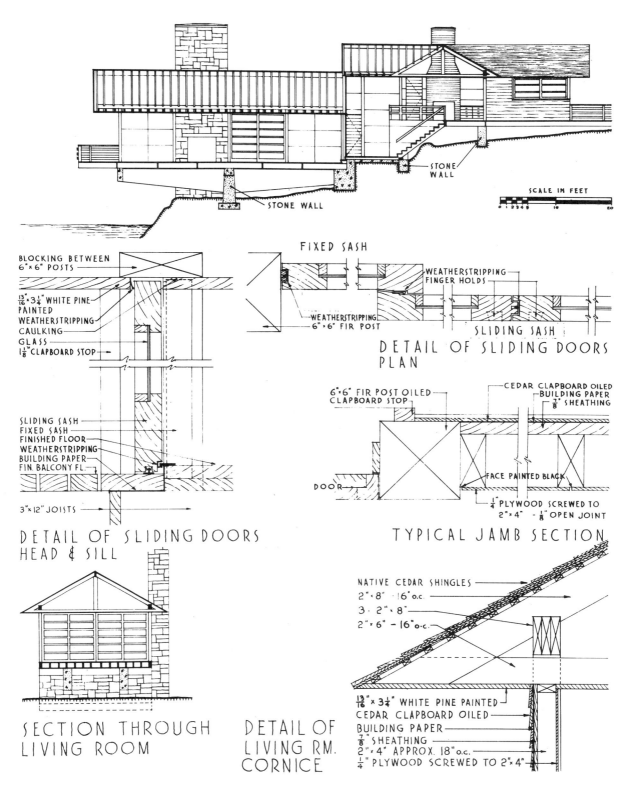

SCALE IN FEET
0 1 2 3 4 5 .... 10 20

STONE WALL

STONE WALL

FIXED SASH

WEATHERSTRIPPING
FINGER HOLDS

WEATHERSTRIPPING
6"×6" FIR POST

SLIDING SASH

DETAIL OF SLIDING DOORS
PLAN

BLOCKING BETWEEN
6"×6" POSTS

$\frac{13}{16}$"×3$\frac{1}{4}$" WHITE PINE
PAINTED
WEATHERSTRIPPING
CAULKING
GLASS
1$\frac{1}{8}$" CLAPBOARD STOP

SLIDING SASH
FIXED SASH
FINISHED FLOOR
WEATHERSTRIPPING
BUILDING PAPER
FIN. BALCONY FL.

3"×12" JOISTS

DETAIL OF SLIDING DOORS
HEAD & SILL

CEDAR CLAPBOARD OILED
BUILDING PAPER
$\frac{7}{8}$" SHEATHING

6"×6" FIR POST OILED
CLAPBOARD STOP

DOOR

FACE PAINTED BLACK

$\frac{1}{4}$" PLYWOOD SCREWED TO
2"×4" − $\frac{1}{8}$" OPEN JOINT

TYPICAL JAMB SECTION

NATIVE CEDAR SHINGLES
2"×8" − 16" o.c.
3 − 2"×8"
2"×6" − 16" o.c.

SECTION THROUGH
LIVING ROOM

DETAIL OF
LIVING RM.
CORNICE

$\frac{13}{16}$"×3$\frac{1}{4}$" WHITE PINE PAINTED
CEDAR CLAPBOARD OILED
BUILDING PAPER
$\frac{7}{8}$" SHEATHING
2"×4" APPROX. 18" o.c.
$\frac{1}{4}$" PLYWOOD SCREWED TO 2"×4"

Fig. 120. Fortune Rock, construction details.

Fig. 121. Howe and Lescaze. H. F. C. Stikeman Cottage, Sennerville, Quebec, 1931.

Fig. 122. Howe and Louis Kahn. Pine Ford Acres, Middletown, Pa., 1940–42, view of pitched- and flat-roofed units.

Fig. 123. Pine Ford Acres, view of community center.

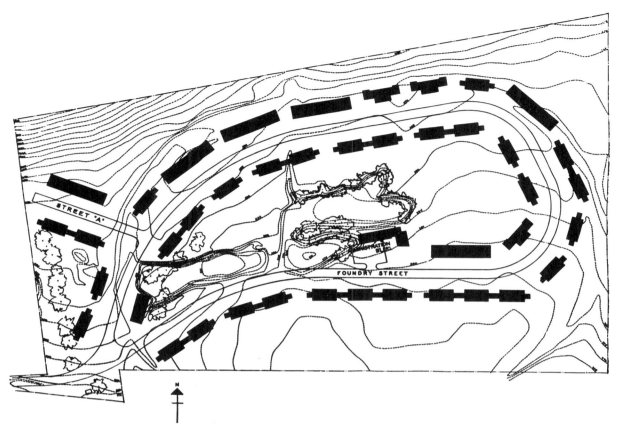

Fig. 124. Howe, Stonorov and Kahn. Carver Court, Coatesville, Pa., 1942–44, site plan.

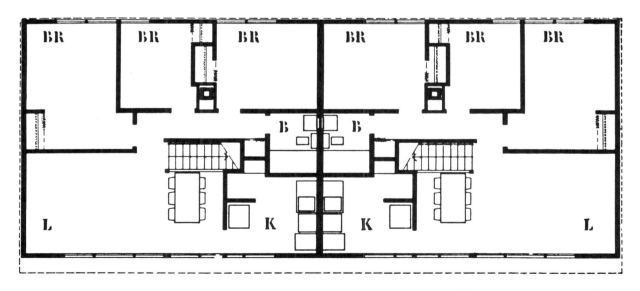

Fig. 125. Carver Court, unit plan.

Fig. 126. Carver Court, typical dwelling unit.

Fig. 127. Carver Court, community center.

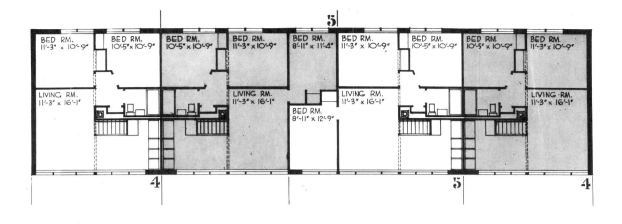

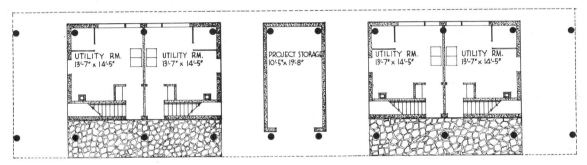

Fig. 128. Lily Ponds, Washington, D.C., ca. 1942, typical unit plan.

Fig. 129. Lily Ponds, model.

Fig. 130. U.S. Consulate, Naples, Italy, ca. 1947, project, model from the front.

Fig. 131. U.S. Consulate, model from the back.

Fig. 132. Howe and Robert Montgomery Brown with the Austin Company. WCAU television studio, Philadelphia, Pa., 1952.

Fig. 133. Howe and Robert Montgomery Brown. Philadelphia *Evening and Sunday Bulletin* office, 1954–55.

been built and occupied." As the gap between the language of modern domestic architecture and the living patterns of American families broadens, the
value of this study has, if anything, increased in the years since it was prepared.
For this reason it is quoted at length here:

> . . . let us review such plans as the row house in Philadelphia, the row
> house in Baltimore, the shoe-box bungalow in New Jersey or Long
> Island, and try to understand why it is that these houses which we have
> tried to improve still seem to be vastly preferred by the average person.
> Why do people prefer the ugliness of dickey-front houses, compressed
> in long rows, surrounded by a sea of concrete, to houses placed on the
> contours, related to sun and breeze, with garden living and community
> facilities? It is true, of course, that many localities offer no alternatives
> in the given price class, but it seems much more important to recognize
> these dwellings as composites of certain amenities accepted as essential,
> for otherwise they would not sell.
>
> The most important advantage that we could find is the provision of
> essential space. . . . [The builder's] client gets a house with space in which
> to put his car, and a basement large enough for storage. . . . To keep a
> house is practically impossible if room is not provided for untidy work
> and storage. Architects may have succeeded in developing closely knit
> actual space for living, but this very space becomes bedlam when the
> bicycle and the baby carriage must be stored in the living room, the
> laundry washed in the kitchen and the chair repaired in the bedroom.[10]

In 1942 Howe and Kahn were joined by Oscar Stonorov, and they formed
the partnership of Howe, Stonorov and Kahn. Stonorov, who had worked
with Howe on the "Children's World" for the 1939 World's Fair, was born in
Frankfurt, Germany, in 1905. He studied at the University of Florence in
1924–25 and at the Ecole Polytechnique in Zurich between 1925 and 1928.
He was a dedicated modernist from the beginning of his architectural career
until his death in 1970, though near the end of his career, political pressure
and general expediency led him to produce some very questionable work
including blatantly pseudo-Georgian town houses as part of his redevelopment work at Society Hill in Philadelphia. In the late 1920s Stonorov had
worked with André Lurçat and Le Corbusier. Along with Willy Boesiger, he
edited the first volume of Le Corbusier's *Oeuvre Complète*.

10. George Howe, Oscar Stonorov, Louis I. Kahn, " 'Standards' Versus Essential Space,"
Forum 76 (May 1942), 308–11.

When Stonorov came to America in 1929, his credentials as a modernist were impeccable, and his influence on such young architects in Philadelphia and New York as Kahn and Norman N. Rice was electric. There gathered about him a number of disgruntled young designers trained in the vocabulary of Beaux-Arts classicism and now eager for insights into the newly imported International Style. Like most other young modernists in America, he got little work. As design consultant to the little-known firm of Tucker and Howell, he did build, by 1931, the Sam T. Weyman Biological Laboratory at the Highlands Museum in Highlands, North Carolina. One of the few American buildings illustrated in Hitchcock and Johnson's *The International Style*, its exaggeratedly thin pipe columns were found by the authors to be "too frail" in appearance and "incongruous" in their juxtaposition to the bulging volumes of the wooden structure itself.[11]

Stonorov was concerned with problems of public housing during the thirties. In 1933–34, in association with Alfred Kastner (and under the direction of the Beaux-Arts architect W. Pope Barney), he designed the Carl Mackley Houses in the Juniata Park district of Philadelphia. The first public housing project to be sponsored by the federal government, it is to this day probably the most successful of its kind in any American city.[12] In 1935 he experimented with the use of steel-frame construction in residential design. In accord with his European Machine Phase predilections, his design did not express the frame at all and was sheathed in brick painted white; in fact, a number of prefabricated, "clip-on," cosmetic facades were available in varying styles including neocolonial, neo-Georgian, and one called "western-colonial."[13]

11. Henry-Russell Hitchcock and Philip Johnson, *The International Style* (New York: Museum of Modern Art, 1932), pp. 222–23.

12. See also chap. 5, n. 40. The use of concrete, especially concrete block, and the elegant fenstration have not yet been surpassed in public housing in this country, and the inclusion of a street below grade for automobiles—not a dank basement tunnel such as Stonorov employed in the neo-Georgian town houses adjoining Hopkinson House, which he built in Philadelphia in 1961–63—make the Mackley Houses a kind of textbook of housing design. Unfortunately, the interior planning, badly hampered by the archaic Philadelphia housing code, does not measure up to the standards set by the exterior. See Albert Mayer, "Critique of the Hosiery Workers' Housing Development in Philadelphia," *Architecture* (New York) 71 (April 1935), 189–94; "Carl Mackley Houses, Philadelphia," *Record* 75 (Feb. 1934), 120–21; "Portfolio of Public Works," *Record* 77 (May 1935), 328–29. See also Howe, "Meaning of the Arts Today." For a recent discussion, see Harold E. Dickson, *A Hundred Pennsylvania Buildings* (State College, Pa.: Bald Eagle Press, 1954), p. 93.

Stonorov also participated in the design of Westfield Acres, Camden, N.J. See *Forum* 69 (May 1938), 372–75.

13. See "Demonstration Houses," *Forum* 63 (July 1935), 26–32.

In 1936–37 Stonorov remodeled and enlarged the farmhouse of his future father-in-law, Frank B. Foster, at Phoenixville, Pennsylvania.[14] More interesting is the house he designed for himself, the Avon Lea Farm, also at Phoenixville. In this rambling house, built in part upon the ruined stone foundations of an eighteenth-century farmhouse, Stonorov's highly theatrical sense of form, his love of bold shapes—so-called free-forms—were given robust expression while, in typical Machine Phase fashion, the expression of construction received only cursory attention.[15]

The first commission of the firm of Howe, Stonorov and Kahn was the design of the Carver Court houses at Coatesville, Pennsylvania (*figs. 124–27*). This scheme, completed in 1943, was developed for the Mutual Ownership Division of the Federal Works Agency. It was intended not only to fulfill a pressing wartime need (in this case intensified because it was to house Negroes emigrating from the south to work in northern industrial communities) but to suggest "solutions for self supporting projects" which might be built after the war.[16] Carver Court was surely one of the finest of the wartime housing projects. Located on the site of a former racetrack just off the Coatesville-Paoli Highway, its double loop of houses reflects the previous disposition of the property. Of the three different unit types employed, the three-bedroom "ground-freed" model is the most interesting; the transverse concrete supporting walls contribute a refreshing generosity of scale to the otherwise simple wooden boxes. Here, and at the later Lily Ponds project, intended for Washington, D. C., Howe and his associates tested their theories of essential space, attempting "to include the many advantages of the basement while eliminating its defects." As Howe and Stonorov wrote:[17]

> In essence, the scheme consists of nothing more than a transposition of the basement to the ground level, with one story of living space above. When developed into a typical four-family unity, some interesting features appear. There is open space between the utility blocks which serves very conveniently as a carport, a shelter for the entrance or a covered play area. These openings also eliminate the distinction between "front" and "back," as there is free circulation through, rather than around, each building. . . .

14. "A Pennsylvania Farmhouse . . ." *Record* 82 (Aug. 1937), 69–72.
15. "House in Chester County, Pennsylvania," *Forum 81* (Aug. 1944), 87–90.
16. "Carver Court," *Forum 81* (Dec. 1944), 109–16.
17. Howe et al., " 'Standards' Versus Essential Space."

Planners, in their attempts to control room orientation, have sometimes resorted to extravagant site development, or have changed the unit types on opposite sides of the street. The "ground-freed" house may be entered with equal ease from either side, permitting the architect to orient rooms and porches as he desires. . . .

It should be hardly necessary to state that the architects make no claim to complete authorship of the "ground-freed" house. The idea is an old one, and a very good one, and its application to housing offers distinct advantages, especially at the present time, when enthusiasm for site planning is tending to obscure the primary importance of the house. It is possible on any project to skimp on roads, planting and other elements, and to bring these up to par at some future date. The house, on the other hand, is completely inflexible once built. And if essential space is omitted at the beginning it can never be added. In view of these simple and inescapable facts, it is time to take another look at the standards and see what they mean in terms of family living.

Lily Ponds, a similar project which was never built, would have been even better: the rhythmic interplay between the round columns and enclosing brick walls yields more intricate spatial effects, and the use of concrete block and brick (demanded by the Washington building code) provide a sense of permanence that almost all the wartime housing projects lacked. (*figs. 128, 129*).

In February 1942 Howe was appointed Supervising Architect of the Public Buildings Administration;[18] he had already served the federal government as a juror for the Smithsonian competition in 1939, as the only modernist member of the P. B. A.'s decidedly conservative advisory board on architectural design,

18. The history of the Supervising Architect's office is briefly summarized in "Forum of Events: Supervisory Architect's Office," *Forum* 72 (May 1945), 76, 80. Howe succeeded Louis A. Simon, who had held the position for 45 years until his retirement. *Architectural Forum* was delighted by Howe's appointment: "One of the profession's most advanced thinkers will undoubtedly bring a forward-looking attitude to this assignment. Because he is respected by traditionalists who will remember his superb Pennsylvania houses and by modernists who will acclaim his PSFS Building, designed with Lescaze, and his Wasserman and Thomas houses, Howe's choice could not be better. Progressives have burned as official Washington fiddled with Roman architecture. They should not assume that Howe will change that over-night, however, He is too wise in the ways of the Capitol to try. Nevertheless the appointment will bring encouragement to the modern group, over the years fewer columns and starling-roost pediments to the Mall." "U. S. Architect No. 1," *Forum* 76 (Feb. 1942), 44 supp. See also *Pencil Points* 23 (Feb. 1942), 54 supp.; *Record* 91 (Mar. 1942), 10.

and in 1941 and 1942 as a part-time consultant to the P. B. A.[19] The symbolic importance of Howe's appointment cannot be overstated. His selection for the highest governmental post in architecture marked a complete break with the official posture that had crippled architectural decision making throughout the 1930s when so much federally sponsored construction was authorized as part of the New Deal. Of all modernist architects, Howe was the most likely choice for this post by virtue of his background and experience and his unique career in traditionalist as well as modernist design. Howe in fact, described himself at this time as "a veteran of the Beaux-Arts who has come through the conflict pretty badly cut up but not decapitated."[20]

Unfortunately, the war effort so curtailed construction that his job was virtually without power in relation to the design of actual buildings. Even the Defense Housing Program which had been part of the mobilization effort had come to an end. A good deal of his time was spent in essential but uninspiring administrative tasks. Most notably among these duties was the assumption of responsibility for the preparation of strategies for the protection of government buildings in the event of enemy attack.[21]

Nonetheless, Howe succeeded in influencing the design of a few "temporary" buildings in the Washington area. One, for the Office of War Information, is pedestrian. Another, residence halls for women government workers, is somewhat more interesting. With so many architects credited, it is difficult to assess

19. In recommending Howe for the job of Supervising Architect, Philip B. Fleming, also a P. B. A. consultant, wrote of Howe's "highly meritorious service in the Public Buildings Administration where his unusual creative ability, sensitive perception of design requirements, as well as his excellent administrative qualities are well recognized by the officials there."

20. Howe, "Contemporary Architecture Compared to Architecture of the Past," speech delivered before the 15th International Congress of Architects, New York University, 12 May 1939. Howe had won the confidence of the academic world as well. He was a member of the committee of the Board of Overseers of Harvard University to visit the Graduate School of Design, and of similar advisory bodies at the University of Pennsylvania, Princeton, and the California Institute of Technology. For aspects of Howe's theories of architectural education during the 1930s, see his letter to Robert M. Brown, 7 March 1930, and W. Pope Barney, "Premises and Conclusions at the Princeton Round Table," *Record* 82 (Sept. 1937), 56–62.

21. A notation in Howe's dossier lists the duties of his office as follows: "Broad direction of the design and preparation of drawings and specifications for the construction of all Federal buildings and building projects, and for the repair, remodeling, and extension of existing buildings in the District of Columbia, involving technical studies of an architectural and engineering character, and the direction of all repairs to existing Federal buildings located outside of the metropolitan area of Washington, D.C."

Other important duties listed are: "Authority to make recommendations to the Commissioner for the employment of broad technical and administrative direction over such services; to represent the Commissioner in conferences with Federal, State and Municipal authorities on matters having to do with planning, design and construction of Federal buildings and building projects."

Howe's contribution toward this design, though he took pride in the clear articulation of the functional parts: the bold stair towers, the prowlike windows of the parlors, and the inviting curves of the entrance porch. It is interesting that *Architectural Forum* regarded them as "perhaps the most successful part of the entire Washington war housing program," noting that their "great merit . . . lies in the completeness of the solution they offer. The buildings are temporary, look temporary—and also look well. Accepting the dormitory scheme, the authorities provided the manifold services which make dormitory life tolerable."[22]

In 1944 Howe was involved in the preparation of preliminary design proposals for a proposed annex to the State Department which was to have been built on the complex site on the west side of Lafayette Square which includes Blair House and Decatur House. While correspondence in Howe's files indicates that block plans, elevations, and perspectives were prepared for three alternatives (the last of which suggesting eventual demolition of Blair House), the drawings appear to have been lost.[23]

Although Howe's actual power was small, his influence toward establishing an official reception to non-neoclassic architecture was enormous. Because of his position and his articulateness as a speaker and a writer, his ideas reached an unprofessional audience at a time when the curtailment of actual construction turned attention to more theoretical issues. As he said in 1945, shortly before retiring from government service: "I am not disclosing a state secret when I tell you that my personal tastes are on the radical side. My opinions are no more binding on Uncle Sam than those of any other single citizen but my administrative position gives them a certain importance. An administrator can't originate much but he can stop almost anything. At least I shall not stand personally in the way of the advanced architectural thinker. The Commissioner of Public Buildings smiles craftily every time I open up on him about modern architecture but I believe he is sympathetic, though with understandable reservations."[24]

Howe used his influence wisely and effectively, encouraging disgruntled architects and planners to look ahead to the postwar period. He told Pennsylvania architects in May 1942:

22. "Washington Housing (West Potomac Development,)" *Forum* 80 (Jan. 1944), 61–62.

23. Howe, "Rough Draft, Submission to the Honorable Secretary of State," 2 May 1944.

24. Howe, "Relation of the Architect to Government." An abbreviated version was published in the Michigan Society of Architects *Weekly Bulletin* 19 (31 July 1945), 1, 3; (7 Aug. 1945), 1, 3.

For the moment we are so engrossed in the overwhelming trade of war, that there seems to be no time for architecture; yet in the war effort itself are being formed the elements of a new architectural era. . . . The very fact that architects are being against their will dispersed through the war construction field is bound to have an incalculable effect on public building design and construction. The economic pressures of post-war readjustment will force us to put our newly acquired techniques to work in the building industry. "All great art," I read recently, "is born of war." The words are from a book by Colonel Von Foertsch, of the German General Staff, on "The Art of Modern Warfare," but they are not the Colonel's words. They are the words of John Ruskin, to whom war was an abomination. Let us, like him, look forward hopefully in the midst of disaster.[25]

Howe also sought to establish an effective, modern, direction for the government's architectural policy. In 1944 he was chairman of a panel that undertook the formulation of some architectural principles to serve as a guide for administrators (see below). From the transcription of the proceedings, Howe prepared a paper, "Architecture. Review of the Situation. October 1944," which, though written in his characteristically complicated style, is nonetheless not only an incisive estimate of the state of American architecture between the two World Wars but a lucid discussion of such basic architectural concepts as scale and function. Interestingly enough, in his presentation of "categories of government structures," and in his specific discussions of building materials, equipment, and the like, Howe assumed that American Beaux-Arts version of the Guadetesque tone, which was to be attempted again and perhaps for the last time in Talbot Hamlin's compendium, *Forms and Functions of Twentieth Century Architecture.*

On 3 February 1945, shortly before he resigned from government service, Howe addressed the Conference on Architecture with Regard to Professional Training and Practice, held at the University of Michigan. His speech was essentially a detailed and somewhat technical evaluation of "the prospects of the architect in relation to the work directed by the Public Buildings Administration." But near the end Howe found himself drawn

to the following conclusions: the architect's relation to government is actually and potentially better than it has been for a long time; he has

25. Howe, untitled talk before the Pennsylvania Association of Architects, Harrisburg, 29 May 1942, 5 pp., ms.

proved himself versatile and adaptable in many fields of war activity and become experienced in government when he was excluded from his normal occupations; the technical and administrative machinery for handling the work of government design is constantly improving; the trend toward large-scale planning should provide ample opportunity for the display of the designer's talents in government work; insofar as the Public Buildings Administration is concerned the policy will be to employ private firms as generally as practicable rather than to expand the permanent staff indefinitely.

All this is to the good but what is perhaps more important is the sense of cohesion and common interest within the architectural profession which has resulted from the difficulties in which it has recently found itself. This sense must be fostered above everything and it must be the constant effort of the profession as a whole to seek the means by which its services, which it knows to be valuable in principle, can be made effective in practice. It is not enough to criticize government and claim to be misunderstood. It is necessary to try to understand the restrictions, the very necessary restrictions, under which administrators work in a democracy, and to find the points at which the interests of government and the architectural profession are common. They are many and can become more by intelligent inquiry and adjustment.[26]

As the Allied war effort grew more successful, many architects turned their thoughts increasingly to the problems and possibilities that a peacetime economy would bring with it—one which, it was fervently hoped, would be more stable and prosperous than that of the thirties. The massive relocations of population and the development of whole new centers of activity made it clear that the existing attitudes toward mechanisms for large-scale physical planning were inadequate if not generally nonexistent. Joseph Hudnut, dean of Harvard's Graduate School of Design, brought these problems to a wide professional audience in his important article, "The Political Art of Planning."[27] This article crystallized for Howe, and for many others, many of the

26. Howe, "Relation of the Architect to Government."

27. Joseph Hudnut, "The Political Art of Planning," *Record* 114 (Oct. 1943), 44–48. "It is a great pity," Hudnut wrote, "that the term *city planner* has come to have so nebulous a meaning nowadays. If I had my way, so imperative a title should never be given to the makers of Utopias; nor should it be given, on the other hand, to that very vocal person, the 'planning expert,' child of the scientific spirit, who opposes to the generous antique tradition bleak wildernesses of data, tabulation and diagram. . . . Of course I know that surveys and reports, statistics and maps, are necessary instruments of planning but these, like the data and calculations of engineers, might

potential problems inherent in the postwar situation and made it clear that a dangerous split was growing between those who programmed and those who implemented. Howe had Hudnut's article before him when he prepared what was to become one of his best-known essays, "Master Plans for Master Politicians," which was first delivered on 27 January 1945 as a talk before the managerial meeting of the short-lived American Society of Architects and Planners.[28]

Here he was once again concerned with what he regarded as the inherent duality of the architect's situation: "as artist his imagination must run ahead of reality. As technician he must work with texts and in laboratories that seem to him and are in fact inadequate." Nonetheless, he insisted that the architect-planner must remain true to his primary role as artist, though "political action must be [his] first interest." Howe continued: "It is rather the fashion nowadays to scoff at plans that are not practical. By practical plans are meant presumably those that fall within the immediate or not too remote social, political, economic and legal possibilities. In an article on 'The Political Art of Planning' Dean Hudnut last year made scholarly fun of the master plans buried in the Planning Library at Harvard. Yet it is obvious from a recent controversy in the public press that even the modest proposals of architect-planners are beyond the scope of the practical-minded.

"There are two great showmen living today who are . . . great architect-planners," Howe went on, referring to Wright and Le Corbusier. "Each foresees a different solution. The American of the plains prophesies the abandonment or rurification of the city, the European on a crowded continent

---

be kept for the discreet and understanding eye of professionals. Most harmful to the cause of planning is that air of satisfied accomplishment with which these are paraded before the public. Propaganda for Planning? That is a vicious propaganda which encourages a pride in means—and leaves ends to the coming generation. . . . What is needed to give consequence and direction to our art of planning is a political process more definite, understood, and resourceful than any which now obtains." Hudnut went on to call for a division between "career planners," who, like career diplomats, "would carry on from year to year the routine business of planning and would build up that funded body of knowledge and experience which might form the common ever-renewed tools of planning." But, he warned, this must not be mistaken for the art of city planning just as air-conditioning must not be mistaken for architecture. The second half of his division, the "policy-making planners, the *architects-of-cities* . . . should be as directly responsible to public opinions as are mayor and alderman. It is in this group that the art of planning—political as well as architectural—should reach its highest expression."

28. Howe, "Master Plans for Master Politicians," *Magazine of Art* 39 (Feb. 1946), 66–68. This was printed in translation in the Italian journal *Metron*. Howe was for a short time vice-president of the American Society of Architects and Planners, men who claimed to "believe that modern design is more than paltry flat roofs and corner windows on little houses." See "Planning Is Politics," *Forum* 82 (March 1945), 7.

prophesies its rebuilding." Their role has been of immeasurable importance; "their impractical plans and words have done indirectly as much as all the practical together to bring the legislative and administrative machinery of planning to the point it has reached today."

Recounting Vitruvius's tale of the planner Dinocrates and his patron, Alexander the Great, Howe sought to "point out that a bold plan dramatically presented is one of the most powerful instruments of political pressure in the hands of any section of society." Howe concluded by defining in precise terms the role of what has since come to be called the urban designer: "As technician [he] . . . must prepare practical plans for the practical-minded. As artist he cannot but stand or fall by master plans for master politicians." And Howe, in preparing the definition, did not overlook the dilemma which urban design has as its corollary. The architect-planner stands between two extremes: between the reality of existing legislation and administrative machinery, which are acknowledged to be inadequate, on the one hand, and the consequences of his own planning philosophy, which carry him far into the realm of political imagination, on the other.

"This realm is peculiarly the architect-planner's. Others whose business it is can work out details of legislation and administration as well, I will venture to say better, than he. Only he can present the image of the end toward which these working instruments are directed. Only he can provide the statesman with graphic projections of the still impossible leading to imaginative political action that will set the machinery moving. Whatever else he does this he must continue to do. He must provide master plans for master politicians."

In 1954 or 1955, Howe prepared a new conclusion to this talk, which, I believe, serves to illuminate not only the development of his viewpoint but also to suggest indirectly that one of his functions in government service may have been to shape policy in a wide area concerned not only with buildings but with issues of planning and redevelopment. In this new ending to the article, which he retitled "Plans Practical and Not Practical," he wrote:

> At the conclusion of World War II it seemed almost as though some sort of master legislative act integrating activities at the Federal, State and local levels . . . [was] about to become effective. The "Advance Planning Program of the Public Buildings Administration" was authorized by the Congress in 1943, and in 1945 Mr. W. E. Reynolds, Commissioner of Public Buildings [and Howe's immediate superior], appeared before a Congressional hearing to urge an appropriation under its provisions. He very properly took the stand that no public building program could be

intelligently undertaken without general surveys of public road, community facility and planning problems in general at the local level which he felt the Federal Government could properly finance. . . .

Under the title "Post-War Urban Redevelopment" [Reynolds] made a clear, concise and comprehensive analysis of urban planning problems in their social, administrative and economic aspects and definitely stated his opinion that national responsibility with respect to them existed. "These problems are not insurmountable," [Reynolds] concluded. "We have the opportunity and we have the ability to do a good job of rebuilding our cities. We cannot avoid some national responsibility to do just that."[29]

Aside from building design, three projects appear to have occupied most of Howe's time in Washington. One concerned supervising the implementation of the President's directive for protecting federal buildings and their contents against enemy attack.[30] The second was the report of the panel on "General Principles to be Considered in the Design of Government Architecture."[31] The third was the formulation of guidelines for the "Urban Research Planning Project," the purpose of which was to determine "urban planning objectives, standards, methods and procedures; and by trial in a particular area to determine how these can be achieved and applied so as to effect the best possible coordination and integration of all undertakings, public and private, affecting or contributing to the development and redevelopment of urban areas."[32]

The possibilities for developing monumental architecture within the stylistic and intellectual context of the International Style was another important concern of Howe's during these years. In a talk in December 1941 at the Fogg Art Museum, Harvard University, in an effort to find a workable framework for a revitalized monumentality, he moved beyond the stylistic battles

29. Howe, "Plans Practical and Not Practical," no date (ca. 1954 or 1955), 2 pp., holograph ms., draft conclusion to updated version of "Master Plans for Master Politicians." The implication is that Howe prepared Reynold's remarks on postwar urban redevelopment.

30. See stenographic transcript of Howe, "Remarks," speech delivered at Training Conference on Protection of Public Buildings and Property . . . , 3 Aug. 1942.

31. The final draft of this report was called "Architecture. Review of the Situation. October 1944." The "panel on architecture consisted of Howe as chairman and Gilbert Stanley Underwood, S. E. Sanders, C. David Persina, and R. S. Hart as members. The report, which was definitely Guadetesque in tone and purpose, appears never to have been completed, at least under Howe's administration. Numerous holograph drafts of the report among Howe's papers indicate that in its final form it was largely a reflection of his own views.

32. "Urban Research Planning Project," 17 pp. typescript, George Howe Collection, Avery.

of the thirties toward a more profound concern for the relationship of art to society.[33] Taking his cue from such theorists as Walter Curt Behrendt, Howe saw art as the reflection of its time: "In its period of confusion it corresponds to the confusion of our lives."[34] He cited many who contributed to this search for a meaningful "expression-form": Aalto, Wright, Albert Kahn, Gropius, and others. Their efforts, "however seemingly eccentric, have been directed to one purpose, and one purpose only, to create a usable expression-form worthy of the name democratic, an expression-form proper to church and state, rich and poor, art and industry. The great sin of eclecticism has not been artistic sterility, but compartmented exclusivism. The meaning of the art of building is that society is one." In architecture, as in life, it is "the proper struggle of man with nature" which is of consequence.

In June 1944 Howe participated in an exchange of letters with John D. Morse, the editor of *Magazine of Art*. This discussion led in September 1944 to a follow-up, "Memorials for Mankind."[35] In reply to somewhat oversentimental statements about war memorials by Archibald MacLeish, the poet, and Charles D. Maginnis, a traditionalist architect, Howe asked a series of pertinent questions (though perhaps his replies fail to transcend the sentimentality of which he was so critical).

Howe did offer a word picture of his ideas for an appropriate World War II memorial. Not surprisingly, it was related in form to his Coast Guard Memorial of 1928, combined, as it were, with Burnham Hoyt's Red Rocks Amphitheatre and Norman Bel Geddes's Corbusian projections of the America of 1960. The principal interest in this word picture was its colossal scale, an "amphitheatre of rocky eminences and on their sides I might set tiers of seats and terraces for multitudes and I might set it upon a vast stepped platform approached by highways from every side."[36]

In 1947 Howe agreed to serve as professional adviser for the competition for the Jefferson National Expansion Memorial in St. Louis. His well-known interest in the capabilities for monumental architectural expression within an acceptable modern design vocabulary and his position as a modernist acceptable to the Beaux-Arts establishment, which even in 1948 was still very much in control, made him the logical choice for the job. "I was called

33. Howe, "Meaning of the Arts Today."

34. Howe, "Two Years of Architecture," book review, *Yale Review* 27 n.s. (Sept. 1937), 204–06.

35. Howe, "Memorials for Mankind," *Forum* 82 (May 1945), 122–24; see also "War Memorials," *Forum* 91 (Dec. 1949), 100.

36. Howe, "Memorials for Mankind."

in," he later recalled, "as professional adviser to divest the event of local implications and possibly as a sort of missing link between past and present."[37]

Howe wrote the program and directed the competition, which, at his recommendation, was to be open to anyone who by "education or experience" was entitled to call himself an architect. The two-stage competition reflected his belief in the complementary but discrete roles of "imagination" and "intellect" in architectural design in particular, and in the creative process in general. In the first stage, the entrants were exhorted to "give their imaginations free rein, leaving the examination of what really can be done to a less exuberant moment."[38] The jury, chaired by William Wilson Wurster, consisted of S. Herbert Hare, Fiske Kimball, Louis La Beaume, Charles Nagel, Jr., Richard J. Neutra, and Roland Wank. The results, save for the bold, innovative arch of Eero Saarinen, which the jury courageously chose, and which was finally built, were not particularly distinguished.[39]

Needless to say, the jury's choice was extremely controversial. Gilmore D. Clarke, the landscape architect, in a prefigurement of the tone of the McCarthy era, accused Saarinen of plagiarizing the "unbuilt central element in the design for a proposed international Exposition to be held in Rome, Italy in 1942," and implied that, issues of plagiarism aside, the "circumstances" suggested that the Saarinen design might well be inappropriate because it was "similar in design to one originally created to glorify twenty years of Fascism in Italy!"[40]

Howe was in Rome at this time, and Saarinen wrote to thank him for having written "the best competition program I have seen" and to report Clarke's attack. It seems that Clarke was "the guy who had most to do with killing the Smithsonian," the competition for which Howe had been a juror in 1939 and in which Eero and Eliel Saarinen, then in partnership, had won first prize. Saarinen reported: "I find there was a design for Mussolini's Fair which, as a minor motif, used an arch in the shape of a half circle."[41]

A few years later, when asked by Douglas Haskell to comment on the recently completed United Nations General Assembly Building in New York, Howe made what was probably his wittiest pronouncement on the subject of

37. Howe, "A Lesson from the Jefferson Memorial Competition," *A.I.A. Journal* 15 (March 1951), 116–19. Howe had previously served on the jury for the Smithsonian Museum competition in 1939; see chap. 7, n. 4.

38. Howe, "Jefferson National Expansion Competition," *Forum* 88 (March 1948), 14–18.

39. Ibid. See also "Jefferson Memorial Competition Winners," *Record* 103 (April 1948), 92–93; "The Gateway Arch . . . Dedicated," *Forum* 28 (June 1968), 32–37.

40. Gilmore D. Clarke, letter to William Wilson Wurster, 24 Feb. 1948.

41. Eero Saarinen, letter to Howe, 26 Feb. 1948.

monumentality. Commenting on Haskell's suggestion that the design "has elements of modern 'popular baroque,' " Howe wrote:

> · So it has been called the Baroque phase of modern architecture? What does Baroque mean? Grotesque, gigantesque, involved, as some might use the word, or, as others might use it, comparable to the works of that brief moment in the history of architecture when "measure yielded to melody, the static to the dynamic"?
>
> I should prefer a more analytical and less emotional adjective. One might call this interior, for instance, the Legislative phase of modern architecture. It seems like a well-meaning social statute adopted after long debate and many compromises, not always consistent. Then there is the last minute "joker" proposed by the Devil, always lurking in the back benches. The Devil, the fallen angel, says Denis de Rougemont, is "comme un artiste qui a perdu son génie et ne croit plus à la peinture, mais qui a conservé son métier et l'envie d'être à l'avant garde."
>
> But perhaps I give M. Léger too much stature.[42]

In May 1943 Howe became the first modernist architect to be made a Fellow of the American Institute of Architects. The citation was brief and surprisingly apt: "Upon the increment of ideas of creative individuals depends the evolution of our concept of design. In George Howe we have a happy combination of teacher, writer and creator, whose endeavors have extended the mental horizons of the profession. American architecture faces an international destiny. Relationships already established by Mr. Howe are richly suggestive of our opportunities and responsibilities toward a convalescent humanity."[43]

Howe's tenure of office in Washington can be principally noted for accomplishments in two important areas. In terms of the stylistic preferences of the governmental bureaucracy it marked the beginning of the shift away from the stripped classicism of the 1930s toward an acceptance of the formal vocabulary of the International Style. It also established Howe as a leading spokesman for American architecture and a leading force in the reconciliation between the seemingly conflicting beliefs of modernist architects, still in the minority, and the profession at large.

42. Howe, letter to Douglas Haskell, editor of *Forum*, 19 Sept. 1952. Reprinted in slightly different form in "UN Assembly. How Do Architects Like? First Reaction: Most of Them Don't," *Forum* 97 (Dec. 1952), 114–15.

43. "Citation to George Howe on being Made a Fellow of the American Institute of Architects," *A.I.A. Journal* 2 Aug. (1944), 77. See also *Forum* 81 (Nov. 1944), 214.

On 14 September 1945, Howe, claiming illness, tendered his resignation. With no future plans in sight, he could take with him only the admonition of his superior, W. E. Reynolds, that "it will be a great mistake for you to retire from the architectural profession to which you contribute so much."[44]

Howe's disappointment in his governmental career lingered on in the years immediately following his departure from Washington. He was commissioned in 1945 to design the Italian Campaign Memorial in Rome, but no trace of the design has been found.[45] He traveled and he tried to write a book, which he titled "Of Houses and Human Bondage. Reflections on Modern Architecture." He became increasingly dissatisfied with his marriage, and he and Maritje Howe were divorced in 1948.[46] Howe came close to remarriage a number of times. Especially serious was his romance with Virginia Biddle, a society columnist and a woman of dazzling charm, who described him as one of the ten most exciting men in Philadelphia: "urbane, with natural sophistication and a smooth approach to life."[47] To the world at large, he sustained his personal image. Reluctant to assume the role of elder statesman, Howe seemed unwilling to allow age and position to crowd out his pleasure in life.

In 1947 Howe was appointed Resident Architect at the American Academy in Rome. While at the Academy, he undertook preliminary studies for a new building for the United States consulate in Naples (*figs. 130, 131*). This design, which can now be studied only from photographs of the model, consists of a seven-story office block with a one-story compound behind. Though the office slab is symmetrical, the handling of such key elements as the entrance and roof terrace is not; overall, the effect is of a hybrid form of stripped classicism and cubism reminiscent of northern Italian modernist work of the late 1930s, and of Eric Mendelsohn's work in Israel. The scheme relies

44. W. E. Reynolds, letter to Howe, 14 Sept. 1945.

45. In a letter to Charles S. Cunningham, 10 May 1954, Howe wrote about this project: "since then [1945] nothing has been done."

46. Howe was 62 years old. Helen Howe West writes: "Why Ma and Pa found it necessary to divorce late in 1948 quite eludes me. I suppose Pa had a more than usually pressing girl who was determined to marry him. It seemed absurd to me (I had advocated a divorce in the 1920's and had my ears properly boxed for even using the dirty word), although I full well understood that their marriage had been on the rocks for a long time—but it did seem silly, as I kept pointing out—Ma was not a bit demanding and provided him a safety factor with which he could fend off predatory females. He didn't get the point and Ma acted like an offended Victorian. There were many girls in Father's life and it wasn't always easy sailing for Ma." *George Howe, Architect* (Philadelphia: William Nunn, 1973), p. 55; see also pp. 27, 58–59. See also William Stix Wasserman, letter to author, 8 Jan. 1974, which discusses Howe's romantic life at this time.

47. Virginia Biddle, "The Philadelphia Scene/The Ten Most Exciting Men in Philadelphia," *Philadelphia Evening Bulletin,* 30 Nov. 1952.

for its compositional strength on the exact detailing of the windows, which emphasize the wall as skin, and on their proportions suggesting the frame behind. It seems more than likely that this design, never before published but well known to American architects traveling in Rome at the time, influenced the reshaping of modern design into neoclassical modes in the early 1950s. Aspects of Kahn's AFL-CIO Medical Service Plan Building in Philadelphia and Johnson's Kneses Tifereth Israel Synagogue in Port Chester are related to Howe's project.[48]

Howe arrived at the Academy in May 1947 and remained there for more than two years, with occasional return trips to the U.S. While at the Academy he recommended Louis Kahn for a fellowship, enabling his former partner, who still had not found that direction which was to make his the towering American architectural talent of the 1960s, to visit Europe for the first time since the late 1920s. Kahn succeeded Howe as Resident Architect in 1950–51, the first year Howe was at Yale.[49]

In August 1949, Howe, while still at the Academy, was invited to become chairman of the Department of Architecture at Yale University. He assumed the position on 1 January 1950.[50] The department had not changed essentially since before the war, and by 1950 it lacked leadership. As Benjamin Thompson, a student there during the early forties and later a prominent architect closely connected with the Graduate School of Design at Harvard stated, "Yale was a good school. It never did have a serious formulation of its purpose, but it exposed you to many influences, which was fine."[51] Everett V. Meeks, formidable and resolutely antimodern, was dean of the School of Fine Arts for many years until his death in 1947. He had provided the school with strong direction until, near the end of his career, he faltered under pressures to accept modernist architecture as the formal basis for teaching design in the school. In the 1930s Yale and the University of Pennsylvania were the leading Beaux-Arts schools in the nation. Within the department itself, and especially after

48. See Scully, *Louis I. Kahn,* and John M. Jacobus, *Philip Johnson* (New York: Braziller, 1962).

49. Louis Kahn, et al., "On the Responsibility of the Architect," *Perspecta* 2 (1953), 45–57.

50. Charles Sawyer, at the time Dean of the School of Fine Arts at Yale, recalls that Kahn "initially suggested . . . Howe. . . . Also, I consulted Eero Saarinen, then a member of our University Council Advisory Committee, Ed Stone, who had been Chief Visiting Critic, Harold Hauf, and I think, Carroll Meeks and Henry Pfisterer." Letter to author, 9 Feb. 1974. In accepting the invitation, Howe, then at the American Academy, wrote to Sawyer: "I had no intention of entering the academic field but had rather made up my mind to live in Europe and take up a long deferred project to write a book." Handwritten letter, 31 Aug. 1949.

51. Thompson was quoted in "The Talk of the Town: New Store," *The New Yorker,* 28 Dec. 1963, p. 26.

Meeks's death, a succession of chief critics, including Wallace Harrison, Richard M. Bennett, and Edward D. Stone, was not able to make up in variety what the department lacked in overall commitment and direction. When upon Meeks's retirement Charles Sawyer was appointed dean and Harold Hauf chairman of the architecture department, it was hoped that their strong administrative abilities would provide the requisite leadership to cope with the influx of veterans who enrolled in the school and also return to the teaching program some of the luster of the prewar years. It did not, and by 1949 the students and, to a considerable extent, the faculty, were discontented and not a little envious of the brilliant Harvard scene which, ironically, was by then well past its peak of vitality, though it would take many years for this to become obvious. At the instigation of Louis Kahn, who was senior critic in residence at the time, Sawyer invited Howe to accept the chairmanship made vacant by Hauf's decision to retire to private practice.[52] It was felt that the luster of Howe's reputation would establish a new tone.

Howe seized the opportunity to cap his career in an unconventional way: aside from the European emigré modernists, no distinguished talent associated with the modern movement in America had as yet been offered a position of such importance in American architectural education. Howe brought to Yale his wisdom, his experience, what Wilder Green, a former student, has described as his "constructive cynicism and sophistication."[53] Above all, Howe brought his charm. To a faculty rent by conflicts, some petty and personal, many truly reflective of the state of American architecture at the time, he was able to apply, as he had in the difficult early days of modernism in America, the soothing balm of aristocratic geniality—too often, it would soon become

52. Hauf's appointment had been announced on 28 Oct. 1947. He was assisted by Edward D. Stone, who was "Senior Critic in Residence." Louis Kahn, Paul Schweikher, Carl Koch, and Gardiner Dailey were appointed as visiting critics in residence. Kahn was appointed chief critic in 1948. Shortly thereafter he undertook the "collaborative" project, traditionally a project given in the third year involving cooperative work with students in the painting and city planning programs. Interestingly enough, Kahn chose as the program the design of a headquarters for UNESCO, the design of which would involve an enormous column-free space, marking Kahn's first concerns with the design of long-span structures which was to have its earliest important manifestation in his design for the Yale Art Gallery, 1951–53. Kahn was reappointed as chief critic for the School in October 1949.

Sawyer writes: "Harold Hauf was an excellent administrator—manager of the Department; but he was not an innovator and some of our alumni in architecture and members of the Council Committee felt that our Department lacked the image and specific identity of Harvard or M. I. T." At the same time, Sawyer notes that though "there was general agreement that the School needed to move away from the Beaux Arts tradition which had been its hallmark during the administration of my predecessor, Everett Meeks, there was also a rather strong resentment against following too closely in the direction of Harvard." Letter, 9 Feb. 1974.

53. Wilder Green, telephone conversation with author, Jan. 1974. See also Sawyer, letter, 9 Feb. 1974.

apparent, at the expense of a genuine solution to the problems at hand.

Howe's arrival at Yale in February 1950, virtually coinciding with the installation of Josef Albers as chairman of the Department of Art in July 1950 (he had been a visiting critic at Yale since October 1949), marked the beginning of the university's re-ascendancy in the visual arts.[54] Howe and Albers admired each other immensely, and there are certainly similarities between Albers's ambiguously complex, spatially interwoven drawings of the early fifties and the complex geometric projections which Howe used to construct for relaxation.[55] In any case, the excitement of Albers's new teaching techniques, and the hostile reaction of the vestigial Beaux-Arts faculty was complemented, less dramatically, by Howe's innovations in the Department of Architecture.

Howe's view of the department's philosophical position was highly critical. Later, he recalled the situation as he had found it:

1. The first year students were being neglected by the administration. [Their teacher, Eugene Nalle,] was working under great difficulties, in quarters usually known as the "snake pit," and under an imposed program of the direst and most unimaginative kind.

2. The second year students were being projected into a planning program of the crassest two-dimensional functional nature. They were confused and discontented. This discontent was spreading to the first

54. Yale University News Bureau, Release 479, 22 Feb. 1950. Because architecture was a department in the School of Fine Arts, and because Sawyer had come to Yale in 1948 "with a specific commitment to develop some inter-relationship and interaction between the various aspects of the visual arts," it was necessary that the new chairman for the Art Department be acceptable to the Architecture Department as well. Howe was very enthusiastic about Albers and "assisted" Sawyer "in persuading [him] to come to Yale. . . . There was excellent personal rapport between Albers and Howe, although the real interaction between the departments was less than I had hoped and anticipated." Sawyer, letter, 9 Feb. 1974.

55. Howe's lifelong interest in mathematics increased in the late thirties and became for him a principal source of relaxation, stimulation, and fascination. See his "Introduction to the Subject," talk delivered at Museum of Modern Art symposium "De Divina Proportione," 11 March 1952, typescript. In 1938 he noted his pleasure in the following popular scientific books: *Mathematics for the Millions* and *The Evolution of Scientific Thought.* "George Howe," in Harvard University, *Class of 1908, Secretary's Seventh Report* (Cambridge, Mass., 1938). At his death his library included: Gyorgy Kepes, *The Language of Vision* (annotated); Alfred North Whitehead, *Science and the Modern World* (annotated); Le Corbusier, *The Modulor;* Richard Stevens Burington and Charles Chapman Torrance, *Higher Mathematics; Review of Metaphysics* (1953–54); *The Philosophy of Nietszche;* Henri Frankfort, et al., *Before Philosophy;* Matila C. Ghyka, *Esthétique des Proportions dans la Nature et dans les Arts;* Oswald Spengler, *The Decline of the West,* vols. 1 and 2; D'Arcy Wentworth Thompson, *On Growth and Form;* George Gamow, *One, Two, Three . . . Infinity;* Norbert Weiner, *Cybernetics;* Alfred North Whitehead, *The Aims of Education* (annotated); Erich Heller, *The Disinherited Mind;* Lincoln Barnett, *The Universe and Doctor Einstein;* William James, *The Varieties of Religious Experience.*

year students to such a point that a large number of them, in 1951, said they had rather go to another school than into second year design at Yale. I received protesting petitions and delegations.[56]

In the third and fourth years things were even worse, with students "in general, incapable of three-dimensional thinking and prone to 'slap an elevation' on a plan at the last minute."[57]

Howe's personal success at Yale was enormous from the start. Sardonic, cynical, and good natured, by the sheer magnetism of his presence he seemed to infuse new life into the school. Elegantly, if improbably, dressed in green tyrolean hat, fawn-colored vest, tweed coat, and gray flannels, and armed with a host of clever remarks, he would engage the students in conversation, disarm them, and find out precisely what bothered them. Often he would call to a student straight faced, though with an impish twinkle, and say to him something like: "Do you know, statistics show that eighty-five percent of New York businessmen like to fornicate by north light? After lectures or juries, he would usually invite a group of students to his rooms at Jonathan Edwards College for an informal session of conversation and drinking. These he called meetings of the Digressionist Club. Wilder Green, Peter Millard, James Jarrett, and Earl Carlin were among the students who constituted the Digressionist membership.

But Howe's preferred method of communication was the formal lecture, delivered from time to time during the school year. These lectures and a few reports and memoranda constitute the clearest records of what Howe was attempting to achieve at Yale. Shortly after taking office, Howe addressed the alumni on 22 February 1950 about a problem which had long concerned him: the duality of imagination and intellect in architecture as manifested in the conflicting roles of the architect as artist and technician. This talk established the basis of his regime at Yale—insistence on the role of architecture as an artistic discipline involved with issues of administration, planning, and simple problem solving. He said, "We must not lose sight of the fact that the primary purpose of architectural schools is to create architects not to prepare draftsmen for office work." Design is paramount, and "over-emphasis on technological preparation must not be allowed to interfere." A mean between technical studies and design must be found. The purpose of an architectural school, the training of artists must not be lost, but an "artist who is not technically competent in his art is no artist."[58]

---

56. "Memorandum to Dean Sawyer," 4 Nov. 1954. Peter Millard largely confirmed Howe's assessment of the situation in conversation with author, 17 Jan. 1974.

57. Howe, ibid.

58. Howe, untitled lecture, quoted in Yale University News Bureau, Release 479, 22 Feb. 1950.

Howe elaborated on his philosophy of architectural education in a talk delivered before the Department of Architecture on 20 September 1951. Using the same title Charles Herbert Moore had used thirty years before, "Training for the Practice of Architecture," he spoke of his intention to develop a "course of training . . . peculiarly Yale's, based on no doctrine or theory but worked out from day to day by experience. When our course of training becomes so stabilized it will be time to begin again from the beginning."

Howe reiterated his belief in the dual concomitants of architectural form, imagination and intellect, going on to define the practice of architecture as "the occupation, with intent to create significant form, of producing designs for and producing the execution of, any and every sort of work constructed for the use of man." To this end all considerations, economic, technologic, and sociologic, were to be directed. Only when the two streams of imagination and intellect unite do we have style. Style is not made, but discovered. It is "full of the thoughts and feelings . . . of the day and when it is discovered becomes the property of a whole culture, to draw on in its turn."[59]

Howe delivered one of his most important talks before the third-year class on 5 October 1953 as an introduction to their first major design problem that term, a bank. It contained the key to that philosophy of design which Howe had been developing since his earliest concern in the thirties with spatial flow, which he came to call "the path of the feet and the eyes." This doctrine, an explicit criticism of Giedeon's conceptual emphasis on spatial flow, was soundly based on faith in the perceptual capabilities of architects and ordinary people alike. It grew from Howe's belief that "in thinking of human scale" one should think of man "as an eye suspended in space some five feet above the surface of the earth, on plane or mountain or some artificial eminence created by man. Think of man especially as a mobile eye, supported on a pair of feet, and remember that the roving eye can experience only that to which the feet conduct it. So we come to the notion of the path of the feet and the eyes, by which the living experience of architecture is determined, and the notion of going in and going out, the transition from natural space to man-defined space."

Howe stressed his claim that

> thinking of structure from the beginning as an experience in following the path of the feet and the eyes immediately frees the mind from memory overlays to follow direct experience in relation to an immediate new situation. This leads at once to a consideration of the functional significance

59. Howe, "Training for the Practice of Architecture," *Perspecta* I (1952), 1–5.

of man. We have to admit that man may be sometimes nobly and sometimes not nobly (let's not say ignobly) functional. Whichever he may be in any particular case it must be the intention of architecture to enhance his dignity. So we come to the notion of pageantry and ceremony, pageantry as a passing through, approach, ceremony as pause; whether to and through the portal of a cathedral to pause at the altar rail or to and through the grape arbor to pause in the darkly sober interior of the now generally vanished outhouse.[60]

Howe ranked among his most important contributions to Yale his discovery of Eugene Nalle and their collaborative development of

a system of ordered exercises which would prepare the minds of the students *in general* for independent thought and work. If such a system is not stultifying in music or medicine I could not conceive that it would be so in architecture. With this end in view I joined the first year staff, abandoned the imposed program, and started experimenting with such general ideas as space, movement in space, composition, color, drawing, and so forth, without regard to specific function or dry contemporary technics.

All this was largely an attitude in my mind, but Mr. Nalle enthusiastically embraced it and developed it over a period of four years into the system of preparation which now exists.[61]

Nalle, a man of intense dedication, was a Texan who had come to Yale as a graduate student after World War II but never completed his training as an architect. Badly injured in an airplane crash during the war, his looks and manner couldn't have been less like Howe's. Howe, who was by nature inclined to delegate details to others, recognized Nalle's almost obsessive and untiring

---

60. Howe, "Talk to Third Year Students," 5 Oct. 1953. This talk is echoed remarkably by Philip Johnson in his "Whence and Whither: The Processional Element in Architecture," *Perspecta* 9–10 (1965), 167–78.

61. Howe, "Report to the President by the Retiring Chairman," July 1954. Sawyer confirms Howe's view of the basic design program. He writes: "In the initial stages, (Howe) had considerable success. Projects were clarified, simplified and arranged in a sequence adapted to the experience of students at that level; there was more concern both for draughtsmanship, for the analysis of space, and for simpler forms of construction. Wally Harrison had said to me earlier that 'Yale turns out too many talking architects,' a situation Howe set out to remedy. While considerably more time was demanded of the students, they seemed to respond affirmatively to the discipline. In the process, however, George did stir up some resistance on the part of the resident design faculty and the architectural historians who felt that their own contributions to the program were being minimized, but there was no apparent antagonism to Howe personally; he was generally respected by students and faculty alike." Letter, 9 Feb. 1974.

dedication to his ideals and to students. He strengthened his position on the faculty and made him "the foundation stone" of his "teaching structure." By 1953 Howe had succeeded in establishing a combined College and professional course for Yale students, leading to a B.A. and B. Arch. degree in six years and entrusting the first two years of the architectural program (the middle two of the combined program) to Nalle's direction. "These two years of architectural design," Howe wrote in his annual report for 1952–53, "have finally been combined into a systematic lower school discipline in preparation for greater freedom in the Third and Fourth years." Included in this program was an "integration of engineering design and historical background with architectural design" which Howe optimistically felt "to be on the way to realization."[62]

Nalle's philosophy and his techniques of teaching have become obscured by the events that followed Howe's retirement in 1953. What does seem clear is that Howe established the philosophical structure for the program and that Nalle concerned himself with its implementation. Tremendous emphasis was placed on the relationship of small elements of the building fabric. The expression of joinery became a fundamental concern in the design process. Nalle's inarticulate and uncommunicative nature caused him to be regarded by some as an almost Zenlike figure of remarkable depth. King-Lui Wu, then beginning his teaching career, says that Nalle, having put the students into the darkness, offered them one magnificently glowing light at a time, never revealing to them the complexity and interdependence of the issues. Howe of course would counterbalance Nalle's single-mindedness, and he saw to it that others like Philip Johnson, Louis Kahn, and Buckminster Fuller were at hand to present a diversity of viewpoints.

In addition to Nalle's specific strengths and limitations in the studio, his and Howe's attitudes toward the relationship of a professional program to the university as a whole is a critical one. They sought to legislate the exposure of architecture students to disciplines outside design by proposing the establishment of special courses in which these disciplines would be presented to students in the context of an overall architectural approach. Their position, which many on the university faculty considered a fundamentally anti-intel-

62. Howe, "Annual Report of the Chairman, 1952–53," 3 June 1953, 2 pp., typescript. Visiting faculty included Frederick Kiesler, Elbert Peets, Pietro Belluschi, R. Buckminster Fuller, Harwell Hamilton Harris, and Paul Schweikher. Permanent staff and faculty included Eugene Nalle, Christopher Tunnard, Louis Kahn, Robert Coolidge, and King-Lui Wu. With regard to Howe and Sawyer's restructuring of the Yale College architecture major, see Charles Sawyer, letter to Dean William C. DeVane, 29 Oct. 1952 (George Howe Collection, Avery Library, Columbia).

lectual attitude, and which seems so much a contradiction of Howe's beliefs as developed over a lifetime, was articulated by Howe in his final report to President A. Whitney Griswold:

Glib verbal knowledge is a dangerous possession, I am convinced, to the budding visual artist, whose proper medium of expression is the image, not the word, whose natural endowment is intuition, not intellect. To apprehend the futility of aesthetic theory as a tool for the creation of architecture it is necessary only to read Borissavlievithc's long, exhaustive and dull dissertation on the subject. Filled with sketchy theories of all kinds, the Yale major is convinced that talking architecture, science, economics, sociology, is the way to create three-dimensional form in the Modern World.

So the first step in reeducating the aspirant architect seemed to me, in consultation with Mr. Nalle, to be to remove him from the possibility of using the language of words and to force him to use only the visual language of form, in other words to set him tasks to perform having to do with space, projections, value and color contrasts, and so forth. All the so-called "contemporary" problems, around which the verbiage of modern architecture has gathered, together with all the familiar associative images presented by everyday life and current publications, could no longer be argued about and imitated. This unusual circumscription of the design program was enthusiastically embraced by Mr. Nalle and developed by him for beyond anything I had conceived. But the circumscription is more apparent than real. By a series of progressive exercises, well within the scope of the novice's understanding, the student is freed from the excessive number of variables to be considered in the design of, say, a house, and can develop his own interpretations without reference to precedent of any kind, as his personality unfolds. Furthermore there is ample opportunity to discuss the philosophy of building as a trade, a science and an art, instead of kitchen equipment, furniture design, industrial products and the rest, which are always being thrust under the student's nose without the intervention of his instructors. Last but not least the student becomes proficient in his trade of drawing, lettering, composition, projections and space presentation without the necessity of attending separate courses in drafting, perspective, watercolor and the rest, as is the general custom.

The real meaning of this discipline cannot be expressed in words. Only an examination of the results produced can convey any impression of its fundamental interest. It is laborious and long, lasting two years, and in this day of short cuts has been criticized on that score. Suffice it to say, however, that it has proved its worth. The students become competent craftsmen, able to secure employment in good offices at an early stage in their training, and in the last two years of their professional course are intellectually able to associate whatever cultural background they may have acquired at any stage in their education with the intuitional function of visual design. They are no longer blind imitators of stylistic modern models but, within their natural capacities, creators in their own right.[63]

More succinctly, then, Nalle's methods involved the students directly with wood and masonry construction, often using the actual materials in the drafting room in a manner many felt more appropriate to the engineering laboratory or to the contractor's shed.

Howe's tenure as chairman was circumscribed by Yale's compulsory retirement age of sixty-eight and in 1952, two years before he was to retire, he suggested that Paul Schweikher, who had taught under Hauf, be invited to succeed him. Schweikher rejoined the faculty in 1953, first as critic and then in 1954 as chairman.[64] Schweiker, a man of very different temperament

63. Howe, " Report to the President by the Retiring Chairman." For a student's view of Yale during the term following Howe's retirement, but just before the dam burst, see Edwin A. Kent, "Graduate Schools: V. School of Fine Arts; New Trends," *Yale Daily News,* 31 Oct. 1954. The closest one is now able to come to Nalle's own philosophy of design is his article "Whole Design," in *Perspecta* 1 (1952), 6–7. In it one can sense some of the compelling urgency of his approach, his belief that "architecture, with its irrationally complex yet deep roots of personal discipline, demands an extremely broad and viable outlook. It must encompass intuitive sensibility to the immediate situation observable in short range fact; this must be combined with a 'moral behavior' (in the largest sense of the word) beyond egocentric sentimentality which demands a continual intellectual wrestling with theory—a philosophic study of relationships between the inner and outer worlds of reality." For a further discussion of this period at Yale and Nalle and Howe's relationship, see my forthcoming article, "Yale: 1950–65," scheduled for publication in *Oppositions* 4 (Fall 1974).

64. "Schweikher Appointed Professor of Architecture," Yale University News Bureau, Release 871, 22 June 1953. Sawyer recalls the sequence of events as follows: "As George Howe approached the age for mandatory retirement, we began a search for a successor. Because the profession was then in one of its periodic and comparative booms, the options were rather limited. . . . Howe himself suggested Paul Schweikher, who had served as a visiting critic during the previous year, apparently with excellent results. Saarinen, who had been a contemporary of Schweikher's in architecture at Yale, supported him and we had favorable reports from our architectural alumni in the Chicago area. . . . While his reputation was as something of a 'loner' he seems to have been generally respected by his contemporaries . . . I liked him personally—and I still do. We thought we were fortunate in his acceptance of the Chairmanship," Letter, 9 Feb. 1974.

from Howe, was brusque and impatient; he also tended to confuse his personal philosophic commitments—then moving from Wright to Mies—with the best interests of the department's curriculum. His professional practice was burgeoning and he was out of New Haven a great deal of the time. Even more than Howe, he relied on Nalle, but without Howe's abilities to modify Nalle's single-mindedness, to gloss over his abrasive manner. Not surprisingly, in November 1954, just five months after his retirement to Philadelphia, Howe was asked by Dean Sawyer to come back to New Haven to meet with the faculty members separately and prepare a report.

The faculty's principal criticism was focused on Nalle, whom, according to Howe's report, they regarded as "dictatorial, unfair and vindictive, confused, narrow, psychopathic." In response to these charges, Howe cited instances of student enthusiasm for Nalle although he did not acknowledge the accusations with a direct refutation. As to claims that the "whole method of instruction evolved by Mr. Nalle, at my suggestion, is too analytical, not free enough, distorted, unhumanistic, contrary to the Yale ideal of the free exchange of ideas," Howe ventured total disagreement, going on to claim that the principle of "integrated teaching in various fields under the leadership of architecture, in an architectural school" is thoroughly sound and should be continued by whatever means are possible.

Howe's view was simplistic, defensive, and bitter, that of a tired, disengaged man leaning on his charm. He concluded his report:

> When I was in New Haven, I listened patiently, answering only here and there with a protest that not the new Chairman but the old was responsible for much of what they found to criticize. That, they said, was somehow different. Why? Only, I suspect, because they were used to his weird ways. However that may be, the longer I think about it the more indignant I become at the parochial behavior, the petty vanity, the lack of generosity and understanding, of patience and forebearance, the seemingly unconscious disloyalty to their beloved Yale of my former colleagues.
>
> None of this, smiling diplomat that I am, will I say to their faces. I shall tell them only that I have reported their sentiments to you as best I could and retire from the scene. They complained that you and Paul [Schweikher] would not listen to them. One of them said to me that he felt better already after talking to me. If that is the feeling of others my purpose in injecting myself into the argument will have been fulfilled.
>
> On reading over this hasty script I find I have failed to mention one

interesting point. When the Department was really in confusion a few years ago the humanists found no fault with the system. Only the idea of a professional discipline seems to shock them. Shall I laugh or cry?[65]

Howe was right in at least one respect. It had been his charm and commitment to excellence which acted as the bonding agent. Now, with it gone, everything began to fall apart.[66] The situation continued to decline after his visit. As Calvin M. Trillin reported in the *Yale Daily News,* the criticism made by the undergraduate majors centering around Nalle's first- and second-year design program was four-fold: "1) inadequate criticism by the instructors, 2) the arbitrary grading of creative projects by one man, 3) the absence of diversity and depth within the course, and 4) the insufficient number of instructors."[67]

Yale undergraduates majoring in architecture took the equivalent of five courses in the school, all graded by Nalle despite the fact that Schweikher, in the fall of 1954, had agreed to participate more regularly in the grading processes. It was, however, neither the student protests over grading nor the resentment of the faculty over Nalle's high-handed tactics and his single-minded attitudes toward form that forced the issue, but the visit of the National Architectural Accrediting Board which, casting a disapproving eye on the entire situation and especially on Nalle's huge burden of responsibility, ultimately left University Provost Edgar Furniss "with the impression that more funds should be devoted to the department."[68]

On 22 February 1955 the University announced its intention to investigate the controversy, whose central issue, aside from personalities, seemed, according to Trillin, to be one of "diversity as opposed to regimentation."[69] Despite Schweikher's implied support of Nalle, the students and some of the faculty demanded administrative reform which included reinstatement of the open-jury system in the third and fourth years and use of a grading committee in

65. Howe, "Memorandum to Dean Sawyer."

66. Ibid. See also Calvin M. Trillin, "Architecture, Yale's Latest Controversy," *Yale Daily News,* 3 March 1955, p. 2.

67. Trillin, "Students, Faculty, Hit Architectural School," *Yale Daily News,* 18 Feb. 1955, pp. 1, 4.

68. Quoted in "Regimented Approach? Controversy Sweeps Architecture School," unsigned editorial, *Yale Daily News,* 18 Feb. 1955, p. 2. See also "Architectural School Listed by Accrediting Board on Provisional Basis, 56–57," *New York Times,* 6 Jan. 1957, p. 73. This article was prepared long after the Board's decision had become known to the University.

69. Trillin, "University to Investigate Architecture Controversy," *Yale Daily News,* 22 Feb. 1955, p. 1. For a defense of the school by a fourth-year student, see Walter Kaplan, "Communication. Student Vindicates Architecture Policy," *Yale Daily News,* 26 Feb. 1955, p. 2.

the first and second years. In addition, more instructors were to be hired, thereby reducing Nalle's teaching load and his influence as well.[70] Thus the issue of Nalle's teaching methods, never openly aired, was camouflaged in administrative reform.[71] The desire of the University to gloss over the conflicts was aided by Howe's death on 16 April 1955. Without a champion, the agony of his rejection must have become almost unbearable when Schweikher's position was unquestionably weakened. For Nalle, his authority over the first and second year program was ended. In 1956 Schweikher resigned; Nalle was able to stay only a little longer.[72] By 1958 the School of Fine Arts

70. Trillin, "Architecture Students Win Grading Reforms," *Yale Daily News,* 25 March 1955, p. 1. Sawyer writes: "Eugene Nalle, [Howe's] chosen instrument in carrying out the basic program, bore the brunt of this criticism. Nalle, although apparently an effective and dedicated teacher, was no diplomat himself, and tended to be contemptuous of the academics and the non-professional aspects of the curriculum. Gradually, the students divided into cliques: Nalle's ardent supporters and his detractors." Letter, 9 Feb. 1974.

71. For Schweikher's description of the situation, see Trillin, "Architecture, Yale's Latest Controversy." The essence of Nalle's controlled approach to learning is clearly seen in Schweikher's exposition of the prevailing teaching philosophy as one of "the discipline of orderly acquisition, coming to know a few things well in a step by step procedure. It uses discipline as a kind of checkrein to the unlearned, uninformed, impulsive gush (the rush of notions to the head) that is so often mistaken for the ingenuity of creative action but results as frequently in formless juxtaposition." Kahn, who along with Carroll Meeks and King-Lui Wu formed the core of the opposition to Schweikher, commented in the same article that "students should be given a consciousness of the whole. They should be presented with a wider span of criticism. They should never be allowed to lose sight of the whole problem of architecture during each of their four years. They should not be taught one part one year, one part the next, etc. The present conception is that a short program will lead to more learning. I believe that no man is big enough to impose a single approach."

Sawyer writes: "Why then the 'collapse' of the Department . . . under Schweikher's Chairmanship? In general Schweikher followed closely the pattern which George Howe had established; they both believed in a rigorous discipline in the basic design stages. Where George could enforce it with a smile and the aura of his own personality, Paul gave the impression of being rigid, unyielding, and unwilling to listen to others. He was a staunch supporter of Gene Nalle, then under sharp attack from faculty and students which had come to the attention of the University administration. Quite unwisely, I think, Schweikher placed Nalle in overall charge of third year design, in addition to his responsibilities for the first two years, and since the latter had neither professional stature or the tenure to protect himself from his critics, this only added to his burdens. When the students rebelled, Schweikher assumed this responsibility himself, but by that time, 'the fat was in the fire,' and in a remarkably short time the whole morale and effectiveness of the Department deteriorated. . . . The basic program, which had seemed innovative and adventurous in Howe's administration, now appeared to students and critics sterile and academic, although the form was essentially the same. . . . While the personal rapport between Albers and Schweikher was excellent, there was no longer any real association between the Departments." Letter, 9 Feb. 1974.

72. Nalle was replaced as head of the first year at the end of the 1954–55 academic year by T. Gorm Hansen. See Trillin, "Committee Sanctions Architecture Revisions," *Yale Daily News,* 31 May 1955, p. 1. See also "Architecture Report to Get Official Study," idem., 12 May 1955, p. 1.

was completely reorganized, emerging as the School of Art and Architecture with a new dean, Gibson A. Danes, and a new chairman for architecture, Paul Rudolph, under whose direction Yale was propelled into a position of international prominence in architectural education.[73]

Other aspects of Howe's chairmanship enjoyed a more lasting influence. Principal among these were his exchange of letters with the philosopher Paul Weiss, then developing his ideas on the arts in general which are recorded in his books, *Nine Basic Arts* and *The World of Art;* the founding of *Perspecta, The Yale Architectural Journal;* the deflection of Yale's building policy from the revivalism of the prewar period toward an adventurous pursuit of that which is most innovative in modern design.

Perspecta's first issue appeared in the summer of 1952. Generously underwritten by Howe and others, it immediately exhibited a professionalism that has come to distinguish it from other student magazines and from the so-called professional journals as well. *Perspecta's* origin, according to Howe's preface to the first issue, grew out of his

> custom to listen to the complaints of my students and discuss with them the problems of contemporary architecture beyond the limits of the drafting room.
>
> When I returned from a weekend in the summer of 1950 I reported to them that Mies van der Rohe had said to me "We know what design is." When I returned from a New Year's excursion in 1951 I reported to them that Frank Lloyd Wright had said to me "I am the background." While expressing their admiration of these two eminent architects the students refused to accept their judgments as final.
>
> Yet, inexperienced as they are in life and even in their trade, they were unable to offer alternatives to these expressions of personal satisfaction. So we came to the conclusion that they should create a medium of expression for themselves through which the potentialities of con-

73. See J. G. Fritzinger, Jr., "Arts Division Replaced in Major Readjustment," *Yale Daily News,* 18 Oct. 1955, p. 1. This marks the first of a series of administrative moves eventually leading to the creation in 1958 of the posts occupied by Danes and Rudolph. Schweikher's resignation is documented in "Schweikher to Submit Resignation from Top Architecture Post," *Yale Daily News,* 8 Feb. 1956, p. 1; "Schweikher Leaves as Architecture Department Head," *New York Times,* 23 Feb. 1956, p. 25. See also Peter F. Hannah, "A Year's Progress. Yale Architecture Controversy: Results?," *Yale Daily News,* 16 March 1956, p. 16; "Dr. Danes Named Dean, P. Rudolph Architecture Department Chairman," *New York Times,* 12 June 1957, p. 29.

temporary expression in architecture might be explored without pro-grammatic implications.

The first number of *Perspecta* is but a beginning. It proposes to estab-lish the arguments that revolve around the axis of contemporary archi-tecture on a broader turntable, encompassing the past as well as the present: and extendable to the future. To all architects, teachers, students *Perspecta* offers a place on the *merry-go-round*.[74]

Perspecta has fulfilled Howe's hopes, and, in subsequent issues has main-tained the highest standards of architectural journalism: idiosyncratic and controversial, chameleonlike and without strangling editorial bias, it is, to this day, a serious and provocative journal of opinion, more an indication than a reflection of the multiple directions of architectural thought in our time. The first three issues truly illuminate the vitality of the years of Howe's chairman-ship.[75] Especially in the first two years of his tenure, Yale was freewheeling and indulgent of innovation and controversy.[76] Howe was able to accommo-date Nalle's earthiness as well as Philip Johnson's sophistication and for-malism.[77] Johnson, then a critic at the school and frequent member of its architectural juries, was so enthusiastic he claimed that were he to go to archi-tecture school over again, Yale would have been the place "because it is a greater madhouse than the rest and has fine 'gentlemen' working there."[78] Howe, together with Paul Weiss, nursed, indulged, and stimulated Kahn, not only as architect but as philosopher. The completion of the Art Gallery and Design Center and the publication in *Perspecta 2* of Kahn's early critical

74. Howe, "Preface," *Perspecta* 1 (1952), 1.

75. Perhaps the most splendid written document of the Yale scene in the early fifties is the con-versation, "On the Responsibility of the Architect," *Perspecta* 2 (1953), pp. 2–5. A compilation of conversations held in a studio apartment shared by a number of students and combined to give the impression of one conversation, it is a key document.

76. Edwin Gilbert's novel, *Native Stone* (Garden City: Doubleday, 1956), is set at Yale in the time of Howe's chairmanship, and in it both he and Kahn are portrayed. The character Matthew Pierce is modeled on Howe ("tall, frosty-eyed chairman with the inimitable aura of dark elegance," p. 108), as is the character Vernon Austin.

77. In addition to helping to found *Perspecta,* Howe also encouraged students to meet in-formally with architects. Often he would arrange for certain architects, normally inaccessible to students, to visit the School. Frank Lloyd Wright was one of these.

Sawyer writes: "While Johnson was an occasional visiting critic in Howe's tenure, I don't think that he was especially influential or their relationship especially close. He did serve as something of a gadfly with the students and there was considerable disagreement among them as to his effectiveness as a teacher. He was interested in and active in the support of the Program in Typographic Design under Alvin Eisenman, and subsequently of Perspecta." Letter, 9 Feb. 1974.

78. Johnson, quoted in "The Next Fifty Years," *Forum* 94 (June 1951), 165–70.

design statements, in *Perspecta 3* of his "Order is Design," and in *Perspecta 4* of his "Architecture is the Thoughtful Making of Spaces" mark the beginning of his maturity as an architect. Buckminster Fuller, also, was present and indulged. His influence on Kahn's design for the Art Gallery is obvious, and the story of his "Architect-Painter Collaborative" teaching project of 1952 is documented in *Perspecta 2*.[79]

Much has been written about Kahn's Art Gallery; yet while there is no doubt that the design was a milestone both in his development and in the evolution of modern architecture beyond the timidities of form characteristic of the 1940s, Howe's role in the building's conception and in its implementation remains undefined. For one thing, it was Howe who secured the commission for Kahn. The University had already become resigned to a modern design, largely through the efforts of Philip L. Goodwin, who had begun preparing designs as early as 1941. As Kahn himself pointed out in 1954, Goodwin "fought the battle for modern architecture at Yale and he won!"[80] By 1950 Goodwin, in semiretirement, did not want the job, and he recommended Philip Johnson, the director of architecture at the Museum of Modern Art and, as yet, virtually untried as an architect. But Howe intervened and convinced Yale's new president, A. Whitney Griswold, that Kahn, more experienced and already a highly respected, though as yet unfulfilled architect, ought to be given the job. Griswold agreed, and Kahn, in association with Douglas Orr and in consultation with Howe, was awarded the design. It is Howe who is credited with the organizing conception of the building, its extreme flexibility. Toward implementating that idea, Howe further contributed the idea of the "pogo panels"—five-foot-wide, floor-to-ceiling panels, arrangeable in series, with spring-mounted, synthetic rubber-tipped feet—which made the building truly flexible on a day-to-day basis. The building remains a triumph for Kahn and for Yale as well: a unique first statement for

---

79. For a general discussion of the interrelationship between Howe, Nalle, and Kahn during Howe's tenure at Yale, and for the effect of Fuller on the design of the Yale Art Gallery, see Scully, *Louis I. Kahn,* pp. 18–21; R. Buckminster Fuller, "The Yale Collaborative. The Cardboard House," *Perspecta* 2 (1953), 28–35.

80. For Goodwin's design, see "Art Gallery Extension," Yale Associates *Bulletin* 10, no. 2 (Dec. 1941), 1–3. Goodwin's scheme was still alive in 1950; see "Big Windows at Yale," *Forum* 92 (March 1950), 149. Howe's role in securing the commission for Kahn is touched on by Scully in his *American Architecture and Urbanism* (New York: Praeger, 1969), p. 214.

Kahn, is quoted in George Sanderson, "Extension: University Art Gallery and Design Center," *Progressive Architecture* 35 (May 1954), 88–92. See also *Yale Daily News,* 6–7 Nov. 1953, esp. Henry S. F. Cooper, "The Architect Speaks," and Vincent Scully, "Somber and Archaic; Expressive Tension;" "Gallery Fulfills Designer's Dreams," *Yale Daily News,* 9 March 1955, p. 1.

the university, marked by boldness and what was described at the time as a show of "determination to return to design fundamentals."[81] Moreover, Howe can surely be credited with starting Griswold on that path as a patron of architecture, which, perhaps more than any other, is his legacy to Yale.[82]

Howe retired from Yale in June 1954. At a party attended by two hundred friends, colleagues, and students, he was presented with a painting by Josef Albers and with a medal designed by the students, inscribed on one side with his motto, *illegitimus non est carborundum* (which he chose to translate, "Don't let the bastards grind you down"), and on the other with *George Howe, Architectus Optimus, Philadelphiae, Cantabrigiaeque Alumnus In Medaillis Yalensium Haerens.*[83] He returned to Philadelphia and concentrated his energies on his private practice with Robert Montgomery Brown and on related professional activities. His design for the television studios of station WCAU, Philadelphia, had just been completed, (*fig. 132*) and ground was broken in August for the new headquarters of the Philadelphia *Evening and Sunday Bulletin,* an enormous structure, including two basements and track facilities for twelve railroad cars of newsprint rolls, set behind a 200-foot parking plaza facing Pennsylvania Station and stretching 1,000 feet along Market Street (*fig. 133*). Both buildings are in a distinctly minor key, though the *Bulletin* building, reflecting Wright's administration building for the Johnson Wax Company, gives strong definition to the street and makes the parking lot a surprisingly pleasant amenity.

Ever since his return to nongovernmental life in 1945, Howe's interest in the practice of architecture was minimal. He was, however, becoming more enthusiastic about his role as an elder statesman, and in addition to his academic responsibilities, he continued to speak out on professional issues, lecture, and sit on advisory boards.[84] His principal activities focused on Philadelphia, which, under the leadership of Edmund Bacon, chairman of its Planning Commission, was undergoing what was to become known as a "renaissance."

81. Sanderson, "Extension."

82. See Walter McQuade, "Building Years of a Yale Man," *Forum* 118 (June 1963), 88–93.

83. Scully writes: "The word should be *illegitimis;* it was incorrectly cut by the engraver. Earl Carlin and I had the honor of making the presentations. We also gave him a large reproduction of a painting by Bouguereau of some nymphs dragging a satyr into the water, and we told him that it represented 'other conspicuous virtues' of his. He seemed to treasure it most of all and went off clutching it."

84. Typical of these pronouncements are his comments on the United Nations Assembly Building; see n. 46 above and text.

In particular, Howe became embroiled in controversy concerning Penn Center, although his role was peripheral and his name appears to have been used to gloss over what has since been criticized heavily. Howe was asked to sit on and chair a Citizens Advisory Board of Design, appointed by the Pennsylvania Railroad. The other members were Bacon and Robert Dowling.

The story of the "battle for Penn Center," key to the success of Bacon's overall planning strategy, and of the failure of ideals in the face of the "hard reality" of the Uris Brothers' sponsorship of the project has been documented by James Reichley.[85] Howe's role was that of conciliator; recognizing the pressures of the moment and the Uris Brothers' insistence on a "quick profit," he tried to salvage as much as he could of the intended grandeur of Bacon's initial plan. Kahn, already recognized as Philadelphia's leading architect, was the fly in the ointment. Critical of Bacon and his methods—"A frustrated architect. A planner who thinks he is a politician—Kahn described his own initial scheme as "an attempt to recreate Pisa" while calling the Bacon-Dowling compromise, with its simplistic plan of off-set slabs, "two-step architecture."[86] But it was against the first Uris Brothers design submission, prepared by Emery Roth and Sons, architects of New York, that Kahn directed the principal force of his attack: in school, he said, the design "would have received the mark of zero." Howe and Bacon, reserving objections to the bland appearance of the proposed design, recommended that the railroad (whom, it should be remembered, they represented as part of a Board of Design) reject the design because it lacked provision of subterranean concourses, which were, from the first, the organizing feature of the overall planning concept. Dowling did not join in their dissent. Kahn continued to hammer away at the Uris scheme, and Bacon, realizing, as Reichley explains it, "that the railroad was using him as an ornament," resigned from the Board of Design. Howe, friendly to the directors of the railroad and to Bacon, persuaded him to "stick it out."

Ground was broken for the first Uris building on 24 November 1953. Its design is marginally superior to earlier submissions, but it failed to suggest a meaningful connection with future development and with the pre-existing structures in the immediate vicinity. By January 1954 many concerned, including Bacon, Howe, and even Dowling, felt that, as Reichley writes, "some-

85. James Reichley, "Philadelphia Does It: The Battle for Penn Center," *Harper's* 214 (Feb. 1957), 49–56; see also Howe's opening address at the Regional Meeting, Middle Atlantic Conference, A.I.A., 22 Oct. 1953.

86. Reichley, "Philadelphia Does It." Kahn's own plan for Penn Center can be seen in *Perspecta* 2 (1953), 21–22.

thing had to be done to save the project from disaster." It was Philadelphia's reform mayor, Joseph M. Clark, Jr., who ameliorated the situation by throwing his weight in favor of a coordinated development of Penn Center. Within a few months the possibilities for some artistic success seemed more favorable, and with the election of a new president of the railroad, James M. Symes, the idea of a coordinated development, and especially of an underground concourse was firmly fixed. By June, Clark was so in command that a "proposal to establish aesthetic control over future construction by a board of art experts [was] set aside on technical grounds"—and although George Howe for one believed it would have a "deadening effect on the development," Clark nonetheless made it clear that the days of the railroad's public-be-damned dominance were a thing of the past, and for Kahn, it was clear that some effort would be made to make something better than run-of-the-mill on this key site. But, of course, it was too late for disaster to be avoided—it could only be ameliorated. Penn Center, despite all attempts, is still the "two-step" architecture that Kahn so trenchantly predicted it would be.

Howe reflected:

> We have done as well as we are able. It is the product of our plans and schemes and dreams, and when it is finished it will already have begun to change. The city has always beaten us—and itself—and it always will, because it will grow more quickly than we are ever able to grow either separately or together. But then a part of its growth is our very effort to tame it, isn't it, so how can you say that we ever fail? I think it is Henry James who somewhere speaks of the American city—not this city, but there is a similarity to all our cities, you know, just as they are all different—as a bold, bad beauty; poor bold, bad beauty who is constant only in her inconstancy and whom we resent at the same moment as we pursue. Well, how do you deal with a bold, bad beauty? You must improvise, James says—I am not sure if James is saying this or if it is merely myself, but let us say that it is James—always improvise. And in the improvisation, there is the fun.[87]

The evolution of the dilemma of Penn Center forced Howe toward a realization of the dilemma of city design in a time when city planners and others relatively untrained in the language of shapes were very much in control. The "architect's relation to urban design" is a "disquieting" one, he told the 1953

87. Howe, quoted in Reichley, "Philadelphia Does It."

Regional Meeting of the Middle Atlantic Conference of the American Institute of Architects.[88]

> Planning as a part of urban design should be treated as an art, not as a science. Under the pressure of analytical conclusions, founded on the dubious economic and social premises of accepted practice, without imagination or consideration for form, the architect, as artist, when called to design the three-dimensional urban reality, finds the distribution, size and shape of the elements he has to deal with practically predetermined. What is worse, this unfortunate is often obliged to share in the analytical process knowing full well that Ol' Man Dollar, he don't say nothin', he just keeps rollin' along.

Finding Christopher Tunnard's scientific definition of planning as outlined in his book *The City of Man,* a "false and feeble faith in the organization of science and art, with science coming first," Howe went on to reflect on his experiences as chairman of the Citizens Advisory Board of Design for Penn Center, a board

> supposed to control, with persuasive rather than authoritarian hand, the three-dimensional form of a large private project. . . . On the shape of this project, I was assured, the Board was to exercise a decisive influence. Needless to say the Board found everything of importance had been decided before its appointment. Its actual function was to make a *fait accompli* acceptable by suggesting features that would make a commercial complex appear to be dedicated to gracious living, for which, I may add, no money had been provided.
> So the architect concerned with urban design finds himself a sort of modern alchemist, striving perpetually to condense the philosopher's stone and liquid gold from the vaporous substance of credit money and statistical projection.

Almost as soon as the "battle for Penn Center" was concluded, a new one erupted concerning the Independence Mall, just then being completed. Early in 1955 Howe was asked by the Philadelphia Chapter of the American Institute of Architects to prepare a "report on the use of the land facing Independence Mall and Independence Mall Historical Park" with special reference to "the character of the architecture that shall be recommended to prospective

88. Howe's was the opening address; see n. 85.

builders" in these areas.[89] Emphasizing the need to encourage a rich mixture
of uses in the area "so the memorial areas will become a source of daily instead
of occasional inspiration in the leisure hours of the surrounding inhabitants,"
he felt "impelled to utter a warning about the possibility of a Colonial 'revival' " while at the same time stressing the desirability of preserving existing
buildings wherever possible, especially the "fine nineteenth century buildings
along Chestnut and Walnut Streets." These buildings, perhaps the most unique
in Philadelphia, are even to this day regarded with suspicion—especially by
those "misguided Colonial enthusiasts" who see Philadelphia's historical position in a very limited way. The best of them, including Frank Furness's
Guarantee Trust and The National Bank of the Republic, have fallen, as
Howe, virtually alone among architects, warned they would.[90] In his report
Howe was insistent that

> these nineteenth century buildings, unlike the Colonial pastiches [of the
> twentieth century], do harmonize with the old buildings being preserved
> in the Historical Park. They harmonize with them by right of historic
> contrast and creative evolution. To wander about among structures of
> successive styles and periods is to feel the exhilaration of moving in
> architectural history. The nineteenth century buildings were designed
> by some of the most dedicated and original architects our country ever
> produced. . . .
>
> So we too should follow the genius of our time in recommending to
> prospective builders the character of the architecture they should create.
> Their buildings should be 'modern' in design, as that term is compre-
> hensively understood, and tall within limits. Tall buildings are the neces-
> sary expression of economic health today. They have the further
> advantage of screening the backs and sides of other tall buildings behind
> them, which are such unhapppy blemishes on our city scenes. I consider
> it most fortunate that the first new building being erected on Chestnut
> Street is a light thirteen-story glass structure. The modest edifices of our
> forefather's time should not be overborne by great masses of brick and
> stone clothed in detail suitable only to another scale of life. . . .
>
> We may hope, of course, that every architect employed to design a
> building in the areas will be a genius. As to this hope all I can say is,

89. Howe, "Report on the Use of the Land Facing Independence Mall and Independence
National Historical Park," 28 March 1955, 4 pp., typescript.

90. For a fuller account of this systematic destruction, see James F. O'Gorman, et al., *The
Architecture of Frank Furness* (Philadelphia: Museum of Art, 1973).

trust in God and keep your powder dry. If we don't like him the only thing we can do is shoot him. I almost got shot myself in 1932.[91]

Howe died on 17 April 1955 on the eve of his departure with Dean G. Holmes Perkins of the School of Fine Arts, University of Pennsylvania, for Turkey, where they were to help organize an architectural school under the direction of UNESCO.[92] He died amidst disappointing circumstances: his work at Yale was being repudiated; his efforts to save Penn Center from architectural mediocrity had failed; his warnings about the destruction of Philadelphia's fabulous heritage of nineteenth-century architecture were falling on deaf ears. Despite these disappointments, his position in American architecture was an eminent one, the achievements of his career were recognized, and he himself was admired and even loved.

91. Howe, "Report on the Use of the Land."
92. At his death Howe's estate showed a value of $97,290 (Philadelphia *Evening Bulletin*, 23 March 1956). He was awarded a doctor of fine arts degree posthumously by the University of Pennsylvania in June 1955. The obituary notices were numerous.

Epilogue

My interests in George Howe go back a number of years to when I first became aware of his importance in the formulative stages of the International Style in America. It occurred to me then that someone of my generation, trained at Yale in the 1960s where Howe's and Kahn's influences were still very much present, yet presumably divorced from the battle of the styles (International and otherwise) and the unpleasantness of the legacy of Howe's last years there, should reinvestigate the recent history of American architecture, especially the critical developments of the 1920s and 1930s, and in so doing attempt to construct a viable framework for the absorption into our culture of the events of the period. It also occurred to me that America's architecture, especially in the 1920s, was intimately connected with every phase of our national life; not in the simple cause-and-effect relationship that has been assumed by such writers as John Burchard and Albert Bush-Brown, but in the rather more complex interaction and parallelism of important developments in politics, literature, and the fine arts. Further investigation has not disappointed me, and this book—biography, history, and criticism—is intended to reflect these concerns.

Howe's provocative career seems to me a unique key to understanding American developments in architecture during the first fifty years of this century. This work is not intended as a final statement of the events of the recent past but rather as a beginning one. America is faced with problems remarkably like those that she faced in the 1930s, when her architects struggled to make the International Style their own. Now, in the decadence of that style (when some are already thinking of its revival), American architects are searching once again for an approach to building that can relate to a different pace of life without losing sight of the magnificent achievements of that earlier phase: to make out of imagination and intellect a new, responsive architecture.

The International Style, through its brilliant gestures, created very persuasive images of modern life. But as its fifty-year history, now draws to a close, architects are calling into question many of its premises, such as its romance with the machine and the apocalyptic moral fervor of so many of its proponents. Yet these premises and this moral tone are still regarded by some as fundamental principles of modern architecture. Not so for Howe.

For this reason, if for no other, the story of his career in general, and of his work on PSFS in particular, tends to indicate that, at least for one architect, certain broad and permanent values could mesh with the spectacular mechano-morphological cubism of the International Style as it reached its zenith in the later 1920s. That is to say, Howe's contact with the forms and intentions of the style surely opened up a whole new life in architecture for him, but he brought something to it as well. He brought a simple concern for "fundamental principles" of building, which many International Style architects disregarded and some often just plain lacked.

The great Philadelphia architects of the last 100 years have always shared this concern for high, possibly even extreme stylistic expression combined with a respect for sound building. From the first of them, Frank Furness, whose crude and violent forms expressed the bravado of the nouveau riche boldness of his era, through Wilson Eyre, Paul Cret, George Howe, Louis Kahn, Romaldo Giurgola, and Robert Venturi, each has struggled to articulate a language of form at once comprehensive and particular. Just as Furness turned our eyes to his own special perceptions of the Gothic while infusing them with the raw power of the Industrial Age, and Venturi asks us to look at Mannerism and the highway strip so that we can make a more integral peace with our cultural pluralism, so Howe, skeptical and therefore too often cut off from decisive action, forces us to see beyond the surfaces of buildings to their underlying principles: to reassess the narrowly conceived revolutionary shibboleths of a generation or so ago in the light of more fundamental architectural values. Louis Kahn, in many ways a spiritual successor to Howe, seems to understand better than any other architect today those Beaux-Arts theories of architecture that inform both his work and Howe's. These Kahn learned from Paul Cret and from his years of association with Howe. In his actual building, Kahn has not always been able to find suitable expression for his theoretical convictions, and his growth has been slow. But it seems fitting that today it is Kahn who speaks for an architecture of "meaningful form" and "meaningful spaces," an architecture that seeks to use what Howe called "imaginative gifts" for what he also called a "penetration of the meaning of things."

Furness, Eyre, Cret, Howe, Giurgola, Kahn, and Venturi perhaps constitute a Philadelphia School.[1] And in Vreeland, Weinstein, Robertson, Pasanella, and others of us who have responded to this tradition as it was articulated by Howe and Kahn at the architecture schools of Penn and Yale, it may be that

1. This is suggested by Vincent Scully in his *American Architecture and Urbanism*, p. 99. The idea of a "Philadelphia School" was first brought to the attention of contemporary readers by Jan C. Rowan in his "Wanting to Be," *Progressive Architecture* (1961).

at last a coherent direction for our architecture is beginning to emerge—a sense of common purpose based upon principles other than those of simple parochialism or regionalism, one in which High Hollow, PSFS, Square Shadows, and Fortune Rock will always hold central and honorable places.

Abbreviations

AIM	Arthur I. Meigs
GH	George Howe
H & L	Howe and Lescaze
MMH	Mellor, Meigs and Howe
RMB	Robert Montgomery Brown
WL	William Lescaze
WM	Walter Mellor

A & D	*Arts and Decoration*
Barbey	Gilles Barbey, "William Lescaze: Sa carrière et son oeuvre de 1915–1939," *Werk* 58 (Aug. 1971), 559-65
CL	*Country Life* (U.S.)
Coffin	Lewis A. Coffin, ed., *American Country Houses of Today* (New York: Architectural Book Publishing Co., 1935)
Creese	Walter Creese, "American Architecture from 1918 to 1933, with Special Emphasis on European Influence" (Ph.D. diss., Harvard, 1949)
Dickson	Harold B. Dickson, *One Hundred Pennsylvania Buildings* (State College, Pa.: Bald Eagle Press, 1954)
Forum	*Architectural Forum*
"George Howe"	"George Howe, An Architectural Biography," *T-Square* 2 (Jan. 1932), 20-23
Giolli	Raffaello Giolli, "William Lescaze," *Casabella* 10 (Jan. 1937), 10-21
HB	*House Beautiful*
HG	*House and Garden*
Hitchcock	Henry-Russell Hitchcock, "Howe and Lescaze," in Alfred Barr et al., *Modern Architecture, International Exhibition* (New York: Museum of Modern Art, 1932)

Hopkins	Alfred Hopkins, ed., *Moderne Amerikanische Landhäuser* (Berlin: Wasmuth, 1926); U. S. edition, *American Country Houses of Today* (New York: Architectural Book Publishing Co., 1927)
Howe, "PSFS Branch Offices"	George Howe, "The Philadelphia Saving Fund Society Branch Offices," *Forum* 42 (June 1928), 881-86
Jordy	William H. Jordy, "PSFS: Its Development and Its Significance in Modern Architecture," *JSAH* 21 (May 1962), 47-83
Jordy and Stern	William H. Jordy and Robert Stern, "PSFS," "PSFS" issue of *JSAH* 21 (May 1962)
Jordy and Wright	William H. Jordy and Henry Wright, "PSFS," *Forum* 120 (May 1964), 124-29, 143
JSAH	*Journal of the Society of Architectural Historians*
McAndrew	John McAndrew, ed., *Guide to Modern Architecture: Northeast States* (New York: Museum of Modern Art, 1940)
McGrath	Raymond McGrath, *Twentieth Century Houses* (London: Faber, 1934)
Mock	Elizabeth Mock, ed., *Built in U.S.A. 1932–44* (New York: Museum of Modern Art, 1944)
New York Yearbook	New York Architectural League, *Yearbook*
Philadelphia Yearbook	Philadelphia Chapter A. I. A. and T-Square Club, *Yearbook*
Record	*Architectural Record*
Robin and Barmacho	A. Robin and Barmacho, "Howe and Lescaze," *L'Architecture d'Aujourd'hui* 4 (Nov.–Dec. 1933)
Sartoris	Alberto Sartoris, *Gli Elementi dell' Architettura Funzionale* (Milan: Hoepli, 1935)
Stern	Robert A. M. Stern, "PSFS-Beaux-Arts Theory and Rational Expressionism," *JSAH* 21 (May 1962), 84-95
West	Helen Howe West, *George Howe, Architect* (Philadelphia: William Nunn, 1973)
Work of MMH	*A Monograph of the Work of Mellor, Meigs and Howe* (New York: Architectural Book Publishing Co., 1923)

List of Works

Only a small portion of Howe's personal and office records remains. These records have been generously donated to the Avery Architectural Library at Columbia University, New York, by his daughter, Helen Howe West, and his long-time associate, Louis E. McAllister, and constitute the core of the George Howe Collection. To these materials I have added the correspondence and other pertinent materials that have accumulated during the research and writing of this book.

In the List of Works the date given for an individual building designed by Howe or his partners is the date of completion, unless there is some doubt, in which case the date of its first appearance in an architectural publication is used. For supplementary dating evidence I have relied on Howe's office correspondence and on recollections of his clients and professional associates. As often as possible I have also included the date when work was begun on the design of the project.

Bibliographical references are generally confined to illustrated articles that treat the building as a work of architecture. Full references to periodicals are given only when the article carries a by-line. The reader eager to assemble the fullest bibliographical overview of a given building is referred to Writings by George Howe as well as to the textual footnotes.

I have ventured to assign initiating design credit for those projects executed during Howe's four partnerships. These attributions are sometimes quite clearly documented, as in PSFS; often they are based on such collateral evidence as architect–client relationship, as in the Howe–Fraley Residence. Always these factors are balanced by my own judgment of the work in question from the point of view of style.

1912	"Le Modele Type d'un Billet de Banque de Mille Francs," student project, Ecole Nationale des Beaux-Arts, Paris.
	Credit: GH. *Bibliography:* Ecole Nationale des Beaux-Arts, *Les Concours d'Architecture de l'Année Scolaire,* 1911–1912 (Paris: Vincent, 1912), pl. 30.
	Project issued 3 Feb. 1912; due 30 Feb. 1912. For it Howe received the *Prémière Seconde Médaille.*
1912	"Un Institut Océanographique," student project, Ecole Nationale des Beaux-Arts, Paris.
	Credit: GH. *Bibliography:* ibid, pls. 176–77.
	Project issued 31 Jan. 1912; due 30 March 1912. For it Howe received the *Prémière Seconde Médaille.*
1912	"Un Hôtel des Postes," student project, Ecole Nationale des Beaux-Arts, Paris.
	Credit: GH. *Bibliography:* Ecole Nationale des Beaux-Arts, *Les Concours d'Architecture de l'Année Scolaire,* 1912–1913 (Paris: Vincent, 1913), pls. 22–25.
	Project issued 18 July 1912; due 5 Oct. 1912. For it Howe received the *Première Médaille.*

1913 George Howe House (1), Chestnut Hill, Pa., renovation.

Credit: GH. *Bibliography:* Harold D. Eberlein, "Current Tendencies in the Arrangement of Interiors," *Record* 36 (Nov. 1914), 394–420, esp. 418.

1914 "In the Luxembourg Gardens," drawing.

Credit: GH. *Bibliography: Philadelphia Yearbook,* 1914.

1914 "Hôtel Lallemand, Bourges," drawing.

Credit: GH. *Bibliography:* ibid.

ca. 1914 Kermit Roosevelt House, Oyster Bay, L. I., N. Y., additions and renovations.

Credit: GH.

1914–16;
1923 (garage);
1928 (swimming pool)

High Hollow, George Howe House (2), 101 West Hampton Ave. (now Hampton Rd.), Chestnut Hill, Pa.

Now the Samuel Paley Conference Center of the University of Pennsylvania.

Credit: GH of Furness, Evans & Co. *Bibliography: Record* 39 (June 1916), 562–67. Paul Cret, "A Hillside House," *Record* 48 (Aug. 1920), 83–106; reprinted in *Work of MMH,* pp. 14–32. *HB* 52 (July 1922), 32. *Amer. Architect* 123 (14 Feb. 1923), 145. *CL* 44 (June 1923), 65. *HG* 44 (19 Aug. 1923), 73. *HB* 54 (Oct. 1923), 352; (Dec. 1923), 584, 587. Alwyn T. Dovell, "Combining One Material with Another," *HG* 45 (Jan. 1924), 46. *HB* 55 (April 1924), 378–79. John Taylor Boyd, Jr., "Imagination and Knowledge are Combined in Modern Building," *A & D* 22 (April 1925), 29–31. C. Matlack Price, "The Country House in Good Taste," *A & D* 23 (Oct. 1925), 42–44. Hitchcock, p. 149.

1915 Overmantel by Jean Goujon, drawing.

Credit: GH. *Bibliography: Philadelphia Yearbook,* 1915.

1916 Farm building for Alfred Mellor, Cunningham, Mass.

Credit: MMH (WM). *Bibliography: Work of MMH,* pp. 193–94.

1916–17 Mrs. A. J. Antelo Devereux House, Dark Harbor, Me.

Credit: MMH (WM, AIM). *Bibliography: Forum* 35 (Aug. 1921), pls. 24–27. *Work of MMH,* pp. 121–24.

1916–17 Heatly C. Dulles House, Villanova, Pa.

Credit: MMH (WM). *Bibliography:* Edmund B. Gilchrist, "House for Heatly C. Dulles," *Record* 48 (Jan. 1920), 3–17; reprinted in *Work of MMH,* pp. 74–88. *HB* 51 (June 1922), 560–61. *HG* 44 (Dec. 1923), 72–73.

1916–18 John F. Meigs II House, Ithan (Radnor), Pa.

Credit: MMH (AIM). *Bibliography: Amer. Architect* 111 (4 April 1917), pl. *Work of MMH,* pp. 107–11. Coffin, p. 59.

1916–18;
1921 (garden and architecture)

Francis S. Mc Ilhenny House, Montgomery Ave., Chestnut Hill, Pa.

Credit: MMH (AIM). *Bibliography:* Arthur I. Meigs, "The Design of a House at Chestnut Hill, Philadelphia," *Forum* 31 (Oct. 1919), 119–22; reprinted in *Work of MMH,* pp. 33–60. Charles S. Keefe, ed., *The American House* (New York: UPC Book Co., 1922), pls. 174–77. *New York Yearbook* (1923). *Amer. Architect* 123 (14 Feb. 1923), 141. *HG* 43 (April 1923), 91. *HB* 56 (Oct. 1924), 346; (Dec. 1924), 595. *HG* 55 (March 1929), 122–23; this article gives Meigs full credit. R. W. Sexton, ed., *American Country Houses of Today* (New York: Architectural Book Publishing Co., 1930), pp. 79–81. Dickson, p. 87.

ca. 1920–21;
1928 (enlarged)

Garth, Robert T. McCracken House, through-block site between Kitchens Lane and Westview St., Germantown, Pa.

Credit: MMH (AIM). *Bibliography:* C. Matlack Price, "Attaining the Ideal in the Small House," *A & D* 15 (Sept. 1921), 28–86; abridged in *Work of MMH,* pp. 61–64. *CL* 40 (Oct. 1921), 61. *New York Yearbook,* 1922. *Philadelphia Yearbook,* 1922. *Amer. Architect* 121 (15 Feb. 1922), pls. within pp. 127–43. *HB* 51 (April 1922), 327; (July 1922), 29. Augusta Owen Patterson, *American Homes of To-Day* (New York: Macmillan, 1924), p. 310. *New York Yearbook,* 1926. Talbot F. Hamlin, *The American Spirit in Architecture* (New Haven: Yale, 1926), pp. 265, 335. *HG* 49 (April 1926), 94. *Philadelphia Yearbook,* 1928. *A & D* 29 (Aug. 1928), 64. Arthur I. Meigs, " 'Garth,' House of Robert T. McCracken," *Record* 64 (Nov. 1928), 355–78.

1920–21

The Peak, Mrs. Arthur V. Meigs Estate, intersection of Lancaster, Radnor-Chester, and Newton Rds., Radnor, Pa.

Credit: MMH (AIM). *Bibliography:* Arthur I. Meigs, "Permanence on the Estate," *CL* 41 (March 1922), 51–55; reprinted in *Work of MMH,* pp. 96–106. *CL* 43 (April 1923), 52–58.

1920–22

Christopher L. Ward House, Centerville, Del.

Credit: MMH (WM). *Bibliography: Work of MMH,* pp. 112–20. *HG* 44 (Aug. 1923), 64–65.

1921

Four-house development, Germantown Ave., Chestnut Hill, Pa.

Credit: MMH. *Bibliography: Amer. Architect* 126 (22 Oct. 1924), pls. 141–43.

1921

Farm buildings for Morris E. Leeds, Clonmell, Chester County, Pa.

Credit: MMH. *Bibliography: Work of MMH,* pp. 190–92.

1921

Howe-Fraley Residence, 10 West Chestnut Hill Ave., Chestnut Hill, Pa.

Credit: MMH (GH). *Bibliography: Philadelphia Yearbook,* 1924. *Amer. Architect* 126 (2 July 1924), pls. 1–7. *Record* 56 (Nov. 1924), 401, 402, 424, 425. *CL* 48 (July 1925), 60–62.

1921   Swimming pool for Charlton Yarnall, Devon, Pa.

Illustrated as a sketch in *Work of MMH*, it may never have been built.

Credit: MMH (AIM). *Bibliography: Work of MMH*, p. 212.

1921–23   H. F. C. Stikeman House, West Hampton Ave. (now Hampton Rd.), Chestnut Hill, Pa.

Credit: MMH (GH). *Bibliography: Work of MMH*, p. 211. *Philadelphia Yearbook*, 1924. *Amer. Architect* 125 (2 Jan. 1924), pls. *Record* 56 (Nov. 1924), 422–23. Hopkins, pp. 110–11.

1921–24;
1928 (swimming pool)
              Arthur E. Newbold Estate, Laverock, Pa.

Credit: MMH (AIM, GH). *Bibliography: Philadelphia Yearbook*, 1922. *Amer. Architect* 121 (15 Feb. 1922), pls. Arthur I. Meigs, "The Development of the Estate of Arthur Newbold, Esq.," in *Work of MMH*, pp. 196–207. Arthur I. Meigs, "The Farm as a Picturesque Asset," *CL* 43 (April 1923), 52–58; reprinted in *An American Country House*, pp. xxviii–xxx. *Architecture (N.Y.)* 50 (Aug. 1924), pls. 124–28. Arthur I. Meigs, *An American Country House* (New York: Architectural Book Publishing Co., 1925). *New York Yearbook*, 1925. *Philadelphia Yearbook*, 1925. *Amer. Architect* 122 (6 May 1925), 425–28. *CL* 49 (Aug. 1925), 51–57. Lewis Mumford, "The Architecture of Escape," *The New Republic* 43 (12 Aug. 1925), 321–22. *CL* 49 (Dec. 1925), 84. *Amer. Architect* 129 (20 Jan. 1926), 185–90. *HB* 61 (Jan. 1927), 52–53; 62 (July 1927), 43. *Philadelphia Yearbook*, 1929. *CL* 55 (Jan. 1929), 47–55. Vincent J. Scully, *American Architecture and Urbanism* (New York: Praeger, 1969), p. 178.

ca. 1922   Benjamin A. Illoway House, Bell's Mill Rd., Chestnut Hill, Pa.

Credit: MMH (GH). *Bibliography: Record* 56 (Nov. 1924), 426–28. *Architecture (N.Y.)* 53 (Jan. 1925), pls. 86–88. *CL* 50 (Sept. 1926), 52–53.

ca. 1923–24 Willowbrook Farms, Robert Holmes Page Residence, Paoli, Pa.

Credit: MMH. *Bibliography:* HB 57 (April 1925), 377–80. R. W. Sexton, ed., *American Country House of Today* (New York: Architectural Book Publishing Co., 1930), pp. 29–30.

1924   Philadelphia Saving Fund Society, renovation to main office, 7th and Walnut Sts., Philadelphia, Pa.

Credit: MMH. *Bibliography: Jordy*, n. 27.

1924   Philadelphia Saving Fund Society, branch office (North Office), 11th St. and Lehigh Ave., Philadelphia, Pa.

A twin of the office listed below.

Credit: MMH (GH). *Bibliography:* Howe, "PSFS Branch Offices." *Philadelphia Yearbook*, 1925. Jordy and Stern.

1924   Philadelphia Saving Fund Society, branch office (South Office), Broad and
              McKean Sts., Philadelphia, Pa.

              Credit: MMH (GH). *Bibliography:* ibid.

1924;
ca. 1930 (extended)

              Charles J. McManus House, Germantown, Pa.

              Credit: MMH (GH?). *Bibliography: Philadelphia Yearbook,* 1925. *CL* 47
              (April 1925), 57–59. C. Matlack Price, "Progress and Precedent in Small
              House Design," *HB* 58 (Sept. 1925), 209–18. *The Architect* 5 (Oct. 1925),
              pls. 21–24. *Record* 60 (Nov. 1926), 392–93, 413–15. Hopkins, pp. 102–
              11. *Forum* 59 (Dec. 1933), 498–505.

1924–28   United States Coast Guard Memorial, Arlington National Cemetery, Ar-
              lington, Va.

              A photograph of this design was dated 1924 by Howe.

              Credit: GH; Gaston Lachaise, sculptor. *Bibliography:* "George Howe."

1925   Carl E. Siebecker House, Bethlehem, Pa.

              Credit: MMH (GH). *Bibliography: Amer. Architect* 129 (5 March 1926),
              pls. 43–48. Hopkins, pp. 105–09.

ca. 1925   Open-air auditorium, Fairmount Park, Philadelphia, Pa.
              An undated photograph of a drawing of this scheme is among Howe's
              papers. The scheme's inclusion there as well as its compositional symmetry
              and the use of a classical vocabulary suggest Howe's Beaux-Arts influence.
              Provision for ample car parking, as well as the elaborate plans contem-
              plated for Philadelphia for the U.S. sesquicentennial celebration in 1926,
              suggest the dating.

              Credit: MMH.

1926   Philadelphia Saving Fund Society, branch office (West Office), 52nd and
              Ludlow Sts., Philadelphia, Pa.

              A twin of the office listed below.

              Credit: MMH (GH). *Bibliography: New York Yearbook,* 1927. *The
              Architect* 8 (May 1927), 191, 193. Howe, "PSFS Branch Offices." Jordy
              and Stern.

1926   Philadelphia Saving Fund Society, branch office (Logan Office), Broad and
              Ruscomb Sts., Philadelphia, Pa.

              Credit: MMH (GH). *Bibliography:* ibid.

1926   Philadelphia Saving Fund Society, branch office and office tower (1), 12th
              and Market Sts., Philadelphia, Pa., project.

              Credit: MMH. *Bibliography:* Jordy and Stern.

1926–28   Goodhart Hall, Bryn Mawr College, Bryn Mawr, Pa.

              Credit: WM, AIM (MMH). *Bibliography: Philadelphia Yearbook,* 1926.
              Arthur I. Meigs, "Goodhart Hall," *Record* 65 (Feb. 1929), 105–06, 167–
              74.

1927 Ralph J. Baker House, Harrisburg, Pa.

Credit: MMH. *Bibliography: Philadelphia Yearbook,* 1928, 1929. *The Architect* 9 (March 1928), 731–39.

1927 Orville H. Bullitt House, "Oxmoor," Fort Washington, Pa.

Working drawings for this house were deposited in the Howe Archives in 1974 by Mr. and Mrs. Bullitt.

Credit: MMH (GH). *Bibliography: HG* 65 (Jan. 1934), 47.

1927 Robert F. Holden House, Haverford, Pa.

Credit: GH. *Bibliography: Record* 63 (Jan. 1928), 105–12. Clare Ledoux, "Spanish Influence in a Unique Modern Home," *A & D* 31 (July 1929), 56–57, 82. Creese, pt. 3, pp. 20–21.

Record credits this house to MMH; Ledoux credits it to H & L.

1927 Robert McLean House, Whitemarsh Valley, Pa.

Credit: MMH (AIM, GH). *Bibliography:* Robert McLean, "A Few Recollections of George Howe," in West, pp. 35–36.

1927 James P. Magill House, Germantown, Pa.

Credit: MMH. *Bibliography: Creese,* pt. 3, p. 20.

1927 Philadelphia Saving Fund Society, temporary banking offices, 8 South 12th St., Philadelphia, Pa.

Credit: MMH (GH). *Bibliography:* Howe, "PSFS Branch Offices." Jordy and Stern.

1928 George Howe House (3), 2 Bell's Mill Rd., Chestnut Hill, Pa., renovation.

Credit: GH. *Bibliography:* Howe, notes for a slide lecture, no date, ca. 1930.

1928 President's Room, Amos Parrish & Co., New York, N.Y.

Credit: H & L (WL). *Bibliography: Amer. Architect* 135 (5 Jan. 1929), 46–47. *HG* 57 (Feb. 1930), 82.

1928 James M. R. Sinkler House, "Milfern," Sugartown and Goshen Rds., Westchester, Pa.

Credit: H & L (GH). *Bibliography: Philadelphia Yearbook,* 1929. Creese, pt. 3, pp. 20–21.

1928 George F. Tyler House, Elkins Park, Pa., renovation.

Credit: GH. *Bibliography: Philadelphia Yearbook,* 1928. *Record* 66 (Nov. 1929), 445.

1928 Airport, Camden, N.J., project.
Credit: MMH (GH). *Bibliography:* Eleanor Madeira, "George Howe," in West, p. 17.

1928 Christopher Columbus Memorial Lighthouse, Dominican Republic, competition.

Credit: H & L (GH). *Bibliography:* Albert Kelsey, ed., *Program and Rules of the Second Competition for the Selection of an Architect for the Monu-*

mental Lighthouse (Washington, D.C.: Pan American Union, 1930), p. 124.

The two-stage competition was organized in 1927 and judged in April 1929. Therefore it is unlikely that Lescaze participated in the design.

ca. 1928 War Memorial, Somme American Cemetery, Bony, Aisne, France.

Credit: GH (MMH); Sidney Waugh, sculptor. *Bibliography: New York Yearbook,* 1928. "George Howe." John Harbeson, "Battle Monuments Abroad," in Fairmount Park Association, *76th Annual Report,* (Philadelphia, 1948), pp. 18, 23–40.

ca. 1928 William Stix Wasserman House (1), Whitemarsh, Pa., project.

Credit: GH (MMH?).

1929 Mrs. Herbert M. Dreyfus Apartment, New York, N.Y.

Credit: H & L (WL). *Bibliography: HG* 57 (Feb. 1930), 86.

1929 Office of Howe and Lescaze, Philadelphia.

Credit: H & L. *Bibliography: Record* 69 (Jan. 1931), 33–34.

1929 Museum for R. Sturgis Ingersoll, Pennlyn, Montgomery County, Pa., project.

Credit: H & L. *Bibliography:* Ingersoll, letter to Helen Howe West, April 1972; quoted in West, pp. 32–33.

1929 Monument in honor of the 27th and 30th Divisions, A. E. F. Kemmels, near Vierstataelt (near Ypres), Belgium.

Credit: GH; Sidney Waugh, sculptor. *Bibliography:* "George Howe." Harbeson, ibid., pp. 23–40.

1929 Oak Lane Country Day School, East of N. Broad St. near Second St. and Oak Lane Rd., Philadelphia, Pa.

Demolished ca. 1960.

Credit: H & L (WL?). *Bibliography:* Henry-Russell Hitchcock, *Modern Architecture: Romanticism and Reintegration* (New York: Payson and Clarke, 1929), pl. 54. "Ein Kindergarten," *Die Form* 5 (1 Jan. 1930), 15–17. "The Little Red Schoolhouse of Tomorrow's Memories," *U.S.A.* 1 (Spring 1930), 30. "Nursery Building," *Record* 67 (April 1930), 360–63. Talbot F. Hamlin, "Architecture," in Herbert Treadwell Wade, ed., *The New International Yearbook* (New York: Dodd, Mead, 1931), pp. 52–58. Herbert Hoffman, "Kleinkinder Schule in Philadelphie," *Moderne Bauformen* 30 (1931), 578–80. Howe, "Modernism in School Architecture," *The American School and University Yearbook* 4 (New York: American School Publishing Corp., 1931), pp. 93–96. Hitchcock, p. 151. Robin and Barmacho. McGrath, 1934, p. 118. Sartoris, pl. 549. Giolli. McAndrew, p. 95. William Lescaze, *On Being an Architect* (New York: Putnam, 1942), p. 243. Dickson, p. 91. Barbey. *Encyclopedie de l'Architecture* (Paris: Morancé, n.d.), pls. 40–43.

1929   Philadelphia Saving Fund Society, main building, 7th and Walnut Sts.,
            Philadelphia, Pa., renovations.

            Credit: GH. *Bibliography:* Jordy, n. 7.

1929   Philadelphia Saving Fund Society, branch bank and office building (2),
            12th and Market Sts., Philadelphia, Pa., project.

            Credit: GH. *Bibliography:* Jordy and Stern. Jordy and Wright.

1929   Office for William Stix Wasserman, Philadelphia, Pa.

            Credit: H & L. *Bibliography: Philadelphia Yearbook,* 1929. *Record* 69
            (Jan. 1931), 33–35.

1929   William Stix Wasserman House (2), Whitemarsh, Pa., project.

            Credit: H & L. *Bibliography: Philadelphia Yearbook,* 1929. C. Adolph
            Glassgold, "House of William Stix Wasserman, Esq., Whitemarsh, Pennsyl-
            vania," *Forum* 53 (Aug. 1930), 230–32. Talbot F. Hamlin, "Architecture,"
            in Herbert Treadwell Wade, ed., *The New International Yearbook* (New
            York: Dodd, Mead, 1931), pp. 52–58.

ca. 1929 Unidentified showroom and shoe factory.

            Credit: H & L (WL?). *Bibliography:* Frederick Kiesler, *Contemporary Art
            Applied to the Store and Its Display* (New York: Brentano's, 1930),
            p. 144.

1929?   Mrs. Leopold Stowkowski Apartment, New York, N.Y.(?).

            Credit: H & L (WL). *Bibliography:* "Drawing Room," in Herbert Hoffman,
            Modern Interiors (London: Studio, 1934), p. 54. Adolph Glassgold,
            "Stowkowski Apartment," *Forum* 53 (Aug. 1930), 227–29.

1930   Desk and chair design.

            Credit: H & L (WL). *Bibliography: HG* 59 (April 1931), 72.

1930   Ben Herzberg Apartment, New York, N.Y.

            Credit: H & L (WL). *Bibliography: Record* 67 (March 1930), 59–60.
            The Studio 5 (Jan. 1933), 25, 30.

1930   C. Phillips Apartment, New York, N.Y.

            Credit: H & L (WL). *Bibliography: U.S.A.* 1 (Spring 1930), 42.

1930   Mrs. George French Porter House, Ojai, Calif.

            Credit: H & L (WL). *Bibliography: Amer. Architect* 137 (March 1930),
            56. *Record* 68 (Nov. 1930), 440.

ca. 1930 Unidentified interior.

            Credit: H & L. *Bibliography:* Roberto Aloi, *L'Arredamento Moderno*
            (Milan: Hoepli, 1934), pl. 445.

1930–31   Museum of Modern Art, New York, N.Y. (prototypical site), six prelimi-
            nary designs.

14 May–2 June 1930, schemes 1–3. Aug. 1931, schemes 4 and 5. Sept. 1931, scheme 6.

Credit: H & L. *Bibliography: Howe, A Modern Museum* (Springdale, Conn., 1930); reprinted in an altered form in *Record* 80 (July 1936), 43–50, as were schemes 5 and 6. *Pencil Points* 13 (Oct. 1932), 713.

1931 Hattie Carnegie Shop, New York, N.Y.

Credit: H & L (WL). *Bibliography: Creative Art* 9 (Sept. 1931), 241–46.

1931 William Burnlee Curry House, Dartington Hall, Totnes, South Devon, England.

Credit: H & L (WL). *Bibliography: HG* 65 (Feb. 1934), 56–57. *Review* 77 (March 1935), 108. *Forum* 67 (Oct. 1937), 345, 356. Barbey.

1931 Hessian Hills School, Mt. Airy Rd., Croton-on-Hudson, near Harmon, N.Y. Extensively remodeled, now part of synagogue complex.

Credit: H & L (WL?). *Bibliography:* "Ultra-Modern Design Accepted for School," *New York Times,* 30 April 1931, p. 26. "Will Erect Functionalist Building," *Art Digest* (5 June 1931), p. 10. Hitchcock, p. 52. "New School Plans Are Exhibited Here," *New York Times,* 28 Feb. 1932, sec. 2, p. 6. Harold Sterner, "International Architectural Style," *Hound & Horn* 5 (April-June 1932), 452–60. *The American School and University Yearbook* 5 (New York: American School Publishing Corp., 1932–33), p. 35. Robin and Barmacho. McGrath, p. 118. Sartoris, pls. 546–47. Giolli. McAndrew, p. 46. *Forum* 73 (Oct. 1940), 201–02.

1931 Philadelphia Saving Fund Society, branch bank and office building (3), 12th and Market Sts., Philadelphia, Pa. *Credit:* H & L.

Bibliography, 1931–1939

Philadelphia Yearbook, 1931. *Richard A. Seltzer Co., *PSFS* (renting pamphlet; Philadelphia, 1931). *Howe, "A Design for a Savings Bank and Office Building," *T-Square Club Journal* 1 (March 1931), 10–13. Hitchcock, pp. 143–55. Henry-Russell Hitchcock and Philip Johnson, *The International Style: Architecture Since 1922* (New York: Museum of Modern Art, 1932), p. 159. *"The Saving Fund Society Building," *Forum* 56 (Jan. 1932), 97–101. *Leslie S. Tarleton, "Electricity and the Architect," *T-Square Club Journal* 2 (Jan. 1932), 26. Henry-Russell Hitchcock, "Architecture Chronicle: The Brown Decades and the Brown Years," *Hound & Horn* 5 (Jan.–March 1932), 272–77. Harold Sterner, "International Architectural Style," *Hound & Horn* 5 (April–June 1932), 452–60. Catherine Bauer, "Architecture: In Philadelphia," *Arts Weekly* 1 (23 April 1932), 151–54. Douglas Haskell, "The Filing-Cabinet Building," *Creative Art* (June 1932), 446–49. *"PSFS: Hollow Metal Equipment," *Metalcraft* 9 (July 1932), 10–11. *John E. Cornwall, "A Tool Goes to Work in Philadelphia," *Building Investment* 7 (Aug. 1932), 18–20.

1931 (cont.)   *"The Unusual Philadelphia Savings [*sic*] Fund Building," *Engineering News-Record* 109 (10 Nov. 1932), 549–52. *Forum* 57 (Dec. 1932) contains these articles: "A New Shelter for Savings," pp. 483–89, with statements by Howe and Lescaze; Howe and Lescaze, "Planning, Engineering Equipment: The PSFS Building," pp. 543–46; Purdy and Henderson, "Structural Engineering," pp. 547–48; and R. Berkley Hackett, "Mechanical Equipment," pp. 548–50. *"Philadelphia's Fancy," *Fortune* 6 (Dec. 1932), 65–69, 130–31. "Le Philadelphia Saving Fund Building," *La Technique des Travaux* 9, pt. 1 (Feb. 1933), 101–06. *"The Philadelphia Savings [*sic*] Fund Society Building," *Architectural Review* (March 1933), 101–06. *Donald Deskey, "The Rise of American Architecture and Design," *The Studio* 5 (June 1933), 266–73. *Guido Harbers, "Das Neue Burgogebaude PSFS," *Der Baumeister* (June 1933), 195–202, pls. 61–63. *S. Giedion, "Vers un Renouveau Architectural de l'Amerique," *Cahiers d'Art* 8 (Aug. 1933), 237–43. Robin and Barmacho. Roberto Aloi, *L'Arredamento Moderno* (Milan: Hoepli, 1934), pl. 581. Henry-Russell Hitchcock, "Wright and the International Style," in Holger Cahill and Alfred Barr, Jr., *Art in America in Modern Times* (New York: Museum of Modern Art, 1934), pp. 70–72. Philip Johnson, ed., *Machine Art* (New York: Museum of Modern Art, 1934), figs. 81, 257. R. I. B. A., *International Architecture 1924–1934* (London: R. I. B. A., 1934), p. 99. "Architecture Room," Museum of Modern Art *Bulletin* 1 (Jan. 1934), 4; PSFS was the subject of an exhibition at the museum, which included photos of the building as well as a typical office unit and furniture. *Howard Robertson, "An Office Building in Philadelphia," *Architectural & Building News* 137 (12 Jan. 1934), 66–68. *J. P. Mieras, "PSFS," *Bouwkundig Weekblad Architecture* 55 (2 June 1934), 258–63. *"PSFS," *Oeuvres* (Aug. 1934), 14–16. Sartoris, pls. 550–52. *Manne Carlman, "En Modern Bank–Och Kontors–Gijggnad 1 USA," *Byggmastaren* 14 (Jan. 1935), 3–8. E. F. Longees, "William Lescaze Defines Design," *Modern Plastics* 12 (April 1935), 20–22, 58–59. Sheldon and Martha Cheney, *Art and the Machine* (New York: McGraw-Hill, 1936), pp. 9, 23, 40, 148. "Clock Designed by Howe and Lescaze . . . Manufactured by Cartier, for the PSFS," *Industrial Arts* 1 (Spring 1936), 83.

Bibliography, 1937–1973

Giolli. "PSFS," *Architectural Review* 81 (March 1937), 126. "P.S.F.S. Bank and Office Building," *Record* 81 (April 1937), 126. "Le Philadelphia

---

*In March 1936 Lescaze compiled a list of magazines which had published articles on PSFS. In addition to the asterisked articles above, the list included: (American) *Heating and Ventilating,* July 1932; *The New Yorker,* Dec. 1933; *Office Management,* Aug. 1933; *Living Art,* Jan. 1934; *A & D,* June 1934; *Vassar Review,* June 1934; "Otis Elevator Pamphlet," n.d. (English) *The Banker,* Feb. 1936. (French) *Art Applique,* Aug. 1934. (German) *Schweizensche Bauzeitung,* 26 Aug. 1933. (Swiss) *Werk,* Oct. 1933. (Argentine) *Neustra Arquitectura,* May 1933. (Japan) "Japanese Magazine," June 1933.

Saving Fund Building," *L'Architecture d'Aujourd'hui* 9, pt. 1 (Jan. 1938), 16. "PSFS," *L'Architecture d'Aujourd'hui* 10 (June 1939), 24–25. McAndrew, p. 94. Mock, pp. 100–01. "Design Analysis: The Vertical Style," *Forum* 83 (July 1945), 105–13. "PSFS TV Tower (McAllister & Braik, Architects)," *Phil. Yearbook,* 1949. Frederick Gutheim, "The Philadelphia Saving Fund Society Building: A Re-Appraisal: The Old Beauty," *Record* 106 (Oct. 1949), 88–95, 180, 182. Alberto Sartoris, *Encyclopedie de l'Architecture Nouvelle* (Milan: Hoepli, 1954), pls. 765–67. Bruno Zevi, *Architecture as Space* (New York: Horizon, 1957), pp. 192, 194. Henry-Russell Hitchcock, *Architecture: Nineteenth and Twentieth Centuries* (Baltimore: Penguin, 1958), p. 381. John Peter, *Masters of Modern Architecture* (New York: Braziller, 1958), p. 145. George B. Tatum, *Penn's Great Town* (Philadelphia: Pennsylvania, 1961), pp. 131–32, 203, fig. 136. Vincent J. Scully, *Louis I. Kahn* (New York: Braziller, 1962). Jordy and Stern. Jordy and Wright; see also letters to the editor in *Forum,* June and July 1964. Vincent Scully, *American Architecture and Urbanism* (New York: Praeger, 1969), p. 154. Barbey. Earle W. Bolton, Jr., "Memo," in West, pp. 30–32.

1931   H. F. C. Stikeman Cottage, Sennerville, near Montreal, Quebec.
                Credit: H & L (GH).

1931   Trans-Lux Theatre, New York, N.Y.
                Credit: H & L (WL). *Bibliography: Record* 70 (Aug. 1931), 118–20. Frederick Arden Pawley, "Design of Motion Picture Theatres," *Record* 71 (June 1932), 429, pl.

1931   Emigrant Savings Bank and office building, E. 42nd St. (between Fifth and Madison Aves.), New York, N.Y., project.
                Credit: H & L. Rendering signed H & L, July 1931; another rendering signed WL, July 1931. *Bibliography:* Alberto Sartoris, *Encyclopedie de l'architecture nouvelle* (Milan: Hoepli, 1954), vol. 3, pl. 761.

1931   Arthur Peck House, Paoli, Pa., project.
                Credit: H & L (WL). *Bibliography: Phil. Yearbook,* 1931. *Record* 70 (Nov. 1931), 369, 372.

1931   Maurice Wertheim House, Cos Cob, Conn., project.
                Credit: H & L (WL).

1931?   Charles Harding Apartment, New York, N.Y. (?)
                Credit: H & L (WL). *Bibliography: T-Square Club Journal* 1 (April 1931), 23.

ca. 1931   Unidentified interiors.
                Credit: H & L (WL). *Bibliography: A & D* 41 (Oct. 1934), 8–9.

ca. 1931   Unidentified interior.
                Credit: H & L (WL). *Bibliography: A & D* 43 (Jan. 1936), 19.

1931–32 Frederick V. Field House, New Hartford, Conn.

    Credit: H & L (WL?). *Bibliography: Record* 70 (Nov. 1931), 373; 72 (Nov. 1932), 326–29. *Forum* 59 (Nov. 1933), 400–04. Robin and Barmacho. Philip Johnson, "The Modern Room" and "The Modern House," in Holger Cahill and Alfred Barr, Jr., *Art in America in Modern Times* (New York: Museum of Modern Art, 1934), pp. 72–76. McGrath, pp. 117–18. Coffin, p. 112. Sartoris, pls. 553–54. Ula Jackson, "A New American Phenomenon—Luxurious Smaller Houses," *A & D* 44 (Feb. 1936), 11. McAndrew, p. 22. *Forum* 73 (Oct. 1940), 242. Creese, pt. 3, p. 27. Barbey.

1931–32 Philadelphia Saving Fund Society, garage, 12th and Filbert Sts., Philadelphia, Pa.

    Credit: H & L. *Bibliography:* McAndrew, p. 94. *Record* 90 (July 1941), 94.

1931 (Dec.)–1932 (Jan.)

    Housing development for Chrystie-Forsyth Sts., New York, N.Y., project.

    Credit: H & L. *Bibliography:* Hitchcock, pp. 145–46, 154–55. "Explain Houses on Stilts / Architects at Luncheon Say Rent Would Be $10.95 a Room," *New York Times,* 10 Feb. 1932, p. 43. "Proposed Chrystie-Forsyth Housing Development for New York City," *Record* 71 (March 1932), 194–95. "Proposed Housing Development," *Forum* 56 (March 1932), 265–67. "A Slum-Substitute for New York City," *American City* 46 (March 1932), 112. "The Trend of Affairs," *Technology Review* 34 (March 1932), 248. "Proposed Housing Development for Chrystie-Forsyth Streets," *Shelter* 2 (April 1932), 21–23, Harold Sterner, "International Architectural Style," *Hound & Horn* 5 (April–June 1932), 452–60. "Model Housing," editorial, *New York Times,* 3 May 1932, p. 18. "Backs Housing Plan for Chrystie-Forsyth Area / East Side Chamber of Commerce Gives Its Approval to Project for 24 Model Buildings," *New York Times,* 7 May 1932, p. 21. John E. Cornwall, "A Tool Goes to Work in Philadelphia," *Building Investment* 7 (Aug. 1932), 18–20. Giolli.

1932 Unidentified drawing room.

    Credit: H & L. *Bibliography: Arts Weekly* 1 (18 March 1932), 32.

1932 Belmont-Lincoln Hotel, Park Ave. and 42nd St., New York, N.Y., project.

    Credit: H & L (WL).

1932 Fifty Small Houses, project.

    Credit: H & L.

1932 Storefront for Dorothy Gray, New York, N.Y., project.

    Credit: H & L (WL).

1932 Office building for Amos Parrish & Co., New York, N.Y., project.

    Credit: H & L (WL).

1932?   Wilbour Library, Brooklyn Museum, Eastern Pkwy. at Washington Ave., Brooklyn, N.Y.

       Credit: H & L (WL). *Bibliography: Amer. Architect* 147 (Dec. 1935), 14–15.

1932–34   Square Shadows, William Stix Wasserman House (3), Butler Pike, White-marsh, Pa.

       Presently the Agnus Dei School.

       Credit: GH. *Bibliography: Forum* 62 (March 1935), 195–205. *Fortune* 12 (Oct. 1935), 34, 59–65. *Pencil Points* 18 (Jan. 1937), 34; (April 1937), 252. *Forum* 67 (Oct. 1937), 346. James Ford and Katherine Morrow Ford, *The Modern House in America* (New York: Architectural Book Publishing Co., 1940), pp. 61–62. McAndrew, p. 98. *Forum* 73 (Oct. 1940), 252. Katherine Morrow Ford, "Modern is Regional," *HG* 79 (March 1941), pt. 1, p. 35. Dickson, p. 94. Vincent J. Scully, *American Architecture and Urbanism* (New York: Praeger, 1969), p. 178.

1933   Auditorium, Connecticut College, New London, Conn., project.

       Credit: H & L (WL).

1933   Frank V. Storrs Office.

       Credit: H & L (WL). *Bibliography: A & D* (Oct. 1934), 11.

1934–35   Robert F. Welsh House, Laverock, Pa.

       Credit: GH.

       Earle W. Bolton, Jr., has told me that this house was based on a system of precast masonry units called Rothston, in which Mr. Welsh had become interested after seeing them at the Chicago Fair. Welsh was a very unco-operative client, and the result was so compromised that Howe never allowed it to be published. Copies of the drawings for the house have been secured for the Howe Archives through the assistance of Welsh's son, Andrew.

1935   Maurice J. Speiser House, 2005 Delancey Place, Philadelphia, Pa.

       Credit: GH. *Bibliography: Forum* 64 (Feb. 1936), 122–25. Katherine Morrow Ford, "An Old Town House Can Lend Itself to Modern Living," *Christian Science Monitor,* 23 July 1940, p. 6. McAndrew, p. 94.

1936–41   Philadelphia *Evening Bulletin* office, Juniper and Filbert Sts., Philadelphia, Pa., renovation.

       Credit: GH (with Louis McAllister). *Bibliography: Record* 82 (Nov. 1937), 75–79. *Forum* 70 (Jan. 1939), 51. McAndrew, p. 94. *Record* 89 (Feb. 1941), 46–49.

1936–37   Isaac D. Levy House, Germantown, Pa.

       Credit: GH. *Bibliography: Record* 82 (Nov. 1937), 124–26. *HG* 75 (April 1939), pt. 2, p. 20.

1937–39   Fortune Rock, Mrs. Clara Fargo Thomas House, Northeast Harbor Rd. near Ellsworth, Somes Sound, Mount Desert Island, Me.

Credit: GH. *Bibliography: Forum* 71 (Dec. 1939), 446–54. James Ford and Katherine Morrow Ford, *The Modern House in America* (New York: Architectural Book Publishing Co., 1940), pp. 59–60. McAndrew, pp. 27–28. *Royal Architectural Institute of Canada Journal* 17 (April 1940), 60–63. *Forum* 73 (Oct. 1940), 253, 255; 74 (March 1941), 200. Mock, pp. 44–45. Sir Charles Reilly, "Some Contemporary American Buildings," *Architect's Yearbook* 1 (London: Elek, 1945), pp. 120–31. George Nelson, "Houses in the Sun," *Holiday* 7 (Jan. 1950), 90–97. Bruno Zevi, *Storia dell'Architettura Moderna* (Turin: Ernandi, 1950). *L'Architecture d'Aujourd'hui* 24 (Oct. 1953), 68–69. John Jacobus, *Twentieth Century Architecture: The Middle Years, 1940–65* (New York: Praeger, 1966), pp. 44–45. Vincent J. Scully, *American Architecture and Urbanism* (New York: Praeger, 1969), p. 178. Eleanor Madeira, "George Howe," in West, pp. 26–27.

1937   Hodgson House, unknown location, Maine, additions (project?).

Credit: GH. *Bibliography:* West, p. 53.

ca. 1937   Richard W. Hale House, Dover, Mass., renovation.

Credit: GH. *Bibliography:* West, p. 53.

1938   Mrs. Anna H. Donnelly House, Cottrell Rd., Saunderstown, R.I.

Credit: GH and RMB (RMB). *Bibliography:* McAndrew, p. 99.

1938   Arts center, Wheaton College, Norton, Mass., competition.

Credit: GH. *Bibliography: Forum* 69 (Aug. 1938), 143–58. Talbot F. Hamlin, "Competitions," *Pencil Points* 19 (Sept. 1938), 551–65. Museum of Modern Art *Bulletin* 5 (Feb. 1938), 2–3 (the competition was the subject of an exhibition at the museum, 28 June–12 Sept. 1938).

Howe's entry was not awarded any prize.

1939   America at Home, New York World's Fair, Queens, N.Y.

Credit: GH. *Bibliography: Forum* 73 (July 1940), 37.

1939   "Children's World," New York World's Fair, Queens, N.Y.

Credit: GH with Oscar Stonorov, Herbert Spiegel, Cornelius Bogert. *Bibliography: Forum* 70 (June 1939), 440. Ellen Madeira, "George Howe," in West, pp. 23–24.

1939   Prototypical house for *Life* magazine, Amityville, L.I., N.Y.

Credit: GH & RMB (RMB?). *Bibliography: Forum* 73 (July 1940), 10–11.

1940–42   Pine Ford Acres, Middletown, near Harrisburg, Pa., defense housing.

Credit: Howe and Kahn. *Bibliography: Forum* 75 (Oct. 1941), 216–17; 76 (May 1942), 306–08; 84 (Jan. 1946), 110–11.

1941   Beaumont Newhall House, Scarsdale, N.Y., project.

Credit: GH.

1942	Information center, Office of War Information (temporary), Washington, D.C. Now demolished. *Credit:* GH. *Bibliography: Forum* 77 (Nov. 1942), 64.
1942	West Potomac women's residence halls (temporary), Public Buildings Administration, Washington, D.C. Now demolished. *Credit:* GH, supervising architect; Gilbert Stanley Underwood, consulting architect. *Bibliography: Record* 92 (July 1942), 40–43. *Forum* 80 (Jan. 1944), 61–62.
ca. 1942	Lily Ponds, Washington, D.C., defense housing for the Alley Dwelling Authority, project. A revised scheme was built by Stonorov and Kahn. *Credit:* Howe and Kahn. *Bibliography: Forum* 76 (May 1942), 310; 80 (Jan. 1944), 64.
1942–43	Carver Court, Coatesville, Pa., defense housing for the Mutual Ownership Division of the Federal Works Agency. *Credit:* Howe, Stonorov and Kahn. *Bibliography:* Mock, pp. 66–67. *Forum* 81 (Dec. 1944), 109–16. *South African Architectural Record* 31 (Jan. 1946), 23. *Philadelphia Yearbook,* 1949. *Forum* 94 (April 1951), 123. Vincent Scully, *Louis I. Kahn* (New York: Braziller, 1962).
ca. 1947	United States Consulate, Naples, Italy, project. *Credit:* GH. *Bibliography:* West, p. 58.
1947?	U.S. war memorial, Italy. *Credit:* GH.
1952	WCAU television studio, City Line Ave., Philadelphia, Pa. *Credit:* GH and RMB with the Austin Company. *Bibliography: Forum* 97 (Sept. 1952), 148–51. *Progressive Architecture* 34 (Sept. 1953), 75–114.
1954–55	Philadelphia *Evening and Sunday Bulletin* office, including Philadelphia National Bank branch office, 30th and Market Sts., Philadelphia, Pa. *Credit:* GH and RMB.
1955	Wholesale food distribution center, project. *Credit:* GH and RMB.

Writings by George Howe

1904–07 Harvard *Lampoon*. Drawings and writings in vols. 48 (1904), 38; 49 (1905), 228, 252; 50 (1905–06), 43, 71, 76, 129, 245; 51 (1906), 100–01, 129, 153, 160 (a parody of "To a Skylark" called "To a Bartender"), 185, 220, 246–47, 273, 276, 281; 52 (1906–07), 42–43, 45, 72, 153, 274; 53 (1907), 12, 14–15, 40–41, 63, 91, 96–97, 98, 139, 154, 165, 178, 276.

1914 "George Howe," Harvard University, *Class of 1908, Secretary's Second Report*. Cambridge, Mass., 1914.

1920 "George Howe," Harvard University, *Class of 1908, Secretary's Third Report*. Cambridge, Mass., 1920.

1923 "George Howe," Harvard University, *Class of 1908, Secretary's Fourth Report*. Cambridge, Mass., 1923.

"Four Buildings," *A Monograph on the Work of Mellor, Meigs and Howe*. (New York: Architectural Book Publishing Co., 1923), pp. 169–72.

1924 "Foreword," Philadelphia Chapter A. I. A. and T-Square Club, *Yearbook*. Philadelphia, 1924.

"Notes on the Planning of Grounds and Buildings," *Architectural Forum* 41 (Aug. 1924), 45–47.

1928 "George Howe," Harvard University, *Class of 1908, Secretary's Fifth Report*. Cambridge, Mass., 1928.

"The Philadelphia Savings [*sic*] Fund Society Branch Offices," *Architectural Forum* 48 (June 1928), 881–86.

1929 "Modern Decoration." Lecture delivered at the Philadelphia Art Museum, 20 April 1929. 5 pp., typescript

1930 "Modern Architecture," *U.S.A.* 1 (Spring 1930), 19, 20, 23.

"What Is This Modern Architecture Trying to Express," *American Architect* 137 (May 1930), 22–25, 106, 108.

"The Meaning of Modernism in Architecture," *Proceedings of the 63rd Annual Convention of the A.I.A.* (Washington, D.C., 1930), pp. 25–28. Written 19 May 1930.) Excerpts printed in "Modernist & Traditionalist," *Architectural Forum* 53 (July 1930), 49–50.

Letter to Stacy B. Lloyd, PSFS, 29 April 1930. Printed in Jordy and Stern, pp. 95–96.

Letter to James M. Willcox, PSFS, 26 May 1930. Printed in Jordy and Stern, pp. 96–97.

Letter to James M. Willcox, PSFS, 25 July 1930. Printed in Jordy and Stern, pp. 98–99.

Letter to James M. Willcox, PSFS, 30 July 1930. Printed in Jordy and Stern, p. 100.

"Architectural Analysis of the Proposed Building for the Philadelphia Saving

1930   Fund Society at 12th & Market Streets." Undated memo, ca. July 1930.
(cont.)   Printed in Jordy and Ctern, pp. 100–01.

"Architectural Design of the Proposed PSFS Building at 12th & Market
Street." Undated memo, probably ca. July 1930. Printed in Jordy and Stern,
pp. 101–02.

"Organic or Ornamental?" Speech delivered at the Town Hall Club, New York,
14 Nov. 1930. 2 pp., typescript.

"Job: 1200 Market Street." Memo to James M. Willcox, PSFS, 2 Dec. 1930.
Printed in Jordy and Stern, p. 102.

"A Fair Future to the T-Square Club Journal!," *T-Square Club Journal* 1
(Dec. 1930), 3.

1931   "Modernism in School Architecture," *The American School and University
Yearbook* 4 (New York: American School Publishing Corp., 1931), pp.
93–96.

"A Further Vague Pursuit of Truth in Architecture," *T-Square Club Journal* 1
(Feb. 1931), 13–28.

"A Design for a Savings Bank and Office Building," *T-Square Club Journal* 1
(March 1931), 10–13.

Letter to the editor, dated 17 May 1931, *T-Square Club Journal* 1 (May
1931), 34.

"Points of View," *Creative Art* 8 (June 1931), 469. Part of an exchange of
letters with Ely Jacques Kahn. Dated 13 May, it was written in response to
Kahn's letter as well as Frank Lloyd Wright's article in the May issue of
Creative Art.

Letter to the editor, dated 13 June 1931, *T-Square Club Journal* 1 (June 1931),
32.

"Comment," *T-Square Club Journal* 1 (Oct. 1931), 5.

"Resistances to Architectural Experiment," 5 Nov. 1931. 6 pp., typescript.
(Museum of Modern Art Library, vertical file).

"Architectural Deflation or the Practical and the Aesthetic in Modern Archi-
tecture," privately printed (New York, 1931). Address delivered before the
Department of Architecture, College of Fine Arts, New York University,
13 Nov. 1931. Quoted in "Bids Architects Find Uses for Idle Land," *New
York Times,* 14 Nov. 1931, p. 19. A 7-page typescript is included in the
Howe Archives.

"Points of Architecture." Letter to the editor, Philadelphia *Public Ledger,* dated
8 Dec. 1931. Signed Howe & Lescaze. 6 pp., typescript.

"Modern Architecture, the Universal Language. A Synthesis of Economics and
Aesthetics." Speech delivered at the University Club, Philadelphia, 4 Dec.
1931. 6 pp., typescript. There is a slightly different version, delivered at
Princeton University, 15 Dec. 1931. 7 pp., typescript.

"Statement," intended for the Philadelphia *Record,* 20 Dec. 1931. 1 p., typescript.

"George Howe of the Firm of Howe & Lescaze, Architects, Says." Undated
press release about modern principles of architectural design, functionalism,
Radio City, and PSFS, ca. 1931. 2 pp., typescript.

"Planning Low-Cost Housing." Undated typescript, ca. 1931 (Museum of Modern Art Library, vertical file).

1932   "The T-Square," *T-Square* 2 (Jan. 1932), 5.

"George Howe, an Architectural Biography," *T-Square* 2 (Jan. 1932), 20–23. This unsigned article was probably written by Howe.

"A Letter from the President of the T-Square Club," *T-Square* 2 (Feb. 1932), 5.

"Moses Turns Pharaoh," *T-Square* 2 (Feb. 1932), 9. Reprinted in *USA Tomorrow* 1 (Jan. 1955), 11.

"Introduction of Mr. George Gove, Secretary of the N. Y. State Housing Board." Address delivered at the luncheon given by Howe and Lescaze on the occasion of the private viewing of the exhibition of modern architecture at the Museum of Modern Art, 9 Feb. 1932. 3 pp., typescript.

"Why I Became a Functionalist." Paper read before the Symposium of the Museum of Modern Art, 19 Feb. 1932. 5 pp., typescript (Museum of Modern Art Library, vertical file). A portion of these remarks are included in "Symposium: The International Architectural Exhibition," *Shelter* 2 (April 1932).

"Functional Aesthetics and the Social Ideal," *Pencil Points* 13 (April 1932), 215–18. Howe's draft manuscript was originally titled "Functionalism and the Social Ideal."

"Creation and Criticism—Two Book Reviews," *Shelter* 2 (April 1932), 27. Reviews of Frank Lloyd Wright, *An Autobiography,* and Henry Russell Hitchcock and Philip Johnson, *The International Style: Architecture Since 1922.*

"Encouraging Student Tendencies." Statement evaluating thesis projects of students at the Princeton School of Architecture, probably June 1932. 1 p., typescript.

"Modern Architecture—Its Principles and Advantages." Talk delivered over WIP Radio, 30 June 1932. 8 pp., typescript.

Letter to the editor, Philadelphia *Evening Bulletin,* 28 Jan. 1932.

"Diary on Mexican Trip," Oct. 1932. Printed in West, pp. 86–114. This is a trip Howe took with William Stix Wasserman, whose recollections of it are quoted in West, *George Howe,* pp. 45–52.

"To Maxwell Levinson from George Howe," *Shelter* 2 (Nov. 1932), 125. Letter dated 13 July 1932.

"To B. F. [Buckminster Fuller] from George Howe," *Shelter* 2 (Nov. 1932), 128. Letter dated 6 Sept. 1932.

"Statement," *Architectural Forum* 57 (Dec. 1932), 484.

George Howe and William Lescaze, "Planning, Engineering, Equipment. The PSFS," *Architectural Forum* 57 (Dec. 1932), 484.

"Architectural Design." Unidentified talk, ca. 1932. 4 pp., typescript.

"The Branch Bank and Office Building of the Philadelphia Saving Fund Society." Press release, ca. 1932.

"Space, Time and Delancey Place." "Poem written on the occasion of the twenty-fifth wedding anniversary of Anna and Leonard Beale, celebrated in 1932 in Philadelphia under a two-story high silver-lined tent over the backyard of their city residence at 2025 De Lancey Place." Published in 1951 (see below).

1933   "George Howe," Harvard University, *Class of 1908, Secretary's Sixth Report.* Cambridge, Mass., 1933.

1936   "Abstract Design in Modern Architecture." Speech delivered before the College Art Association, Museum of Modern Art, 9 April 1936. Printed in *Parnassus* 8 (Oct. 1936), 29–31.

"Introduction." For a talk delivered by Frank Lloyd Wright, 22 Oct. 1936. No indication of place or occasion. 3 pp., typescript.

1937   "Two Views of Modern Architecture," *Yale Review* 27 (Sept. 1937), 204–06. Reviews of Walter Gropius, *The New Architecture and the Bauhaus,* and Walter Curt Behrendt, *Modern Building.*

1938   "George Howe," Harvard University, *Class of 1908, Secretary's Seventh Report.* Cambridge, Mass., 1938.

1939   "Contemporary Architecture Compared to Architecture of the Past." Speech delivered before the 15th International Congress of Architects, Symposium on Contemporary Architecture, Institute of Fine Arts, New York University, 12 May 1939. 7 pp., typescript.

"The Modern House. The Architect's Point of View." Preliminary draft script of broadcast on WABC Radio, 18 Nov. 1939, as part of the CBS–Museum of Modern Art series of broadcasts, "What Does Modern Art Mean to You?" Typescript.

"Going In and Coming Out—The Fundamental Architectural Experience." Speech delivered at the Philadelphia Art Alliance, 21 Nov. 1939. 12 pp., typescript.

1940   "Le Corbusier." 3 pp., typescript. Written in answer to "Le Corbusier Considers the New York Skyscraper," which appeared in *Legion d'Honneur* 10 (Oct. 1939), 283–86.

"Traditionalist Architecture and Integrated Building." Address delivered at the opening of the comparative exhibition of work by conservative and progressive architects, "Versus," at the Architectural League of New York, 5 March 1940. 10 pp., typescript, dated 20 Feb. 1940 and revised 28 Feb. 1940. Printed in *The Octagon* 12 (March 1940), 16–18; *Architectural Forum* 72 (April 1940), supp. 22–24. Excerpts printed in *Magazine of Art* 33 (April 1940), 235.

"Two Architect's Credos: 'Traditional versus Modern,'" *Magazine of Art* 33 (April 1940), 234–35.

"New York World's Fair, 1940," *Architectural Forum* 73 (July 1940), 31–42. Text and captions by Howe.

"The Development of Metal as a Structural Element." Talk delivered at Logan Hall, University of Pennsylvania, 18 Sept. 1940. Printed in *Bicentennial Conference. Studies in Arts and Architecture* (Philadelphia: University of Pennsylvania, 1941), pp. 93–98.

1941   "The Meaning of the Arts Today." Speech delivered at the Fogg Art Museum, Harvard University, 16 Dec. 1941. Printed in *Magazine of Art* 35 (May 1942), 162–67, 190.

1942   Untitled talk, dated 25 May 1942. Delivered before the Pennsylvania Association of Architects, 29 May 1942. 6 pp., typescript.

George Howe, Oscar Stonorov, and Louis I. Kahn. " 'Standards' Versus Essential Space. Comments on Unit Plans for War Housing," *Architectural Forum* 76 (May 1942), 308–11.

"Remarks." Speech delivered at the Training Conference on Protection of Public Buildings and Property, Protective Construction Unit of the Supervising Architect's Office, Public Building Administration, Washington, D.C., 3 Aug. 1942. Typescript.

1944 "Private and Public Administration Buildings." In Paul Zucker, ed., *New Architecture and City Planning* (New York: Philosophical Library, 1944), pp. 37–43.

"Speech." Delivered as chairman of forum discussion, Museum of Modern Art, 24 March 1944.

"Rough Draft, Submission to the Honorable Secretary of State," 2 May 1944. 3 pp., typescript with holograph revisions. Concerns construction of a new building for the Department of State.

"Memorials for Mankind." Sept. 1944. Printed in *Architectural Forum* 82 (May 1945), 123–24.

"Architecture. Review of the Situation." Oct. 1944. Typescript.

"Monuments, Memorials and Modern Design—An Exchange of Letters," *Magazine of Art* 37 (Oct. 1944), 202–07.

"The Importance of Aesthetics." Speech read at the monthly meeting of the Washington Chapter, A.I.A., 2 Nov. 1944. 3 pp., typescript.

1945 "Master Plans for Master Politicians." Speech delivered before the initial meeting of the Society of Planners and Architects, New York, 27 Jan. 1945. Printed in *Magazine of Art* 39 (Feb. 1946), 66–68; reprinted as "Piani Maestri per i maestri della politica," *Metron* 25 (1948), 12–15.

"The Relation of the Architect to Government." Speech read at the Conference on Architecture with Regard to Professional Training and Practice, University of Michigan, 3 Feb. 1945. Printed in Michigan Society of Architects, *Weekly Bulletin* 19 (31 July 1945), 1, 3; (7 Aug. 1945), 1, 3.

"Cliche Expert." Letter to the editor, *Architectural Forum* 83 (Sept. 1945), 66, 71.

"Reflection. Fortress of Learning. Letter to a Librarian." Holograph manuscript, Oct. 1945. Probably an early version of "Building Technics and the Mathematics of Change in Time," 8 pp., typescript.

"Master Plans for Master Politicians," *Architectural Record* 98 (Dec. 1945), 95–99; *Magazine of Art* 39 (Feb. 1946), 66–68.

"Building Technics and the Mathematics of Change in Time." 6 pp., typescript of unpublished review of Fremont Rider's *The Scholar and the Future of the Research Library*. This review was intended for publication in the *Technology Review* (F. G. Fassett, Jr., editor, to Howe, 27 Dec. 1944).

"Of Houses and Human Bondage. Reflections on Modern Architecture." 30 pp., incomplete typescript for a book containing foreword and two chapters, ca. 1945.

1946 "Flag Staff for a Memorial," *Beaux-Arts Institute of Design Bulletin* 22 (Oct. 1946), 13.

1947   "Statement." Michigan Society of Architects, *Weekly Bulletin* 21 (24 June 1947), 1–2. Text of talk delivered at Princeton University's bicentennial celebration, 1947.

1948   "George Howe," Harvard University, *Class of 1908, Secretary's Eighth Report.* Cambridge, Mass., 1948.

"Jefferson National Expansion Competition," *Architectural Forum* 88 (March 1948), 14–18.

"On Viewing the Results of the Competition," *Progressive Architecture* 29 (May 1948), 68.

Untitled poem about Christmas, 24 Dec. 1948. 2 pp., typescript.

1949   "Flowing Space: The Concept of Our Time." In Thomas H. Creighton, ed., *Building for Modern Man* (Princeton: Princeton, 1949), pp. 164–69.

"Greetings from Sackless Santa Claus." Undated poem, ca. 1949. Holograph manuscript.

1950   Untitled lecture, 22 Feb. 1940. Yale University News Bureau, release 479.

"Sun-witch to the Sun." Poem, *The New Yorker,* 2 Sept. 1950, p. 24.

1951   "A Lesson from the Jefferson Memorial Competition," *A.I.A. Journal* 15 (March 1951), 116–19.

"Confusion of an Architect on First Reading About Space and Time." Poem, *Architectural Record* 109 (May 1951), 14. The first three stanzas of "Space, Time and Delancey Place," written in 1932.

"Saint to the Chimney Swallow." Poem, *The New Yorker,* 30 June 1951, p. 22.

"Talk." Delivered before the student body, Department of Architecture, Yale University, 20 Sept. 1951. Printed as "Training for the Practice of Architecture—A Speech Given Before the Department in September 1951," *Perspecta* 1 (1952), 114.

"New Leaf from an Old Poem." Poem, *The New Yorker,* 22 Dec. 1951, p. 65.

1952   "Gate-house Control Tower for an Industrial Plant," *Beaux-Arts Institute of Design Bulletin* 28 (Jan. 1952), 12.

"Old Cities and New Frontiers," *A.I.A. Journal* 17 (Jan. 1952), 33–36.

"Introduction to the Subject." Talk delivered at the symposium "De Divina Proportione," Museum of Modern Art, 11 March 1952. Typescript.

"Preface," *Perspecta* 1 (1952), 1.

Letter to Douglas Haskell, 1952, included in part in "UN Assembly. How Do Architects Like? First Reaction: Most of Them Don't," *Architectural Forum* 97 (Dec. 1952), 114.

1953   "Fortune Rock." Information sheet prepared for *L'Architecture d'Aujourd'hui,* 1953. 1 p., typescript.

"The Architect and the Philosopher. A Dialogue by Correspondence." Written with Paul Weiss, professor of philosophy, Yale University. Howe's letters are dated 4 May, 25 May, 28 May, 8 June, 16 June, 25 June 1953. Weiss's letters are dated 7 May, 30 May, 1 June, 11 June, 19 June, 29 June, and 19 Nov. 1953.

"Why Then?—Why Now?" Speech delivered at the opening of the exhibition "Philadelphia Architecture in the Nineteenth Century," at the Philadelphia Art Alliance, 15 May 1953. Printed in West, pp. 66–79.

"Preface. Architecture and Creative Evolution," *Perspecta* 2 (1953), 1.

"Some Experiences and Observations of an Elderly Architect," *Perspecta* 2 (1953), 3–5.

"Talk to Third Year Students." Delivered 5 Oct. 1953. 3 pp., mimeographed typescript.

"Opening Address." Delivered at the Regional Meeting of the Middle Atlantic Conference, A. I. A., 22 Oct. 1953. 10 pp., typescript.

1954   Untitled talk. Delivered before the students of the Graduate School of Design, Harvard University, 1954. 11 pp., typescript.

"Newspaper Plant, Cawneer Company Plant," *Beaux-Arts Institute of Design Bulletin* 30 (Feb. 1954), 2–3.

"Will Democracy 'Plan'?" *Comment, the Living Arts* (March 1954), 3–5.

"Plans Practical and Not Practical," no date (ca. 1954–55), 2 pp., holograph manuscript. Draft conclusion to updated version of "Master Plans for Master Politicians."

1955   "Report on the Use of the Land Facing Independence Mall and Independence National Historical Park." Speech delivered to the Philadelphia Chapter, A. I. A., 28 March 1955. Printed in West, pp. 84–86.

Index

Works and writings appear at the end of entries for individuals.

DATE DUE
